Systemic Transformation, Trade and Economic Growth

Contributions to Economics

http://www.springer.de/cgi-bin/search_book.pl?series=1262

Peter Michaelis/Frank Stähler (Eds.)
Recent Policy Issues in Environmental and Resource Economics
1998. ISBN 3-7908-1137-8

Jessica de Wolff
The Political Economy of Fiscal Decisions
1998. ISBN 3-7908-1130-0

Georg Bol/Gholamreza Nakhaeizadeh/Karl-Heinz Vollmer (Eds.)
Risk Measurements, Econometrics and Neural Networks
1998. ISBN 3-7908-1152-1

Joachim Winter
Investment and Exit Decisions at the Plant Level
1998. ISBN 3-7908-1154-8

Bernd Meyer
Intertemporal Asset Pricing
1999. ISBN 3-7908-1159-9

Uwe Walz
Dynamics of Regional Integration
1999. ISBN 3-7908-1185-8

Michael Carlberg
European Monetary Union
1999. ISBN 3-7908-1191-2

Giovanni Galizzi/Luciano Venturini (Eds.)
Vertical Relationships and Coordination in the Food System
1999. ISBN 3-7908-1192-0

Gustav A. Horn/Wolfgang Scheremet/Rudolf Zwiener
Wages and the Euro
1999. ISBN 3-7908-1199-8

Dirk Willer
The Development of Equity Capital Markets in Transition Economies
1999. ISBN 3-7908-1198-X

Karl Matthias Weber
Innovation Diffusion and Political Control of Energy Technologies
1999. ISBN 3-7908-1205-6

Heike Link et al.
The Costs of Road Infrastructure and Congestion in Europe
1999. ISBN 3-7908-1201-3

Simon Duindam
Military Conscription
1999. ISBN 3-7908-1203-X

Bruno Jeitziner
Political Economy of the Swiss National Bank
1999. ISBN 3-7908-1209-9

Irene Ring et al. (Eds.)
Regional Sustainability
1999. ISBN 3-7908-1233-1

Katharina Müller/Andreas Ryll/Hans-Jürgen Wagener (Eds.)
Transformation of Social Security: Pensions in Central-Eastern Europe
1999. ISBN 3-7908-1210-2

Stefan Traub
Framing Effects in Taxation
1999. ISBN 3-7908-1240-4

Pablo Coto-Millán
Utility and Production
1999. ISBN 3-7908-1153-X

Frank Riedel
Imperfect Information and Investor Heterogeneity in the Bond Market
2000. ISBN 3-7908-1247-1

Kirsten Ralf
Business Cycles
2000. ISBN 3-7908-1245-5

Michele Bagella/Leonardo Becchetti (Eds.)
The Competitive Advantage of Industrial Districts
2000. ISBN 3-7908-1254-4

Frank Bohn
Monetary Union and Fiscal Stability
2000. ISBN 3-7908-1266-8

Jaime Behar
Cooperation and Competition in a Common Market
2000. ISBN 3-7908-1280-3

Michael Malakellis
Integrated Macro-Micro-Modelling Under Rational Expectations
2000. ISBN 3-7908-1274-9

continued on page 290

Natalja von Westernhagen

Systemic Transformation, Trade and Economic Growth

Developments, Theoretical Analysis and Empirical Results

With 22 Figures and 40 Tables

Physica-Verlag
A Springer-Verlag Company

Series Editors
Werner A. Müller
Martina Bihn

Author
Natalja von Westernhagen
European Institute for International Economic Relations
at Potsdam University
August-Bebel-Str. 89
D-14482 Potsdam
Germany
n_v_westernhagen@web.de

Printed with the financial support
of Deutscher Akademischer Austauschdienst (DAAD)

ISSN 1431-1933
ISBN 3-7908-1521-7 Physica-Verlag Heidelberg New York

Cataloging-in-Publication Data applied for
Die Deutsche Bibliothek – CIP-Einheitsaufnahme
Westernhagen, Natalja/von: Systemic transformation, trade and economic growth: developments, theoretical analysis and empirical results / Natalja von Westernhagen. – Heidelberg; New York: Physica-Verl., 2002
(Contributions to economics)
ISBN 3-7908-1521-7

Physica-Verlag Heidelberg
a member of BertelsmannSpringer Science+Business Media GmbH

Softcover Design: Erich Kirchner, Heidelberg

SPIN 10887640 88/2202-5 4 3 2 1 0 – Printed on acid-free and non-aging paper

Acknowledgement

This Ph.D. proposal was carried out with the support of a DAAD scholarship within the European Institute for International Economic Relations (EIIW) at the University of Potsdam under the supervision of Prof. Dr. Paul. J.J. Welfens. I would like first of all to express my gratitude to Prof. Dr. Paul J.J. Welfens for his advice and involvement during the research period. Thanks also to Prof. Dr. Hans Gerhard Strohe, the second Ph.D. supervisor, for his critical comments regarding issues of econometrics and also to Prof. Dr. Klaus Schoeler for taking on the position as head of the commission at the Ph.D. exam and to Prof. Dr. Klaus Gloede for his participation in the exam.

I would like also to express my gratitude to Prof. Dr. Rolf J. Langhammer for his support during my one year research stay at the Kiel Institute of World Economics (IfW). I am especially grateful to Dr. Matthias Luecke for his commitment, advice and our discussions during the stay at the Kiel Institute of World Economics and afterwards as he began his activities at the International Monetary Fund in the position of Senior Economist.

Thanks also to Dr. Roland Doehrn for constructive discussions that were particularly helpful during my research stay at the Rine-Westphalia Institute for Economic Research (RWI) in Essen.

Also many thanks to the colleagues at the institute for their input and students who assisted me with my Ph.D. work at the EIIW.

I am also grateful to the DAAD for the financing of my research proposal.

Especially warm thanks to Karsten v. Westernhagen, my husband, who finished his Ph.D. shortly before me, for his tolerance, advice and support. Finally thanks to my parents and parents-in-law, who were all a very active part of the process.

Contents

1 Introduction

1.1 Description of the Problem

The transition process has been the major challenge for the Commonwealth of Independent States (CIS) and Central and Eastern European countries (CEECs) since the end of the 1980s (EBRD, 1999, 2000; CBRF, 1997, 1998, 2001). The process of transition and economic opening up is a complex one, whose goal is restructuring the economy and the establishment of a functioning market economy. According to SACHS (1996, p. 128) systemic transformation means: *„...the institutional, legal, political and administrative change of the economic system from state-ownership and market allocation of resources."* The distorted economic systems of CIS and CEECs, inherited from socialist times has made transition no easy task (KRASNIKOVA, 2001; BRODSKII, 1998). Distortions in combination with transition relevant factors caused sharp output declines in both CIS and CEECs.

Such distortions as an extensive way of development, distorted sectoral structures, lack of private property, state monopoly, soft budget constraints etc. prohibited the efficient functioning of socialist economies (IMF, et al., 1991). Following the extensive way of development, CIS and CEECs experienced insufficient technological change and had poor preconditions for adopting new technologies and carrying out innovation activities. The extensive growth backtracked these economies in their development and was the major reason for the collapse of the Soviet economic system. Moreover, CIS and CEECs have inherited very distorted sectoral structures with oversized industrial sectors dominated by large state-owned monopolies. In the socialist economic system, services, the consumer goods production sector, and the agriculture sector were, to a significant degree, neglected. Therefore, the elimination of sectoral distortions, inducement of pro-competitive pressures, privatization and the restructuring of large state-owned enterprises became the major challenges in the early stages of transition. The lack of private ownership and soft budget constraints common in Soviet times, represented a serious obstacle in the implementation of a market environment. It is essential that governments of transition economies create a healthy competitive environment through implementation of efficient competition policies, introduction of property rights, hardening budget constraints, promotion of corporate governance, enforcement of bankruptcy legislation etc. (EBRD, 2000). Competition discipline can also be considerably induced through openness of the economy and foreign direct investment (FDI).

Distortions were more severe in the case of CIS than in some CEECs such as Hungary and Poland. The extent of distortions distinguished initial conditions for

CIS and CEECs at the beginning of transition, which determined the speed and success in policy reforms. According to their initial conditions, countries have chosen either fast ways of reforms like „shock therapy" in Poland or more „gradualist approach" like Hungary.

Both „shock therapy" and the „gradualist approach" mean reforms in terms of liberalization, stabilization, privatization and institutional reforms. The sequence of these reforms is subject to debate. The first decade of transition has shown that those countries which carried out rapid liberalization reached sustained macroeconomic stabilization and through comprehensive privatization, created a sufficient basis for more sophisticated institutional reforms. Such countries also managed to overcome output declines and to achieve sustained economic growth (EBRD, 2000). Thus not all transition countries were equally successful in market reforms. One can distinguish between more advanced transition economies and less advanced ones.

In this study we compare more advanced transition economies such as Hungary and Poland with less successful CIS countries - Russia, the Ukraine and Belarus. The success of Hungary and Poland in market reforms is a potential model for CIS countries (GRINBERG, 2000). Such reforms as liberalization, stabilization, privatization and institutional changes eliminate distortions of the socialist system and create preconditions for a functioning market economy (KOLODKO, 2001; SKLYAR, 1999; GRISHIN, 2000). A functioning market economy presents in turn a precondition for sustainable economic growth in these countries and for their successful integration into the world economy (ABALKIN, 2000).

Reaching sustainable economic growth and catching up to the income levels of developed market economies is a major long run goal of transition countries. In order to derive conclusions on options for future growth strategy for CIS and CEECs one should first look back into historical developments connected with economic growth in these countries. One notices that a major deficit of the socialist system lied in insufficient technological progress and inefficient innovation activities (IMF et al., 1991; OECD, 1994). The theories of economic growth such as neoclassical growth theory, new growth theory, the theory of technological gap as well as empirical evidence on modern economic growth can help in understanding links between technological change and economic growth (SOLOW, 1956; ROMER, 1986, 1990; BARRO/SALA-I-MARTIN, 1995a; ABRAMOVITZ, 1986; FAGEBERG, 1994; etc.).

New growth theory provides aspects of particular importance for the transition economies. Considering technological progress as a driving force of economic growth, it places an accent on learning by doing, knowledge spillovers and externalities and investment in R&D activities. In the context of new growth theory, human capital plays a crucial role in economic growth (LUCAS, 1988, 1990, 1993; ROMER, 1990; NUREEV, 2000). A broad human capital basis speeds up the opening up of economies, attracts new investment, speeds up learning by doing and increases productivity through spillovers and externalities and hence improves domestic absorptive and innovative capabilities. Although in the former Soviet states the expenditure on public education was rather high, the human capital should be better adopted to the requirements of the market economy. The backlog could be compensated through increased attention towards training, e.g. through better incentives for firms to provide on-the-job training. It is particularly important with the introduction of new equipment, such as IT/personal computers (PCs), which could, in the future, provide for a shift towards more skill- and R&D-intensive exports (EBRD, 2000). New growth theory also provides better insights into the role of openness of the economy and FDI for the future economic growth of the transition economies.

The theoretical analysis for CIS and CEECs shows that capital building and technological progress are essential for long run growth of these countries and their catching up. In the early stages of transition, imitation rather than innovation activities will have to be discussed. Since at the start of the transition CIS and CEECs can not afford the costs of innovation, they can use the „advantage of backwardness" and catch up technologically through imitation activities. But at the same time the countries face uncertainty as to how to create sufficient absorptive capabilities for new technologies and which policy measures are adequate to induce domestic innovation.

When discussing growth opportunities for countries richly endowed with natural resources such as Russia, it is also necessary to discuss the reasons and consequences of the „Dutch Disease" and immiserizing growth (SACHS/WARNER, 1995, 1999; KRUGMAN, 1987; VAN WIJNBERGEN, 1984). Russia, which exports predominately oil and gas may experience the consequences of the „Dutch Disease". The „Dutch Disease" refers to a condition where the manufacturing sector is subverted to the tradable natural resource sector. Since the manufacturing sector plays a crucial role in economic growth, the „Dutch Disease" can considerably diminish the countries future growth prospects (GAVRILENKOV, 2000). Additionally, exporting natural resources from a large country like Russia could have an impact on the world prices of these resources thus worsening the terms of trade. In the case of immiserizing growth Russia would experience welfare losses (LINDERT/PUGEL, 1996). Analyzing the policy options for Russia, this study takes into account the risks connected with the „Dutch Disease" and immiserizing growth.

In this study a special focus is placed on the importance of external factors for economic growth such as openness of the economy and FDI. Before the transition, CIS and CEECs were closed economies and were largely isolated from the world market (IMF et al., 1991). Trade among these countries occurred mostly in the frame of a closed trading block known as the Council for Mutual Economic Assistance (CMEA). Countries within the CMEA were highly integrated and overspecialized; their exports were strongly oriented towards the demand of the CMEA market. In the CMEA trading block Russia played the role of a leading trading partner, providing for exports of natural resources to the other CMEA countries which were strongly dependent on them. Economic isolation and the absence of pro-competitive pressures from the side of the world market negatively affected the quality of exports from the CMEA countries. This was clearly seen after the collapse of the Soviet Union, exports from CIS and CEECs being uncompetitive on world markets due to their failure to meet international standards and requirements.

Trade among CMEA has also considerably affected the specialization pattern of CIS and CEECs. Specialization and integration among CMEA countries occurred mostly for political reasons and not according to comparative advantages. Therefore, with the set up of the transition there was a need to adjust the specialization pattern according to the requirements of demand in world and domestic markets, respectively. The change in the specialization pattern is closely connected with the change in the regional distribution of trade since the specialization pattern strongly depends on with whom a country trades and on the scope of technological spillovers and externalities coming through trade and FDI.

FDI presents one more important factor which alongside openness of the economy, plays a crucial role in the success of the transition process and future economic growth in these economies. Due to the fact that the early stages of transition were accompanied with sharp output declines, the CIS and CEECs did not possess sufficient financial resources in order to finance the transition process, modernize production and infrastructure, replacing obsolete machines and equipment (BULATOV, 2001; GLAZ'EV, 2000; KOSSOV, 1998). Mostly neglected for political reasons in the past, FDI gained considerably in importance with the transition (UNCTAD, 1998, 1999). FDI should play a decisive role in regards to the modernization of production and the tradable sector. However FDI's most important role is as a channel for technology transfer and knowledge spillovers.

Since technological progress is essential for economic growth, openness of the economy and FDI are considered as the most significant factors for the transfer of technology (OECD, 1998). Both openness of the economy and FDI could bring about considerable positive growth effects. This requires detailed discussion with a basis in modern theory and empirical findings. However, one should point out that in certain cases they have also been associated with negative effects (GROSSMAN/HELPMAN 1991a; RODRIK, 1995; AGHION/HOWITT, 1998). Knowing these possible negative effects allows countries to direct domestic policies appropriately to avoid these pitfalls.

Success in transition depends not only on openness per se, but also on changes in the geographical distribution of foreign trade towards more trade with the West and structural adjustment[1] in terms of realizing comparative advantages, through

---

[1] According to SACHS (1996, p. 128) structural adjustment means: "...the initial reallocation of resources in the economy following the introduction of market forces."

more capital- , skill- and R&D-intensive trade. Reorientation of foreign trade towards the West will speed up economic growth through larger volumes of trade and a larger pool of technological spillovers. More capital- , skill- and R&D-intensive specialization of trade would allow transition economies to become more involved in intra-industry trade, which prevails among the majority of OECD countries and inducing a pro-competitive effect and technological catching up (GRUBEL/LLOYD, 1975; KRUGMAN, 1990; HELPMAN, 1998). The same holds for FDI. Whether it contributes to economic growth or not, not only the amount of FDI is important, but also into which sectors it is attracted. There is much to be said for the adjustment of comparative advantages within the CIS countries. The main problem of the CIS countries lies in the high proportion of commodities in their exports (EBRD, 1999, 2000; UN/ECE, 2000a,b; EUROPEAN PARLIAMENT, 2001). Moreover, FDI is predominately directed into traditional sectors of the economy (UNCTAD, 1999). The interplay between openness of the economy, FDI as and its effects on economic growth are important for the development of policy options and the sequencing of policy reforms.

Since geographical patterns of foreign trade in the former socialist countries were more based on political imperatives, it diminished the possibility for growth in these countries. Opening up also induces a regional reorientation of trade. Regional patterns of trade in a well-functioning market economy normally correspond to economic, geographical, and cultural aspects (GROS/ DAUTREBANDE, 1992; WANG/WINTERS, 1992; BALDWIN, 1993; HOLZMANN/ZUKOWSKA-GAGELMANN, 1998). Such regional pattern reflects principles and factors which are of crucial importance for the healthy development of trade relations between trading partners and leads to an increase in trade and hence in economic growth. Regional patterns of trade emerging instead according to political reasons prohibits the „optimal" development of trade relations and diminishes prospects for an increase in volumes of trade and hence in economic growth. Since the CIS and CEECs before the transition traded predominately with the other CMEA countries, there existed a considerable trade potential with Western market economies in the early stages of transition. It is crucial to examine the trade potential existing between the countries of the CIS, CEEC and OECD. A gravity model makes the estimation of trade potential possible. The gravity model approach allows the empirical determination of unrealized potential in trade between CIS, CEECs countries and OECD countries and hence to make conclusions on their progress in opening up.

A similar gravity model approach can be used for FDI (DOEHRN/VON WESTERNHAGEN, 2001). FDI was neglected to a large extent in socialist countries and now represents a new phenomenon for transition economies. The gravity model allows us to estimate potential FDI inflows into these countries and make conclusions about contributions of FDI to gross fixed capital formation and their importance for transformation process and the long run. The gravity model approach for foreign trade and FDI is an empirical part of this work. The evidence on market reforms, theoretical analysis of economic growth, the role of openness and FDI for economic growth and empirical results obtained with the gravity model could help to develop policy options on the future growth strategy for the investigated CIS and CEECs.

1.2 Goals and Structure of the Work

The goal of this analysis is to explore the reasons for economic growth decline in selected CIS and CEECs in the past, to compare progress in reforms in more advanced transition economies such as Hungary and Poland, with the CIS and to develop a growth strategy for CIS and CEECs for the future.

The work covers theoretical, empirical and policy aspects. During the analysis the following questions were raised:

- What were the reasons for economic growth decline in the CIS and CEECs in the early stages of transition?
- Which reforms form the preconditions for further economic growth? The sequencing of these reforms.
- What does growth theory say about the past growth experience of CIS and CEECs and on the future options for a viable growth strategy?
- Which role do external factors such as openness of the economy and FDI play in future economic growth?
- What does the gravity model say on the changes in the geographical pattern of foreign trade and on unrealized potential in FDI? What is the direction for the future?

The work consists of six chapters. At the beginning of each chapter the contents are summarized. At the end of every chapter some tentative conclusions are made. The structure of the work is represented by the Figure 1.

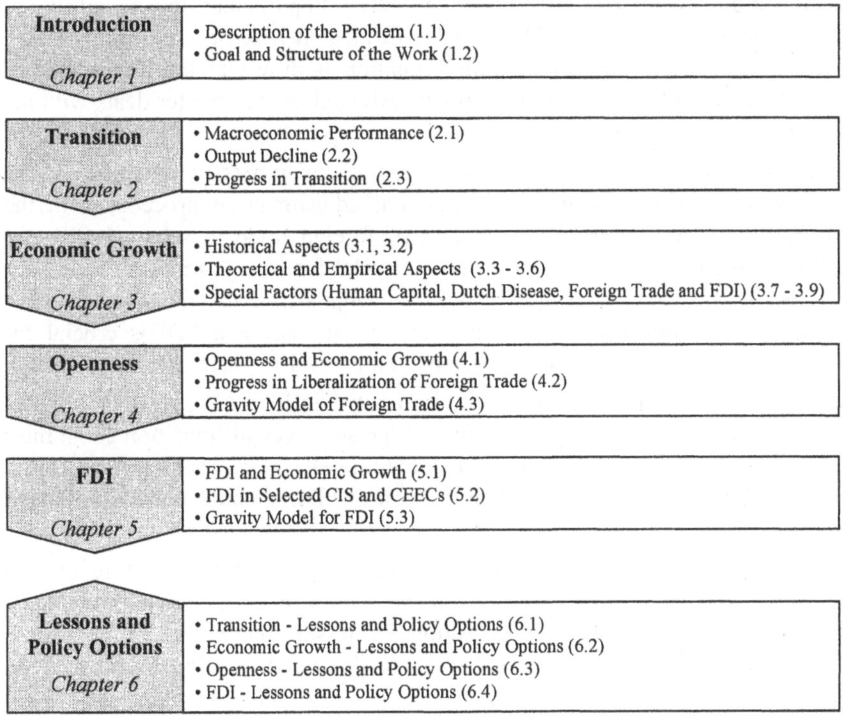

Figure 1: Structure of the Work

The work starts with an introduction which describes the central problem of the analysis(section 1.1) and further determines the goals of the work and it's structure (section 1.2).

The second chapter deals with transition problems. It gives an overview of the macroeconomic performance in the investigated countries at the period of transition (section 2.1), describes the factors of output decline (section 2.2) and compares the investigated countries in their progress towards market reforms (section 2.3).

The third chapter deals with theoretical considerations of economic growth and develops key points for future growth strategies in selected CIS and CEECs. It starts with consideration of historical aspects such as extensive growth strategy in the former USSR and the faults made in the sphere of science and innovation. It proceeds further with a detailed theoretical analysis, which compares the neoclassical approach with new growth theory, based upon which points of reflections for CIS and CEECs are found and finally, discusses additionally the theory of technological gap (sections: 3.3; 3.5; 3.6). Empirical evidence on modern growth theories is also covered by this chapter. At the end of the chapter special factors of economic growth are considered. In particular, the crucial role of human capital is emphasized. The problem of „Dutch Disease" and immiserizing growth is also discussed. Additionally, attention is drawn to the importance of foreign trade and FDI for economic growth. Altogether this chapter deals with the basic problems of economic growth.

The fourth chapter begins with the analysis of the impact of openness of the economy on economic growth and structural adjustment. It proceeds with the analysis of progress in the liberalization of foreign trade in selected CIS and CEECs. At the end of the chapter a gravity model for foreign trade is carried out for selected CIS and CEECs. It should be emphasized that a comprehensive analysis of economic opening up and the role of trade and FDI is crucial for understanding problems and policy options in the transition countries considered.

The fifth chapter deals with the relationship between FDI and economic growth. In this chapter the impact of FDI on growth perspectives of transition economies is discussed. Section 5.2 covers the situation with FDI in selected CIS and CEECs, section 5.3 presents an empirical investigation of FDI potential, carried out using the gravity model.

The sixth chapter represents lessons and policy options for the future growth strategy of selected CIS and CEECs. In the section 6.1 the lessons and policy options of transition are covered. In section 6.2, lessons and policy options which follow from the economic growth theory are discussed. Section 6.3 deals with lessons and policy options regarding openness of the economy. Finally, section 6.4 covers the lessons and policy options regarding attracting FDI.

2 The Challenges of Transition. Analysis for Selected CIS and More Advanced CEECs

The transition from a centrally planned economy to a market-based system was a major challenge for Commonwealth of Independent States (CIS) as well as for Central and Eastern European countries (CEECs) in the 1990s. Transition economies were confronted with problems which, taken together, had a powerful impact on their economies. Thus the beginning of the 1990s was marked by macroeconomic imbalances, structural problems, and large changes in external economic relations. In the first stage of transformation all transition economies experienced sharp declines in real GDP. Output declines were caused on one hand by the distortions inherited from the centrally planned system and by the shocks connected with the transition process itself on the other. The transition from centrally planned to market economy was associated with three shocks with which the countries had to cope. The first shock was connected with the breakup of the Council for Mutual Economic Assistance (CMEA); the second with the disintegration of the USSR during 1990 - 1991; and thirdly the collapse of central planning had a powerful impact on output performance and external developments in the transition economies. Not all transition countries were able to overcome difficulties and to improve their output performance at an equally successful pace.

Countries like Hungary and Poland represented some of the most advanced transition economies in 2000, whereas three CIS economies (Russia, Ukraine, and Belarus) are considerably lagging behind in this process. Thus the transition experience of most advanced CEECs is of significant importance for CIS countries, as they have to confront similar problems. We compare the progress in transition and perspectives for further economic growth of these three CIS economies with more advanced transformation economies like Hungary and Poland.

This chapter consists of four sections. The first section describes the tendencies in macroeconomic performance during the period of transition. In the second section both transition relevant factors of output decline and factors inherited from the centrally planned system are discussed. At the end of this section some conclusions are made on lessons of output decline and future growth perspectives. The third section deals with the progress in transition of the selected CIS and CEECs. Two alternative approaches to transition such as shock therapy and gradualism are considered in this section. Further discussion addresses the comparison of the investigated countries in progress in reforms. The core reforms like liberalization, stabilization, privatization, and institutional reforms are covered in this section. At the end of the chapter conclusions are made on different behavior patterns of the investigated countries in transition and the focus is made on factors which are essential for success in transition.

2.1 Macroeconomic Performance of Countries During the Period of Transition

Table 1 represents an overview of the main macroeconomic indicators describing the performance of the investigated transition economies during the transition period (EBRD, 1999). The performance of countries during the transition is reflected in tendencies in output, industrial output, investment, employment and productivity, inflation, and fiscal and external developments. All transition economies had to cope with similar problems at the start of transition, but not all managed to rapidly adjust to the new economic environment and improve macroeconomic performance. Major common tendencies of macroeconomic performance are shown in Table 1.

In the early years of transition all transition economies experienced a sharp decline in output, accompanied by the fall in industrial output and investment (EBRD, 1999). But since 1994 in Hungary and since 1992 in Poland there has been continuous growth of these indicators. Gross fixed investment in these countries grew rapidly during the last years of transition, providing for new equipment necessary to replace the most obsolete. Rapid restructuring and new investment stimulated the growth of industrial output. At the beginning of the 21th century Hungary and Poland were the fastest growing countries among the transition economies; they recorded growth rates of output of 4 - 7 percent. In 1998/99 in Russia and Ukraine growth of investment and industrial output remained negative, although in Ukraine the speed of decline diminished considerably. In Russia the only year with growth prior to the 1998 crisis was 1997, where GDP output was 0.8 percent and growth in industrial output 1.9 percent, followed by output decline in 1998. Belarus is the only country among the investigated CIS states with positive growth performance in the 1990s. There has been output growth of 1.8 percent in Belarus since 1998, reaching a peak of 11.4 percent in 1997. The positive output performance was accompanied with growing industrial output and growing investment. It is doubtful that the official statistics in Belarus reports correct figures on growth performance. Belarus exhibited very high inflation rates along the whole path of transition and in general achieved little progress in reforms so that the growth can not be sustained.

Most transition countries faced rapid growth of inflation and increasing unemployment rates. The rise of inflation was caused by the rapid liberalization of prices on the one hand, and by inflationary monetary policy on the other. Insufficient tax revenues forced countries to adopt monetary financing of budget. While in Hungary and Poland the disinflation was achieved successfully, in Russia the foundations for sustained macroeconomic stability remained weak and caused reversal in 1998, where the inflation level even doubled in the short period of time. In Ukraine the inflation during the last few years has been acceptable. In Belarus the disinflation policy was never successful as bank landing to state enterprises always took place (EBRD, 1999).

Output decline in the transition economies was accompanied by an increase in unemployment. In most advanced transition economies the unemployment increased in the first years of transition and remained largely unchanged for many years. One would suppose high unemployment was a result of structural adjustment but the evidence shows that most privatization occurred without a high rise in unemployment. This shows that unemployment mainly reflects structural unemployment, wage rigidities, and lack of regional mobility. Unemployment in Ukraine and Belarus still remains artificially low because of so called hidden unemployment in state enterprises.

With the output decline there was also a decline in labor productivity. Advanced transition economies, once output started recovering, entered a phase of deep economic restructuring with rapid productivity growth caused first of all by new investment, where foreign direct investment played a considerable role in providing technology transfer and more advanced methods of economic management. Especially rapid among the transition countries was the productivity growth in Hungary and Poland, while in Russia the productivity growth fell by 40 percent between 1990 and 1994, and has since remained close to zero.

Significant fiscal imbalances were another problem of transition. The fiscal imbalances were the result of poor labor administration, erosion of the tax base, development of barter trade, and tax evasion. Poor fiscal performance was also reinforced by the presence of soft budget constants in the form of tax arrears for favored enterprises.

Most transition economies also experienced high current account deficits. The first sharp increase in deficits was connected with the collapse of the CMEA, where the exports to these countries slumped and imports became more available. As the exports started to reorient towards Western markets in 1993 - 1994 the current account deficit decreased, but increased again during 1995 - 1998, partly reflecting growing capital inflows into the region (and higher imports of equipment by foreign enterprises). In a pragmatic view a deficit greater than 7 percent of GDP represents a serious warning signal, as one could doubt the ability of a country to pay off long-term liabilities in the future. The only country with a positive current account is Russia. However, Russia suffered from high capital flight.

Table 1: Macroeconomic Data for Selected CIS and CEECs

	1991	1992	1993	1994	1995	1996	1997	1998 Esti-mate	1999 Projec-tion
Hungary									
GDP	-11.9	-3.1	-0.6	2.9	1.5	1.3	4.6	5.1	3.0
Industrial output growth	-18.3	-9.7	4.0	9.6	4.6	3.3	11.0	10.6	na
Gross fixed investment	-10.4	-2.6	2.0	12.5	-4.3	6.3	8.8	11.4	na
Unemployment[1]	7.4	12.3	12.1	10.4	10.4	10.5	10.4	9.1	na
Inflation[2]	32.3	21.6	21.1	21.2	28.3	19.8	18.4	10.3	8.0
Current account balance	0.8	0.9	-9.0	-9.4	-5.6	-3.7	-2.1	-4.8	-5.4
Poland									
GDP	-7.0	2.6	3.8	5.2	7.0	6.1	6.9	4.8	3.5
Industrial gross output	-8.0	2.8	6.4	12.1	9.7	8.7	10.8	5.0	na
Gross fixed investment	-4.4	2.3	2.9	9.2	16.9	20.6	21.9	14.5	na
Unemployment	11.8	13.6	16.4	16.0	14.9	13.2	10.5	10.4	na
Inflation	60.4	44.3	37.6	29.4	21.6	18.5	13.2	8.6	6.5
Current account balance	-2.6	1.1	-0.7	2.5	4.6	-1.0	-3.1	-4.5	-5.5

Table 1: Macroeconomic Data for Selected CIS and CEECs (cont.)

	1991	1992	1993	1994	1995	1996	1997	1998 Esti-mate	1999 Projec-tion
Russia									
GDP	-5.0	-14.5	-8.7	-12.7	-4.1	-3.5	0.8	-4.6	0.0
Industrial gross output	-8.0	-18.0	-14.1	-20.0	-3.3	-4.0	1.9	-5.2	na
Gross fixed investment	na	na	-25.8	-26.0	-7.5	-18.5	-5.0	-6.7	na
Unemployment (annual average)	0.0	4.8	5.3	7.1	8.3	9.2	10.9	12.4	na
Inflation	161.0	2,506.1	840.0	204.4	128.6	21.8	10.9	84.5	45.0
Current account balance	na	na	na	3.4	2.3	2.8	0.7	0.9	5.5
Ukraine									
GDP	-11.6	-13.7	-14.2	-23.0	-12.2	-10.0	-3.2	-1.7	-2.5
Industrial gross output	-4.8	-6.4	-8.0	-27.3	-12.0	-5.1	-1.8	-1.5	na
Unemployment	0.0	0.3	0.3	0.3	0.5	1.3	2.3	3.7	na
Inflation	161.0	2,730.0	10,155.0	401.0	181.0	39.7	10.1	20.0	17.0
Current account balance	na	-2.9	-2.4	-3.7	-3.2	-2.5	-3.0	-2.8	-1.3
Belarus									
GDP	-1.2	-9.6	-7.6	-12.6	-10.4	2.8	11.4	8.3	1.5
Industrial gross output	-1.0	-9.4	-10.0	-17.1	-11.7	3.5	18.8	11.0	na
Gross fixed investment	4.4	-18.1	-15.4	-17.2	-28.7	7.2	14.7	9.4	na
Unemployment (end-year)	0.1	0.5	1.4	2.1	2.7	3.9	2.8	2.3	na
Inflation	93.0	1,559.0	1,996.0	1,960.0	244.0	39.3	63.4	181.7	155.0
Current account balance	na	na	-30.4	-13.2	-2.4	-3.6	-5.9	-6.6	-4.8

Source: EBRD (1999), Transition Report 1999

Unemployment[1] in percent of labor force for all five countries.

Inflation[2] for all five countries as a change in year-end retail/consumer price level, in percent

2.2 Output Decline

One of the major developments all transition economies experienced at the early 1990s was the decline in output. Although all investigated economies experienced sharp output decline in the first two years of transition, the behavior of growth path was rather different in these countries. In the more advanced transition economies like Hungary and Poland the output since 1989 followed a U-shape pattern with a minimum reached in 1990 - 1991 (see Table 2). By contrast, output decline in the investigated CIS countries was deeper and more sustained with signs of recovery only in 1996 in Belarus, in 1997 in Russia and with further output decline in Ukraine. The upturn of the growth path in Poland started already in 1992 and in Hungary two years later. The growth path in CIS countries could be described in the 1990s as an L-shape as there was continuous decline since 1991 (EBRD, 1999).

The output decline in the investigated transition economies can be described by various factors. First of all, the distorted economic environment inherited from central planning contributed mostly to the poor output performance and final collapse in the early 1990s. Secondly, the shocks connected with transition were responsible for the sharp output declines the countries experienced at the beginning of the 1990s. Thirdly, the economic recovery in some transition economies and sustained recession in others are to be explained by the different progress in transition: different policy choices, different speed, and success of reforms.

Table 2: Growth in Real GDP in Selected CIS and CEECs

	1989	1990	1991	1992	1993	1994	1995	1996	1997	1998	1999	Estimated level of real GDP in 1998	Year growth started
Hungary	0.7	-3.5	-11.9	-3.1	-0.6	2.9	1.5	1.3	4.6	5.1	3.0	95	1994
Poland	0.2	-11.6	-7.0	2.6	3.8	5.2	7.0	6.1	6.9	4.8	3.5	117	1992
Russia	na	-4.0	-5.0	-14.5	-8.7	-12.7	-4.1	-3.5	0.8	-4.6	0.0	55	1997
Ukraine	4.0	-3.4	-11.6	-13.7	-14	-23.0	-12.2	-10.0	-3.2	-1.7	-2.5	37	------
Belarus	8.0	-3.0	-1.2	-9.6	-7.6	-12.6	-10.4	2.8	10.4	8.3	1.5	78	1996

Source: EBRD (1999), Transition Report 1999

2.2.1 Factors of Output Decline Inherited from the Centrally Planned System

The centrally planned system had highly distorting effects on the economies of CIS and CEECs which, to a large extent, turned to be a major reason for the collapse of output in these countries. Therefore, the understanding of these problems is crucial for successful growth performance in transition countries.

- *Extensive growth.* Since the 1960s the Soviet economy exhibited deteriorating growth performance which was a major cause of its demise in 1991. Thus, according to official statistics, the average annual rate of growth of net material product (NMP) fell from 7.8 percent in the second half of the 1960s to 5.6 percent in 1971 - 1975, 4.3 percent in 1976 - 1980, and 3.2 percent halfway through the 1980s, with the final collapse in the 1990s (IMF et al., 1991). The major policy approach of the Soviet Union was an accelerated industrialization, where the Soviet Union was relying on an extensive approach to development by using it's broad resources. Emphasis was laid on the rapid mobilization of capital, labor, and raw materials, and less on the productivity of inputs. The extensive nature of Soviet growth (that is an increase in the quantity rather than „quality" or productivity of inputs) was reflected in the high share of investment in national income in comparison to market economies, high labor participation rates, and excess labor moving from agriculture to industry. But rapid accumulation of capital found it's limit as the share of income available for consumption had fallen to a „politically acceptable" level. Thus in the late 1960s the fixed capital stock had also begun to decline. EASTERLY/FISCHER (1994), examining the relevance of capital accumulation, explains the decline of Soviet growth rate by the declining marginal product of capital. He also finds a low elasticity of substitution between capital and labor, which is supposed to worsen the problem of the diminishing returns to capital. Deepening of capital led from the particular time period to the decreasing productivity of capital. Demoralization of population and the breakdown of discipline also contributed to the decline in labor productivity.
- *Structural distortions.* The Soviet Union and the CMEA countries in general have faced distorted sectoral structures (BLANCHARD, 1997). The economy of the Soviet countries was highly industrialized but neglected services. For example, the total share of services in Poland in 1989 accounted for 36% of employment, in comparison with 53% relevant for eight poor OECD countries (BERG, 1995). Additionally, most investment in industry was directed to the rapid expansion of heavy industry and was accompanied by relatively slow growth of consumer goods production. Agriculture also became a neglected sector of the economy. Investment in heavy industry was to a large extent directed at large scale weapon production, which was supposed to guarantee both national security and military influence abroad.

- *Large state-owned enterprises.* Industry was dominated by large state-owned enterprises. There were too few small enterprises. In Poland firms with fewer than 100 employees represented 1.4% of total 1989 employment, compared to 14% in West Germany and 32% in Italy (BERG, 1995). One can not compare large enterprises in the former USSR with that of the US, for example, although both were characterized by large economies of scale. The difference lies in corporate organization and governance. While US companies were strongly decentralized, the state enterprises in the former USSR had highly centralized structure which prohibited initiative and innovation „from below" (WELFENS, 1999a).

- *State monopoly.* There was a high concentration of large state owned enterprises, with, in many cases, only one or two producers of a particular good in the entire country, which led to state monopolization of the market. Monopolized production structures allowed the capture of monopoly rents without promoting innovation activities and efficiency gains of enterprises. Supplier structures were also highly monopolized, a reason why socialist firms tended to avoid outsourcing (WELFENS, 1999a).

- *Lack of private ownership.* There was mostly lack of private ownership and absence of profit-orientation so that most firms faced massive inefficiencies (IMF el at., 1991; ESTRIN/WRIGHT, 1999).

- *Soft budget constraints.* BERG (1995, p. 5) argued: *„Soft budget constraint can be summarized as a situation in which the government sets prices as a fixed markup over costs".* Moreover, soft budget constraints means that firms have access to credits from state-owned banks at preferential rates. Soft budget constraints include price control, enterprise-specific taxes, subsidies, and control over allocation of credit to the enterprises. Therefore in the Soviet system potential information content of relative and absolute prices was largely ignored as a result of soft budget constraints. There was weak motivation to increase productivity. There was no bankruptcy law, and the system of contracts was underdeveloped. The problem of soft budget constraints is more detailed discussed by BAI/WANG (1988), BERGLOF/ROLAND (1998), KORNAI (1998, 1999), MASKIN (1999).

- *Artificially low unemployment.* The extensive approach to development and soft budget constraints implied high labor participation rates, which reached artificially high levels in comparison to market economies. Thus in the early 1970s it peaked at a record level of over 85 percent, which is considerably above the levels in Western Europe and the United States (IMF et al., 1991).

- *Closed economies.* Foreign trade occurred in the frame of a closed trading block (mostly among the former CMEA countries) which considerably influenced the specialization pattern of these economies and the geographical distribution of their foreign trade. CMEA was a trading block organization, formed in 1949 for the newly emerged centrally planned economies. Despite a growing role of foreign trade over time, the authorities tried to limit the influence of external conditions on the economy. Thus households and enterprises were largely isolated from the world economy. Foreign trade was carried out by foreign trade organizations whose function consisted of exporting enough to pay for the imports needed under the plan, and to ensure that changes in world prices weakly corresponded to domestic prices, mainly through „price equalization schemes" (various taxes and subsidies) which helped to artificially hold domestic prices fixed (IMF et al., 1991).

- *Underdeveloped financial sector.* The monetary system consisted of a state bank (Gosbank) whose function was to give credits to enterprises according to the plan, to take deposits from households, and to issue currency (IMF et al., 1991; KORNAI, 1994). There was no competitive banking system (with an independent central bank) which could contribute to an efficient functioning of the private economy. Capital markets and security markets were also not developed.
- *Underdeveloped fiscal policy.* Fiscal policy was an object of the plan activities as government carried out a redistributive function among the enterprises and households and reallocated the investment from one enterprise to the other through taxes and subsidies. Thus the enterprises' surpluses were transferred to the budget or the central funds and were then redistributed in the form of investment to the other enterprises. In many cases poor performing enterprises were subsided by better performing enterprises, thus equalizing the whole pattern of enterprises and leaving no possibility for the exaggerated growth of one of them (DMITRIEV/KARCEV, 1996).
- *Collapse of control.* Over 90 percent of the economy was directly controlled by the state, the coordination role of a „market system" was entirely suppressed. The precise control required for detailed plans for the inputs and outputs of all branches of the economy. As the system became even more complicated, the state was not able to provide for sophisticated control, which contributed considerably to the collapse of the whole system (KOTZ, 1997).

2.2.2 Transition Relevant Factors of Output Decline

Transition was also accompanied by a number of challenges and reforms that also contributed to sharp output declines:

- *The change in the role of government.* The coordination of economic activity by the government was not abruptly replaced by coordination through market structures. The lack of marketing experience of state-enterprises in the situation of a break-up in the supplier chain and at the same time absence of further governmental credits contributed to the situation of „transformation recession", where the old mechanism had already collapsed but was not yet replaced by the new one (KOTZ, 1997; KORNAI, 1994).

- *Macroeconomic imbalances and persistence of inflation.* At the beginning of transformation all former republics of the Soviet Union faced a question whether to remain in the ruble area or to introduce their own currencies. Although the conducting of monetary policy was a new challenge for the emerging states, the other problem connected with inflationary bias inherited in the ruble area pointed to the necessity of establishing an independent monetary system. An inflationary bias was caused by the „free rider" problem, where each state with it's own central bank had an incentive to increase credits at a rate faster than the average. The establishment of independent currencies in the former republics of the Soviet Union was accompanied by excessive inflation, which had a negative impact on output growth. Additionally, because enterprises were not subject to a hard budget constraint, monetary growth also accelerated. There is the inverse relationship between inflation and output growth (RANDALL/HANOUSEK, 2000; BRADA/KING/KUTAN, 2000; FISCHER/SAHAY/VEGH, 1998; AGENOR/MCDERMOTT/PRASAD, 1999). There were some signs of medium term recovery in those countries where inflation was reduced. In other states the economic activity continued to weaken. Monetary policies in postcommunist Russia are more detailed discussed by NIKOLIC (2000).

- *Macroeconomic imbalances, namely fiscal deficits.* Liberalization of prices and inflation led to the erosion of the tax base. Moreover, there were growing difficulties in asserting fiscal control in new economic circumstances (EBRD, 1999).

- *Large structural adjustment.* Liberalization of prices was needed to develop a healthy price mechanism where prices carry out the role of signals in a market economy and are responsible for improvements in the efficiency of resource allocation. From the other side quick liberalization of prices leads to a large structural shift from traditional production to the sectors that were previously in „shortage". At the early stage of liberalization there is high uncertainty about relative prices. Additionally, the lack of property rights, legal infrastructure, and unstable macroeconomic environment can lead to the situation where cutbacks in production in the traditional sector are taking place faster than the emergence of new production. The backlog between „old" and „new" production contributes to the so called „transformation recession" and is responsible for the declines in aggregate output (ANDERSON/CITRIN/LAHIRI, 1995; BOONE/GOMULKA/LAYARD, 1998).

- *Demand shock in military sector.* The industrial production in the USSR was highly concentrated on arms and other military goods (GADDY, 1996). The USSR, for political reasons, also supplied developing countries with export credits directed mainly at the financing of arms exports. As a result, the USSR had accumulated large claims on developing countries that turned out to be largely illiquid. The USSR, given balance of payments problems in the second half of the 1980s as most developing countries were unable to repay their debt, stopped extending new export credits. Thus, from the late 1980s the provision of these credits was sharply reduced, having a negative impact on the military industrial complex in the countries' receipt of credits. From the other side there was also a decline in domestic demand in Russia itself. Thus defense spending in Russia dropped from over 8 percent of GDP in 1991 to 5.5 percent of GDP in 1992, and the share of industrial output in defense-related industries fell from 40 percent in 1991 to 30 percent in 1992 (ANDERSON/CITRIN/LAHIRI, 1995). This tendency was reflected in the balance of payments, both in the reduction of exports and in related export credits.

- *Reduction in overall grants and subsidies.* The USSR gave grants and subsidies to the other Soviet republics and CMEA countries which, in the case of some Asian republics, accounted for 15 to 20 percent of their GDP. Subsidies also took place in the form of low prices (compared to world market prices) for energy and raw materials. The USSR subsidized the other CMEA countries after the 1973 - 1974 oil price hike because it would have otherwise experienced terms of trade losses. The terms of trade between its exports (raw materials-mostly energy products) and its imports (mainly machinery and equipment) were less favorable to the USSR than if world prices had been applied (CHRISTENSEN, 1994). These transfers have been considerably reduced since 1993, which caused output losses in the CMEA states by reducing their ability to pay for imported inputs (ANDERSON/CITRIN/LAHIRI, 1995).

- *Deterioration of terms of trade.* Liberalization of foreign trade and external transactions moved the prices of tradables, including energy and raw materials, towards world levels. As a result the terms of trade deteriorated for 14 states (excluding Russia) by some 23 percent in 1992, followed by a further worsening of over 10 percent in 1993 - 1994. As was estimated at 1990 levels of trade, a 30 percent deterioration in the terms of trade contributed to an average 13 percent loss in GDP in the 14 states (excluding Russia). Russia could not fully explore its improvements in terms of trade because of the reduction in the volume of inter-republican trade (ANDERSON/CITRIN/LAHIRI, 1995).

- *Growth of competition from imports.* The competition with imports rapidly increased with the openness of the economy and liberalization of external markets, as domestic firms were not able to compete in unfamiliar circumstances (CHRISTENSEN, 1994).

- *CMEA trade shock.* The CMEA was abolished at the beginning of 1991 and CMEA export markets were lost for the former USSR countries (GACS/PECK, 1996; KORNAI, 1994). The collapse of CMEA trade was caused by market-related reforms in some CEECs and to a large extent by planning and management crisis in Russia, as Russia was no longer able to provide control over economic transactions and to hold together regions asserting greater autonomy. The reorientation of Russia's exports towards the convertible currency area was also an important factor (CHRISTENSEN, 1994). The USSR could not full take advantage of the abolition of the CMEA, although it implied a 40 - 45 percent improvement in the terms of trade with the other CMEA countries[2]. Thus, only 20 percent of the USSR's 60 percent of trade with CMEA countries in the second half of the 1980's was with CMEA countries outside of the Baltic states and other countries of the former Soviet Union (ANDERSON/CITRIN/LAHIRI, 1995). RODRIK (1992) estimates the impact of the dissolution of the CMEA on CEECs. According to his estimations Soviet trade shock accounts for just about all of the cumulative decline in Hungary and between a quarter and a third of the decline in Poland. Thus, three elements of shock: (a) deterioration of terms of trade; (b) a market-loss effect; and (c) a removal of the import subsidy effect had a severe consequences for the CEECs (RODRIK, 1992). GACS (1995) points out that a quick reorientation of Hungary's and Poland's trade towards the West had compensated for the decline in trade with the Soviet Union in a considerably short period of time. The negative effect of CMEA trade also consisted of a distorted comparative advantage pattern and distorted regional distribution of trade developed as a result of closed trade in the frame of CMEA. CMEA block countries were highly integrated with each other and had little interaction with the rest of the world. The trade was based on planning rather than market principals and did not reflect comparative advantages of these countries, as well as it did not correspond to geographical, economic, and cultural principles.

- *The shock of inter-state trade.* The disintegration of the Soviet Union during 1990 - 1991 caused the break-up of traditional trade and financial relations between former Soviet republics and contributed further to the shock. The former republics of the Soviet Union were characterized by a high degree of specialization and were highly integrated with each other. Interstate trade accounted for 70 to 75 percent of the Soviet republics' trade. The economies also had an integrated infrastructure. During 1990 - 1991 the republics began to erect trade barriers against each other. Thus Russia imposed trade restrictions on imports of food and consumer goods coming from countries pursuing independence. Russia also imposed restrictions on some of its exports. The exports of Russia to other countries of the former Soviet Union decreased from 79 percent in 1991 to 37 percent in 1993. The exports of Ukraine and Belarus from 71 percent to 28 percent and from 72 to 43 percent respectively. The settlement system has also deteriorated since the

[2] After the CMEA was abolished, the trade should be carried out at world market prices and to be settled in convertible currencies, what provided for terms of trade gains for the USSR in trade with former CMEA members (CHRISTENSEN, 1994).

disintegration of the Soviet Union. First, the monetary overhang in the Russian economy led to loss of confidence in the ruble. Second, in early 1992, in order to introduce more control over the payments transactions, the Russian authorities instructed that all settlements be carried out only through the central banks of each state. This kind of centralization led to the situation in which, in the first half of 1993, commercial banks in Russia still could not open correspondent accounts with banks of the other states in the ruble area. Third, the new states introduced national currencies and at the initial stage had few convertible currency reserves for settlement with Russia. All these factors together led to the increase in barter transactions and compensation deals with the associated inefficiencies becoming more important (CHRISTENSEN, 1994). In 1997 in Russia the amount of transactions through barter trade and some other nonpecuniary settlements accounted for 70%, which represents a serious obstacle for economic growth as information incorporated in the monetary pricing system is mostly ignored (WELFENS, 1999a).

- *Backwardness of the financial sector.* Financial sector backwardness is one of the obstacles to growth. A well functioning financial system is of prime importance for new investment, especially for small and medium-sized enterprises in the service sector that were in „shortage" in the Soviet times. In many successor states of the Soviet Union, thousands of money-losing state firms are kept alive by credits. A banking system which deals as a conduit between the saving rate and fixed investment in the real sector, and which especially supports the private sector, is not really the case in the investigated CIS countries. There is still reluctance to lend to private firms. The developments in banking and financial sector in CIS and CEECs are considered by ANDERSON/BERGLOF/MITZSEI, 1996; ANDERSON/ KEGELS, 1998; BONIN et al., 1998, BUCH, 1996; BLEJER/SKREB, 1999; RAJAN/ZINGALES, 1998).
- *The lack of institutions.* The institutional change had also caused adjustment costs and was connected with output losses. As the central planning was abolished, the base for all transactions was no longer mandatory delivery targets, but the contractual system. The absence of the „culture" of contracts contributed to the growth of informal relations, loss of reputation, and chaos, and resulted in „disorganization" that was associated with output losses. The reforms at the early stage of transition were slowed by the lack of corresponding institutions and the lack of legal infrastructure (LEIJONHUFVUD/RUEHL, 1997; KORNAI, 1994).

2.2.3 Output Decline and Determinants of Future Growth

The centrally planned system itself was the poor mechanism of control and „equalization" which was mostly responsible for the deterioration and final collapse of the Soviet Union, which spread throughout the other CMEA member states. The major failures of the system were based on the lack of private property, control for prices and investment, soft budget constraints, and lack of competition, all of which together excluded the possibility of efficiency for enterprises. Minimization of costs, profit seeking, and better quality were not necessary goals as they contradicted with Soviet plans. The innovation activities, improvements in productivity so necessary for sustainable economic growth, were to a large extent neglected in Soviet enterprises. Additionally, nearly autarky pattern of foreign trade is also associated with welfare losses for the CMEA block countries. Moreover, high level of integration and specialization without taking into account comparative advantages led to a distorted structure of foreign trade and to the necessity of changes in the comparative advantage pattern during transformation according to economic, geographical, and cultural principles. An underdeveloped financial system and the lack of institutions and legal environment represent serious obstacles in the way of transformation. The transformation from centrally planned to market economy is in general more complicated, as it demands basic changes in the „old" distorted system and supposes first of all to rebuild the old enterprises and institutions and then to introduce new ones. There are also a number of obstacles in the way which are responsible for so called transition recession.

The decline in output during the transformation period was to a large extent caused by the transitional costs of systemic change. Therefore the recovery in output would depend on how soon the growth in new industries and services and private sector activities would prevail over the declines in traditional industries and the state sector. The speed of recovery will closely depend on the speed of structural adjustment. Especially important are the factors crucial for the investment in new sectors (BLANCHARD, 1996). Thus recovery is expected to be enhanced by liberalization, stabilization, privatization, and improvements in legal infrastructure and institutional environment, where a special role should be devoted to the financial institutions (SACHS/WARNER, 1996; SELOWSKY/ MARTIN, 1997).

2.3 Progress in Transition

The transition from a centrally planned economy to a market-based system opened to the world is connected with a number of necessary policies. All transition economies have to face the challenges in establishing liberalization, macroeconomic stabilization, privatization, and the development of institutions.

The transition economies experienced different progress in transition. The large discrepancy in reforms is first of all to be explained by various policy choices the countries have to admit, as well as by the speed in which these reforms were implemented, which is influenced by the difficulty of the reform itself. By nature, liberalization and privatization are reforms that are relatively easy to implement, where the government is supposed to reduce control over prices and create conditions for transferring the ownership of enterprises from the government to private individuals. Creation of institutions which are supposed to support markets and private enterprises, on the other hand, takes time as it requires not only the establishment of a legal environment but also acceptance by the population and the capacity for rule enforcement.

2.3.1 Shock Therapy versus Gradualism

With respect to the speed of market reforms it is possible to point out two approaches which countries have chosen during transformation. The approach that pursues rapid changes in terms of liberalization, stabilization, and privatization, as well as institutional reforms, was called „shock therapy". The rapidity of the introduction of reforms in transition economies and the choice between „shock therapy" and „gradualist approach" is detailed discussed by KATZ/OWEN (2000) and AGHION/BLANCHARD (1994). Poland represents a bright example of „quick" reforms. In the late 1990s Poland is ranked among the most advanced transition economies. Rapid growth of „shock therapy" is based on the quick establishment of functioning markets, quick restructuring of enterprises, and the creation of conditions for new business set-ups, which in turn creates high demand for market institutions. The argumentation against „shock therapy" especially points to the exaggeration of social problems accompanying rapid adjustment, where the situation might occur in which the downsizing of „old" enterprises is quicker than an increase in employment from new businesses. The lack of market institutions would also represent a danger for macroeconomic stability and would remain a problem until there are no further changes in this direction.

An alternative to „shock therapy" is the „gradualist approach" to liberalization and privatization. The „gradualist approach" allows for a more balanced structural adjustment. The „old" enterprises in the state sector of the economy can continually cut-up their activities and provide for better reallocation of resources from the state to the emerging private sector. The downsizing of state enterprises occurs at the rate equal to the rate of growth in the private sector. This approach also allows market institutions to develop in line with markets and the private sector. Hungary performed a successful transformation using the „gradualist approach". However, it is not possible to distinguish which path of reform promises better results. It depends, first of all, on the intent to implement quick changes and secondly, on the initial conditions prior to transformation. Thus in Hungary many of the institutions and practices of a market economy were established long before the start-up of the transformation. Under the surface of communist rule, from the early 1980s onwards, legal small business grew very rapidly. However for Hungary the step by step „gradualist approach" was a right decision because otherwise „shock therapy" would have jeopardized many of Hungary's achievements: high living standards, international banking credibility, political and personal freedom, and already well functioning market institutions and enterprises (HARE/REVESZ, 1992). Most CIS countries choose the „gradualist path" as well. Although it should not serve as an excuse for the very slow reform paths which some of the CIS countries exhibit.

2.3.2 *Progress in Reforms*

The progress in reforms has varied considerably across countries. Hungary and Poland have managed to achieve strategic goals of transformation and are among the most advanced transition economies. Rapid liberalization, sustained macroeconomic stabilization, and comprehensive small-scale privatization have led a profound basis for further institutional reform as private enterprises and voters create demand for market functioning institutions.

To judge the progress in transition one should take into account the initial conditions prior to the process of transformation. CIS countries were more strongly effected by the distortions of central planning than some other CMEA countries. Thus in CEECs central planning was introduced only after 1945, making the transition process potentially easier than for CIS countries which were almost 70 years under the centrally planned system. Additionally, Hungary and Poland were among the wealthier countries than the considered CIS countries prior to the Second World War. In these countries the elements of market economy were never completely eliminated. Thus Hungary and Poland were distinguished by a larger initial private sector; Poland was distinguished by the importance of agriculture in the economy. Moreover countries in Central and Eastern Europe were characterized by less trade dependence on CMEA than Western CIS countries. Thus, the CEECs have managed to achieve competitiveness in Western markets for at least a few selected goods. Additionally, proximity to the EU represented an important advantage in terms of access to markets and financial flows, but first of all in terms of the proximity to modern democratic and business-oriented societies (EBRD, 1999). CEECs have also rapidly reallocated their trade towards the Western markets, which also played a role for the subsequent recovery. Given the better initial conditions and the intent to join the EU, CEECs experienced significantly better performance during the transformation process than CIS countries and have already managed to reach some of the strategic goals and to overcome economic challenges which emerged at the beginning of transition. The transition for CIS countries was substantially aggravated by the Russian transformation crisis, which contributed to reversals in price and trade liberalization.

In Table 3 the progress in transition is summarized for the Central and Eastern European as well as for CIS countries[3]. Table 3 shows the EBRD transition indicators, which explanation is represented in section 2.5. Appendix.

---

[3] See also SACHS (1996) on progress in reforms.

Table 3: Progress in Transition in Central and Eastern Europe, the Baltic States and the CIS, 1999

			Enterprises			Markets and trade			Financial institutions	
Countries	Population (millions, mid-1999)	Private sector share of GDP in %, mid-1999 (EBRD estimate)[1]	Large-scale privatization	Small-scale privatization	Governance and enterprise restructuring	Price liberalization	Trade & foreign exchange system	Competition policy	Banking reform & interest rate liberalization	Securities markets & non-bank financial institutions
Albania	3.2	75	2	4	2	3	4	2	2	2-
Armenia	3.7	60	3	3+	2	3	4	2	2+	2
Azerbaijan	7.6	45	2-	3	2	3	3+	1	2	2-
Belarus	10.2	20	1	2	1	2-	1	2	1	2
Bosnia and Herzegovina	4.3	35	2	2	2-	3	3-	1	2+	1
Bulgaria	8.2	60	3	3+	2+	3	4+	2	3-	2
Croatia	4.5	60	3	4+	3-	3	4	2	3	2+
Czech Republic	10.3	80	4	4+	3	3	4+	3	3+	3
Estonia	1.4	75	4	4+	3	3	4	3-	4-	3
FYR Macedonia	2.0	55	3	4	2	3	4	1	3	2-
Georgia	5.4	60	3+	4	2	3	4	2	2+	1
Hungary	10.1	80	4	4+	3+	3+	4+	3	4	3+
Kasakhstan	14.8	55	3	4	2	3	3	2	2+	2
Kyrgyzstan	4.8	60	3	4	2	3	4	2	2+	2
Latvia	2.4	65	3	4	3-	3	4+	3-	3	2+
Lithuania	3.7	70	3	4+	3-	3	4	2+	3	3-

Table 3: Progress in Transition in Central and Eastern Europe, The Baltic States and the CIS, 1999 (cont.)

			Enterprises			Markets and trade			Financial institutions	
Countries	Population (millions, mid-1999)	Private sector share of GDP in %, mid-1999 (EBRD estimate)[1]	Large-scale privatization	Small-scale privatization	Governance and enterprise restructuring	Price liberalization	Trade & foreign exchange system	Competition policy	Banking reform & interest rate liberalization	Securities markets & non-bank financial institutions
Moldova	4.3	45	3	3+	2	3	4	2	2+	2
Poland	38.8	65	3+	4+	3	3+	4+	3	3+	3+
Romania	22.4	60	3-	4-	2	3	4	2	3-	2
Russian Federation	146.7	70	3+	4	2-	3-	2+	2+	2-	2-
Slovak Republic	5.4	75	4	4+	3	3	4+	3	3-	2+
Slovenia	2.0	55	3+	4+	3-	3	4+	2	3+	3
Tajikistan	6.2	30	2+	3	2-	3	3-	1	1	1
Turkmenistan	4.9	25	2-	2	2-	2	1	1	1	1
Ukraine	50.7	55	2+	3+	2	3	3	2	2	2
Uzbekistan	24.2	45	3-	3	2	2	1	2	2-	2

Source: EBRD (1999), Transition Report 1999

2.3.2.1 Liberalization

In terms of liberalization there was a wide variation across more advanced transition economies and CIS countries in the path and extent of market liberalization. According to the EBRD transition indicators, liberal markets can be defined as having a score of 3- on price liberalization (most prices free except for housing rents and infrastructure tariffs) and 4- on trade liberalization (full current account convertibility). Both Hungary's and Poland's performance is evaluated with a score of 3+ on price liberalization and 4+ on trade liberalization (see Table 3). Both countries have experienced comprehensive price liberalization where most state procurement at non-market prices was largely abolished. Trade liberalization reached the standards of advanced industrial economies with the removal of most all trade barriers and WTO membership. The rapid performance of more advanced transition economies in internal and external liberalization stands in contrast to the more uneven and gradual liberalization in CIS countries.

The link between liberalization and initial conditions is analyzed by KRUEGER/CIOLKO (1998).

Russia has attempted to liberalize both domestic and external markets early, but due to growing imbalances was unable to sustain these reforms. Russian progress on price liberalization was estimated with the score of 3- and on trade liberalization with the score of 2+ (see Table 3). BERKOWITZ/DE JONG/HUSTED (1998) also point to a considerable progress in price liberalization in Russia. Although substantial progress in price liberalization was reached, the progress in external liberalization remains uneven with some export and import controls being abolished and with almost full current account convertibility, but without a fully transparent exchange regime. Ukraine liberalized more gradually than Russia but also reversed these reforms. The performance of Ukraine is marked by a score of 3 for both price and trade liberalization, where in trade liberalization the removal of almost all quantitative and administrative import and export restrictions was reached as well as almost full current convertibility (EBRD, 1999). The progress in liberalization in Belarus still remains far from complete. The scores 2- for price liberalization and only 1 for trade liberalization reflect its backward position (see Table 3). Price controls for important product categories are still present and state procurement at non-market prices is still substantial.

2.3.2.2 Stabilization

There were also large discrepancies between these two groups of countries in terms of macroeconomic stabilization and degree of financial discipline (FISCHER/SAHAY/VEGH, 1996; ASLUND/BOONE/JOHNSON, 1996). CIS countries were „late" stabilizers because they adopted the stabilization program at the end of 1993, where Hungary and Poland had already adopted this program in 1990 (EBRD, 1999). A measure of the strength in the macroeconomic stabilization has been a moderate level of inflation (less that 30 percent) and a sustainable fiscal deficit (less than 5 percent of GDP). A positive impact of macroeconomic stabilization on output was found by HAVRYLYSHYN/ ISVORSKI/VAN ROODEN (1998). Most countries experienced exaggerated inflation growth with the onset of transformation. Most of the investigated countries achieved moderate rates of inflation by the end of 1997. The exceptions were Russia, which experienced growth of inflation during 1998 as a result of weak stabilization policies, and Belarus, where inflation remained high during the whole time of transition as a result of inflationary soft lending to favored enterprises and soft loans (EBRD, 1999). The problem of fiscal deficit was never solved in Russia. The key problem of Russian economy is a low level of tax collection. Thus, e.g. personal income tax being one of the major sources of fiscal revenues in developed countries accounted for from 2.2 to 2.9 percent of GDP in 1995 - 1997, where at the same time it was reported that household incomes in 1997 reached 62 percent of GDP. Tax evasion remains very high by the Russian population, which is especially remarkable among the rich population. Thus in 1997 the richest group of population paid only 16.7 percent of what they were obliged to pay (GAVRILENKOV, 1999).

Russia, while having reached substantial success in liberalization, has never achieved the appropriate level of macroeconomic stability (SACHS, 1995). Stabilization in Russia was to a large extent based on external sources with little success in reforming public financing and appears to be short-lived and fragile (GAVRILENKOV, 1999). Success in both liberalization and stabilization requires adopting public financing to the requirements of a market economy and the imposing of hard budget constraints on enterprises. Liberalization leads to the rapid erosion of the state's old tax base in the state enterprise sector, caused by the shift in relative prices and increased competition from private sector and imports from abroad. Stabilization requires the government to cut subsidies to these enterprises and to accept the costs of economic restructuring. There are different types of soft budget constraint. The most common ones are budgetary subsidies to producers and soft governmental loans. In Russia production subsidies amounted in 1998 to 6.5 percent of GDP (EBRD, 1999). Some countries also try to support state-owned enterprises through alternative forms of support for enterprises, such as tax arrears and non-payment of utility bills. Non-payment of utility bills, especially bills of state-owned energy producers, reflects the old situation in which heavy industry was supported by low administered pricing for energy inputs. This alternative form allows loss-making enterprises to continue to exist and is responsible for the inefficient use of resources, including excessive employment and sales of products at prices below costs and hence undermines macroeconomic stability.

2.3.2.3 Privatization

Privatization is expected to accompany liberalization and stabilization to reach sustainable reforms. The goal of privatization was first of all to replace state ownership by private ownership, and secondly to improve the functioning of the enterprises after the privatization in terms of restructuring and more efficient management. There was substantial progress made in small scale privatization in almost all investigated countries. In Hungary, Poland, and Russia small enterprises were completely privatized. Ukraine and Belarus were also rather successful in this. Most of privatized small enterprises were in trade and service sectors. Different is the situation with large enterprises. Hungary had privatized more than 50 percent of state-owned large enterprises. Poland and Russia more than 25 percent. Ukraine's success was limited by some sales and the progress in Belarus is insufficient with little private ownership of large state-owned enterprises (EBRD, 1999). Important with privatization is the sale of shares to strategic investors because there is evidence that performance in such enterprises is much better than in companies with insider ownership. Hungary sold most of it's large enterprises to strategic investors. Poland created substantial conditions for strategic investors without providing special ownership privileges to enterprise insiders. The CIS countries, on the other hand, mostly gave privatization advantages the to the insider owners (EBRD, 1999; ESTRIN/WRIGHT, 1999; FRYDMAN et al., 1996; AGHION/BLANCHARD, 1996; HANSON, 1997; LESHCHENKO/REVENKO, 1999).

2.3.2.4 Institutions in Transition

The development of institutions that support markets and private enterprises is essential for successful transition (BRUNO/LUIGI, 1996). The impact of economic institutions on economic growth and technological change is argued by HUANG/XU (1999). At different stages of transition different institutions matter. At the initial stage, accompanied by high macroeconomic instability, government is supposed to secure basis market reforms and to support the creation of market functioning institutions. At the initial stage, the role of government is to secure public finances, to protect property and contract rights, and to provide for initial reforms like liberalization and privatization. After the implementation of basis reforms, the role of government would then change towards more coordination responsibilities rather than direct economic governance, and supporting institutions such as competition policy, bankruptcy, corporate governance, and regulation of infrastructure and finance would gain in importance (EBRD, 1999).

The progress of more advanced transition economies in institutional reforms is also considerably higher than in CIS countries. The main differences lie in the implementation of hard budget constraints, promotion of corporate governance, competition policy, banking reform with the establishment of a two-tier system and an independent central bank, and the creation of security markets and non-banking financial institutions. In all these reforms the CIS countries receive no more than 2 points (EBRD, 1999). Still less effort was made in Belarus on the hardening of budget constraints and promotion of corporate governance. In Russia and Ukraine, which exhibit moderate credit and subsidy policy, the implication of bankruptcy legislation remains rather weak and little progress is made to strengthen competition and corporate governance. Limited progress was made in these countries in banking reform; in Belarus on the level of establishment a two - tier system; in Russia and Ukraine on the level of liberalization of interest rates and credit allocation. The establishment of security markets and non-banking financial institutions is situated at the initial level (EBRD, 1999).

The substantial progress of Hungary and Poland in institutional reforms shows that these countries stay at the second stage of transformation where most basic reforms are already introduced and there is sufficient demand for institutions. The demand for institutions depends on the amount of years since the start of transition in which liberal markets have been in operation, on a number of years with macroeconomic stabilization, and on the progress in liberalization and privatization.

Because of different economic interests of various economic actors as well as due to the „free-rider problem" (the economic actors are eager to hide their interest on the set-up of institutions) the demand for institutions can not be fully formed through the market alone. This demands governmental supervision. Openness to foreign trade and foreign direct investment may reinforce the establishment of institutions and also work as a control for the balanced development of reforms. Foreign trade especially with non-transition economies stimulates the creation of institutions because there are possibilities to take over the experience of these countries in conducting business, to import norms and rules. Thus, foreign trading partners are more likely to rely on contacts and may help to introduce the „culture" of contracts in transition economies, where a lot of operations are being carried out in an informal business environment. Similarly, foreign direct investment can help to introduce the rules of corporate governance, which maybe emulated elsewhere. Rules and institutions can also be imported via the membership in international organizations (WELFENS, 1999a; BRADA/ SCHOENFELD/SLAY, 1995; ZECCHINI, 1995).

2.4 Tentative Conclusions

Output decline was more severe and prolonged in CIS than in more advanced transition economies like Hungary and Poland. Hungary and Poland were the most successfully growing economies in the 1990s. The success of one and the failure of the other can be explained by the different initial conditions prior to transition, but the major reason lies in different policy choices and hence progress in market reforms. The evidence shows that countries that exhibited earlier liberalization, stabilization, and privatization also exhibited earlier growth.

From the centrally planned system the transition economies inherited a number of structural and macroeconomic distortions. But at the starting point of transition the CIS countries had a more disadvantageous situation than Hungary and Poland, where, e.g., in Hungary market reforms were introduced long before the final collapse of the Soviet system. Proximity to the developed Western economies and the intent to join the EU determined to a large extent great progress in market reforms in these countries.

The experience of more advanced transition economies shows that recovery depends first of all on the speed of structural adjustment, which provides reallocation of resources from „old" state-owned enterprises to the „new" private sector. Structural reforms start with internal and external liberalization and privatization, and ends with the set-up of market institutions which provide a functioning market economy. Macroeconomic stabilization is also crucial for sustained economic growth. Institutional reform is essential for the success of transition as it provides for rules and structures necessary for the functioning of a market economy. From the other side institutional reform can fully be implemented only after basic reforms like liberalization, stabilization, and privatization, as the private sector creates demand for institutions. The analysis witnesses that Hungary and Poland have already surpassed the stage of basis reforms and are at the second stage where the institutional set-up plays a decisive role. On the other hand, CIS countries are situated at the first „basis" stage and were even placed back in reforms during the last period of time, e.g., the failure in stabilization in Russia.

Price and trade liberalization remain incomplete in the CIS countries and markets are to a large extent still non-competitive. Without the signals of free prices and discipline of competitive markets the transition can not be sustained and the performance will remain disappointing. There is still evidence of soft budget constraints in these countries, if not in the way of budgetary subsidies, then in other alternative ways that are indeed even more detrimental to economic efficiency. Incompetitive markets and soft budget constraints are the main obstacles for the improvement of the efficiency of enterprises and their growth. On the other hand, growth of enterprises in the private sector is the basic precondition for the demand for market-based institutions in transition economies. Especially important is the role of financial institutions as they provide for new investment and support the development of the private sector. The set-up of domestic institutions can be reinforced by integration into the world economy. Openness of the economy, foreign direct investment, entrance to the EU, and membership in international organizations can strengthen the demand of local businesses for market-supporting institutions.

More advanced transition economies like Hungary and Poland have managed to more quickly overcome the distortions inherited from central planning and have already implemented most important market reforms and achieved levels comparable to the advanced industrial countries. Progress in reforms explains the quick recovery of these countries. The higher integration of these economies into the world economy, a rapid reorientation of their economic relations towards the West, and especially the intent to join the EU, which allowed the adoption of rules and norms typical for market economies, the reinforcement of market reforms, and the strengthening of demand for market institutions, all played an important role in this process. The CIS countries are still lagging behind in most of the market reforms. They are still very cautious to open their markets to the world, to create equal competition conditions for state and private firms, and to give equal rights in privatization to strategic and insider investors. All this factors as a detriment to the competitive abilities of the domestic enterprises in the world markets and negatively affects innovation activities and the efficiency of domestic enterprises. One way out of this situation is to increase the integration into the world economy via openness of foreign trade and foreign direct investment and to gain membership in international organizations. The integration into the world economy is important in the sense that it would allow the import of rules and institutions, the adoption of the „culture" of economic behavior, the reinforcement of market reforms, and what is of major importance, the imitation of technological activities essential for economic growth and the catching-up process towards the income levels of advanced countries.

2.5 Appendix

Classification System for Transition Indicators

Large-scale privatization

1 Little private ownership.

2 Comprehensive scheme almost ready for implementation; some sales completed.

3 More than 25 percent of large-scale enterprises' assets in private hands or in the process of being privatized (with the process having reached a stage at which the state has effectively ceded its ownership rights), but possibly with major unresolved issues regarding corporate governance.

4 More than 50 percent of state-owned enterprises and farm assets in private ownership and significant progress on corporate governance of these enterprises.

4+ Standards and performance typical of advanced industrial economies: more than 75 percent of enterprise assets in private ownership with corporate governance.

Small-scale privatization

1 Little progress.

2 Substantial share privatized.

3 Nearly comprehensive program implemented.

4 Complete privatization of small companies with tradable ownership rights.

4+ Standards and performance typical of advanced industrial economies: no state ownership of small enterprises; effective tradability of land.

Governance and enterprise restructuring

1 Soft budget constraints (tax credit and subsidy policies weakening financial discipline at the enterprise level); few other reforms to promote corporate governance.

2 Moderately tight credit and subsidy policy but weak enforcement of bankruptcy legislation and little action taken to strengthen competition and corporate governance.

3 Significant and sustained actions to harden budget constraints and to promote corporate governance effectively (e.g. through privatization combined with tight credit and subsidy policies and/or enforcement of bankruptcy legislation).

4 Substantial improvement in corporate governance, for example, an account of an active corporate control market; significant new investment at the enterprise level.

4+ Standards and performance typical of advanced industrial economies; effective corporate control exercised through domestic financial institutions and markets, fostering market-driven restructuring.

<u>Price liberalization</u>

1 Most prices formally controlled by the government.

2 Price controls for several important product categories; state procurement at non-market prices remains substantial.

3 Substantial progress on price liberalization: state procurement at non-market prices largely phased out.

4 Comprehensive price liberalization; utility pricing which reflects economic costs.

4+ Standards and performance typical of advanced industrial economies: comprehensive price liberalization; efficiency-enhancing regulation of utility pricing.

<u>Trade and foreign exchange system</u>

1 Widespread import and/or export controls or very limited legitimate access to foreign exchange.

2 Some liberalization of import and/or export controls; almost full current account convertibility in principle but with a foreign exchange regime that is not fully transparent (possibly with multiple exchange rates).

3 Removal of almost all quantitative and administrative import and export restrictions; almost full current account convertibility.

4 Removal of all quantitative and administrative import and export restrictions (a part from agriculture) and all significant export tariffs; insignificant direct involvement in exports and imports by ministries and state-owned trading companies; no major non-uniformity of customs duties for non-agricultural goods and services; full current account convertibility.

4+ Standards and performance norms of advanced industrial economies: removal of most tariff barriers; WTO membership.

<u>Competition policy</u>

1 No competition legislation or institutions.

2 Competition policy legislation and institutions set up; some reduction of entry restrictions or enforcement action on dominant firms.

3 Some enforcement actions to reduce abuse of market power and to promote a competitive environment, including break-ups of dominant conglomerates; substantial reduction of entry restrictions.

4 Significant enforcement actions to reduce abuse of market owner and to promote a competitive environment.

4+ Standards and performance typical of advanced industrial economies: effective enforcement of competition policy; unrestricted entry to most markets.

Banking reform and interest rate liberalization

1 Little progress beyond establishment of two-tier system.

2 Significant liberalization of interest rates and credit allocation; limited use of directed credit or interest rate ceilings.

3 Substantial progress in establishment of bank solvency and of a framework for prudential supervision and regulation; full interest rate liberalization with little preferential access to cheap refinancing; significant lending to private enterprises and significant presence of private banks.

4 Significant movement of banking laws and regulations towards BIS standards; well-functioning banking competition and effective prudential supervision; significant term lending to private enterprises; substantial financial deepening.

4+ Standards and performance norms of advanced industrial economies: full convergence of banking laws and regulations with BIS standards; provision of full set of competitive banking services.

Securities markets and non-bank financial institutions

1 Little progress

2 Formation of securities exchanges, market-makers and brokers; some trading in government paper and/or securities; rudimentary legal and regulatory framework for the issuance and trading of securities.

3 Substantial issuance of securities by private enterprises; establishment of independent share registries, secure clearance and settlement procedures, and some protection of minority (e.g. investment funds, private insurance and pension funds, leasing companies) and associated regulatory framework.

4 Securities laws and regulations approaching IOSCO standards; substantial market liquidity and capitalization; well-functioning non-bank financial institutions and effective regulation.

4+ Standards and performance norms of advanced industrial economies: full convergence of securities laws and regulations with IOSCO standards; fully developed non-bank intermediation.

3 Economic Growth in Selected CIS and More Advanced CEECs: Aspects of Future Growth Strategy

The Soviet Union has never been a leading technological nation. Its rapid catching up after World War II was first of all to be explained through the advantage of backwardness that the Soviet Union experienced in the form of a low output per capita. Growth had been stagnant since the 1970s (WELFENS, 1992a). The reasons for decline of growth were too strong reliance on extensive growth and the erosion of incentives to work in the official economy, which resulted in low productivity growth. Insufficient technological progress due to an inefficient scientific sector in the planned economy on one side and poor interplay between scientific sector and production on the other determined low productivity growth and stagnating of the economy. Therefore, there was lack of technological progress in the leading sectors of civilian production and diminishing returns to capital. We will look into these and other problems in more detail subsequently.

This chapter consists of 10 sections. The chapter is structured in such a way as to show growth developments in the former Soviet Union from the historical perspective and to discuss theoretical applications for the present situation in the Commonwealth of Independent States (CIS) and Central and Eastern European countries (CEECs), as well as to show future growth perspectives for these countries. The first section covers the problems and characteristics of the extensive growth strategy of the former Soviet Union. Since the main detriment lay in technological progress, the faults made in the field of science and innovation come to light in the second section. The third section deals with theoretical approaches to economic growth in general. In the forth section empirical evidence on modern growth theory is discussed. Further in the fifth section reflections are made in respect to the application of growth theory to the case of CIS and CEECs. Since catching up with developed market economies is the major goal of transformation countries, the aspects of technological gap theory and the papers of new growth economists on technological catching up are reflected upon in section six. Further sections regard the role of special factors for economic growth in CIS and CEECs. Section seven describes the role of human capital which is essential for further growth. Section eight covers the dangers of „Dutch disease" for economic growth. The problem of „Dutch disease" is especially relevant in the case of countries which are richly endowed with natural resources, such as Russia. Additionally, the importance of foreign trade and foreign direct investment (FDI) like the main channels of technology transfer is strengthened in section nine. Discussions on foreign trade and FDI are proceeded with in the following chapters. At the end some conclusions on further growth strategy for CIS and CEECs are made.

3.1 Extensive Growth in the Former USSR

Being once a successfully growing economy whose speed of economic growth was especially high after the World War II, the Soviet Union has collapsed politically and economically in the late 1980s. Russia, other CIS, and CEECs were strongly hurt by the destructive developments. The impact on the CIS countries was especially long and hard. Prolonged recession began in the late 1980s and is still persistent in some of those economies. The socialist crisis and transformational recession have caused these countries to fall back half a century in their development. Therefore, in the year 2000 (at the start of the new century) the CIS countries were standing at the beginning of a „new" growth process whose success depends strongly on the speed of the positive market reforms, political will, and desire to cooperate with the international society.

What were the reasons for the decline of the Soviet economic growth? Was the strategy of development chosen by Soviet leaders wrong, and what are those faults which proceeded the collapse of the Soviet Union? Several economists investigated the growth experience of the Soviet Union. Common opinion was that the reason for the collapse of the Soviet system was due to a large extent to an extensive strategy of development (EASTERLY/FISCHER, 1992; WEITZMAN, 1970; DESAI, 1976; BERGSON, 1978, 1987, 1991a,b; OFER, 1987; CAMPBELL, 1991).

The extensive strategy of development realized by the Soviet Union relied on an increasing usage of inputs, and neglected growth of productivity and technological progress.

CAMPBELL (1991) points out that the Soviet Union at the beginning of the century was a technologically backward country and the main goal of Soviet leaders after New Economic Policy (NEP) in the twenties was *„...to catch up with and surpass (dognat' i peregnat') the advanced capitalist countries in a historically short period of time"* (CAMPBELL, 1991, p. 117). The extensive strategy was also called the „mobilization" approach as it was supposed to mobilize the resources to reach high growth rates. The major elements of the Soviet strategy consisted of a high rate of investment, technological catch up, mobilization of labor (from rural areas), and use of rich endowments of natural resources.

Table 4 represents the data on GNP, inputs, and productivity in the former USSR estimated by OFER (1987)[4]. Extensive growth strategy in combination with centralized decisionmaking yielded good results, especially at the beginning of the

[4] The Soviet official data on economic growth was highly exaggerated and for that reason rejected by both Western and later Soviet economists. A lot of Western researchers estimated the data on the Soviet growth experience.

20th century. The results seemed to be even better given the background of depression and stagnation experienced in the comparable period of time by the Western market economies. Thus, in the period 1928 - 1940, the average Soviet growth rate reached 5.8 percent and per capita growth was 3.6 percent (see Table 4). The annual growth rate of GNP in the whole period from 1928 till 1985 was 4.2 percent, or 4.7 percent excluding the five World War II years. Per capita growth of GNP in this period was 3.0 percent or 3.3 percent, respectively. But the most important feature revealed by Table 4 is the decline in growth rates over time. The deceleration of Soviet growth began in the 1960s. In the 1950s GNP was growing at the rate of 5.7 percent, while in the 1960s it fell to 5.2 percent per year. In the 1970s it fell further to 3.7 percent, and at the end of the decade growth reached 2.6 percent. GNP per capita remained on the same level of 3.9 percent during the 1950s and 1960s, but fell in the 1970s to 2.7 percent, and at the end of the decade accounted for only 1.8 percent. In the period of 1980 - 1985 the average growth of GNP was about 2.0 percent per year and GNP per capita was 1.1 percent per year. Thus, when in 1985 Mikhail Gorbachev became secretary general of the Soviet Union, the problem of growth decline was obvious. The target for economic growth during the first years of Gorbachev's regime was too ambitious to really be achieved as the growth rate was supposed to reach 4 percent a year. According to CAMPBELL (1991), the actual growth rate during the second half of the eighties did not exceed ca. 1 percent per year. At the end of the decade it turned out to be negative and a prolonged recession set in, the positive outcome of which remains questionable.

Table 4: GNP, Inputs, and Productivity in the Former USSR, 1928 - 1983 (annual rates of growth)

	1928-1985[a]	1928-1940	1940-1950[b]	1950-1985	1950-1960	1960-1970	1970-1975	1975-1980	1980-1985
1. Gross national product	**4.2 (4.7)**	**5.8**	**2.2**	**4.3**	**5.7**	**5.2**	**3.7**	**2.6**	**2.0**
2. Combined inputs	**3.2 (3.4)**	**4.0**	**0.6**	**3.6**	**4.0**	**3.7**	**3.7**	**3.0**	**2.5**
3. Labor (man-hours)	**1.8 (1.9)**	**3.3**	**0.7**	**1.4**	**1.2**	**1.7**	**1.7**	**1.2**	**0.7**
4. Employment	1.9 (2.0)	3.9	0.3	1.5	1.6	2.1	1.5	1.2	0.7
5. Capital	**6.9 (7.5)**	**9.0**	**0.4**	**8.0**	**9.5**	**8.0**	**7.9**	**6.8**	**6.3**
6. Land	0.8 (0.8)	1.6	-1.3	1.1	3.3	0.2	1.0	-0.1	-0.1
7. Total factor productivity[c]	**1.1 (1.2)**	**1.7**	**1.6**	**0.7**	**1.6**	**1.5**	**0.0**	**-0.4**	**-0.5**

Table 4: GNP, Inputs, and Productivity in the Former USSR, 1928 - 1983 (annual rates of growth) (cont.)

	1928-1985[a]	1928-1940	1940-1950[b]	1950-1985	1950-1960	1960-1970	1970-1975	1975-1980	1980-1985
8. GNP per hour worked	2.4 (2.6)	2.4	1.5	3.0	4.4	3.4	2.0	1.4	1.3
9. GNP per employed	2.3 (2.5)	1.8	1.4	2.8	4.0	3.0	2.2	1.4	1.3
10. GNP per unit of capital	-2.4 (-2.6)	-2.9	3.4	-3.3	-3.5	2.6	-3.9	-3.9	-4.0
11. Population	1.3 (1.4)	2.1	-0.8	1.3	1.8	1.3	0.9	0.8	0.9
12. GNP per capita	**3.0 (3.3)**	**3.6**	**2.9**	**3.2**	**3.9**	**3.9**	**2.7**	**1.8**	**1.1**
13. Investment	7.3 (8.1)	9.6	5.6	7.0	11.4	6.8	5.4	4.3	3.2

Source: Ofer (1987)

[a] *Figures in parentheses in this column are calculated on the basis of only 50 years, excluding the World War II years.*

[b] *This period covers World War II years and the following reconstruction period; therefore many of the figures are averages of extremely different magnitudes. For example, GNP stagnated over 1940 - 1944 and grew at 3.6 percent per year over 1944 - 1950; the corresponding figures for population growth are -2.7 and 0.5 percent, respectively, giving 2.7 and 3.1 percent per year for growth of GNP per capita for two subperiods.*

[c] *Figures in parentheses in this line (except for 1928 - 1985) are CIA estimates of total factor productivity, based on an alternative set of weights: 0.558 for hours, 0.412 for capital, and 0.03 for land (CIA, HB, 1984, p.68). For 1980 - 1985 the weights are 0.512, 0.458, and 0.03 respectively (CIA, HB, 1986, p.70).*

One could divide the Soviet growth experience in two stages: from 1928 to 1960 it was a successful stage of economic growth, and from 1960 to 1985 there was the slowdown with elements of recession. The rapid growth at the first stage could be explained by the catching up process which the USSR experienced. As a follower country the USSR could use the „advantage of backwardness" and through technology transfer from advanced industrial countries catch up to a higher level of output. In the years of early industrialization, the USSR indeed carried out a rather outward-oriented economic policy and took advantage of the possibilities to import equipment and technology from more advanced Western economies.

BERGSON (1978), who carried out several studies devoted to the Soviet growth experience, compares average annual growth rates of the USSR and the United States in the period 1928 - 1958. According to his estimations the USSR surpassed the United States in growth terms growing at an annual rate of 4.1 percent a year in contrast to only 2.9 percent in the United States. These figures show that the USSR experienced a rapid catching up process while the United States represented an advanced market economy and for that reason did not grow rapidly. There was also the impact of the Great Depression. But did the USSR really reach the output level of the United States or at which stage of the catching up process did the country face relative stagnation? BERGSON (1978) estimates comparative volume of output in the USSR and the United States. He finds that the USSR lagged far behind the United States in 1955 in terms of total output. According to his estimations the Soviet GNP accounted for only 28 percent of that of the United States if valued in rubles, and 45 percent if valued in dollars. In per capita terms the comparison was also not in the favor of the USSR because of the larger population. Thus, in per capita terms the USSR accounted for only 23 percent of that in the United States in rubles and 38 percent in dollars. The figures for per capita consumption are 19 and 31 percent. The per capita nonconsumption of the USSR represented 36 percent of that in the United States in rubles and 53 percent in dollars.

Thus, the development strategy of the Soviet Union did not really compensate for the „late start". The diminishing growth tendency after the 1960s and later a prolonged recession led to the result that at the beginning of the 21th century the CIS countries are again in the position of „latecomers", as they were a century ago. The Soviet development strategy also did not, or to be more exact, it especially did not provide sufficient consumption levels. The goal of the Soviet Union to reach the „abundance of material and cultural goods for the whole population", or what in other words means to reach high living standards, was not realized. According to BERGSON (1991a), USSR was practically at the bottom of the scale of standards experienced in the OECD in terms of per capita consumption in 1985. The position of the USSR was below Portugal and a little above Turkey, whose level was the lowest among the OECD countries. BERGSON explains low consumption per capita level in the USSR through a low productivity level. What were the reasons for growth decline in the USSR and the collapse of the system?

OFER (1987) points out that Soviet growth was generated by the increase in inputs and declining growth of overall input of productivity. During the period 1928 - 1985 inputs grew at 3.2 percent on average and contributed 76 percent of total GNP growth, while total factor productivity grew at only 1.1 percent and contributed to only 24 percent of total growth (see Table 4). Productivity had completely stagnated an even retreated in the 1970s. For this reason relative contribution of inputs to growth increased and inputs became the sole component of growth since the 1970s. Capital was the main driving force of growth among the inputs. Labor inputs grew at a rate substantially higher than population growth during this entire period. While the population grew on average at a rate of 1.3 percent, labor in man-hours increased at a rate of 1.8 percent and employment at a rate of 1.9. High employment in the Soviet Union was to a large extent due to the high rate of participation in the labor force. Thus, in 1980 the Soviet participation rate was 86.6 percent in comparison to 66.5 and 70.9 percent in E-OECD and the US, respectively. The extremely high participation rate in the Soviet Union was due to the high participation rates of women. But what is more important is the diminishing tendency in labor inputs during the whole period. Thus, labor in man-hours growing at 1.8 percent during the period 1928 - 1940, grew at only 0.7 percent in 1980 - 1985. The same is valid for employment. The growth rate of employment diminished from 3.9 percent p.a. in 1928 - 1940 to only 0.7 percent in 1980 - 1985. The reason was a continuous decline in the population growth. Thus, the population growth has diminished from 2.1 percent p.a. in 1928 - 1940 to 0.9 percent in 1980 - 1985. Sharp declines in labor growth implied that capital became the only source of economic growth.

The Soviet growth strategy was characterized by very high rates of investment, leading to a high growth rate of the capital stock. Thus, in 1975 the capital grew at the annual rate of 8 - 9.5 percent. Such a growth rate could lead to doubling of the size of capital every 8 - 9 years. With the policy change (reduction of planned growth rate of investment) in 1976, the growth rate was allowed to be a little bit lower at approximately 6 or 7 percent, which is still very high by international comparisons (OFER, 1987). Giving definition to the extensive growth, OFER (1987, p. 1806) states: *„Extensive growth may be defined as a growth path along which capital grows at a (much) faster rate than output. Given the relatively slow growth of labor, this path will be followed whenever overall productivity growth is lagging. A necessary condition for rapid growth is that the share of investment in GNP grow monotonically, for it takes a larger share of a slower-growing GNP to keep the growth rate of a faster-growing capital stock constant. Only productivity growth at a rate that equalizes the growth rates of output and capital can avert this outcome, and its absence is what makes Soviet growth extensive"*. CAMPBELL (1991) also claims that the lack of productivity growth was a main factor of output decline. He underlines that the capital stock grew much faster than labor supply and even faster than output growth. In the late 1970s, when productivity growth turned out to be negative, output was growing at a more than proportionate growth in expenditure in inputs. And due to insufficient labor growth the capital was the only source of growth.

To sum up, the extensive model depended to a large extent on continued growth of inputs. With the further expansion it became more difficult to keep up the growth of inputs. There were demographical reasons caused by the decline of population growth, on the one hand, and it became impossible to transfer ever more labor from the rural to the urban sector, on the other. This holds at least for the Soviet economy, whose share of employment in agriculture in 1990 consisted of 12.9% (9,728 thousand) of total employment (75,325 thousand). There was also a need to replace obsolete capital. The capital intensity in the Soviet Union was very high. The problem was that the high ratio of capital to worker was based on the strategy of „capital deepening" instead of developing new capital assets. Such a strategy of permanently increasing the amount of capital in combination with the diminishing tendencies in population growth had no success. On the other hand it became more difficult to maintain output growth only through the increase of the capital stock. A major problem was the low productivity growth of the capital equipment producing sector. The productivity could solve that problem, as it could provide for more output per unit of inputs. But the productivity in the Soviet Union remained low and exhibited diminishing tendencies of growth. Since the late seventies it turned negative, which was the main reason for output decline in the Soviet Union.

BERGSON (1978, 1987, 1991b) investigates in a number of studies the productivity in the USSR and compares it to the experiences of the US and other Western European countries. He often compares the Soviet growth with the experience of the United States. The reason for comparisons made between two countries was mostly due to the Cold War. But the other reason is that both countries are very similar as they are both of continental dimensions, rely on economies of scale, and to a limited degree on foreign trade; they also are relatively well-endowed with natural resources. In absolute terms the United States had a much higher output per worker than the USSR. Thus, in 1960 output per worker in the USSR accounted for 26 or 41 percent of that in the United States (BERGSON, 1978). He emphasizes that productivity turned out to be especially low for the economy in general because of resource misallocation between farm and nonfarm sectors. The analysis showed that efficiency was especially low in agriculture. He also compares the USSR with other Western countries such as France, Germany (FRG), the United Kingdom, and Italy. For the year 1960 he finds that the USSR was most comparable to Italy in terms of productivity, which had the lowest productivity level among the investigated Western economies (BERGSON, 1978). He also made comparisons for the year 1975 for four communist and seven entrepreneurial market economy (EME) countries (BERGSON, 1991b). Among communist countries are the USSR, Hungary, Poland, and Yugoslavia. Among EME countries are the USA, FRG, France, the UK, Japan, and Spain. In the four communist countries, output per worker for 1975 was 29.5 to 34.3 percent below that of EME countries. Similar estimations were made for the year 1960 for the same four Soviet countries and seven OECD countries with close results (BERGSON, 1987). Comparison of socialist and market economies represents a difficult task since they have different economic and statistical systems. Deflation and quality aspects are particularly cumbersome.

In investigating productivity BERGSON (1978) analyses not only output per worker in absolute terms, but the growth of output per worker as well. He analyses the growth of output per worker as an impact of diverse conditioning factors: first, the increase in the stock of reproducible capital; second, improvement in the quality of labor; third, technological progress including both innovations in productive technologies and gains in productive efficiency due to redesign of the specific working arrangements (institutions, policies, and practices) by which the economy is organized. He emphasizes the relative importance of investment for productivity growth, on the one hand, and labor quality improvement and technological progress, on the other. Under the assumption that the backward countries should catch up in terms of productivity, meaning the lower the level of productivity the faster productivity growth, the results for the USSR might be surprising. In terms of productivity growth the USSR in 1960 with a rate of growth of 2.4 percent is outpaced by two Western countries, namely France and Germany, with annual growth rates of 3.9 percent and 3.4 percent, respectively. Italy and Japan, which were close to the USSR in the stage of development, have also experienced much higher rates of productivity growth, namely 4.4 and 5.9 percent, respectively. The USSR surpassed the UK and the US, which were the most advanced Western economies and are not comparable to the USSR in their stage of development. The productivity in the UK and the US grew at 1.8 and 1.6, respectively. The above figures witness that productivity growth in the USSR falls within the range of the Western countries. The two least advanced Western economies such as Italy and Japan exhibited much higher productivity growth. What was the reason that the USSR did not experience a long term catching up process in terms of productivity?

BERGSON (1978) comes to the conclusion that the growth of productivity in the USSR was mostly due to the increase in capital investment. The other factors of productivity growth such as investment in human capital and technology had relatively low importance. BERGSON also compares the capital investment cost of productivity growth of the USSR with that of Italy and Japan, which resemble the catching up process of the USSR[5]. The capital investment costs in the USSR are much higher than in Italy and Japan, and even higher than in France and Germany, although the latter represent more advanced economies. It is astonishing insofar as the capital investment cost of productivity growth turns out to be higher the more advanced the country is, and lower the less advanced the country is. Other sources of productivity growth, which could compensate the costs through

[5] The capital investment cost of productivity growth indicates how much capital investment is needed to increase productivity by one percentage point (BERGSON, 1987).

higher productivity gains, have been relatively weak in the USSR. This particularly concerns labor quality improvement and technological progress. BERGSON argues that especially modest technological progress was primarily responsible for the poor productivity performance. As far as labor quality is concerned the USSR had managed to reallocate sufficient resources and made much investment in education. For that reason, the labor quality looked favorable compared to that in Western countries. BERGSON blames economic working arrangements in the USSR to be responsible for low technological progress. The lack of innovation incentives and the complex bureaucratic process through which the innovation activities should pass before they will be implemented in the economy, slowed technological change. To sum up, behind poor productivity performance of the former Soviet Union stood low technological progress which was weak due mostly to insufficient incentives for innovation.

WEITZMAN (1972) offered another explanation for the extensive growth in the USSR. He argues that the decline in output was not caused because the share of investment in GDP hit a ceiling, but mainly because of the decline of the marginal product of capital, which used to be the only growing input. He argues that post-1945 Soviet growth corresponded to a constant elasticity of substitution (CES) production function with elasticity of substitution significantly less than one. His finding was that the elasticity of substitution of capital to labor was about 0.4 percent, and the residual which reflected technological change was growing at a constant rate of about 2 percent annually. Technological change, which accounted for 15 to 25 percent of average output increases, did not play such an important role in the Soviet Union as in other economies. In a situation of low technological change and scarce labor, low elasticity of substitution of capital to labor could lead to a decrease in output growth. Elasticity of substitution less than one makes it difficult to increase output through more inputs of one factor as the diminishing returns to capital rapidly set in. This situation as argued by WEITZMAN reflects the case of the Soviet Union as more capital was needed to compensate for scarcity of labor inputs very well.

WEITZMAN also tries to compare the Soviet case to the US. He applies the same CES function to the data of the US economy. The CES function did not fit the US case and produced a very high standard error. WEITZMAN argues that the reason for the „error" could be due to „the undetected swings of technological change". Technological change was, however, much higher in the US economy than in the Soviet Union. Making conclusions on further growth prospects for the USSR WEITZMAN (1972, p. 685) says: *„Instead of capital, labor and technical change will have to be increasingly relied upon as alternative sources of future economic growth".* He emphasizes that future growth should actually rely more on technological change as there is little possibility to increase labor in the near future due to predictions of demographers as well as a low possibility of increasing industrial population through transfers of population from agriculture. The Soviet system provided little possibilities for innovation as risk and uncertainty were eliminated by the planning system, which discouraged innovation on the local level.

DESAI (1976) has estimated CES function for the Soviet Union as well. He agrees that the CES constant returns to scale production function fits the production relationship in the Soviet economy. The elasticity of substitution of capital to labor is less than one. According to DESAI's estimations the parameter of technological change is higher than the 2 percent estimated by WEITZMAN and accounts for 3.5 or 4 percent. In this case a high rate of technological change reflects a process of catching up and corresponds the widespread view about the generally low level of Soviet technology.

To sum up, the investigation of WEITZMAN so far differs in the explanation of Soviet growth as it does not predict the diminishing of the total factor productivity as in other studies but explains the decline of Soviet output growth through diminishing returns to capital. Although WEITZMAN strengthens more diminishing returns to capital and not poor technological performance of the Soviet Union, if one looks behind the low elasticity of capital to labor, one will see that it might actually be due to poor technological progress in the Soviet Union. OFER (1987), analyzing the article of WEITZMAN, points out that a declining marginal productivity of capital might be a result of weak R&D activities and misdirection of R&D, as well as insufficient investment policy. He argues that it is the responsibility of R&D to provide for labor-saving innovations and the lack of such technologies in the new capital is a reason that a lot of labor-intensive workplaces were created without the possibility of those to be filled. This argumentation corresponds to that of WEITZMAN, as he agrees that the only way to reach output growth is to rely increasingly on technological change. OFER (1987) pays attention to the fact that the CES function estimated by WEITZMAN included neutral or disembodies technological progress. In the case of embodied technological progress high rates of investment could indeed lead to more economic growth. But the evidence shows that investment in the Soviet Union embodied only a small technological element which was connected with poor technological performance of the Soviet Union in the past.

3.2 Science and Innovation in the Former USSR

Low technological progress was not the goal of the Soviet government but the outcome of the system. A number of factors contributed to the collapse of Soviet science. Soviet science was of an extensive character and did not generate substantial returns (BALZER, 1995; SCHNEIDER, 1994). Although until the late 1970s in terms of the number of scientists and engineers per million of population and R&D expenditure the Soviet Union matched the figures of leading nations of the world, Soviet science turned out to be rather ineffective and regressed substantially during the 1980s and 1990s. In the 1960s R&D expenditure in the Soviet Union grew, on average, 10 - 12 percent annually and for S&T personnel, 7

- 8 percent. But R&D expenditure growth fell to only 5.1 percent in the mid 1970s, and has decreased considerably since the 1980s as a result of the overall crisis (OECD, 1994). Extensive growth, which lasted till the late 1970s, resulted in the creation of an extremely large R&D base which was greater than those of most OECD countries and made Russia famous, especially in the spheres of basic research and military technologies.

Ineffectiveness of the Soviet science was based on a number of factors. The high military orientation of Soviet science due to self-sufficiency in the military sphere is one of the most important ones. Even by the end of the 1980s 20% of the total defense budget and 75% of the federal science budget was directed towards spending on science in military sector (SIMANOVSKY, 1998; OECD, 1994). Investment in the military sector under priority of the space and weapons programs brought only little economic pay-off. Although the military sector was much more innovative than the civilian sector, the innovation activities were negatively affected by a number of factors. Thus, the high secrecy of military research led to the duplication of research and waste of resources, i.e. almost every field of the defense complex had their own laser system (defense industry, shipbuilding, nuclear industry, aviation, etc.). High concentration of production also had negative impact on innovation activity in the military sector. Thus, in 1993 there were nearly no small enterprises in the defense sector, at the same time medium sized enterprises accounted for less than 6 percent. Military R&D was carried out separate from industry and not within the major industrial companies like it is, for example, in the United States.

The civil sector, which could bring more economic pay-off, was to a large extent neglected. The civilian sector had never had high priority, although in 1988, before conversion, 30 percent of all R&D expenditure in the defense sector went to civilian R&D, and due to the lack of incentives and mechanisms for adopting technologies, defense technologies were never put to their best use in the civilian sector (OECD, 1994)[6]. In many cases civilian products were constructed to operate for military purposes. Moreover, low quality components or in some cases defective components which could not be used any more in military production were used in civilian production. Security-related information barriers prevented the transfer of technologies from the military to the civilian sector. As a result a large technological gap appeared between the military and the civilian sector. The gap even increased in the period of crisis because the government tried to support high priority military areas first. In the early 1990s the question of conversion

---

[6] OECD (1994, p. 166): *"A lot of science-intensive civil products were manufactured at defense enterprises. Such as civil aircraft, ships, telecommunication system, electronics, and about half of all mechanical durable goods produced in the country: all televisions, radios, tape recorders, cameras and video cameras, and as much as 70 to 80 per cent of washing machines, refrigerators, etc."*

became crucial[7], but because of the large technological gap it was impossible to overcome the gap between military and civilian sectors in a short period of time. The transfer of technologies from the military to the civilian sector was to a large extent prohibited by the inability of civilian enterprises to transfer and adopt technologies, the inability of the civilian sector to innovate, the lack of equipment, and the need to retrain personal. On the other hand, military technologies did not really correspond to the needs of civilian production. This especially concerns technologies which are important in the market economy. Thus, military production has never faced the problem of low production costs. It was oriented towards military rather than civilian consumers in terms of demand for quality and design. Conversion was also aggravated by the location of the defense sector (in Russia from 50 to 75 percent of science in the defense sector is concentrated in Moscow and St. Petersburg) and it's organizational separation from industry (OECD, 1994).

The demilitarization and conversion of military enterprises had a negative impact on R&D in the CIS countries, despite the fact that it was a positive development in the 1990s. The inability of civilian enterprises to adopt new technologies and reduce the military sector at the same time led to a quasi-loss of many technologies and experiences. But in spite of conversion, R&D in the investigated CIS countries remains excessively militarized. Table 5 presents defense expenditure and trade in arms in selected countries. Military expenditure as a percent of GDP in Russia, although reduced since 1992, still remained rather high in 1997 and accounted for 5.8%. It is approximately two times as large as that of the United States, whose share is the largest among the developed market economies and was equal to 3.3% in 1997. According to the World Bank figures represented in Table 5, the share of military expenditures in GDP in Ukraine has almost doubled since 1992 and represented 3.7% in 1997. This share is higher than that of the United States.

While in Russia the tendency to reduce military activities is seen in the reduction of the military expenditure share as a percentage of GDP and in the reduction of armed forces personnel as well as the export of arms, in the Ukraine all these indicators had increased in 1997 in comparison to 1992. Rather high in Ukraine is the share of exports of arms from the total exports and accounts for 3.5%, which is comparable to the United States, whose share was 4.6% in 1997 (see Table 5). The United Kingdom had the next highest share among the developed market economies of 2.3% in 1997. In Belarus military expenditure did not change considerably and was 1.7% in 1997. There was reduction in armed forces personnel but astonishing large was the share of arms exports from total exports, which was equal to 6.7%, the highest share in the investigated sample of CIS countries. Defense expenditure and trade in arms are at a low level in Poland and Hungary and are comparable to those of the most developed market economies.

[7] For further readings on conversion in Russia see BZHILIANSKAYA (1996).

High military expenditures for several CIS countries could be partly explained through differences in collecting data in NATO countries and CIS countries. Thus, while military expenditure for NATO countries is based on the NATO definition and excludes civilian-type expenditure of the defense ministry, the data for CIS countries covers those expenditures of the ministry of defense in those countries and could include also civilian-type expenditure (World Bank, 2000).

Table 5: Defense Expenditure and Trade in Arms

	Military expenditure				Armed forces personnel				Arms trade			
	% of GNP		% of central government expenditure		Total thousands		% of labor force		Exports % of total exports		Imports % of total imports	
	1992	1997	1992	1997	1992	1997	1992	1997	1992	1997	1992	1997
Russia	8.0	5.8	28.0	30.9	1,900	1,300	2.5	1.7	5.9	2.6	0.0	0.0
Ukraine	1.9	3.7	...	8.4	438	450	1.7	1.8	0.0	3.5	0.0	0.0
Belarus	1.9	1.7	4.9	4.8	102	65	1.9	1.2	0.0	6.7	0.0	0.0
Poland	2.3	2.3	8.8	5.6	270	230	1.4	1.2	0.2	0.2	0.0	0.4
Hungary	2.1	1.9	3.8	4.3	78	50	1.6	1.0	0.4	0.0	0.0	0.5
United States	4.8	3.3	21.1	16.3	1,920	1,530	1.5	1.1	5.6	4.6	0.3	0.2
Japan	1.0	1.0	6.3	6.6	242	250	0.4	0.4	0.0	0.0	0.9	0.8
Germany	2.1	1.6	6.3	4.7	442	335	1.1	0.8	0.3	0.1	0.6	0.2
United Kingdom	3.8	2.7	9.3	7.1	293	218	1.0	0.7	3.3	2.3	1.3	0.7
France	3.4	3.0	7.6	6.4	522	475	2.1	1.8	0.9	2.0	0.2	0.1
Italy	2.1	2.0	3.9	4.1	471	419	1.9	1.7	0.3	0.3	0.2	0.2
Australia	2.5	2.2	9.2	8.6	68	65	0.8	0.7	0.1	0.0	2.1	1.4
Belgium	1.8	1.5	3.7	3.2	79	46	1.9	1.1	0.3	0.1	0.2	0.2
Sweden	2.6	2.5	5.3	5.4	70	60	1.5	1.3	1.5	1.1	0.3	0.5
Austria	1.0	0.9	2.4	1.9	52	48	1.4	1.3	0.2	0.0	0.1	0.3
Switzerland	1.8	1.4	7.2	5.8	31	39	0.9	1.0	1.2	0.1	0.7	0.4
Finland	2.2	1.7	4.3	4.3	33	35	1.3	1.3	0.0	0.1	2.1	1.2

Source: World Bank (2000), World Bank website: http://www.worldbank.org

Disproportions between military and civilian sectors were accompanied by the disproportions between fundamental and applied research. Being strong in one area, Soviet science was weak in the other. Soviet scientific activity was especially strong in fundamental research and in theoretical fields, by contrast it was rather weak in applied work, innovation, and diffusion. For example, in the former USSR civilian R&D like computers and consumer electronics was considerably lagging behind progress in fundamental science and military and space R&D and hence was far below world standards (BOESMAN, 1993)[8]. High success records in math and science were accompanied by low skill levels in the social sciences, psychology, and business. BALZER (1995) argues that the gap between fundamental/theoretical and practical science may represent one of the most difficult vestiges of the old system to overcome.

One important feature of Soviet research was externalized R&D and engineering (R&D&E). Production in the Soviet Union was not organized in combination with innovation activity. Instead, R&D was carried out by the Soviet Academy of Sciences and other research institutions. Thus, innovation and production were two separate activities managed by the government. The relation between both was more one-sided than balanced with intensive one-way links running from R&D to production. It was R&D for industry rather than R&D in industry as it is common in market economies. Feedback from production was rather weak and hence did not leave much possibilities for learning by doing or learning by using. Moreover, the enterprises were deprived of the ability to accumulate knowledge. Knowledge was accumulated by research institutes and design and engineering bureaus. The S&T system in the former Soviet Union was branch oriented and the flows between branches were modest, thus preventing technology transfer between different branches (RADOSEVIC, 1999). RADOSEVIC (1999) argues that the main problem of socialism was its inability to innovate in the long run, and the separation of R&D&E from production was to a large extent responsible for such an outcome.

High isolation of Soviet science from the world due to political reasons was responsible for weak technology transfer from other countries. Soviet scientists had to rely, to a large extent, only on their own resources and achievements. As a result some unique inventions were created, but on the other hand a large technological gap appeared between the leading Western economies and the Soviet Union, especially in civilian technologies (OECD, 1994). Isolation from world technologies deprived the Soviet Union of numerous growth possibilities which are related to trade and FDI as routes of technology transfer. FDI in particular provides new technologies, brings organizational knowledge, and leads to high productivity improvements in foreign investment enterprises (RADOSEVIC, 1999).

---

[8] For a more detailed sectoral analysis of Russian R&D see GOKHBERG (1997).

Additionally, most research institutions in the Soviet Union were state organizations. As a result, there was a state monopoly over innovations. There were no incentives for individual creative activity as the appropriation of innovation rents was irrelevant and technology was considered as a „free good". Restriction of intellectual property rights and the neglecting of individual interests were the major factors of poor innovation performance and decline in R&D effectiveness (OECD, 1994; SIMANOVSKY, 1998; RADOSEVIC, 1999). Moreover, innovation activity was impaired through the inefficient and inflexible organizational structures of Soviet science. Thus, the organization of Soviet science was vertical or had „branch" subordination. The supervision role was carried out by the USSR Academy of Sciences or some other ministries or agencies. As a result this „departmental" approach led to high inflexibility and insufficient reallocation of financial, material, and human resources as well as to long bureaucratic procedures (SIMANOVSKY, 1998). Ministries were not interested in introducing innovations, since the priority was to fulfill plan tasks. Thus, governmental ownership on inventions, bureaucratic structures, and plan pressures rather than risk-taking activities were responsible for the unfavorable climate for innovations and for the growing incapacity of Soviet science to innovate and adopt new technologies.

These and others reasons were accountable for the collapse of Soviet science. The collapse was reinforced by the dissolution of the Council for Mutual Economic Assistance (CMEA), the dissolution of the Soviet Union, common economic crisis of CIS countries, which led to the reduction in R&D expenditure, decreases in salary in the R&D sphere, reduction of scientific personnel, and internal and external brain drain. The dissolution of CMEA in 1991 had a large impact on Soviet science and led to the severing of all R&D programs and projects that were carried out within the organization. Moreover, it led to the break-up of technological areas, which accounted for about 20 - 25% of world technological exchanges (SIMANOVSKI, 1998).

The break-up of the Soviet Union had a substantial negative impact. First of all, the wholeness of the R&D complex was destroyed. It had a negative impact on technology and science in emerging CIS states due to the high integration of research in the former Soviet Union. Thus, scientific research, design, project organization, and technology transfer were carried out in different republics (i.e. research was performed in Russia, development in Belarus, and technology transfer took place in the Ukraine). After the dissolution of the Soviet Union research centers ended up in different states. Some research institutes carried out their research on the territory of the whole Soviet Union and lost their wholeness after the break-up of the Soviet Union. The emerging CIS states had to adjust the science sector to their own needs, since the integrated framework of the USSR did not really correspond to their needs. The other 12 nations of the former Soviet Union account for approximately 12 percent of total researchers of a particular republic. Moreover, due to the high concentration of science in three republics, namely Russia, the Ukraine, and Belarus, the other republics stand before the necessity of reinforcing their own scientific potential (SIMANOVSKI, 1998; OECD, 1994; BOESMAN, 1993)[9].

Overall economic crisis also affected the R&D sector of the former Soviet Union. Table 6 represents the dynamics of some indicators on R&D in selected CIS countries. Since 1990 the spending on R&D has considerably decreased in CIS countries. In Russia R&D spending during the period from 1990 to 1995 had fallen from 2.5 percent to only 0.8 percent of GDP. R&D spending in Ukraine and Belarus had also reduced. R&D spending in Ukraine accounted for 1.2% of GDP in 1995 in comparison to 1.8% in 1990. R&D spending in Belarus was only 1% of GDP in 1995 instead of the 3% in 1990 (see Table 6). The situation had drastically changed to the worth in electronic industry, space industry, and aviation industry (SIMANOVSKY, 1998). The number of people employed in the science and science research sector diminished nearly by half in the period from 1990 to 1995. In Russia the drop was 41%, in Ukraine 43% and 55% in Belarus. Since 1990 there has been a tendency of diminishing wages. Wages in the scientific sector became much lower than those paid in many other sectors of the economy. Thus, in Russia the monthly wage in science and science research was 116% of the economy average. It was continuously falling until 1992, where it was 67% of the economy average. From 1992 to 1995 it went up but the increase was insignificant with an average monthly wage of only 75% in 1995. Approximately the same is true for Ukraine and Belarus. In the Ukraine monthly wage diminished from 127% in 1990 to 85% in 1992 and then increased to 107%. In Belarus it decreased from 128% in 1990 to 88% in 1992 and reached 108% in 1995. The general trend was a considerable decline of wages of people working in the science sector.

---

[9] BOESMAN (1993, p. 610): *"Science and technology (S&T) resources and capabilities in the former Soviet Union are heavily concentrated in Russia, particularly in Moscow and St. Petersburg. Russia has about two-thirds of the researchers and major research institutes, and almost 60 percent of all research organizations, of the former Soviet Union. The second major concentration, about 17 percent, is in the Ukraine, mainly in Kiev. Belarus is third with about 4 percent. The other 12 nations of the former Soviet Union account for approximately 12 percent of total researches and 20 percent of total research organizations".*

Table 6: Indicators of R&D in Some CIS Countries

	1990	1991	1992	1993	1994	1995
Expenditure on Science and Scientific Research (% of GDP)						
Russia	2.5	2.0	1.0	1.1	1.0	0.8
Ukraine	1.8	1.7	1.4	1.0	1.8	1.2
Belarus	3.0	2.5	0.8	0.8	0.8	1.0
Expenditure on Science and Scientific Research (growth rate in percent)						
Russia	...	-1.8	-23.2	-5.6	-8.4	-12.5
Ukraine	...	...	...	...	...	...
Belarus	...	-0.9	-23.3	-19.2	-12.4	-9.5
Employment in Science and Science Research (thousands)						
Russia	3,130	3,075	2,307	2,237	1,833	...
Ukraine	632	631	480	438	394	363
Belarus	103	101	79	60	53	46
Monthly Nominal Wages in Science, Research and Development (percent of economy average)						
Russia	116	97	67	75	86	75
Ukraine	127	99	85	92	108	107
Belarus	128	117	88	96	99	108

Source: The World Bank (1996), Statistical Handbook 1996

Table 7 compares science and technology in selected CIS countries, Hungary, and Poland with that of the developed market economies. From the table it is seen that although CIS countries had a relatively large number of scientists and engineers in R&D in the period from 1987 to 97, the efficiency of the R&D personnel was not very high. Thus, in this period Russia had 3,587 scientists and engineers in R&D per million people, which is comparable to Sweden, Japan, and the United States. It lagged considerably behind in the number of scientific and technical journal articles, which was only 17,180 for Russia but 142,792 for the United States, 39,498 for Japan, 32,980 for the United Kingdom, 30,654 for Germany, and 23,811 for France. The number of patent applications filed in Russia was many times lower than in nearly all developed market economies in 1997. Thus, the number of patent applications filed by residents in Russia was equal to 15,277, and by non-residents to 32,943. The number of patent applications filed by residents and non-residents in Japan in 1997 was 351,487 and 66,487, in the United States 125,808 and 110,884, in Germany 62,052 and 113,543, and in France 18,669 and 93,962, respectively. The same is true for the Ukraine and Belarus, where the above discussed indicators are even lower than in Russia. R&D expenditure as % of GDP in the investigated CIS countries was relatively low in the period form 1987 to 1997. In Russia R&D expenditure in this period was only 0.88%, in Belarus 1.07. R&D expenditure in developed market economies was much higher. Thus, in Sweden it was 3.76%, in Japan 2.80, in Finland 2.78, in the United States 2.63, Switzerland 2.60, Germany 2.41, France 2.25, and Italy 2.21. If one were to take R&D expenditure as a measure of R&D potential then the investigated CIS countries would fall in the group of such countries as Cuba (0.82), India (0.73), Brazil (0.81), Chile (0.68), and China (0.66).

The share of high-technology exports as a percentage of manufactured exports is also low in the investigated CIS countries with the exception of Russia. Thus, in Russia this share in 1998 was 12%, which is comparable to Austria (12%), Australia (11%), Italy (8%), and Belgium (8%) and much lower than that of the United States (33%), the United Kingdom (28%), Japan (26%), France (23%), and Finland (22%). In Belarus the share is only 4% and close to that of Poland, which is 3%. Hungary in turn exported many high-technology products. The share of high-technology exports in Hungary in 1998 was 21%, which is close to Sweden (20%), Finland (22%), and France (23%). R&D expenditure in both Hungary and Poland was rather low and equaled 0.68 and 0.77, respectively. The number of scientific and technical journal articles and patent applications is also not especially high in Hungary and Poland. Low R&D expenditure and low economic benefits of the research activities in the investigated CIS countries, Hungary and Poland, show that the systemic failures were crucial and that the transformation crisis contributed considerably to the poor performance of the R&D sector in transition economies.

Table 7: Science and Technology in Selected Countries

	Scientists and engineers in R&D	Technicians in R&D	Science and engineering students	Scientific and technical journal articles	Expenditures for R&D	High-technology exports		Royalty and license fees		Patent applications filed[a]	
	per million people 1987-1997[b]	per million people 1987-1997[b]	% of total tertiary students 1987-1997[b]	1995	% of GNP 1987-1997[b]	$ mill 1998	% of manufactured exports 1998	Receipts $ mill 1998	Payments $ mill 1998	Residents 1997	Non-residents 1997
Russian Federation	3,587	600	50	17,180	0.88	2,449	12	28	2	15,277	32,943
Ukraine	2,171	575	42	2,489	...	...	...	...	...	4,692	28,036
Belarus	2,248	266	48	...	1.07	204	4	1	1	755	25,280
Hungary	1,099	510	32	1,469	0.68	3,891	21	46	215	774	29,331
Poland	1,358	1,377	28	3,895	0.77	684	3	22	195	2,401	30,137
United States	3,676	..	19	142,792	2.63	170,681	33	36,808	11,292	125,808	110,884
Japan	4,909	827	21	39,498	2.80	94,777	26	7,388	8,947	351,487	66,487
Germany	2,831	1,472	47	30,654	2.41	63,698	14	3,252	4,893	62,052	113,543
United Kingdom	2,448	1,017	34	32,980	1.95	64,461	28	6,724	6,123	26,591	121,618
France	2,659	2,873	37	23,811	2.25	54,183	23	2,336	2,717	18,669	93,962
Italy	1,318	798	30	14,117	2.21	17,066	8	477	1,155	2,574	88,836
Australia	3,357	797	24	9,747	1.80	1,564	11	275	1,010	8,937	39,274
Belgium	2,272	2,201	41	3,996	1.60	11,115	8	645	1,099	1,687	84,958
Sweden	3,826	3,166	38	7,190	3.76	13,725	20	1,114	939	7,893	107,107

Table 7: Science and Technology in Selected Countries (cont.)

	Scientists and engineers in R&D	Technicians in R&D	Science and enginee-ring students	Scientific and technical journal articles	Expenditures for R&D	High-technology exports		Royalty and license fees		Patent applications filed[a]	
	per million people 1987-1997[b]	per million people 1987-1997[b]	% of total tertiary students 1987-1997[b]	1995	% of GNP 1987-1997[b]	$ mill 1998	% of manufactured exports 1998	Receipts $ mill 1998	Payments $ mill 1998	Residents 1997	Non-residents 1997
Austria	1,627	812	33	2,807	1.53	5,877	12	99	811	2,681	108,543
Finland	2,799	1,996	39	3,246	2.78	8,124	22	106	411	4,061	105,376
Switzer-land	3,006	1,374	34	5,896	2.60	12,030	16	..	..	5,814	107,038

Source: The World Bank (2000), World Bank website: http://www.worldbank.org

a. *Other patent applications filed in 1997 include those filed under the auspices of the African Intellectual Property Organization (31 by residents, 26,057 by nonresidents), African Regional Industrial Property Organization (7 by residents, 25,724 by nonresidents), European Patent office (44,604 by residents, 53,339 by nonresidents), and Eurasian Patent Organization (258 by residents, 26,207 by nonresidents). The original information was provided by the World Intellectual Property Organization (WIPO). The International Bureau of WIPO assumed no liability or responsibility with regard to the transformation of these data.*

b. *Data is for the latest year available; see Primary data documentation for most recent year available.*

c. *Total for residents and nonresidents.*

The brain drain, which can be divided into internal and external brain drain, represents another problem that contributed to the weakness of the research sector in the investigated CIS countries. The internal brain drain characterizes the movement of research personnel from the governmental sector to non-R&D activities in the private sector. External brain drain stands for the emigration of scientists and students abroad on a temporary basis or taking up permanent residency. Internal brain drain is considered as an economic problem, as there are no incentives to stay in the research sector, mostly due to low wages or reduction in the defense sector. Internal brain drain has negatively influenced the research sector in many ways. I.e., a lot of specialists had to leave the defense sector. By the beginning of 1997 research staff in the defense sector had fallen by 53 - 60% compared with 1991. This had a negative impact on famous research schools and design and engineering centers, as well as on the quality of the remaining personnel as about 40% of doctors and candidates of science had left the R&D sector of Russia's military complex (SIMANOVSKY, 1998). POOPER (1993) argues that internal brain drain should not generally be considered to be negative. The state sector in the Soviet Union was oversized, the movement of specialists from state to private sector could indeed increase the productivity of the economy. Important is that the shrinking of the R&D personnel is not drastic and that there remain incentives for young people to go to the scientific sector. If such incentives are absent, the overall decline of the R&D personnel could be a threat for further economic growth of the country, as R&D normally provides the main impulse for technological progress.

External brain drain might be more severe as the most talented people leave the country. As STREPETOVA (1995) points out, the increasingly supranational nature of knowledge, increasing interdependence in the global economy, and the increasing contribution of „foreign" human capital to economic progress are the main reasons for which researchers and technical staff became more mobile. POOPER (1993) considers emigration of scientists from Russia a normal phenomenon in the era of increasingly internationalized scientific networks. The emigration in Russia has dramatically increased since the end of 1980s. Thus, between 1987 and 1990, the annual number of immigrants increased 10,7 times. Between 1992 and 1993, the increase was 11%. About 60% of emigrants came form the most economically active, industrious, and employable population (STREPETOVA, 1995). The emigration mostly affected expert staff and skilled workers. Most of the emigration of scientists was to the United States and Western Europe. During the period from 1990 to 1993, about 4,500 Russian scientists (mainly mathematicians, physicists, computer programmers, and biologists) took permanent residence (PRA) in the United States. In the period from 1975 till 1995 about 50% of US demand (marginal) for mathematicians was satisfied by immigrants from the former Soviet Union. About 40% of the top-level theoretical physicists from the former USSR and about 12% of the highly skilled experimental physicists have gone abroad temporarily or permanently. Among the emigrants to the United States 80% were engineers, followed by natural scientists (about 10%), by mathematicians (about 8%), and computer specialists (about 2%) (STREPETOVA, 1995).

The emigration can be dangerous for transition economies as it robs the countries of some of their best scientists in the time of transition, and they therefore face a constraint for growth. It reduces the growth rate of the effective human capital remaining in the economy and hence causes reduction of the home country's per capita income growth.

POOPER (1993) has analyzed the costs and benefits of emigration in the short and long run. In the short run, emigration could have large negative effects on the economy since it deprives the country of the ability to absorb foreign technologies, particular of the disembodied variety. In the long run the danger is to loss the ability to innovate which represents a prime engine of economic growth. Benefits in the long run are connected with the return of researchers and maybe their students, who bring back with them much new „tacit" knowledge. Thus, they will contribute to the general store of domestic technical knowledge. Of course, the desire to return would to a large extent depend on the opportunities and prospects the researchers face in their home country. An attractive environment could be an incentive for foreign researchers to come to Russia. To provide such an environment and reverse immigration, to get a net inflow of foreign researchers and students, is an important task of policymakers.

The crucial factors responsible for the collapse of the Soviet science can be summarized as follows:

- Soviet science was (disregarding some exceptions) extensive and inefficient (OECD, 1994; SCHNEIDER, 1994; BALZER, 1995).
- Soviet science was highly militarized (OECD, 1994; SIMANOVSKY, 1998).
- The research in most civilian industries was stagnant (OECD, 1994).
- There was a large technological gap between military technologies and civilian technologies, which created considerable difficulties during conversion (OECD, 1994).
- Strong emphasis on fundamental/theoretical research and underdeveloped applied science BOESMAN, 1993; BALZER, 1995).
- Separation of production from R&D sector. Production is not a major source of innovative activity (RADOSEVIC, 1999).
- Isolation from world technologies. Absence of welfare gains from trade and technology transfer through FDI (OECD, 1994; RADOSEVIC, 1999).
- Poor incentives for innovation activities (governmental supervision of innovations, lack of intellectual property rights, long bureaucratic procedures, and plan pressures rather than risk taking activities) (OECD, 1994; SIMANOVSKY, 1998; RADOSEVIC, 1999).
- Dissolution of COMECON (SIMANOVSKY, 1998).
- Break-up of the Soviet Union (BOESMAN, 1993; OECD, 1994; SIMANOVSKY, 1998).
- Economic crisis (reduction in R&D expenditure, reduction in wages and personnel in R&D field) (SIMANOVSKY, 1998).
- Internal and external brain drain (POOPER, 1993; STREPETOVA, 1995).

The present position of the investigated CIS countries as well as Hungary and Poland in the R&D sphere is rather weak. If high and sustained growth is to be achieved attention of policy makers to the problem of R&D should have a high priority. To some extent the brain drain is normal in the modern world of intensified research contacts. From this perspective it is an important task of the government to create incentives for foreign researchers and students, which could contribute to growth in the transition countries. The technological backwardness could allow the countries to take advantages from imitation of technologies already available to developed nations, rather than innovate, which demands high capital intensity and skilled human resources as well as a complex research base in the CIS countries and the transition economies. Increasing capital intensity and broadening the human will take time.

3.3 Neoclassical versus New Growth Theory

Much of the discussions on the Soviet growth experience in Western literature has taken place in the light of neoclassical growth theory. Nevertheless, new growth theory could also provide important insights into the reasons of output decline in the Soviet Union and can deal as a yardstick to show new directions of development for the CIS countries and CEECs.

The major goal of transition economies is to converge with the income per capita levels of the most advanced OECD countries. For this reason, they should follow, in principal issues, the growth strategy chosen by the most advanced Western economies. EASTERLY/FISCHER (1992) argue that Soviet extensive growth experience with the absence of technological change and diminishing returns to capital, where capital was the only possible source of economic growth, fits well with the neoclassical model, while new growth theory corresponds better to the growth experience of Western economies.

Let us look at the differences between the two theories. The most important contribution to the neoclassical theory was the work of ROBERT SOLOW (1956). A description of SOLOW's model can be found in standard text books, i.e. BARRO/SALA-I-MARTIN (1995a) and JONES (1995a). SOLOW's theory helped to clarify the role of accumulation of physical capital and emphasized the importance of technological progress as the main driving force of sustained economic growth (JONES, 1998) (for detailed description of the neoclassical model see section 3.11.1. Appendix A).

Figure 2 shows the differences between neoclassical and new growth theories. The most important assumption of neoclassical growth theory is the *exogenous technological change*. That means that the determinants of technological change are not considered by the neoclassical growth theory (for example the R&D activities of firms does not influence the technology available to firms). Technology improves exogenously and the same technological opportunities are available to all countries of the world. The neoclassical theory implies *constant returns* to all inputs (factors) and *diminishing returns to capital.* The neoclassical growth theory implies only *level effects* and generates *transitional dynamics.* As a result of diminishing returns to capital each additional unit of capital increases the output by less and less. A country investing more moves from one *steady state* to the next *steady state* with a higher per capita level. The neoclassical model predicts the *convergence* of countries to the steady state values. Here it is important to distinguish between absolute and conditional convergence. The hypothesis of absolute convergence assumes that poor economies tend to grow faster than rich economies approaching steady state without making any difference in characteristics of economies. Conditional convergence relaxes the assumption of similar parameters (for example consider economies with different initial stocks of capital per person and different saving rates) and hence similar steady state positions. Thus, the important prediction of the neoclassical model is that each economy converges to its own steady state and the speed of convergence relates inversely to the distance from the steady state.

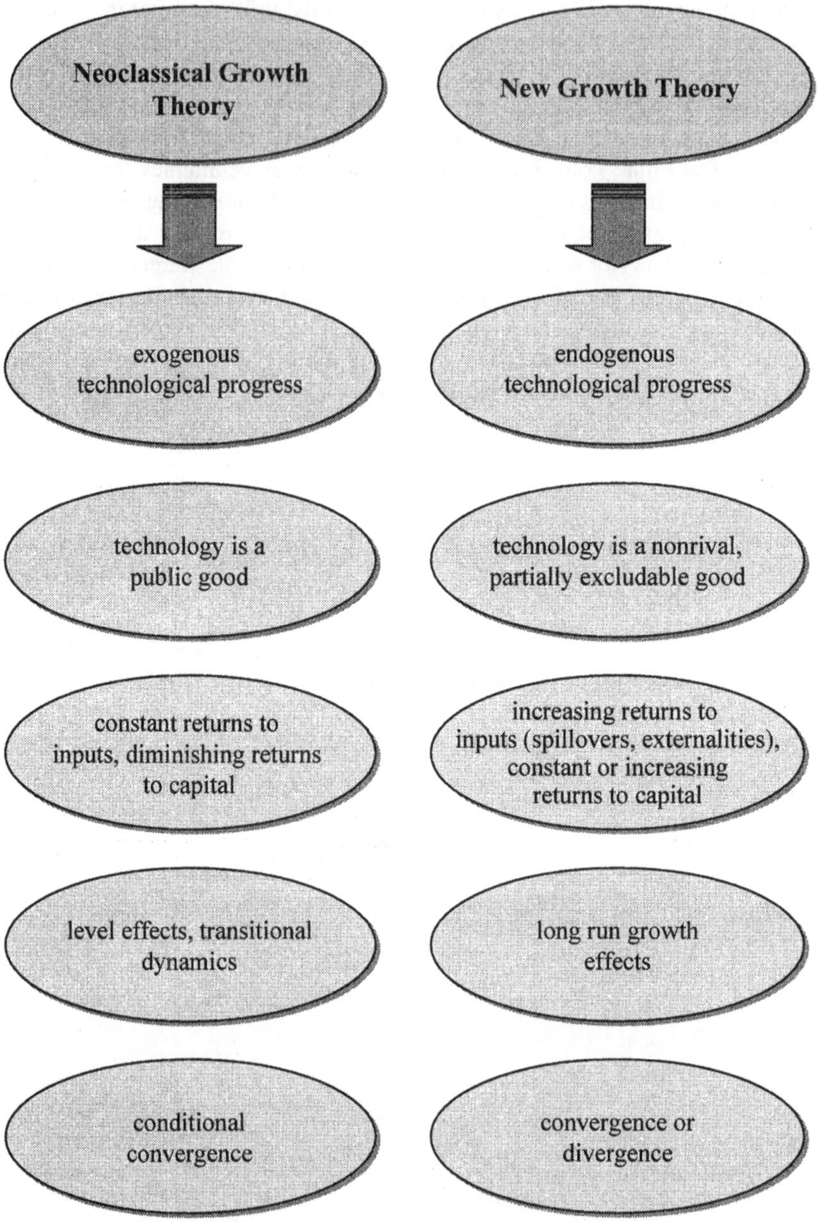

Figure 2: Neoclassical versus New Growth Theory

The new growth theory was first introduced by ROMER (1986). As ROMER (1994, p. 3) points out, „*The phrase „endogenous growth" embraces a diverse body of theoretical and empirical work that emerged in the 1980s. This work distinguishes itself from neoclassical growth emphasizing that economic growth is an endogenous outcome of an economic system, not the result of forces that impinge from outside"*. ROMER (1990) provides new understanding of technology as a *nonrival, partially excludable good* which is different from the neoclassical understanding of technology as a public good. The nonrival and partially excludable nature of technology implies that technological change takes place because of the actions of self-interested individuals, so improvements in technology must confer benefits that are at least partially excludable. The nonrival and partially excludable character of technology implies *„spillover" effects* and *externalities* that lead to increasing returns to scale of the factors of production. Thus, „spillovers" and externalities help to escape from diminishing returns to capital since in models of new growth theory there are constant or increasing returns to capital. Among the assumptions of the endogenous growth model is that countries can grow indefinitely long at different rates and need not converge in income per capita. Thus, new growth theory does not predict obligatory convergence, rather *divergence*. In other words, it says countries can grow at different growth rates for an infinite amount of time. The new growth theory influences *long run rate of growth* in contrast to the neoclassical growth theory, which has only level effects. Thus, new growth theory explains the sustained or long-run growth which countries can exhibit. The distinguished feature of new growth theory is that governmental policies, spillovers, externalities, and most importantly innovations, have long run growth effects. This means that through appropriate governmental policies, investment in physical and human capital, and R&D it is possible to influence the growth possibilities of a country. The neoclassical theory in contrast does not say which policies should be implemented to encourage economic growth since it does not explain the reasons for technological change.

The models of new growth theory due to GROSSMAN (1996) can be divided into three broad groups: AK models of long-run growth, externality based growth models, and innovation based growth models. In the AK models governmental policies are a decisive factor for long run growth. In this model capital accumulation still continues to be regarded as the driving force behind economic growth. Diminishing returns to accumulation of capital are avoided in the sense that total investment is assumed to be larger than total depreciation, thus assuring indefinite accumulation of capital. Such governmental policy was considered by the economists JONES and MANUELLI (1990) as they investigated the impact of tax policy (tax on saving or in other words tax on capital income) and external liberalization of the economy on the interest rate of capital, and hence economic growth. They compare low-tax and high-tax countries where low-tax countries accumulate more than high-tax countries, which provides a higher growth rate for the economy of the low-tax country. Liberalization of trade increases the price of capital goods and hence the rate of return on investment, thus spurring growth. REBELO (1991) also explains differences in growth experiences as a result of cross-country differences in government policies. Such policies as well as high income taxation and poor property rights impose low growth rates.

The externality-based growth models overcome diminishing returns to capital through knowledge spillovers and externalities. The idea that spillover effects contribute to economic growth was first proposed by ARROW (1962) in his famous work about learning by doing. ARROW regards learning as a product of experience. ARROW eliminates the diminishing returns to capital assuming that investment in physical capital creates knowledge spillovers that allow a firm to produce more efficiently. The expression learning by doing or learning by investing is explained by the positive impact of experience on productivity. BARRO and SALA-I-MARTIN (1995a) illustrate the idea of learning by doing in the sense that an increase in the firm's capital stock creates a parallel increase in its stock of knowledge. This process reflects the idea that increase in productivity represents a result of knowledge spillovers coming from investment and experience of production. ROMER (1986) goes further and introduces externalities in his model. Because of the nonrival nature of knowledge, if one firm uses an idea this does not prevent another from using it. Knowledge, once discovered, spreads over the whole economy. According to this point of view accumulation of new capital by one firm leads to the increase in the productivity of capital held by others. This leads to the conclusion that even if each firm taken separately exhibits diminishing returns to capital, investment in capital could generate an externality so that all firms taken together will not experience diminishing returns to capital. The externalities can occur in the case of investment in human capital as well as in physical capital. If the externalities are strong enough, the marginal product of physical or human capital will stay permanently above the discount rate so that growth could be reached through the continuous accumulation of the inputs that generate the positive externalities. One might suppose that because of the special nature of knowledge, ROMER was speaking in his work about investment in knowledge rather than in physical capital. Although investment in knowledge would generate the same kind of externalities that could sustain growth, ROMER was looking at investment in physical capital. LUCAS (1988) developed an alternative externality-based growth model where he emphasizes the importance of accumulation of human capital. He regards growth of the aggregate skill level (the productivity of the education activity) as an explanation for long-run growth.

In models of externality-based growth, the growth in productivity occurs, one could say, quasi accidentally as a side effect of investment in physical or human capital. In innovation-based models innovations are considered as the driving force of technological progress and investment in knowledge as a purposeful activity of technological change. In innovation-based models new technologies originate from investment in R&D carried out by private firms. Private innovation implies the creation of transitory monopoly power because investment in R&D

gives first-mover-advantages so that all these models feature imperfect competition.

R&D activities of private firms generate technological progress that can take the form of either product innovation (new products, products of better quality) or process innovation (new production method) (BRETSCHGER, 1998). Innovation of new products in the consumption sector brings advantages to the consumers in that consumers can choose with increasing innovation among larger amounts of products, so that different tastes of consumers are being satisfied. The consumer choice consists as before from old and new products so that new products do not force the old ones from the market. The opposite takes place in the case of quality innovation, where the old products lose their demand on the market. In the production sector product innovation leads to the increase in the amount of intermediate goods that are demanded for the production of consumer products. A greater variety of intermediate goods proposes that greater amounts of firms are involved in the production of the same product. Therefore a greater variety of intermediate goods causes greater specialization of firms. Process innovation improves production possibilities of firms, increases factor productivity, and changes factor proportions.

Models with an expanding variety of products are discussed by BARRO/SALA-I-MARTIN (1995a) as well as ROMER (1990). Technological progress reveals itself in an expansion of the number of varieties of producer and consumer products in the models with a variety of products. In the „variety models" technological progress is sustained through the assumption that the creation of new products increases the knowledge stock, which lowers the costs of innovation. The products in these models do not disappear from the market so that the more products are invented the more intense is competition, which lowers the costs of inventing new products. The models with improvements in the quality of products are discussed by BARRO/SALA-I-MARTIN (1995a), GROSSMAN/HELPMAN (1991b/1994), and AGHION/HOWITT (1998). In these models technological progress takes place through the improvements in the quality of products. Since consumers are ready to pay more for higher quality products, the firms are always interested in improving the quality of products. The important assumption of „quality models" is that all firms are able to study successful innovations and improve upon them. In other words, these models feature a vertical differentiation of products. Each intermediate product is assumed to have it's own „quality ladder". Each product can be improved an infinite number of times. This „productivity" improvement of a products leads to the effect that new generations of products can provide more product „services" in comparison to the old ones. An example could be desktop computers where the permanent improvement of chips allows much more productive usage of this product over time.

AGHION and HOWITT (1998) provide an integrated model, which can be regarded as either a Schumpeterian model with capital or a Solow-Swan model with endogenous technological progress. The model represents the basic model of creative destruction, which includes capital accumulation. The main difference from the ROMER and GROSSMAN/HELPMAN models considered above is that incentives to perform R&D in the AGHION/HOWITT model are closely linked with the stock of capital. By distinguishing in this model between sectors producing final output, intermediate output, and research, they consider capital as a factor contributing to both research and final output. Capital is broadly distinguished as a combination of human and physical capital. They argue that the role of physical capital as an input to research was ignored. Still, physical capital accumulation in the form of accumulation of high-tech intermediate goods represents an input into research. Since new technologies are embodied into new forms of physical and human capital, they should be accumulated in order to use new technologies. Research, which uses both human capital and physical capital, prevents the rise in cost of research and hence stimulates innovation. Thus, capital accumulation and innovation can be regarded as two aspects of the same process and the policies which influence accumulation of capital would also promote innovation. On the one hand, more innovation promotes capital accumulation since it raises the marginal product of capital. On the other hand, more capital accumulation will stimulate innovation since the costs of innovation will go down providing for higher profits to a successful innovator. As a result, both the incentives to perform R&D and the incentives to accumulate capital have long run growth effects.

3.4 Empirical Evidence on Growth Theory

The empirical evidence on the new growth theory is not yet sufficient. There were some studies which reject the assumptions of the new growth models. Thus, JONES (1995a,b) argues that „scale effects" predicted by many recent R&D-based models of growth are inconsistent with the time-series evidence from industrialized economies[10]. New growth models predict that permanent changes in policy variables lead to permanent changes in the growth rates of countries. JONES points out that, i.e., in the United States average growth rates were not affected by the increase of such variables as investment rates in education or investment rates in equipment and the number of scientists and engineers engaged in R&D, whose growth was considerable during the last half of the century. Although investment rates in education have increased enormously over the past century and investment rates in equipment (computer), as well as the share of labor engaged in R&D, have grown continuously since 1950, the average growth rates in the United States remained the same from 1870 to 1929. He also argues

[10] Economists JONES and HALL argue that we are mainly interested in growth rates because of their impact on levels and hence one should examine economic levels instead of economic growth. For discussion see JONES/HALL (1997).

that differences across countries can not be explained by differences in investment rates, and differences in rates at which individuals accumulate skills alone, as is the case in the AK models and the Lucas model. In other words, the differences in growth rates between countries are not always associated with differences in policies. Thus, between 1960 and 1988 the United States, Honduras, and Malawi all grew at approximately the same rate, although their policies were rather different.

The issues of the new growth theory have been supported by some empirical literature. There were studies which found a positive correlation between investment and long run growth on the one side, and the long lasting effects of policies on economic growth on the other. Thus, LEVINE/RENELT (1992) empirically find a strong correlation between long run growth and the share of investment in GDP. DE LONG/SUMMERS (1991) find that machinery and equipment investment has a strong association with long-run growth. The new growth theory was also supported by studies of BARRO (1991), ROMER (1993b), and EASTERLY (1993), who found strong negative effects of distortionary policies on economic growth. Thus BARRO finds a negative correlation between distortionary investment policies and growth, since government-induced distortions of markets negatively influence future research. ROMER strengthens that trade restrictions, taxes, corruption, bureaucratic red tape, etc. can strongly suppress the number of productive activities in a developing economy and hence have a large negative impact in aggregate output. EASTERLY (1993) found the negative effect of distortionary policies on economic growth.

To some extent empirical observation seemed to approve the existence of conditional convergence. Thus, BARRO/SALA-I-MARTIN (1992) find the evidence of convergence for a sample of 98 countries from 1960 to 1985 in a conditional sense, that is, only if controlling for the determinants of the steady-state (only if such variables as initial school enrollment rates and the ratio of government consumption to GDP are held constant). But the hypothesis of absolute convergence was not confirmed by the broad cross country data (BARRO/SALA-I-MARTIN, 1995a). BROADBERRY (1994) rejected empirically global convergence in manufacturing. This means that countries with different endowments and demand conditions will produce at different technological levels and hence their productivity will differ as well. On the other hand, he found evidence for „local convergence", namely for countries with similar endowments and demand conditions. MANKIW/ROMER/WEIL (1992) in their empirical work with the human capital accumulation in the SOLOW model, also come to the conclusion that countries with similar technologies and rates of accumulation and population growth should converge in income per capita. This convergence should occur more slowly than it is predicted by the SOLOW model (compare 17 years according to the SOLOW model and 35 years in the augmented model of MANKIW/ROMER/WEIL). The results of the empirical work of MANKIW/ROMER/WEIL were criticized by TEMPLE (1999) and DINO-

POULOS/THOMPSON (1999). The result are especially influenced by the assumption of exogenous technological progress in the model of MANKIW/ROMER/WEIL and depend much on the measure of human capital.

3.5 Reflections on Modern Growth Theory Applied to CIS and CEECs

As far as Soviet growth experience is concerned one could assume that diminishing returns to capital, which were obvious in the Soviet Union, support the neoclassical point of view (EASTERLY/FISCHER, 1992). Moreover, technological progress in the Soviet Union had the character of a public good, which in principle was equally given to all state-enterprises. The definition of technological change as a nonrival, partially excludable good can really not be applied to the case of the Soviet Union since state-enterprises did not compete in the sphere of innovation. R&D was carried out by separate research laboratories and R&D results were equally available to a whole range of state-enterprises. The understanding of technology like a public good also corresponds to the neoclassical model.

On the other hand, the distortionary policies as well as the lack of incentives to innovation could be, to a much larger extent, responsible for output decline in the Soviet Union. This aspect speaks in favor of the new growth theory (EASTERLY/FISCHER, 1992). Thus, according to EASTERLY (1993), BARRO (1991), and ROMER (1993b), distortionary policies can have negative long run growth rate effects.

One interesting explanation supplied by the investigation of WEITZMAN (1990) could be that the neoclassical model does indeed describe the Soviet case better, but the new growth theory with endogenous technological change better corresponds to the experience of Western market economies. The neoclassical model in the WEITZMAN study did not work for the US economy data because of higher technological progress, which was not possible to reflect in the neoclassical framework. Thus, endogenous growth can only then take place when there are incentives to innovate or adopt new technologies. If such incentives are absent, there is no endogenous growth. The only source of growth in the absence of technological change will be the increasing accumulation of factors of production. While labor can not grow fast as it is bound by limited population growth, the only driving force of economic growth will be the increasing accumulation of capital until diminishing returns set in. Diminishing returns in the absence of technological change would lead to the decline of output and stagnation of the economy (EASTERLY/FISCHER, 1992).

Technological change is of prime importance for the future growth strategy of CIS and CEECs. That is why the neoclassical model provides little explanation for the future growth policy for these countries, as it does not endogenize technological progress. Due to the neoclassical growth model the countries should invest more to reach higher output per capita level. Neoclassical theory with technological progress, where output per capita is growing in steady state with the rate of exogenous technological progress, does not depart from transition dynamics and does not explain long run growth. Thus, by investing more a country will reach a higher steady state level but not higher growth rates. Additionally, lower population growth would contribute to higher output per capita since in the SOLOW model population does not create knowledge spillovers and hence does not generate growth (for a detailed description of the neoclassical model see section 3.11.1 Appendix A).

Instead new growth theory provides new insights into the sources of technological change and can deal as a yardstick for future the long run growth strategies of CIS and CEECs. Figure 3 emphasizes the respective incentives which new growth theory provides in various approaches. All models of the new growth theory provide implications for long run growth and non-transitional dynamics. According to the AK models adequate governmental policies would allow countries to reach higher growth rates. These models suggest that countries will have incentives for liberalization, lower capital taxation, and stronger property rights, which would have positive long run growth effects.

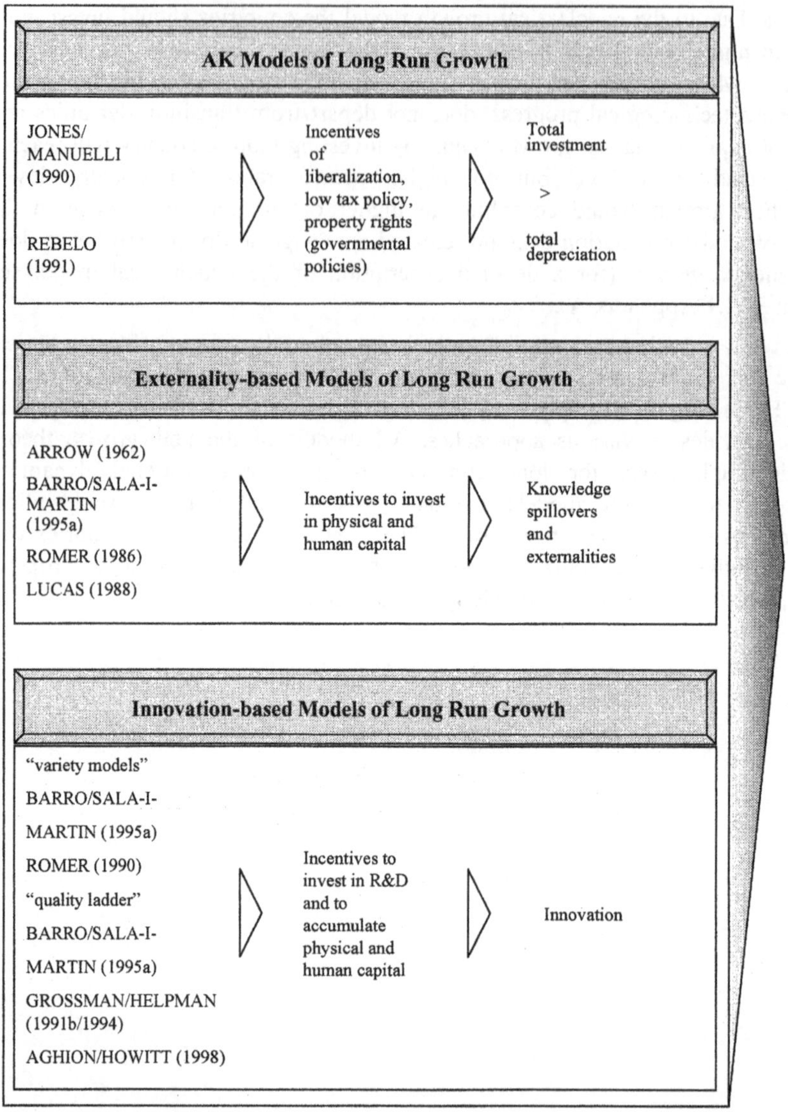

Figure 3: New Growth Theory

Externality-based models are associated with incentives to invest in physical and human capital. Investment in both physical and human capital provides for knowledge spillovers and externalities, which raises the productivity in the whole economy. Much attention should be devoted to learning by doing by making investments and attracting FDI. Just following the strategy of „deepening capital" without increasing „stock of knowledge" does not, as Soviet experience shows, bring positive results. Especially as investment in human capital provides for spillovers and externalities. Thus, multinational corporations (MNCs) investing in economies involve domestic labor, employees and managers, in the process of learning and upgrading their skills, which represents a considerable spillover effect for the domestic economy. Moreover, the countries should create incentives for innovation and adaptation of technologies like the main driving force of technological change. In innovation-based models investment in R&D plays a significant role. Additionally, as AGHION/HOWITT argue, accumulation of physical and human capital promotes innovation and hence contributes to the long run growth as well. Thus, new growth theory provides considerable explanation for future growth possibilities of CIS and CEECs. Much would depend on the willingness to apply them in a political and economic sense and on the willingness to be involved in international technological networks like foreign trade and foreign direct investment, which represent the main channels of technology transfer.

3.6 Catching Up

The most interesting answer that growth theory can provide for CIS and CEECs is how to catch up to the income levels of advanced OECD countries. The possibility of technological catching up was first described by economic historians and later discussed by historically oriented economists and some new growth economists. Technological catching up based on the „advantage of backwardness" poor countries can exploit demands considerable effort from these countries and strongly depends on whether these countries can take advantage of „social capability", „technological opportunity/capability", and „indigenous innovation".

3.6.1 The Theory of Technological Gap

The prime goal of the CIS and CEECs is to catch up to the income levels of advanced OECD countries. Catching up would allow the countries to be wholly integrated into the world economy, to increase trade and financial flows, and to increase economic prosperity.

The question of convergence is controversial in growth literature. Neoclassical growth theory predicts convergence between countries and regions. Neoclassical growth theory explains long run growth as an outcome of exogenous technological progress. Convergence in the neoclassical growth model occurs along the transition path. Due to diminishing returns to capital, the countries converge to their steady state levels. An important implication of this theory is that economies with lower capital stock per person tend to grow faster in per capita terms. In other words, per capita growth rates are inversely related to initial levels of income, so poor countries should grow faster than richer ones.

The recent growth theory explains long run growth with endogenous technological progress. Innovation is considered to be the main driving force of technological progress. Innovation represents the result of the profit-maximizing activities of private firms and therefore makes permanent differences in productivity levels and growth rates between countries possible. Endogenous growth models (such as GROSSMAN/HELPMAN, 1991a) tend to predict divergence rather than convergence.

JONES/BERNARD (1996) criticize that new growth theory overlooks the importance of technology transfer in its approach to convergence. They emphasize that technology transfer, which explains differences in labor productivity across countries, allows countries to converge to the higher level of productivity which leading countries exhibit. JONES/BERNARD point out that the role of technology is also ignored in the empirical literature. Thus, i.e., in their empirical investigations MANKIW/ROMER/WEIL (1992) and BARRO/SALA-I-MARTIN (1992) explain differences in growth rates through differences in capital accumulation under the assumption that economies accumulate technology at the same rate. Adoption and accumulation of technology are assumed away in explaining both relative output levels and growth rates, hence convergence.

GRIES/JUNGBLUT (1997) point out that in models of new growth theory the differences in productivity are explained by differences in innovation activities performed within one country. If one does not allow for transfer of knowledge across international borders then new growth theory describes how a country performs its own R&D activities and makes discoveries. There are models of new growth theory which allow for international integration, but transfer of technologies from other countries occurs without paying any costs, which does not correspond to the real world. In a world lacking international integration one will observe an important scale effect. This scale effect predicts that larger countries will grow faster than smaller ones because they can easier afford the costs of innovation. This prediction obviously contradicts empirical observations and draws on the assumption that no technological transfer occurs across countries. The explanation of productivity growth through innovation activities for middle and low income countries does not correspond to practical evidence. New growth theory seems to better explain the growth possibilities for rich rather than for middle and low income countries. Additionally, recent growth experience of the East Asian countries points to convergence. During the process of catching up the East Asian countries exhibited higher growth rates than industrialized countries, which does not correspond to predictions of new growth theory because new growth theory rejects any kind of convergence.

The importance of technological catching up for growth possibilities of countries has long been emphasized by economic historians and historically oriented economists. The first contributions to the theory of technological gap was provided by GERSCHENKRON (1962), and later formalized by GOMULKA (1971) and CORNWALL (1977). The theory is based on the hypothesis that technologically „backward" countries have an opportunity to converge to technologically more advanced countries by imitation. „The advantage of backwardness" allows for rapid advance. The larger the technological gap in productivity the faster the follower country can possibly grow. Thus, initially more „backward" countries tend to catch up faster. As the technological gap between leader and follower country diminishes the potential to grow will also diminish. It will always be more difficult to increase productivity as the follower country moves closer to the technological frontier because the poll of best-practice technologies becomes smaller as the countries converge.

The main difference of technological gap theory from the neoclassical one is its attitude towards technology. Technological gap theorists see technological differences between countries as the main reason for differences in GDP per capita across countries.

The economists of the technological gap approach, opposed to new growth economists, explain differences in stock of knowledge and technological capabilities of countries through innovation and imitation activities. They argue that new growth theory by means of innovation driven growth process explains the growth possibilities for industrialized countries rather than for middle and low income countries. The industrialized elite performs innovation activities in order not to loose their comparative advantages as technological leaders. On the other hand, developing or catching up countries, because of the lack of sufficient preconditions, can not avoid making innovations. The possibility for these countries to catch up to the frontier is found in imitation rather than innovation. Imitation and adoption of new technologies is usually connected with lower costs and lower risks than innovation, so that catching up countries possess „an advantage of backwardness" GRIES/JUNGBLUT (1997). Because the speed of adoption of innovations is more rapid in relatively low-income countries, the rate of growth of productivity in the particular industry will be higher in the low-income country than it was for a comparable stage of development in the high-income country (CORNWALL, 1977). „An advantage of backwardness" also represents an opportunity for CIS and CEECs to catch up to the productivity levels of OECD countries. The above investigation shows that CIS countries and other transition economies have inherited backward technologies from the Soviet Union era, especially in civil production. Technological activities should also be adapted to market conditions. That is why imitation of „market" technologies, which is connected with institutional, structural, and organizational changes towards market principals, is more appropriate for catching up for these countries than innovation.

The technological gap approach represents an application of Schumpeter's dynamic theory. It analyses economic growth as an interaction of two conflicting forces: innovation, which tends to increase technological gap, and imitation, which tends to reduce it. The opportunity of technologically backward countries to catch up depends on their own effort on the one hand, and on innovative efforts of advanced countries which could increase the gap, on the other hand.

One speaks about the opportunity or possibility for backward countries to catch up and not about the safe outcome of the effort. This possibility is difficult to fulfill. There are a lot of constraints on the way to technological advancement. ABRAMOVITZ (1986) emphasized that a country's potential to catch up is closely connected with the „social capability" of the country. Thus, backward countries can exhibit quick catching up in terms of productivity if they are socially advanced. Identifying the term „social capability" ABRAMOVITZ pays special attention to education, the quality of infrastructure, and to a country's political, commercial, industrial, and financial institutions. ABRAMOVITZ (1986, p.389) noted: *„Social capability, finally, depends on more than the content of education and the organization of firms. Other aspects of economic systems count as well, their openness to competition, to the establishment and operation of new firms, and to the sale and purchase of new goods and services. Viewed from the other side, it is a question of the obstacles to change raised by vested interests, established positions, and customary relations among firms and between employers and employees".* Thus, considering the countries own technological system, those which are open to new technologies, new human capital, and new organizational structure and operational techniques will be successful.

ABRAMOVITZ defined the term „social capability" as referring to the set of factors that support absorbing and exploitation of best-practice technologies from abroad. Additionally, countries should be able to adopt technologies from abroad. He adds that there is an interaction between social capability and technological opportunity. While social capability, which represents the education potential embodied in a nation's population and institutions, provides for implementation of already existing technologies, technological opportunity forces countries to change and to improve existing institutional arrangements using the gained experience. Technological opportunity represents a kind of innovation effort which countries should make to improve the economic environment using knowledge assimilated from abroad.

Therefore CIS and CEECs could, theoretically, exploit the advantage of backwardness and generate growth more rapidly than more advanced countries, provided they possess the sufficient social capabilities which would permit them to successfully exploit technologies already employed by the technological leaders. Success in the adaptation of technologies is limited by the social capability of countries. As ABRAMOVITZ points out, the strength of the tendency to catch up can be weakened or overcome depending on the convergence of production patterns or on an endogenous enlargement of social capabilities. The potential for catching up depends on the following factors: facilities for the diffusion of knowledge (channels of international technical communications, multinational corporations, the state of international trade, and direct capital investment), rate of structural change in the composition of output, of the workforce, of geographical location, of industry, and of population, and macroeconomic and monetary conditions which provide for capital investment and the expansion of effective demand.

BELL/PAVITT (1992) introduced the term „technological capability", which is close to that of ABRAMOVITZ's technological opportunity, and incorporates resources needed to generate and manage technical change. „Technological capability" includes skills, knowledge, and experience, institutional structures, and linkages. „Technological capability" is responsible for the dynamics of industrialization, therefore it is important that it provides resources necessary to generate and manage that dynamism.

BELL/PAVITT (1992) associate accumulation of technology with the cumulative acquisition of „intangible capital" in the form of personal, organizational, and institutional skills. The international competitiveness of a country will evolve along with these national technological trajectories.

Among the factors associated with the successful accumulation of technologies they point out:

- The flow of technology should be closely coupled with the rapid development of indigenous capabilities in business firms.
- Investment in education and training.
- Incentives for innovation and imitation. These features were to a large extent neglected in centrally planned economies. The conditions for imitation should include intellectual property rights, competition pressures, and favorable macroeconomic climate.
- Favorable market conditions. Technological accumulation is likely to profit from a large and continually expanding market. Some financial support and various protection measures might be favorable in a sector-specific perspective to encourage the effective learning in developing countries. Investment in infrastructure is essential for the development of technologies.

FAGEBERG (1994) also points to the fact that latecomers would face larger requirements for capital and other advanced factors than those that prevailed at an early stage[11]. These requirements would demand that latecomer countries develop a new institutional system, which has little or no counterpart in an established industrial country. Thus, catching up requires significant effort and substantial institutional building. Additionally, there should be support from society to

[11] For further discussions see also FAGEBERG (1987, 1988).

introduce changes, i.e., in Russia an important part of society resists changes, which is a significant constraint for a successful catching up process.

FAGEBERG (1994) argues that the role of indigenous technological activities is different from that of technological leaders. Thus, he stresses that innovation activities carried out within a country also represent an important factor for catching up. He points out that imitation and innovation in follower countries are to a large extent combined, as a successful imitation strategy often contains an element of innovation. His empirical investigation where he tested both imitation and innovation proves that innovation represents an important variable for catching up possibilities of countries (FAGEBERG, 1994). Thus, additionally to „social capability", the creation of new technology within a country is of crucial importance. Innovation capabilities are closely connected with the country's capacity to exploit the benefits offered by available technology. The success in exploiting the possibilities offered depends on the country's ability to mobilize resources for transforming social, institutional, and economic structures. Thus, technological change represents a joint outcome of innovation and learning activities within firms as well as a continuous process of interaction and adoption between them and their environment. Thereby each country represents a separate technologic system with its own dynamics. The importance of indigenous technological capabilities increases as a country moves closer to the technological frontier. A high level of innovation means a high share of „new" goods in output and an extensive use of „new" techniques in production. Thus, „new" goods are associated with high prices and „new" techniques with high productivity, so it follows that countries with high levels of innovation also have a higher levels of GDP per capita. Therefore, it is impossible to surpass advanced countries with imitation without using innovation as well.

PAVITT/SOETE (1981) regard innovation and imitation as the forms of survival in a competition world. Innovation allows firms to get high profits and gain an increased market share due to patent protection, secrecy, and time lag in imitation. Innovation is the central feature of competition in the industrial world, where imitation represents an opportunity of survival for developing countries. The importance of „foreign technology" was proven by historical experience during the industrialization of both Europe and the United Sates in the nineteenth century and Japan in the twentieth century. Recent experience of the rapid industrialization of some newly NICs, such as South Korea, supports this view.

PAVITT/SOETE investigate the „windows of opportunity" for countries to catch up[12]. Their main concept is based on the idea of a technology life cycle and the assumption that there are different costs of imitation at different stages of the technology life cycle. The technology life cycle consists of four stages: introduction, early growth, late growth, and maturity. Investigating the level of such criterion as minimum fixed investment required, minimum level of locational

[12] For further readings see also PREZ/SOETE (1988).

advantages required, minimum scientific and technological knowledge required, and minimum relevant skills and experience required, which in different configurations represent different opportunities of entry, they found that entry is easier in the introduction and maturity stages. Entry in the introduction stage is more appropriate in the case of developing countries as the latter is associated with considerable amounts of investment and technology purchase funds. The introduction phase demands little capital and experience, but considerable scientific and technical knowledge, as well as an adequate provision of locational advantages. Thus, given that countries possess a profound stock of general knowledge, which is the case in CIS and CEECs, they can enter relatively easy at the introduction phase. Entry is more difficult in the growth stages, as at these stages tacit knowledge becomes more important than experience and learning-by-doing. Thus, the „window of opportunity" for CIS and CEECs to catch up is to enter new technologies at the introduction phase, because after that the „window of opportunity" will be closed until the cycle goes round.

GRIES/JUBGBLUT (1997) consider the stages of catching up where they pay special attention to sufficient human capital, in the form of essential human, administrative, and organizational knowledge, as a precondition for the successful adaptation and use of advanced technologies in a country. Once the process of upgrading starts up one can distinguish four stages of this process:

The process of upgrading will start slowly at the first stage due to insufficient technological experience and a low endowment of human capital. If the country is able to assimilate higher incomes and accumulate physical and human capital, the process of upgrading will move to the second stage of sustained growth, or even to acceleration. In this stage of growth it is important for a country to direct increases in productivity towards the development of additional comparative advantages and growing export shares. Increasing exports is a necessary instrument in obtaining the import of goods with incorporated technological knowledge. FDI could also speed up the process of upgrading. FDI is an additional source for accumulating the necessary capital for further successful upgrading, and is also a channel for accessing advanced techniques.

The third stage is characterized by the slowdown of technological progress and upgrading. As the countries converge, the pool of uncopied ideas gets smaller and thus, the costs of imitation would become more expensive causing a slowdown of convergence.

The fourth stage is the stage of convergence. As a country adopts more and more advanced techniques the scope of technologies available for imitation will diminish and the countries will converge. But the final gap between catching up and industrialized countries will remain. To close the final technological gap alone by means of imitation is not possible. One should switch from imitation to innovation to become a member of the industrialized club. The importance of human capital becomes clear in this final stage. Sufficient human capital is that force which makes it possible to overcome the slowdown of the upgrading process and provide the switch from imitation to innovation. FDI does not play such an important role in the last stage of upgrading.

The countries that were not able to create the preconditions for upgrading will not be able to keep a leading technological position and will diverge, or even stagnate. The fundamental preconditions for countries in global growth are the stock of human capital, R&D intensities, the investment rate, and the openness of a county. The change of fundamentals could considerably change the position of countries in world competition. Improvement of fundamental conditions could speed up the process of convergence, while deterioration could replace the leading country with the follower.

The process of upgrading is depicted by the following Figure 4.

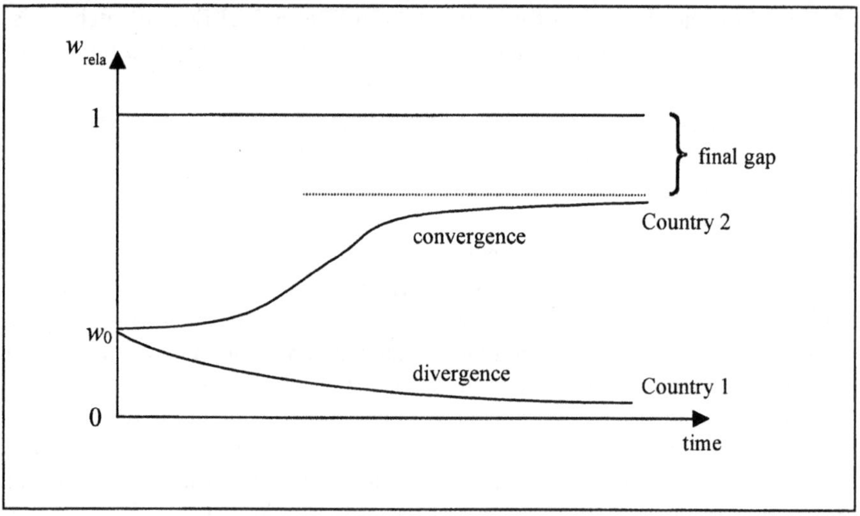

Source: Gries/Jungblut(1997)

Figure 4: Convergence and Divergence

In the picture the horizontal axis shows time. The technological position of the catching up country relative to the industrialized elite is shown on the vertical axis by w. The technological position of the group of industrialized countries is normalized to 1. The time path of these countries is a horizontal line. The other two paths correspond to converging or a diverging countries. Although countries have the same initial technological position they move in different directions due to different initial conditions necessary for successful upgrading. Thus, such initial conditions as human capital abundance, R&D activities, the investment rate, and openness of the economy determine the success of the country in catching up to the industrialized elite.

To sum up, the main assumptions of the technological gap theory we will refer to Figure 5. The figure represents successful catching up and the necessary requirements in order to reach a higher level of GDP per capita or to converge. According to the technological gap theory developed by GERSCHENKRON (1962), GOMULKA (1971), and CORNWALL (1977), a low income country (a country with low GDP per capita) has an „advantage of backwardness," which allows it to grow faster than a high income economy. Fast growth is based on imitation by the catching up country of the best-practice technologies of the industrialized word. Faster growth is explained by the lower costs of imitation and exploiting of this technology and hence higher productivity in comparison to the costs and productivity at the innovation stage.

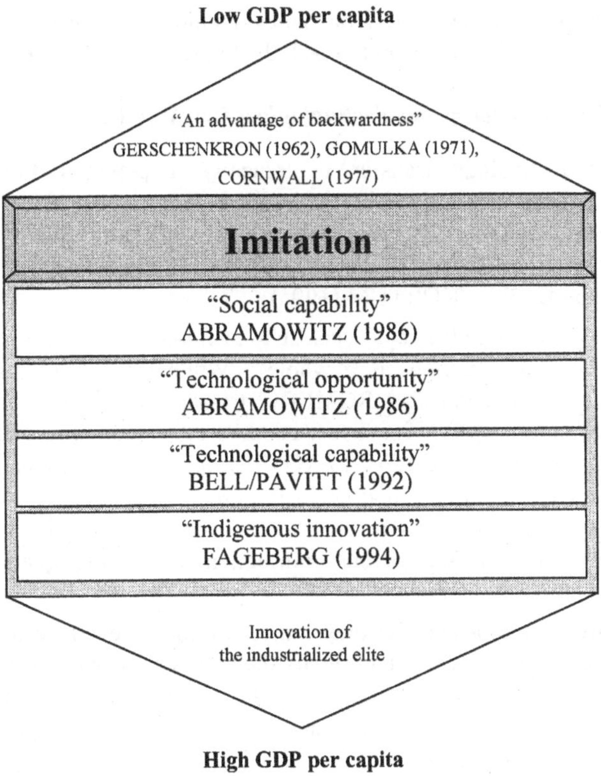

Figure 5: The Theory of Technological Gap

But successful imitation is limited by the „social capability" of the country, which according to ABRAMOVITZ (1986) represents knowledge embodied in people and institutions. „Social capability" is an important precondition for the successful adoption and assimilation of new technologies, but even more important is not only to absorb but also to adopt technologies to new economic surrounding. The adoption demands changes and improvements of respective institutional arrangements and represents the ability to learn from new technologies. Such ability to change and to improve existing institutional arrangements corresponds to the term of „technological opportunity" introduced by GERSCHENKRON (1962) and is close to the term of „technological capability" introduced by BELL/PAVITT (1992). FAGEBERG (1994) also proved empirically that innovation activities of the home country different from that of industrialized elite are important preconditions for successful catching up. Because countries which perform innovations have the highest productivity and the highest GDP per capita, it is difficult to surpass them in level of GDP per capital without surpassing them in innovation. Therefore to close the remaining gap between the industrialized elite and the catching up countries, the latter should switch from imitation to innovation, which would allow them to reach the highest level of GDP per capita.

3.6.2 New Growth Theory and Technological Catching Up

The view that technology transfer is logically a potential force behind convergence has been emphasized by ROMER (1993a) in his „idea gaps", by GROSSMAN/HELPMAN (1991a) in the analysis of North-South trade, by KRUGMAN (1990), BARRO/SALA-I-MARTIN (1995b), and by empirical results obtained by EATON/KORTUM (1995).

ROMER's (1993) term of „idea gaps" is close to technology gap but is more broad as it refers to economic activity as a whole[13]. While technology gap is more associated with manufacturing, ROMER stresses that the more broad understanding of „idea gaps" is important because most economic activity takes places outside of factories. According to ROMER, ideas include numerous forms of economic activity which are all used in the creation of economic value in a modern economy, such as packaging, marketing, distribution, inventory control, payments systems, information systems, transactions processing, quality control, and worker motivation.

Poor countries remain poor because they fail to use ideas generated in industrial nations. Thus, idea gaps draw attention to the interaction and communication between a developing country and the rest of the world. ROMER points out that such channels of knowledge transfer as trade, which also generates gains for both the recipient and the supplying country, and FDI account, historically belong to the most important forms of international flows of ideas. He stresses that in this context the role of multinational corporations as the conduits of idea flows becomes specially important. Multinational corporations bring the ideas from the rest of the world and combine them with domestic resources. Multinational corporations can transfer knowledge through different arrangements with

---

[13] For further discussions see also ROMER (1992).

developing countries, such as FDI, joint ventures, marketing and licensing agreements, and other formal and informal agreements with domestic firms. Developing countries can attain many ideas embodied in imports of capital goods by multinational corporations.

It is a challenge for developing countries to create incentives for the holders of this knowledge to put it into use in these countries. To create preconditions is a special task of local government. The government should create the necessary economic infrastructure to facilitate smooth functioning of the economy and to enable the formation of „absorption capability" of the country. Government should provide for the basic institutional infrastructure and functioning financial system which allows for payments between borrowers and lenders and undistorted and stable monetary and exchange regimes. Government should also encourage the private sector and property rights, and provide for a basic physical infrastructure. All these are the preconditions for creating the appropriate „absorption capacity" of the country, which is a characteristic of an economy and society as a whole. Following technology gap economists, ROMER points out that the „absorption capability" of a country includes human capital, a large institutional framework, and a „national innovation system" of the economy. Institutional framework represents a broad understanding of institutional system, which consists of educational systems, firms, and research institutions, both public and private. ROMER stresses that rapid growth of a country depends on both foreign technology and the „absorption capability" of the country. This point of view overlaps considerably with that of technology gap economists.

GROSSMAN/HELPMAN (1991a) introduce trade into the R&D model, which allows for the diffusion of knowledge and convergence between developing and industrialized countries. Since R&D models argue that new products result from new ideas, trade in goods can help transmit knowledge internationally. The considered model assumes that the world economy innovates by developing new varieties of horizontally differentiated products. GROSSMAN/HELPMAN consider a model of North and South trade which better corresponds with the case of developing countries than with trade in vertically differentiated products. The basic idea of this product cycle model is that the new products being invented in the North are imitated by the South due to relatively lower Southern wages. They treat imitation as an investment activity in the technological capability of the country, which attains an element of innovation as it represents an effort to adapt new knowledge to new circumstances. Innovation, as well as imitation, requires managerial talent, scientists, and technicians. The ability of countries to imitate depends on the local investment in technology and on the stock of knowledge in the North as there are spillovers between the North and South due to international trade. A new product is initially produced in the North until either further innovation (in the quality ladder model) or successful southern imitation (in both variety model and quality ladder model) occurs. As a result of successful imitation the product will be produced in the Southern country. First the products were exported by the North and then due to successful imitation by the South, thereby completing the cycle. This model captures technology driven trade and makes diffusion of technology in new growth models possible. Thus, due to international trade there are positive growth effects for both North and South. Northern producers benefit if Southern producers take over manufacturing, as they then as a result of decreased number of competitors are able to hire some of the laid-off workers and expend their sales and profits. The South benefits from integration as it enforces technological progress and hence increases growth rates. The government could also positively influence the local accumulation of knowledge in the South. GROSSMAN/HELPMAN point out two possibilities. The first represents research subsidy in order to cover the expenses which emerge from the adoption of technologies to local conditions, the second is to relax patent protection which would encourage imitation.

GROSSMAN/HELPMAN (1991b-quality ladder) represent a R&D model which incorporates two widely used types of R&D based endogenous growth models: the „variety only" and the „quality ladder". They showed that both models share identical reduced forms for their simplest variants. In this paper they also discuss the innovation process in a two-country setting. With product improvements taking place in each country, they obtain a long-run equilibrium in intra-industry trade in vertically differentiated products and with inter-industry trade of technologically progressive goods for homogenous, unchanging goods, where the latter is close to the North-South model in the previous paper.

KRUGMAN (1990) as well as GROSSMAN/HELPMAN regard models of technology transfer between North and South. The advantage of developed countries lies in the ability to exploit new technology. He stresses that innovation is a process by which new products are created where technology transfer is the process by which new products are transformed into old products. Innovations are constantly emerging in the developed region and then move to less developed regions in the face of low-wage competition.

BARRO/SALA-I-MARTIN (1995b) have developed a model which combines the features of endogenous-growth models with the convergence assumption of the neoclassical growth model. In their model the world is growing at the growth rate of discoveries and inventions made by technologically leading nations. Follower countries converge to the leading due to cheaper copying and imitation. Successful imitation reduces the pool of uncopied ideas. That means the increase in costs of imitation and decline in the follower's growth rates. BARRO/SALA-I-MARTIN emphasize that this property strongly reminds one of the conditional convergence predicted by the neoclassical model and proved empirically in the cross-country data on economic growth.

EATON/KORTUM (1995) represent a multicountry model of technological diffusion and innovation in which countries converge to a common growth rate. They examined productivity growth since World War II in the five leading research economies: West Germany, France, the United Kingdom, Japan, and the United States, and came to the conclusion that technology differences and not capital accumulation explain differences in manufacturing productivity. Thus, the growth of these countries over the last four decades was more due to their ability to adopt productive technologies developed at home and abroad and not due to capital deepening per se.

They argue that if backward countries did not have the possibility to imitate they would have to rely on their own total factor productivity and be even more innovative then the industrialized countries. This catching up perspective is likely to take a lot of time. At the same time technologically backward countries have the possibility to catch up rapidly by absorbing the most advanced technologies. The empirical finding of EATON/KORTUM was that more than 50% of growth in some OECD countries derives from innovation in the United States, Germany, and Japan. Even the United Sates obtain over 40 per cent of its growth from abroad.

The model developed by EATON/KORTUM implies convergence of economies to a steady state with parallel growth rates under the assumption of international technological mobility. Analyzing the post World War II behavior of manufacturing productivity in Germany, France, the United Kingdom, Japan, and the United Sates, they found confirmation of convergence between these countries after the technological disparity left by World War II.

The special role of integration as a driving factor of technological diffusion is underlined in the above models of technological diffusion developed by new growth economists. ROMER (1993a) in his „idea gaps" points to the necessity for poor countries to use ideas developed in the industrialized world. He thereby strengthens the essential role of foreign trade and foreign direct investment, and the importance of creation conditions for multinational corporations. It is to a large extent the task of the government to provide incentives for foreign firms and investors. The incentives are closely connected with the „technological capability" of the country which consists of human capital, institutional framework, and innovation effort. As GROSSMAN/HELPMAN (1995a,b) point out there are positive growth effects from trade with the North, which enforces technological progress within the Southern country, and provides for higher productivity and growth rates. The same idea is developed by KRUGMAN (1990). As the countries proceed in imitation the gap between them and industrialized countries diminishes, according to BARRO/SALA-I-MARTIN (1995b), and their growth rates become more equal and the countries converge. EATON/KORTUM (1995) found empirical confirmation of convergence for some OECD countries after World War II which they explain through the adoption of productive technologies by these countries and not through capital deepening per se. Foreign technologies seem to play a considerable role even for the United Sates, which according to EATON/KORTUM obtain more then 40% of their growth from abroad.

3.7 The Role of Human Capital for Economic Growth

The importance of human capital for economic growth was first emphasized by the new growth literature. In the framework of the new growth literature human capital determines R&D activities and the technological capability of a country, and hence its long run economic growth. As GRIES/JUNGBLUT (1997) point out in the new growth theory human capital is not simply accumulated like it is in the neoclassical models (MANKIW/ROMER/WEIL, 1992), but provides for spillovers, externalities, and innovation. Human capital plays a role in a number of models of the new growth theory. LUCAS (1988, 1990, 1993), ROMER (1990), HELPMAN (1992), NELSON/PHELPS (1966), EASTERLY/KING/LEVINE/REBELO (1994), KELLER (1966).

In the models of LUCAS (1988, 1933), accumulation of human capital provides for spillover effects, or as LUCAS puts it, „external effect" or external „engine of growth", which contributes to the productivity of all factors of production. Accumulation of human capital increases aggregate knowledge in the economy and prevents the marginal product of capital from showing diminishing returns. The role of human capital, which follows from its „external effect", is the ability to attract other factors of production, such as physical capital, which also contributes to per capita income growth. LUCAS (1990) argues that physical capital does not go to poor (developing) countries because these countries do not possess sufficient endowments of complementary human capital.

In ROMER (1990) and HELPMAN (1992) human capital represents the main contribution to the R&D sector, which generates new goods and ideas. Thus, the greater initial stock of human capital would allow countries to generate new goods and new knowledge faster, and thus provide for faster economic growth.

Human capital also plays a considerable role for the technological catching up of countries. As EASTERLY/KING/LEVINE/REBELO (1994) and NELSON/PHELPS (1966) suggest, a larger stock of human capital would allow a faster absorption and adoption of new technologies and techniques and a more rapid catching up with the technological frontier. NELSON/PHELPS suggest that higher proportions of human capital to tangible capital would allow a society to attain a more dynamic technology and speed up the process of technological diffusion. KELLER (1996), studying the effects of outward-oriented trade policy on technological catching up, emphasizes that the gap between technological leader and follower can not be closed only by outward-oriented policy, but depends on the development of human capital in the follower country.

The problem of human capital is discussed in a number of other studies. HELPMAN/RANGEL (1999) examined the role of two types of human capital, technology-specific experience and general education for the diffusion of technologies, and secondary innovation and learning by firms. IYIGUN/OWEN

(1999) investigate the importance of different kinds of human capital like entrepreneurial and professional skills for different stages of economic development. Thus, entrepreneurial human capital plays a relatively more important role for intermediate income countries, whereas professional human capital is relatively more important in richer countries. As an economy develops, individuals choose to invest more time accumulating professional skills through schooling than accumulating entrepreneurial human capital. Both skills are important components of an economy's human capital stock, but they influence the level of technology and aggregate production in potentially different ways. SCHULZE (1961) discusses social aspects of human capital formation. He stresses that the World Bank and other international organizations should devote more attention and provide more help to developing countries with the formation of human capital since most investment in these countries is in physical and not human capital[14].

The importance of human capital is emphasized by the technological gap theory as well. Developing countries can use the „advantage of backwardness", assuming that they possess „social capability". Human capital represents an important contribution to „social capability" and enables countries to catch up and introduce new technologies and knowledge into the local economies and adapt them to the new economic environment (ABRAMOWITZ, 1986). GRUNDLACH/NUNNENKAMP (1996) argue that the successful application of new technologies by developing countries also depends on local „technological capability", which is not in the least determined by the level of education. „Technological capability" is also discussed by ABRAMOWITZ and represents an ability to select, adopt, and potentially improve imported technologies. „Social capability" with human capital as a base forms a precondition for the „technological capability" of developing countries.

Empirical evidence on the positive effect of human capital on economic growth was provided by BARRO (1991, 1992), and MANKIW/ROMER/WEIL (1992), BENHABIB/SPIEGEL (1994). The important finding of BARRO (1991) suggests that the starting amount of human capital represents a substantial factor for the future growth of developing countries. Therefore, those poor countries will catch up with rich countries which have high human capital per person (in relation to their level of per capita GDP). BARRO finds out that countries with higher human capital tend to have low fertility rates and high ratios of physical investment to GDP. BENHABIB/SPIEGEL (1994) find positive impact of human capital on the growth rate of total factor productivity and hence technological progress and long run growth. In their model human capital influences both the rate of domestically produced innovations, as in ROMERs (1990) model, and at the same time human capital stock is an important determinant for the adoption of technologies from

[14] For further readings on human capital see also GRILICHES (1995) and HELPMAN (1992).

abroad, as in the model of NELSON/PHELS (1966). The assumption that a better educated labor force is also better in implementing and adopting new technologies and thereby generating growth has been empirically confirmed. They find also that levels of human capital play an important role in attracting physical capital, which supports the issues discussed by LUCAS. BENHABIB/SPIEGEL additionally run a regression where human capital enters a standard Cobb-Douglas production function. Opposed to MANKIW/ROMER/WEIL they fail to find a positive impact of human capital accumulation on economic growth. Thus, the final finding of BENHABIB/SPIEGEL is that human capital contributes to growth since it attracts physical capital and promotes technological progress.

FAN/OVERLAND/SPAGAT (1999) analyze the situation with respect to human capital in modern Russia. Educational tradition in Russia suggests that Russia should have a powerful basis for catching up because it is characterized by widespread literacy, numeracy, and technical training. But nevertheless, Russia remains on the level of a middle income developing country. Russia is quite different in human capital from poor developing countries, as the former Soviet Union possessed a considerable threshold of human capital. The problem is that at present it produces the wrong skills for a market economy. The authors argue that Russia's human capital stock will decline to match its standards of living rather than the opposite, that Russia's standard of living will rise to meet it's human capital stock. There are no incentives for Russian young people to invest in human capital. First of all, the Russian educational system is not adjusted to market conditions and represents a deteriorated version of the Soviet system, which is not capable of providing the human capital needed in a market economy. The second important factor is connected with low returns to human capital in the Russian system in the circumstances of an underdeveloped infrastructure which should support the accumulation of human capital. As a result, these conditions are responsible for high internal and external brain drain. Internal brain drain could push a temporary rise in economic output, but together with external brain drain it will seriously undermine long-run economic potential. The authors also argue that the lack of incentives at present for young people to improve their education will negatively influence the next generation. They point out that the restructuring of education is essentially important at the moment. Otherwise the delay in education restructuring will lead to a persistent drop in productivity and would make the inverse process costly. It is essential that the intergeneration continuity of Russia's intellectual tradition not be lost, that it adapt to the requirements of the market economy of the 21st century.

KITAEV (1994) also points out that the former USSR's economy mostly produced specialists in overspecialized technical profiles who previously served the needs of the military-industrial complex, but at present are hardly demanded in the market economy. The abundance of highly qualified specialists in relation to low-skilled workers caused inadequate wage structures where workers with secondary education earn two or three times more than university professors or high-level researchers, whose qualification does not meet the requirements of market demand. Even if the former USSR's educational system does adjust to market requirements, the economy will stagnate due to existing mismanagement and the shortage of personnel capable of operating under market economy conditions. KITAEV points out that, additionally to Western technologies, the CIS countries should acquire know-how in management, marketing, and distribution. A threat for the market economy is the „black" economy, which is widespread across countries of the former USSR.

RUTZENKOV (1995) argues that the inadequate national system of innovation is a greater obstacle for starting catching up than the technological backwardness. The incentives to innovate were suppressed in the former Soviet Union for a long period of time. In this period people forgot what it means to operate in a competitive environment, to carry out risk-taking activities, and to introduce new ideas into the practice. Moreover, the world's experience was mostly neglected due to economic isolation. The changes in social behavior should be accompanied by the institutional changes which are supposed to support catching up and innovation. RUTZENKOV emphasizes that it is not technological backwardness per se which represents the main problem, but the absence of an adequate national systems of production and innovation, as well as the weakness of political will for catching up. The collapse and disintegration of the Soviet Union had a negative effect on production and innovation. As a result, the research intensive branches of Russia's industry are declining, the whole technological system is morally and physically obsolete, and communications and transportation infrastructures are underdeveloped. The „old" industries like steel and machine-building, traditional electrotechnique, traditional chemical industry, and car industry are lagging far behind the world technological frontier. Therefore, the top political/economic priorities which determine the priorities of technology, foreign trade, and investment for Russia and other CIS countries should be domestic and foreign capital accumulation, technological accumulation, and the rebuilding of national production and innovation systems (RUTZENKOV, 1995)[15].

Table 8 summarizes the results of the above studies on Russia and other CIS countries. The results show that although Russia and other CIS countries possess a considerable threshold of human capital, it is not efficient as it does not correspond to market requirements and is excluded from the market system.

---

[15] For further readings on science and education in the former USSR and other Soviet countries see JONES (1994) and KNEZO (1993).

Table 8: Results of Studies on Human Capital in Russia and other CIS Countries

	High-skilled human capital	Human capital adopted to market conditions	Infrastructure	Market institutions	System of innovation
FAN/OVERLAND/SPAGAT (1999)	under-utilization	scarce	low	low	
KITAEV (1994)	under-utilization	scarce	low	low	
RUTZENKOV (1994)			low	low	low

Additionally, low development of infrastructure does not allow for the complete realization of human capital in the economy. The lack of market institutions represents a threat in many ways. First, the market specialists can not be educated, secondly, they can not be adequately employed, hence the well-educated human capital is educated in matter which is obsolete in a market environment and can not be realized. Low innovation represents a threat in the sense that people can not function under the pressure of competition in an innovative environment and take risk onto themselves. The catching up preconditions of CIS countries does not look very promising, except in terms of potential in human capital. In order not to lose the existing potential of human capital it is important to make rash reforms of the educational systems. Otherwise the accumulated knowledge will be lost, since the present economic environment is not able to make use of it. Speed of reforms is also important for other determinants. Speed of reforms can be enhanced by integration with the European Union, as a lot of problems can be decided in the framework of this cooperation. Reorientation of foreign trade towards EU and other world economies would increase the FDI into the transition countries, where the presence of multinational firms would raise the demand for market oriented specialists. FDI would allow for substantial improvements in the physical infrastructure. Integration into the EU and participation in international organizations would facilitate the import of norms and institutions from advanced market economies (Candidate countries into the EU have to fulfill requirements which give them direction and stimulate them towards reforms).

Hungary and Poland have considerably improved their „social capability" through their progress in such reforms as external liberalization, stabilization, privatization, institutional reforms, and prospects to join the EU. CIS countries are partially missing the willingness for reforms and suffer under from distrust and long hesitation to integrate into the world economic society. Low speed and progress in reforms has deepened the economic crisis and left these countries with few choices.

3.8 The Problem of the Dutch Disease

In the situation of economic crisis the possibility to get rich easily becomes especially attractive, an area where the rich endowment of natural resources in Russia could be part of the problem. Thus, in Russia and other CIS countries which have considerable natural resource endowments, revenues from the resource sector could become the main source of income in the economy. In such a setting, economies risk the reallocation of resources from the manufacturing tradable sector towards the non-tradable sector, which could impair long run growth of the economy. This problem of disadvantages caused by abundant natural resources is known as Dutch disease.

What is Dutch disease? The mechanism of the Dutch disease obvious in a three sector economy (a tradable natural resource sector, a tradable (non-resource) manufacturing sector, and a non-traded sector) functions as follows. A large abundance of natural resources leads to higher concentrations of tradable production in the natural resource sector rather than in manufacturing, and shifts capital and labor, which otherwise might be employed in manufacturing, to the non-traded goods sector (SACHS/WARNER, 1995b). Thus, the manufacturing sector gets crowded out by the tradable natural resource sector. This phenomenon was first observed in the Netherlands, therefore it is called the Dutch disease. Natural gas discoveries in the Netherlands considerably reduced the competitiveness of Dutch manufacturing and led to the decrease of it's world market share. The United Kingdom also suffered from the decline in manufacturing as one of the most large West European oil and gas producers. As pointed out by VAN WIJNBERGEN (1984), developing countries producing oil face serious problems with the diversification of their export structure. This problem can also be observed in Russia.

Thus, Dutch disease represents a threat for both the developed and developing world, where it deprives the first of the country's already existing manufacturing sector, and prevents the other from developing it. Why, as KRUGMAN (1987) raises the question, can countries not simply follow their comparative advantages and concentrate on the natural resource sector? According to trade theory, countries should specialize in their comparative advantages. Following this logic, abundance in natural resources represents a comparative advantage which countries should exploit. But still some countries prefer to ignore this advice. The answer is that „*...when the natural resources run out, the lost manufacturing sectors will not come back*" KRUGMAN (1987, p. 49). As for developing countries, the further development of natural resources will move the goal of higher economic growth and prosperity further into the future, since the resource boom (either from a term-of-trade improvement or a resource discovery) experienced by some economies doesn't really stimulate economic growth and in some cases causes its decline (SACHS/WARNER, 1999).

The reason for the Dutch disease lies in poor linkages between the tradable natural resource sector, the non-traded sector, and economic growth. It is a well known fact that the technological progress which represents the main driving force of economic growth is much faster in the manufacturing sector. Due to the new growth theory, endogenous growth is caused by learning by doing, knowledge spillovers, externalities, and innovation. VAN WIJNBERGEN (1984) discusses learning by doing induced technological progress and stresses that learning by doing mostly takes place in manufacturing and so the decline of this sector will permanently lower per capita income. Learning by doing is a precondition for technology adoption and diffusion. Therefore countries which are lagging behind in manufacturing are not able to successfully adopt world innovations and cut off the resources needed to perform indigenous innovation. These would have a negative impact on economic growth and would cause its slow down. Additionally, as stressed by HIRSCHMAN (1958), there are stronger „backward and forward linkages" in the manufacturing sector than in the natural resource sector, and hence stronger impact on other sectors of the economy. The factor of „backward and forward linkages" represents a crucial impulse for the increase of productivity in the rest of the economy.

Thus, in the case of developing countries, *„...a period of retrenchment of non-oil traded goods production will delay the Learning by Doing experience that would improve their comparative advantage (or lessen a comparative „disadvantage") in the production of manufactured goods"* (VAN WIJNBERGEN, 1984, p. 53). In the case of developed countries oil and other natural resource discoveries will cut manufacturing production in favor of the non-traded sector. Moreover, natural resource discoveries can cause real appreciation of the country's exchange rate and thus crowd out its other tradable sectors (KRUGMAN, 1987). The latter is based on treatment of the Dutch disease as a situation where income earnings from the natural resource sector are considered as a pure transfer payment from abroad (KRUGMAN, 1987). As a result of a sufficiently long transfer with an unchanging specialization pattern, there will be a rise in the relative wages of the recipient country with a consequent shift of production abroad (disadvantage in productivity) (KRUGMAN, 1987).

The Netherlands had to deal with the consequences of Dutch disease until the 1990s. SMITS/DE JONG/VAN ARK (1999), investigating the economic growth of the Netherlands in the three technology phases which ran from 1800 to 1913 (steam), from 1890 to 1990 (electricity), and from 1973 to the present (information and communication technology), point out that Dutch disease made it more difficult to transfer and diffuse some technologies. The Netherlands lost its position during the eighteenth century after being at the world technological frontier in the seventeenth century. During this time it lost many of its exports markets (to a large extent during the Napoleonic Wars). The poor industrial situation within the country prevented the successful diffusion of new technologies (stem) and was responsible for the inability to innovate. In the nineteenth century the Netherlands was lagging behind the other Northwestern European countries in productivity growth. In the period 1947 - 73 there was a successful catching up, mostly due to low wages, but it then experienced another slowdown after 1973. In 1979 the Dutch economy was hardly hurt by the second oil crisis as a result of over-expansionary policies during the 1970's and at the same time loss of competitiveness due to huge gas exports (the „Dutch disease"), which caused a serious crisis in the early 1980s. The Dutch productivity gains from the ICT revolution are also questionable as the impact should be low due to a relatively large service sector in comparison with manufacturing (SMITS/DE JONG/VAN ARK, 1999).

SACHS/WARNER (1995b) empirically investigated the relationship between abundant natural resources and economic growth. They found for a sample of 97 developing countries that those economies which had a high ratio of natural resource exports in GDP in 1971 (base year) also had low growth rates during the subsequent period 1971 - 1989. To resource-based exports account agriculture, minerals, and fuels. The interesting question, which they raise in the paper is why natural resource abundance becomes a disadvantage when the countries have more possibilities to finance imports and make investments in the economy. Why doesn't this happen, or why is it not the case on average, taking into account that there are always some exceptions of the rule? SACHS/WARNER discuss in their paper the factors which could make natural resource abundance a disadvantage as they are regarded in the rest of the literature. The disadvantage of natural resource abundance starts with easy riches lead to sloth. This creates further preconditions for an inequality in the society due to high rent-seeking behavior, world prices for primary exports turn out to be lower than for manufacturing, making primary export unattractive, the demand for manufacturing grows faster than demand for primary goods, protectionism becomes, as a rule, stronger against primary goods than against manufacturing goods, there are poor „backward and forward linkages" from primary export to the rest of the economy, and there is weak learning by doing in the primary sector.

SACHS/WARNER develop a number of hypotheses, which explain the negative effect of natural resource abundance on political and economic variables such as trade policy, bureaucratic efficiency, and other determinants of growth. They argue that the effects of resource abundance on growth can be either direct or indirect, depending on other factors influencing growth. Thus, they argue that resource rich countries tend to develop inward-looking economic policies and an ineffective bureaucratic mechanism. Additionally, the possibility to get rich easy from the high rents on natural resources creates a danger of social polarization and income inequality since the political elite is eager to take advantage of resource wealth. Finally, dependence on primary resources makes the country more vulnerable to external shocks. They run a cross-country growth regression, where they specify the effect of natural resource intensity on growth and control for a number of additional variables which are important in explaining growth. These variables are initial GDP, trade policy, investment rates, terms of trade volatility, inequality, and the effectiveness of the bureaucracy. Empirical testing of these hypotheses showed the conformation of the following results. Resource abundance causes bureaucratic inefficiency and protectionism and lowers investment rates. Oppositely, there was no confirmation of the negative association between external shocks (terms of trade volatility), income inequality, and growth. Going further SACHS/WARNER determine how strong the direct impact of natural resource intensity on growth and indirect impact (the impact through other variables) is. The first hypothesis they test focuses on the effect of resource abundance on bureaucratic efficiency. It is supposed that high bureaucratic inefficiency has either a direct negative impact on growth or is indirect through depressing investment demand. A second hypothesis is that natural resource abundance would lead to higher protectionism due to Dutch disease effects. Dutch disease contributes to the disappearance of manufacturing from a country. This in turn creates more incentives to induce protectionist measures to defend the rest of the manufacturing sector. Higher protectionism would cause lower investment rates and hence result in low growth rates. A third hypotheses is based on the assumption that natural resource abundance will increase overall demand, which will result in higher relative prices of investment goods and hence low growth rates. A last hypothesis shows the problem of learning by doing in the context of Dutch disease where natural resource abundance shifts labor away from high learning by doing sectors and hence depress productivity and growth.

The empirical results confirm the negative direct effect of natural resource intensity on economic growth. The direct effect seems to be twice as large as all the indirect effects combined. Among indirect effects the effect on openness appears to be the largest. Thus, variables of natural resource intensity and openness represent important determinants of economic growth. The rest of the indirect effects associated with Dutch disease, although significant, play only a moderate role quantitatively. The large difference between the direct effect compared to indirect effects could be because of measurement bias, as the model tends to overestimate the direct effects.

In their other paper SACHS/WARNER (1999) study the effects of natural resource booms on economic growth. On the evidence from seven Latin American countries they show that resource booms were associated with declining per-capita GDP rather than with economic growth. The historical evidence supports this view since Latin American countries exhibited only small growth during the last thirty years, while East Asian countries, which have poor natural resource endowments, grew very rapidly. The Latin American countries remained the exporters of primary commodities, while East Asian countries became exporters of increasingly capital-intensive and technology-intensive goods.

The logic that natural resource booms can spur growth is based on big push reasoning, which could be a catalyst for low-income countries to overcome the fixed costs of industrialization. The results of this paper support the results of the previous one. Resource scarce countries tend to have a larger service sector and a smaller manufacturing sector as well as a small ratio of exports of manufactured goods to total exports. Thus, Dutch disease had consequences in the reduction of the manufacturing sector, which is essential for economic growth. SACHS/WARNER found the regression estimate of the natural resource effect for eleven Latin American countries. The largest impact of natural resource intensity on growth was in the case of Venezuela. Venezuelan growth was 0.77 per cent lower due to natural resource intensity. This shows the dimension of the effect since Venezuelan growth was 14 per cent lower than it should be (in the case of no natural resources) at the end of a 20 year period ending in 1990. The negative effect on growth was also found in the case of a natural resource boom. Examining the effect of a resource boom on three Latin American countries (Bolivia, Mexico, and Venezuela, where the boom was especially visible) SACHS/WARNER did not find lasting positive effects of this on economic growth, but rather an effect of slowdown and decrease.

Thus, transition economies, and especially Russia, should be very cautious in investing in resource abundant industries because the growth of these industries is not a guaranty for long run growth of the economy. Instead, developing countries concentrating on resource abundant industries reallocate the resources from manufacturing into the non-traded sector. Since the manufacturing sector is associated with special links to growth such as learning by doing, knowledge spillovers, externalities, and strong „forward and backward linkages", decreasing the share of the manufacturing sector can lead to poor growth performance. Moreover, developing countries have strong difficulties with the diversification of their export structures and thus the growth possibilities are being moved further into the future. There is one more problem which such countries as Russia could face. This is the problem of immiserizing growth (for more detailed description see section 3.11.2 Appendix B). Immiserizing growth induces a country to expand its exports, which in the case of a large country can lead to the deterioration of terms of trade and welfare losses. Therefore, for large countries, a diversified export structure could reduce the risks of immiserizing growth as well as the promotion of import replacing instead of export expanding industries (LINDERT/PUGEL, 1996).

There is some risk that Russia could face problems of the Dutch disease with oil and gas prices rising strongly in real terms in 1999/2000. Governmental R&D policy might address this problem by strongly promoting the growth of manufactured exports.

Table 9: The Evidence of Dutch Disease in Russian Economy

	1995	1998
Manufacturing (% of GDP)*	29.3%	29%
Energy sector (electricity and fuels) (% of GDP)*	10.4%	10.7%
Electricity sector (% of GDP)*	3.6%	4,8%
Total employment (mill.)	66,4	63,6
Employment in manufacturing (mill.)	16,006	13,173
Employment in energy sector (electricity and fuels) (mill.)	1,596	1,646
Employment in electricity sector (mill.)	0,750	0,852
Relative price of oil	0,135	0,126

Source: IMF (1999), International Financial Statistics Yearbook, 1999; EBRD (2000), EBRD Transition Report 2000; own calculations

** In basic prices*

Table 9 shows that there is no evidence at present of a Dutch disease in the Russian economy. But, on the one hand, induced investments into the energy sector and tax evasion on the other favor the expansion of the energy sector in Russia and represent the danger of the Dutch disease for the future.

3.9 The Importance of Foreign Trade and Foreign Direct Investment for Technological Catching Up

As technological upgrading represents a challenge for CIS and CEECs to catch up to the income levels of the leading industrialized economies, one should draw special attention to the channels of technology transfer from abroad. Among other sources, trade and FDI are pointed out by many economists as being the main channels of technology transfer (PAVITT/SOETE, 1981, CORNWALL, 1977, LLEWELLYN/PESARAN, 1976, SINGER/REYNILDS, 1975, PACK, 1992, GROSSMAN/HELPMAN, 1991a, GRIES/JUNGBLUT, 1997, ROMER, 1993a). Foreign trade and FDI are crucial channels of technology transfer. They provide for knowledge spillovers and externalities from abroad which raise considerably the productivity level in the domestic economy. They stimulate innovation activities within the domestic economy, and improve its absorptive capacity (ability to imitate advanced forms of technologies). Both have a strong positive impact on human capital, which is an important drive for economic growth from the point of view of new growth theory and is an essential precondition for technology transfer from the point of view of technological gap theory.

PAVITT/SOETE (1981) point out that trade in capital goods and FDI play a specially important role in the international diffusion of innovations. ROMER (1993a) points to the importance of idea flows across national borders for catching up possibilities of developing countries, where he emphasizes the special role of multinational corporations. GRIES/JUNGBLUT (1997) emphasizes the role of foreign trade and FDI as the main channels for technology transfer for the catching up of „backward" countries. GROSSMAN/HELPMAN (1991a) argue that the most important benefit to a country of participating in international trade might be the access that such trade affords to the technological knowledge of the rest of the world. PACK (1992), analyzing the experience of Asian countries in the period 1960 - 1985, emphasizes that productivity growth in Asian countries was not only the result of the technology acquired, but mostly because this technology was embodied in economies that offered strong inducements to export and in which a decrease in costs and improvement in quality were the main prerogatives. He points out that slowly growing economies can not automatically take advantage of their current low income but should make an intensive effort to acquire technology. The countries could learn from technology incorporated in imported products and from externalities appearing from exporting. Therefore, a competitive environment with pro-export structures is an important precondition for the acquisition of knowledge. Additionally, FDI should be encouraged (PACK, 1992). Approximately the same evidence as in Asian economies was true for OECD countries in the post-war period. LLEWELLYN/PESARAN (1976) tested a model for OECD countries in the post-war period and found out that the existence of a technological gap, a strong propensity to invest, and successful export performance were the main factors leading to a rapid rate of growth of manufacturing output in these countries.

CORNWALL (1977) points out that the amount of technological knowledge available for innovation in the imitating country depends to a large extent (among other things) on the creating of subsidiaries by multinational corporations in the countries industrializing late. FDI is important for the expansion of the absorptive capacity of the imitating country (MURELL, 1990; WELFENS, 1992b).

FISCHER/EASTERLY (1992), analyzing the growth perspectives of the former Soviet republics, emphasize that much of the long run growth would depend on the rate of return to new capital. New capital can be provided by foreign investors. Would the former Soviet states be successful in attracting FDI? In this point neoclassical and new growth theory also provide controversial explanations. According to the neoclassical growth model, capital will go to the countries where it is scarce. In the new growth theory capital will be attracted to the countries where it is already abundant because of the strong externalities from the accumulated threshold of capital. LUCAS (1990) and ZEBREGS (1998) point out that foreign capital would go to the countries, which have accumulated more human capital and where political risk has been overcome. GARIBALDI/MORA/SAHAY/ZETTELMEYER (1999) point to the importance of country risk perceptions and institutional obstacles in their econometric analysis as the limiting factors of attracting FDI. In the following chapters special attention will be devoted to foreign trade and FDI and their interaction with economic growth.

3.10 Tentative Conclusions

In this chapter aspects of future growth strategy were analyzed for CIS and CEECs. The analysis started with a historical perspective. Extensive strategy of development in the former Soviet Union and a distortive system of science and innovation represented crucial factors for decline of output growth in the former Soviet Union.

Further research proceeds along a theoretical perspective. Both neoclassical and new growth theory provide insights into the growth experience of the former Soviet Union. On the one hand growth in the former USSR strongly resembles the neoclassical model. Diminishing returns to capital in the situation of low technological change and the politically determined public nature of technological progress support this view. On the other hand, new growth theory puts new light on the reasons of output decline in the former USSR. It explains output decline in the former Soviet Union as a result of distortionary policies which have an effect on long run growth as well as due to the absence of incentives to innovate and adopt new technologies, which are the main preconditions for endogenous change and growth.

The neoclassical growth theory only seems to be partly adequate for the future growth strategy of CIS and other CEECs. The policy implications provided by the neoclassical growth theory are limited to investment/saving policies. New growth theory, where governmental policies, knowledge spillovers, externalities, and innovation influence long run growth, shows broader policy options for future growth strategies and leads to a deeper understanding of the reasons for the output decline in the Soviet Union.

Technological gap between CIS and CEECs and the industrialized elite is large. The technological catching up described in the theory of technological gap and supported by some new growth theorists points to an appropriate option to close the gap. Much emphasis should be made on the creation of preconditions for successful technology transfer. These precondition include social capability, technological opportunity/capability, indigenous innovation, and a majority ownership of foreign investors (otherwise the incentives to transfer the latest technologies is very limited).

Human capital plays a crucial role for economic growth. In the context of new growth theory it generates knowledge spillovers and externalities, promotes innovation, and in the context of the technological gap approach, it is an important precondition for technology transfer.

For the future growth strategy in the case of resource rich countries such as Russia, the Dutch disease problem should be taken into account. The abundance of natural resources does not promote economic growth, but instead has a negative impact. Dutch disease also represents an obstacle for developing countries to diversify their export structure and hence makes catching up difficult.

Channels of technology transfer such as foreign trade and FDI are of great importance for the future growth of the CIS and CEECs since technology represents a driving force of economic growth and rapid catching up depends to a large extent on technology transfers from abroad. The aspects of foreign trade and FDI as well as the role of structural change for growth will be discussed in the following chapters.

3.11 Appendix

3.11.1 Appendix A: Neoclassical Growth Theory

An important contribution to neoclassical growth theory was the work of ROBERT SOLOW (1956). Solow's theory helped to clarify the role of accumulation of physical capital and emphasized the importance of technological progress as a main driving force of the sustained economic growth (JONES, 1998).

Following ROBERT SOLOW (1956, p 65), who wrote: „*All theory depends on assumptions which are not quite true. That is what makes it theory. The art of successful theorizing is to make the inevitable simplifying assumption in such a way that the final results are not very sensitive*„, we will use the assumptions inherent in the Solow model.

The first assumption of the closed economy model is that only one commodity is considered, output as a whole. One consequence of this assumption is that there is no international trade in the model because countries produce and consume only a single good hence the model is applied for the case of a closed economy. In a closed economy, output equals income, and the amount invested equals the amount saved.

Another important assumption of the model is that the technology is *exogenous*- that means that the determinants of the technological change are not considered in this model (for example the R&D activities of firms does not influence the technology available to firms). Technology improves exogenously and the same technological opportunities are available in all countries of the world.

The description of the Solow model can be found in different text books, among them BARRO and SALA-I-MARTIN (1995) and JONES (1998).

The Solow model is based on two main equations, a production function and a capital accumulation equation. There are only two inputs in the production function: physical capital, K, and labor, L (see equation 3.1). The production function may be specified Cobb-Douglas form and is given by

$$Y = F(K, L) = K^{\alpha} L^{1-\alpha}, \tag{3.1}$$

where α is some number between 0 and 1. Notice that this production function is characterized by *constant returns to scale*: if all the inputs double, output will also exactly double. The condition of constant returns to scale implies that output can be written as

$$Y = F(K, L) = LF(K / L, 1) = Lf(k) \tag{3.2}$$

where $k = K / L$ is the capital-labor ratio, $y = Y / L$ is per capita output, and the function $f(k)$ is defined to equal $F(k,1)$. This result means that the production function can be expressed in *intensive form* as

$$y = f(k). \tag{3.3}$$

To apply this to the Cobb-Douglas function it is possible to rewrite the production function in equation (3.1) in terms of output per worker as:

$$y = k^{\alpha}. \tag{3.4}$$

This production function implies diminishing returns to capital per worker: each additional unit of capital increases the output by less and less (see Figure 6).

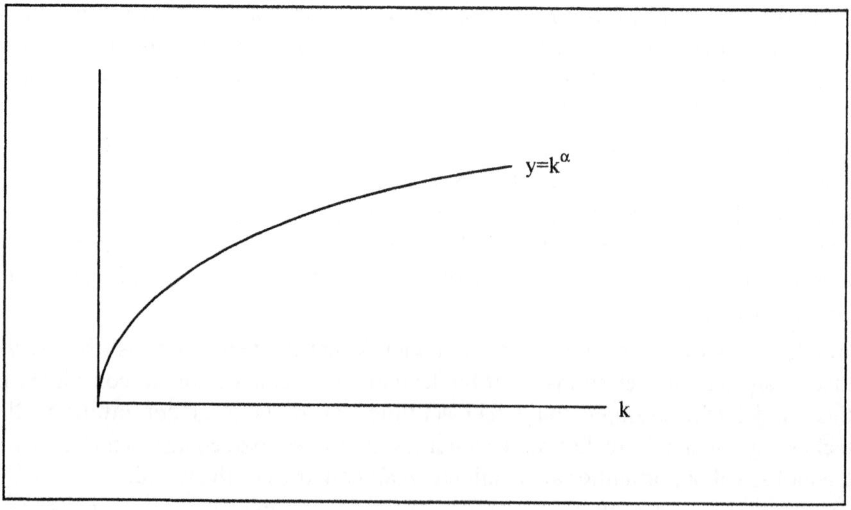

Source: Jones (1998), p. 21

Figure 6: A Cobb-Douglas Production Function

The second key equation of the Solow model is the capital accumulation equation

$$\dot{K} = sY - \delta K, \tag{3.5}$$

where s is a saving rate and δ-the rate of capital depreciation.

According to this equation the change in the capital stock $\dot{K}$, ($\dot{K} = dK/dt$), is equal to the amount of gross investment, sY, less the amount of depreciation that occurs during the production process, δK. The capital accumulation equation in terms of k can be obtained in the following way. Since $k = K/L$, the relative rate of change of k is the difference between the relative rates of change of K and L. That is:

$$\dot{k}/k = \dot{K}/K - \dot{L}/L. \tag{3.6}$$

Under the assumption that population grows at a constant, exogenous rate, $\dot{L}/L = n$ and making substitution of $\dot{K} = sY - \delta K$ one will get

$$\dot{k}/k = sY/K - n - \delta = sy/k - n - \delta. \tag{3.7}$$

Now the capital accumulation equation in per worker terms can be attained:

$$\dot{k} = sy - (n+\delta)k. \tag{3.8}$$

The equation (3.8) is the fundamental differential equation of the neoclassical model. The equation says that the change in capital per worker increases with investment per worker while it decreases with depreciation and with population growth. The term $n+\delta$ is also called effective depreciation rate for capital/labor ratio, $k = K/L$. If the saving rate, s were 0, then k would decline partly due to depreciation of K at the rate δ and partly due to growth of L at the rate n.

The two key equations of the Solow model in terms of output per worker and capital per worker provide insights into the growth path of the economy or in other worlds how output per worker grow in the economy.

These equations are:

$$y = k^{\alpha} \tag{3.9}$$

and

$$\dot{k} = sy - (n+\delta)k. \tag{3.10}$$

In the model of Solow because of the diminishing returns to capital the economy is always approaching a steady state k^*. A *steady state* can be defined as a situation in which the various quantities grow at constant rates. (BARRO/SALA-I-MARTIN, 1995). In the Solow model the steady state corresponds to $\dot{k} = 0$ in equation 3.10. The equation is most easy to analyze if we look at the Figure 7.

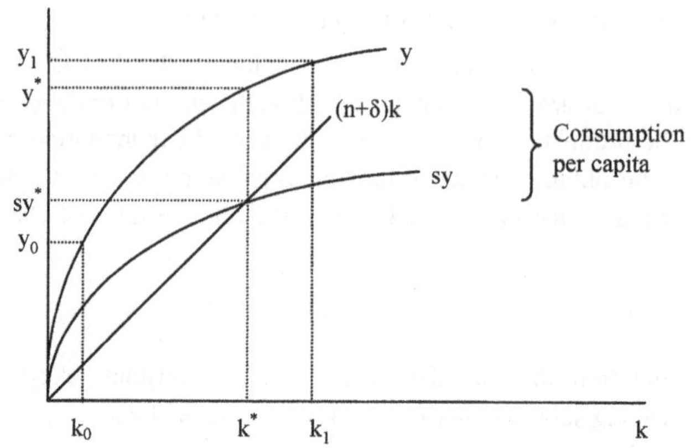

Source: Jones (1998), p. 26

Figure 7: The Solow Diagram and the Production Function

The upper curve is the production function y. The second curve is the amount of investment per person sy. The term $(n+\delta)k$ represents the amount of new investment per person needed to keep the amount of capital per worker constant. Both depreciation and the growing workforce tend to reduce the amount of capital per person in the economy. The steady state value of k is denoted by k^*. The change in the amount of capital per worker is represented as the difference between sy and $(n+\delta)k$ curves. y^* determines the steady state value of output per worker, as a function of k^*. The figure 7 represents also the steady state consumption value as difference between steady state output per worker, y^* and steady state investment per worker, sy^*. The figure illustrates that the economy always approaches a steady state whether it starts below or above its steady state value. Suppose an economy has capital equal to the amount k_0. At k_0 the amount of investment per worker exceeds the amount needed to keep capital per worker constant, so that there is a growth of capital per worker and output per worker correspondingly till the steady state value. If an economy starts to the right of k^* (k_1) the amount of investment does not exceed the amount needed to keep capital per worker constant, so that the capital per worker would decline causing the decline in output per worker till both terms reach their steady state values.

Now it is possible to look how the economy would react on the changes in the investment rate, s, and the population rate, n, and which kind of policy implications it can have? The first case of increase in the investment rate is plotted at the Figure 8 and shows the shift in the level of per capita income from the steady state level k^* to the higher steady state level k^{**}. At the current value of the capital stock, k^*, investment per worker as a result of increase in the investment rate now exceeds the amount required to keep capital per worker constant, and therefore the economy would grow till the new higher steady state level of capital per worker and would reach higher level of output per worker, so that the economy becomes richer than before.

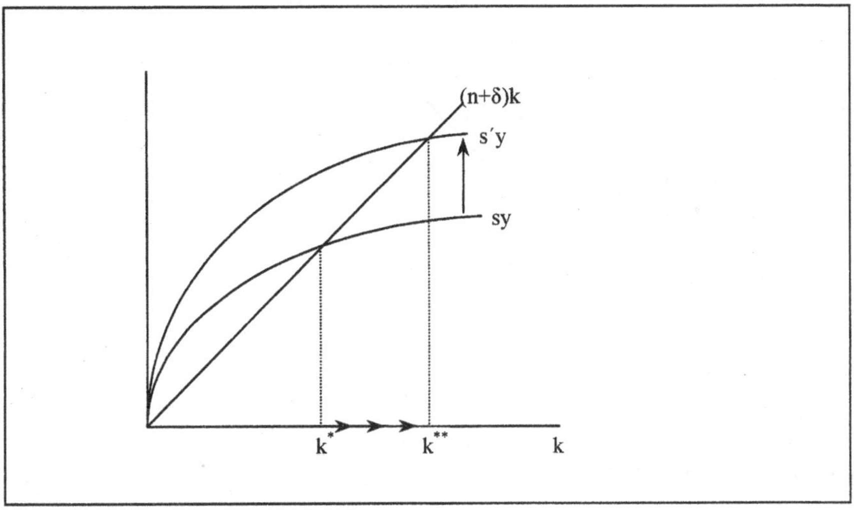

Source: Jones (1998), p. 27

Figure 8: An Increase in the Investment Rate

An increase in the population rate has vice versa opposite impact. An increase in the population rate is reflected by the Figure 9, where the $(n+\delta)k$ curve moves to the left to the new curve $(n'+\delta)k$. At the value of the capital stock k^*, investment per worker does not compensate any more the amount needed to keep the capital-labor ratio constant in the face of rising population. Therefore the capital-labor ratio begins to fall approaching new steady state where the value of output per worker is lower than before.

The conclusion, which is possible to draw from this figure is that countries with higher saving/investment rates tend to be richer and vise versa. Higher investment rates allow countries to accumulate more capital per worker and to reach higher output per worker level. Opposite to that countries with high population growth rates, according to the Solow model tend to be poorer.

What is very important to remark at this stage is that changes in the saving/investment rate, the rate of population growth do not affect the steady state growth rate of output per capita, which is equal to 0. For this reason, the model as presently specified does not provide explanations of the determinants of long-run per capita growth. This model has only *level effects* and provides *transitional dynamics.*

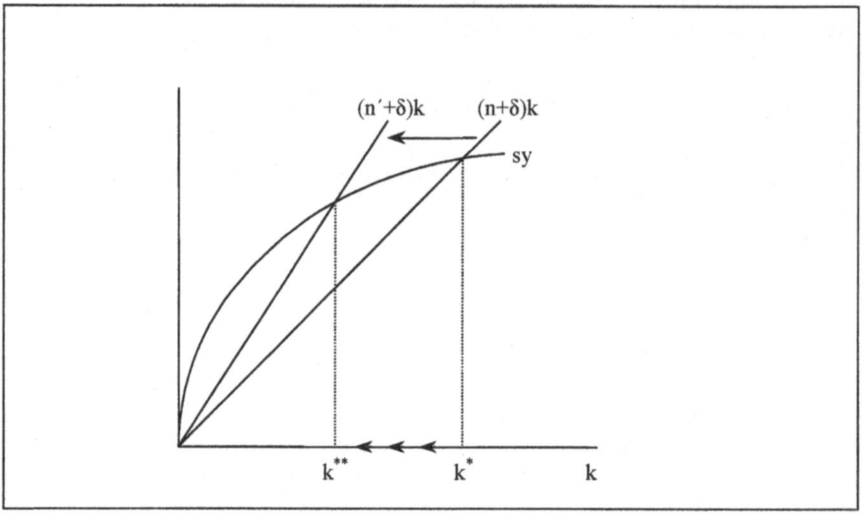

Source: Jones (1998), p. 28

Figure 9: An Increase in Population Growth

One more important conclusion from the Solow model follows from the fact that along the transition path the growth rate of the capital stock would decline with the rise of the capital stock.

To demonstrate this fact we look at the equation of the capital accumulation

$$\dot{k}/k = sk^{\alpha-1} - (n+\delta). \tag{3.11}$$

Because α is less than one, the growth rate of k declines with the rise of k. The same would be valid for output per worker because of proportional relationship between growth rate of y and growth rate of k. An important question arises: whether the result obtained means that the economies with lower capital per person tend to grow faster in per capita terms. In other words does it mean that countries converge to the common steady state level?

The transitional dynamics plotted in the Figure 10 proves clearly this assumption. The growth rate of k ($\dot{k}/k$) is given by the vertical difference between the saving curve, $sy/k = sk^{\alpha-1}$ and the effective depreciation line, $n+\delta$ that does not depend on k and therefore plotted as a horizontal line. Thus, the figure shows how the convergence evolves. The speed of convergence increases the further the economy is from its steady state value. Thus, the further the economy below its steady state value of k the faster the economy grows and the further an economy above its steady state the faster it would decline.

From that it follows that the neoclassical growth theory predicts the *convergence* of countries to the steady state values. One should distinguish between absolute and conditional convergence.

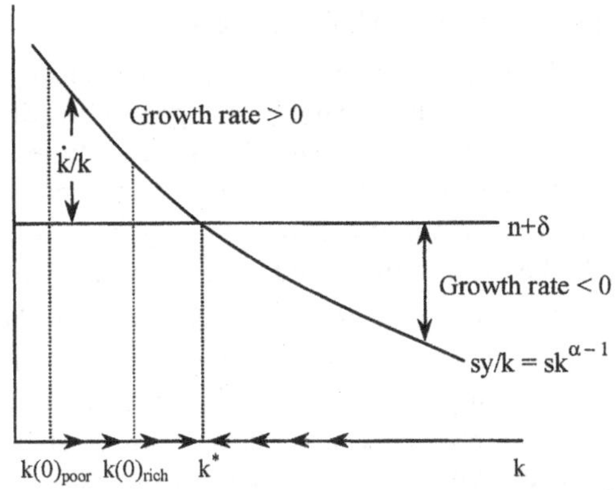

Source: Jones (1998), p. 32

Figure 10: Transition Dynamics

The hypothesis of absolute convergence assumes that poor economies tend to grow faster than rich economies approaching steady state without making any difference in characteristics of economies. One can imagine this if one considers a group of closed economies that have the same parameters as s, n, and δ and also the same production function, $f(\cdot)$. Then the economies would move towards the same steady state values of k^* and y^*. The only difference between the economies is different starting values of capital per person. The model implies then that less-advanced economies - with lower values of k and y will grow faster than more developed economies and thereby will catch up or converge to those with higher capital-labor ratios. But the hypothesis of absolute convergence was not confirmed by the broad cross country data (BARRO/SALA-I-MARTIN,

1995). The data showed that it was more plausible to confine the considered economies to a more homogeneous group (as for example the 20 advanced OECD countries or the continental US states). In this case one speaks about conditional convergence - convergence that relaxes the assumption of the similar parameters (for example consider the economies with different initial stocks of capital per person and different saving rates) and hence similar steady state positions. Thus the important prediction of neoclassical model is that each economy converges to its own steady state and that the speed of the convergence relates inversely to the distance from the steady state. Empirical observations seemed to approve the existence of conditional convergence. BARRO/SALA-I-MARTIN (1992) found evidence of convergence for a sample of 98 countries from 1960 to 1985 in a conditional sense, that is, only if controlling for the determinants of the steady-state (only if such variables as initial school enrollment rates and the ratio of government consumption to GDP are hold constant).

The prediction of conditional convergence in the neoclassical model contradicts with a very important stylized fact, namely the possibility of the economy to exhibit sustained per capita income growth. At the same time as JONES (1998) points out it corresponds to the several other stylized facts. For example it explains differences in per capita income across countries. It generates a constant capital-output ratio of K/L, because both k and y are constant. It generates also a constant marginal product of capital. But it does not support the stylized fact of sustained growth. This model exhibits growth only in the framework of transitional dynamics. The model explains growth only along the transition path from one steady state to the other steady state position. Thus, if the economy begins with a stock of capital per worker below its steady state then it would experience growth of k and y along the transition path to the new steady state level. The closer economy to the approaching steady state the slower growth rate would be diminishing in the steady state to the null (JONES, 1998). Thus the obtained model predicts constant per capita variables in the long run. This feature of the model contradicts obviously with practical evidence and is clearly unrealistic. For example the United States exhibit the positive per capita growth rate for over two centuries what would be impossible to maintain only accumulating capital because of diminishing returns.

The neoclassical economists of the 1950s and 1960s recognized this problem and introduced technological improvements over time into the model. These improvements allowed to escape from diminishing returns and thus enabled the economy to grow in per capita terms in the long run. An important assumption of the neoclassical model is that technological progress is *exogenous*: it falls like „manna from heaven". The neoclassical model does not examine where technological change comes from. It spreads automatically over an economy and represents just a function of time. Of course, such an assumption is unrealistic because the most technological improvements reflect purposeful activity, such as research and development (R&D) carried out by firms or for example universities.

The deeper insights into the sources of technological improvements are provided by the „new" growth theory where it is the major challenge to relax the assumption of exogenous technological progress.

To explain how the model works one assumes that the production function includes labor-augmenting technological progress and that the technology term, $A(t)$, grows at the constant rate x. Then the condition for the change in the capital stock is

$$\dot{K} = s \cdot F[K, L \cdot A(t)] - \delta K . \tag{3.12}$$

One can derive an expression for the change in k over time by dividing both sides of the equation by L:

$$\dot{k} = s \cdot F[k, A(t)] - (n+\delta) \cdot k . \tag{3.13}$$

The only difference from equation (3.8) is that output per person depends now on the level of technology, $A(t)$.

The growth rate from k would take then the following form:

$$g_k = s \cdot F[k, A(t)] / k - (n+\delta) . \tag{3.14}$$

In the equation 3.7 g_k equals the difference between two terms, where the first term is the product of s and the average product of capital, and the second term is $n+\delta$. The only difference from the previous model is that now the average product of capital, $F[k, A(t)]/k$ would increase over time because of the growth in $A(t)$ at the rate x. At the Figure 10 it would be reflected through the shift of the downward-sloping curve $s \cdot F[k, A(t)]/k$ continually to the right what would course the shift in the steady state level of k^* also continually to the right. Now it is possible to compute the growth rate of k in the steady state.

By definition, the steady state growth rate, g_k^* is constant. Because s, n, and δ are also constants, equation (3.14) implies that the average product of capital, $F[k, A(t)]/k$, is constant in the steady state. Since there are constant returns to scale one can rewrite the average product in the form $F[1, A(t)/k]$. As one can now see the average product will be constant only if k and $A(t)$ grow at the same rate, that is, $g_k^* = x$.

Output per capita is given by the following formula:

$$y = F[k, A(t)] = k \cdot F[1, A(t)/k] . \tag{3.15}$$

Since k and $A(t)$ grow in the steady state at the rate x, the steady state growth rate of y equals x. Moreover, since for consumption c it is true that $c=(1-s)\cdot y$, the steady state growth rate of c also equals x. A situation in which capital, output, consumption, and population are growing at constant rate is called a *balanced growth path.*

That is, along a balanced growth path in the neoclassical growth model, output per worker and capital per worker grow at the rate of exogenous technological change, so that

$$g_y = g_k = x\,. \tag{3.16}$$

Opposite to the model without technological progress, and therefore without long run growth in output per worker or capital per worker: $g_y = g_k = 0$ the model with technology shows that technological progress is the source of sustained per capita growth.

The analysis of the model with technological progress proceeds very much like the analysis of the transitional dynamics made in the previous model with the only difference that the variable k is no longer constant in the long run, so that it is more convenient to rewrite the system in terms of variables that remain constant in the steady-state.

Thus, instead of k it is better to work with the ratio $\hat{k} \equiv k / A(t) = K / [L \cdot A(t)]$. Since k and $A(t)$ grow in the steady-state at the same rate the ratio $\hat{k}$ will be constant in steady-state. The variable $L \cdot A(t) \equiv \hat{L}$ is often called the effective amount of labor - the physical quantity of labor, L, multiplied by its efficiency, $A(t)$. The variable $\hat{k}$ is called then the quantity of capital per unit of effective labor.

The intensive form for the quantity of output per unit of effective labor, $\hat{y} \equiv Y / [L \cdot A(t)]$, is given by

$$\hat{y} = F(\hat{k},1) = f(\hat{k})\,. \tag{3.17}$$

The equation for growth rate of $\hat{k}$ is derived analog to the previous model and under the condition that $A(t)$ grows at the rate x has the following form:

$$g_{\hat{k}} = s \cdot f(\hat{k}) / \hat{k} - (x+n+\delta)\,. \tag{3.18}$$

The only difference to the equation (3.7) is the parameter x at the last term on the right-hand side. The term $x+n+\delta$ represents now the effective depreciation rate for $\hat{k} = K / \hat{L}$. That means that under the assumption that the saving rate equals zero, $\hat{k}$ would decline partly because of depreciation of K at the rate δ and partly due to the growth of L at the rate $x+n$.

Then the steady-state value $\hat{k}^*$ satisfies the condition (because g_k is zero in the steady-state)

$$s \cdot f(\hat{k}^*) = (x+n+\delta) \cdot \hat{k}^*. \tag{3.19}$$

The transitional dynamics of $\hat{k}$ are relatively similar to those of k in the previous model. The Figure 11 represents the growth rate of capital per effective worker $\hat{k}$ by the vertical distance between the $s \cdot f(\hat{k})/\hat{k}$ curve and the effective depreciation line, $x+n+\delta$.

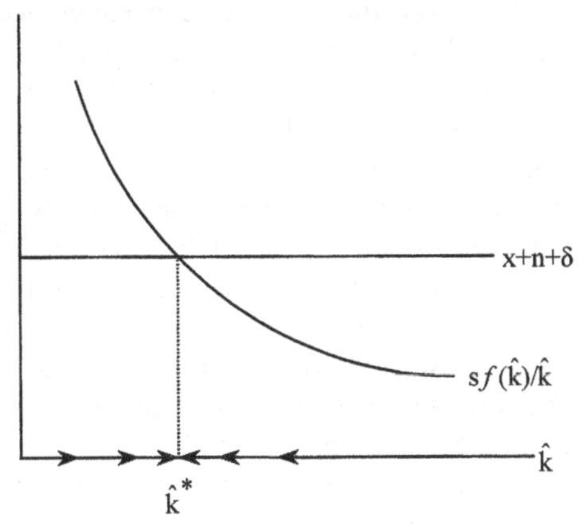

Source: Barro/Sala-i-Martin (1995), p. 36

Figure 11: The Solow Model with Technological Progress

In the steady state, the variables $\hat{k}$, $\hat{y}$, $\hat{c}$ - are constant. Therefore, the per capita variables - k, y, c grow in the steady-state at the exogenous rate of technological progress, x. The growth rate of level variables - K, Y, C equals $n+x$, that is, the sum of population growth and technological change. It is important to emphasize that although the model with technological change explains the sustained growth of per capita variables it does not depart from transitional dynamics. That means that as before the shifts in the level of the saving rate or the level of the production function have level effects but not growth effects. For example the increase in the level of the saving rate would course the increase in the levels of $\hat{k}^*$, $\hat{y}^*$, $\hat{c}^*$ but not the increase of their steady-state growth rates. As before, such kinds of disturbances influence growth rates during transition path from one steady state level to the other. The conclusion is that policy changes in the neoclassical model increase growth rates but only along the transition path. That is, policy changes have no long run growth effects. Through level effects a permanent policy change can permanently raise (or lower) the level of per capita output. Thus the explanation of differences between countries in per capita incomes from the point of view of neoclassical model is based on the principle of transitional dynamics.

The countries achieve a higher per capita income when they invest more and have lower population growth rates both of which allow to accumulate more capital per worker and attain the increase in labor productivity. The neoclassical model provides also an answer to the question why do economies exhibit sustained growth explaining this fact through the exogenous technological progress. Technological progress allows to overcome the diminishing returns to capital and in the long run countries exhibit per capita growth at the rate of technological progress. But the neoclassical growth theory does not give an answer to the evidence of the tremendous variation in country growth rates during the long period of time. In other words it fails to answer: Why do countries grow permanently at different growth rates in the long run if they have the same underlying growth rate for technology? The neoclassical model does not also provides the explanation to the sources of technological progress itself, what is the main question to be considered by the „new" growth theory. Endogenizing technological progress new growth theory explains the variation of growth rates between countries along the long run path.

3.11.2 Appendix B: Immiserizing Growth

Immiserizing growth, which was first analyzed by Jagdish Bhagwati, takes place in the case of a large country, in which willingness to trade has an impact on the equilibrium international price. In the case of a large country, the willingness to export more can lead to a decline in the country's terms of trade so that the country lowers the world price of its exports.

Consequently, a country would have a worthier price for its exports relative to the price that it has to pay for its imports. This situation is called immiserizing growth. Therefore, immiserizing growth can be defined as growth which as a result of increased willingness to trade can cause a decline in the country's terms of trade and has a negative impact on the country's well-being or welfare (LINDERT/ PUGEL, 1996). Figure 12 shows the case of immiserizing growth. In this figure the expansion of wheat production leads to a shift of the country's production-possibility curve (ppc) from S_1 to S_7. This shift of ppc increases the supply of wheat (expands willingness to trade with wheat) at world markets. The increased supply of wheat drives down the relative price of wheat on the world market. In the figure it is a change from 3bu/yd before the trade to only 1 bu/yd after the trade. The terms of trade become so bad that the ability to produce extra wheat does not compensate for losses from the increased relative price of imports of the other good (in this case cloth). Therefore, consumption becomes lower at C_7 than at the consumption point (C_1) which was possible before the trade. Such a situation reflects the consequences of immiserizing growth.

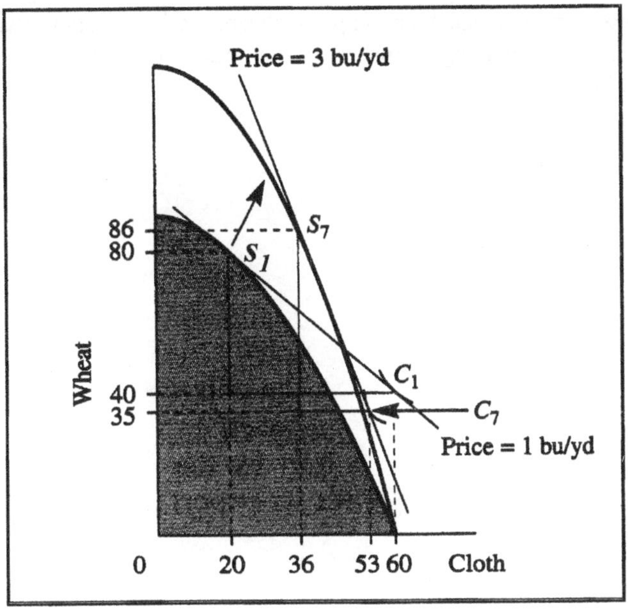

Source: Lindert/Pugel, 1996

Figure 12: Immiserizing Growth in a Large Country

According to LINDERT/PUGEL (1996), immiserizing growth should correspond to the following three conditions: first, the country's growth should have a strong impact on the willingness to expand exports, the supply of which must be large enough to considerably influence the level of world prices; second, the foreign demand for the country's exports should be price inelastic so that a large supply of the country's exports should cause a considerable drop in the international price of the export good; third, the country should be heavily engaged in trade so that the ability to produce more can not compensate for the welfare loss which emerges from the deterioration of terms of trade.

Although these three components taken together appear very seldom in the practice, the possible welfare losses from the decline in terms of trade can promote policy makers to look for decisions which help to avoid this situation. Thus, a diversified export structure lowers the risk of experiencing immiserizing growth. On the other hand, such countries as Russia, which relies much on exports of one (or a few) primary products (e.g. oil in Russia), are much more exposed to such a risk. Additionally, a large country encouraging import-replacing industries instead of export-expanding may improve terms of trade and make imports cheaper for the domestic economy. Keeping in mind the case of immiserizing growth, which makes imports more expensive and exports cheaper, a large country has a reason to promote import-replacing industries which turn world prices in its favor (LINDERT/PUGEL, 1996).

4 Openness of Foreign Trade and Economic Developments in CIS and More Advanced CEECs

The question whether or not openness of the economy has a positive impact on economic growth is not a new one. It can be dated back to the times of Adam Smith. Although the answer seems to be clear in the light of broad empirical and theoretical literature which confirms a strong positive relationship between openness and growth, many countries in the 20th century adopted protectionist policies. Protectionist policies were induced by World War II. Only since the 1980s have the views which support openness begun to dominate among economists. These views were supported by developments in the world economy. The experience of Latin American countries on the one hand showed the inconsistency of import substitution policies and their poor impact on growth. On the other hand, the growth success of Asian countries is mostly explained by strongly outward oriented policies. The collapse of the Soviet Union and the economic integration of Commonwealth of Independent States (CIS) and Central and Eastern European countries (CEECs) into the World economy provided for much discussion on appropriate policy reforms and structural adjustment in these countries. Liberalization of the external sector appeared to be one of the most important requirements of international organizations necessary for these countries to fulfill in order to become „normal" countries of the world economy.

This chapter consists of tree sections. The first section considers the relationship between openness and growth from both theoretical and empirical sides. The importance of economies of scale which lead to intra-industry trade is also discussed in the light of the structural adjustment of CIS and CEECs and increasing trade with the West. The second section highlights the progress of three CIS economies, Russia, the Ukraine, and Belarus, and more advanced CEECs (Hungary and Poland) in foreign trade liberalization. The change in the geographical distribution of their exports during the transformation process is also considered, as well as the adjustment of their specialization patterns in trade with the EU. The third section represents an empirical investigation of foreign trade potential for selected CIS and CEECs. It starts with theoretical considerations of the gravity model for foreign trade. It covers recent studies in this sphere and develops a new specification of the gravity model for considered countries. At the end of the section the gravity model results are discussed. Finally some conclusions are made on the progress of the investigated CIS and CEECs in the opening up of their foreign trade towards the West.

4.1 Openness of Foreign Trade - An Impulse of Growth and Structural Adjustment

This section considers the impact of openness on economic growth. Both static and dynamic gains from openness are discussed. The theoretical considerations on the positive relationship between openness and economic growth are proved by the empirical literature. Finally, this section refers to the importance of scale economies, product differentiation, and intra-industry specialization in modern trade. Economies of scale cause intra-industry trade between advanced market economies. These issues should be taken into account by transition economies adjusting their specialization pattern in trade with the West.

4.1.1 Theoretical Approach to Openness and Economic Growth

In the theoretical literature one should distinguish between static and dynamic gains from trade. Static gains are more associated with traditional trade theory and are linked to the gains from international specialization according to comparative advantages. Dynamic gains are predominately associated with new trade theory. Such gains as economies of scale, increasing returns to innovation and international investment, and knowledge spillovers through trade are the examples of dynamic gains (THIRLWALL, 1999). If one speaks about the impact of static and dynamic gains on growth one could say static gains only have level effects while dynamic gains provide for growth effects. Therefore, one associates traditional trade theory more with neoclassical growth theory, and new trade theory more with new growth theory. The relationship between economic growth and openness is interdependent. It means that not only does openness affect economic growth, but growth also has an impact on foreign trade. Such equations can be estimated using the method of two-stage least squares.

Starting with static gains from trade we will first refer to the effects of openness in the framework of neoclassical growth theory. According to neoclassical growth theory, income per capita grows in the long run at the growth rate of exogenous technological progress. Since technological change is exogenous, trade with other countries does not have an effect on an economy's long run rate of growth. However, openness could have level effects and exaggerate the movement from one steady state to the other higher steady state level. Since investment in capital is the only driving force of economic growth in the neoclassical model, international flows of capital could raise convergence to the steady state level in the case of an open economy (AGHION/HOWITT, 1998).

But static gains from trade, which appear according to increased international capital mobility, are found to be quantitatively rather small. Thus, BARRO/MANKIW/SALA-I-MARTIN (1995) represent a neoclassical growth model for an open economy which leads to a relatively low rate of convergence in the presence of capital mobility. Their argument is that if some types of capital, such as human capital, can only be financed domestically, then open economies converge only slightly faster than closed ones. The study of PAN (1999) also supports this view. He finds that there is a sacrifice of 1.69 percent per year in economic growth rates if a country changes from an open economy to a closed economy. Thus, openness of the economy will lead to faster economic growth. The investigation of PAN (1999) supports the argument of trade and financial liberalization.

GRUNDLACH (1997) finds higher rates of convergence for open economies in comparison to closed ones. He points to the importance of physical capital's share in factor income as a parameter which distinguishes the difference in convergence rates for open and closed economies. He finds that if physical capital's share equals 60 percent, as it is in many developing countries, then convergence rates for open and closed economies differ by a factor of 2.5. His empirical results support this view. He argues that the rate of convergence for open developing countries is equal to 5 percent, while for closed economies it is 1.5 percent.

The next effect of trade on economic growth operates through factor price equalization, or in other words, „equalizing exchange". Factor price equalization follows from the Heckscher-Ohlin trade theory, which was introduced by HECKSCHER (1919) and OHLIN (1933) and later formalized by SAMUELSON (1948, 1949). The Heckscher-Ohlin theorem states: „a country will export goods that are intensive in production in its abundant factors and import goods intensive in its relatively scarce factors" (HECKSCHER/OHLIN, 1991, p. 25). Thus, according to this theory a country specializes according to its comparative advantages which are determined through its relative factor endowments of production. Differences in factor endowments or comparative advantages initiate trade between countries. „The preconditions for initiating international trade may thus be summarized as different relative scarcity, i.e., different relative prices of the factors of production in the exchange countries, as well as different proportions between the factors of production in different commodities" (HECKSCHER/OHLIN, 1991, p. 9). Factor price equalization represents an outcome of the Heckscher-Ohlin theory because: *„If the techniques of production are the same in all countries... trade must continue to expand until an equalization of the relative scarcity of the factors of production among countries has occurred*" (HECKSCHER/OHLIN, 1991, p. 9). Factor price equalization is supposed to speed up convergence. Since equalization of the factor prices is not the same as the equalization of total income, RUFFIN (1988) showed that equalization of the former usually leads to the equalization of the latter.

WARZIARG (1998) points to a more efficient price system in open economies that allows to avoid adverse effects of price distortions on accumulation and growth. Open economies are less likely to have tradable goods prices that differ substantially from those prevailing on world markets because free trade should lead to an equalization of the prices of traded goods across countries (WARZIARG, 1998). A lower degree of price distortions in open economies is according to the so called allocation effect of free trade, based on the tendency of open economies to specialize according to their comparative advantages.

VENTURA (1997) shows in his paper how international trade affects the low of diminishing returns to capital. VENTURA (1997) points out that in the case of factor price equalization, international trade between countries has an effect on the law of diminishing returns to capital, thus diminishing returns to capital apply only to world averages. In a small outward oriented economy which exports goods at world prices, the marginal product of capital is determined by the world's stock of capital. By producing goods and accumulating capital this economy can move production into the more capital intensive export sector, which would allow it to escape from the diminishing returns to capital which would otherwise set in the case of autarky.

The next channel through which openness affects growth is competition. Openness strengthens competition among countries stimulating them to use the available resources in the best way. As an affect of openness countries engage in specialization and exchange, exploiting their comparative advantages. It devotes natural, human, industrial, and financial resources in these countries to their highest and best users and provides higher levels of output. The better reallocation of resources brings gains to both production and consumption. The increased degree of market competition resulting from a wider scale of market interactions yields further gains in efficiency. Efficiency in turn contributes to economic growth and raises incomes. This is confirmed by the fact that in the last decade countries with more opened economies have achieved the annual average growth of others (OECD, 1998). Openness additionally provides for consumer gains which consist of a larger poll of consumer goods so that consumers have a larger and qualitatively better choice at their disposal (THIRLWALL, 1999).

Many economists argue that only in the framework of new growth theory it was for the first time possible to comprehensively analyze the impact of openness on economic growth. Since new growth theory provides for long run growth effects and considers among others the impact of policy instruments on growth, new growth theory made it for the first time possible to analyze the impact of openness on long run growth. More recent studies of GROSSMAN/HELPMAN (1991a, 1994), RIVERA-BATIZ/ROMER (1991), BEN-DAVID/LOEWY (1996, 1998), ROMER (1990), KRUGMAN (1990), AGHION/HOWITT (1998), YOUNG (1991) etc. emphasize various aspects of the growth process and show how international trade may affect them. These models capture some important aspects of openness like the role of openness for innovation, the effect of openness on economic growth through knowledge spillovers and externalities, the role of openness for imitation possibilities of countries, etc. These models are associated with dynamic gains from trade. In these models innovation and knowledge spillovers stand in the center. Moreover, monopolistic behavior determines imperfect competition, economies of scale, and differentiated production.

THIRLWALL (1999) emphasizes that one of the major dynamic benefits from trade is connected with the size of the market. The size of the market allows the countries to realize their economies of scale. In the case of increasing returns to scale, increased market share will lead to gains which are much higher than static gains from more efficient resource allocation. THIRLWALL points out that with increasing size of the market each country can benefit from trade irrespective of the terms of trade.

One of the most important benefits from trade is connected with the access to new technologies (GROSSMAN/HELPMAN, 1994). Countries integrated into the world have an access to a larger technical knowledge base than those which live in isolation.

In the models of new growth theory economic growth often occurs according to knowledge spillovers and externalities. Introduction of international trade into these models would increase the scope of knowledge spillovers and externalities, since it increases market size and raises the equilibrium number of firms, which would induce technological change (AGHION/HOWITT, 1998). GROSSMAN/ HELPMAN (1991a)[16] point to the special importance of participation in world markets, since countries can learn a lot about innovative products and novel methods of production. Commercial transactions, the number of which increases with the openness of the economy, represent an essential source of international information and ideas.

The impact of idea flows on long run growth is considered by RIVERA-BATIZ/ROMER (1991). In their model they distinguish between two cases: first in which trade in goods is not accompanied by the flow of ideas and second, in which trade in goods is induced by transmission of ideas. Their finding supports the view that knowledge spillovers or flows of ideas represent those elements which induce long run growth through trade in goods, but trade in goods does not perform this role per se. They find that only in the case where flows of ideas through trade in goods are possible there is a long run effect on growth. Otherwise trade in goods without flows of ideas does not have any effect on the long run rate of growth.

In the model of BEN-DAVID/LOEWY (1996), countries with similar technological parameters converge to the same growth rates in the long run. The steady state growth rates depend on one hand on the rate of knowledge accumulation by the country itself, and on the other hand on access to the stock of world knowledge which occurs through foreign trade. Thus the extent of foreign trade determines the amount of knowledge spillovers and has an impact on the rate of output growth. BEN-DAVID/LOEWY (1996, 1998) find that liberalization of foreign trade has two effects on the output of countries. First, it has a level effect,

---

[16] For further reading see GROSSMAN/HELPMAN (1991c) and HELPMAN/KRUGMAN (1993).

which allows a country to catch up and even to leapfrog over initially wealthier countries. And additionally, there is a growth effect which takes place in the case of the liberalization of those countries which possess a considerable stock of knowledge.

ROMER (1990) has developed a model where the long run growth rate depends on the stock of human capital, which through knowledge spillovers and externalities supports the productivity of the whole economy. This model has an interesting implication since international trade increases the stock of human capital by the world stock of human capital, and thus can speed up growth. This model explains why poor underdeveloped countries which have a low level of human capital and closed economy do not exhibit growth. On the other hand, countries with a large population can also benefit from international trade because the impact of foreign human capital on the economy is important, but not the increase in labor force or population size or density. One more implication follows from this model, namely for higher knowledge spillovers and externalities which spur growth countries should choose those trading partners which possess a larger stock of human capital.

International trade also raises returns on innovation. Since the incentive to innovate is closely connected with the expectation of receiving monopoly rents, and since there are increasing returns to scale in a Schumpeterian economy, international trade represents a powerful possibility for innovators to increase gains from innovation (AGHION/HOWITT, 1998). Therefore, „*...a Schumpeterian world is one in which international integration increases the incentives for and the benefits from innovation*" (KRUGMAN, 1990, p. 166). Thus participation in world markets raises returns to innovation making the temporary monopoly more attractive for an innovator. Higher monopoly rents will encourage R&D activities, thereby enhancing economic growth. On the other hand, each country can benefit from innovation when temporary monopoly ends and knowledge becomes available to all countries participating in free trade. One more aspect should be pointed out. Since there are fixed costs of innovation, an integrated world can afford more innovations and at the same time capture higher rates of return on innovations. This will increase the amount of technologically improved goods, economic growth, and consumption per capita (KRUGMAN, 1990).

International trade enhances capital accumulation as well. Larger market size and increasing returns to scale make accumulation of capital easier. (THIRLWALL, 1999). For poor developing countries openness often represents the only possibility to accomplish large-scale investment in advanced capital equipment. Empirical evidence on the enhancing role of market size for capital accumulation and its growth effects was provided by ADES/GLAESER (1994). WARZIARG (1998), in his empirical paper, also finds that strong positive effect of openness on economic growth functions, first of all through increased accumulation of physical capital which accounts for more than a half of the total effect. BALDWIN (1992) also finds a large positive effect of openness on the steady-state levels of such factors as human and physical capital. Since steady-state levels of these factors are endogenous, trade policy can affect these levels. Therefore, openness has a dynamic effect on output when the economy moves from one steady state to its new steady state level, which works through accumulation of the factors of production.

International trade also promotes competition. In a Schumpeterian economy, the competition effect on growth is not clear and is more complicated than in a world with perfect competition. On the one hand, according to BEN-DAVID/LOEWY (1998), an open economy exhibits greater competitive pressures and is induced to incorporate more foreign knowledge into its production process, which promotes knowledge diffusion and exaggerates growth. Moreover, as GROSSMAN/HELPMAN (1991a) point out, openness enforces countries to pursue new ideas and introduce new technologies. Generating ideas which are new in the local market does not provide for a competitive position in the world market. Thus countries are forced to generate ideas and technologies which are innovative on a global scale (GROSSMAN/HELPMAN, 1994).

On the other hand, competition plays a role as a force which reduces profits of innovators gained according to increased market size, since market share of any given firm shrinks with the increase of the number of rivals (RODRIK, 1995). Additionally, competition could discourage innovation and hence decrease economic growth, since innovation takes place in a monopolistic environment (AGHION/HOWITT, 1998).

The statement that increased competition will always lead to an increase in the growth rate is actually incorrect. Thus GROSSMAN/HELPMAN (1991a) consider some cases where integration into the world economy means a slow down of the long run growth rate for particular countries rather than an increase. Analyzing the GROSSMAN/HELPMAN (1991a) model, RODRIK (1995) points out that integration may imply a reallocation effect. Since static comparative advantages determine the starting position of a country before opening up to trade, integration may induce the reallocation of resources towards a new competitive position which the country would admit in the circumstances of world competition. If the resources were reallocated towards the „growth sectors" during this adjustment process, the effect of openness on long rung growth would be positive. Otherwise openness can reduce long run economic growth. Thus a country which accumulated a sufficient stock of knowledge would have a comparative advantage in R&D activities. Since R&D activities dominate world research and world production of high-technology goods, an initially lagging country would be forced to specialize in traditional manufacturing. Reallocation of resources towards the production of traditional goods would reduce a country's long run growth rate (GROSSMAN/HELPMAN, 1991a).

Therefore, countries which have a large natural resources sector in which unskilled labor dominates (over skilled workers) may be induced by trade to specialize in activities which reinforce the role of the natural resource sector. This occurs to some extent at the expense of human-capital intensive activities like R&D. Thus trade forces these countries to carry out activities which can slow down their long run growth rate and pulls resources away from R&D intensive activities which speed up long run growth. Additionally, a sacrifice in the growth rate would be exhibited by countries where technological spillovers are national in scope so that the incentive for international cooperation is low. Researchers from these countries would have difficulties in competing with researchers from other countries which have access to a larger knowledge base. Therefore, for such countries catching up before openness could contribute more to long run growth than the risk of opening itself to world competition.

Additionally, a negative „competition effect" also plays a role in the case of North-South trade, when innovators from the North face competition of cheaper products imitated by the South, whereby imitated products represent a serious threat for producers in the North (AGHION/HOWITT, 1998; KRUGMAN, 1990).

A positive impact of integration consists in the fact that an integrated market helps to avoid the duplication of innovation. Innovative firms stand in competition with each other and have to develop novel ideas and technologies. For this reason trade reduces duplication of the research effort. Otherwise, in the absence of trade, each of the economies would devote resources to the development of identical innovations so that the resources taken together would considerably exceed the amount of developed goods. Consequently integration leads to a more productive use of aggregate resources devoted to innovation (KRUGMAN, 1990; GROSSMAN/HELPMAN, 1991a; RODRIK, 1995).

International trade can have an impact on „static and dynamic comparative advantages". International trade can have additional effect on economic growth through the reallocation of resources across sectors induced by comparative advantages. Technological differences between countries also determine to a large extent their comparative advantages. In the most models of traditional trade theory technological change was taken exogenously and hence one speaks about „static comparative advantages". In the Schumpeterian models of economic growth technological progress is endogenous and hence the interaction of endogenous technological change with comparative advantages provides for „dynamic comparative advantages", whereby the pattern of comparative advantages becomes endogenous itself (AGHION/HOWITT, 1998).

International trade inhibits learning-by-doing in less developed countries (LDCs) as well. DAVIS (1991) finds that greater market size speeds up the rate of learning. YOUNG (1991)[17] suggests that LDCs should specialize in goods with

---

[17] YOUNG (1991) considers an endogenous model with learning by doing and spillovers across goods. His finding is that trade between an LDC (a less technologically advanced country) and a DC would lead rather to divergence than convergence. Thus in his model

greater potential for further learning-by-doing. CHUANG (1998) emphasizes that in trade-induced learning both exports and imports contribute considerably to the learning process. Although openness of the economy is an important precondition for learning, rapid learning depends on with whom a country trades and on the technological level from which a country can learn. Therefore, a country should trade more with technologically advanced countries which ensures learning and growth upon a country's own technological abilities.

International trade promotes the diffusion of knowledge. Many economists, e.g. GROSSMAN/HELPMAN (1991a,b), KRUGMAN (1990), ROMER (1992, 1993a), EDWARDS (1992), BARRO/SALA-I-MARTIN (1995a,b), SEGER-STROM/DINOPOULOS (1990), BREZIS/KRUGMAN/TSIDDON (1993), LAL (1992), KUMAR/SIDDHARTHAN (1997), and FEENSTRA (1996) have agreed that more open economies are better able to absorb technologies generated in leading nations. Most of these models consider North-South trade, trade between one developed country and one developing country. While innovation takes place in the advanced nation, poorer countries focus on the imitation of technologies developed by leading nations. In these models trade is directly linked to the growth rate of the imitating country. Imitation here has the role of reducing costs and improving product variety and quality. Since the growth rate depends on the costs of imitation and on the stock of knowledge accumulated by the imitating country, more opened economies are able to capture more new ideas and technologies than closed ones, and hence are more successful in imitation and will catch up faster.

The effects of openness on growth can be summarized as follows:

Static gains

- International capital flows promote economic growth (neoclassical growth framework) (AGHION/HOWITT, 1998; BARRO/MANKIW/SALA-I-MARTIN, 1995; PAN, 1999; GRUNDLACH, 1997).
- Factor price equalization speeds up convergence (HECKSCHER, 1919; OHLIN, 1993; SAMUELSON, 1948, 1949; RUFFIN, 1987; HECK-SCHER/OHLIN, 1991).
- A more efficient price system in open economies stimulates capital accumulation (WARZIARG, 1998).
- International trade helps countries to escape from diminishing returns to capital since the marginal product of capital is determined by the world's stock of capital (VENTURA, 1997).

---

growth rates of LDCs under free trade are smaller than under autarky. Therefore in his model learning that occurs within and between industries does not spillover across borders.

- Competition in perfect markets increases the effectiveness of economies (OECD, 1998).
- Openness brings about consumer gains - a larger poll of consumer goods (THIRLWALL, 1999).

Dynamic gains

- The size of the market allows countries to better exploit their economies of scale (THIRLWALL, 1999).
- International trade provides access to new technologies (GROSSMAN/HELPMAN, 1994).
- International trade increases the scope of knowledge spillovers and externalities and thus speeds up technological diffusion, innovation, and growth (AGHION/HOWITT, 1998; GROSSMAN/HELPMAN, 1991a; RIVERA-BATIZ/ROMER, 1991; BEN-DAVID/LOEWY, 1996, 1998; ROMER, 1990).
- International trade raises both the scope of possible innovations and returns to innovation (KRUGMAN, 1990).
- International trade according to larger market size and increasing returns to scale enhances capital accumulation (THIRLWALL, 1999; ADES/GLAESER, 1994; WARZIARG, 1998; BALDWIN, 1992).
- Competition in a Schumpeterian economy does not obligatorily raise economic growth. On the one hand it induces incentives for knowledge diffusion, innovation, and growth (BEN-DAVID/LOEWY, 1998; GROSSMAN/HEPMAN, 1991a, 1994). On the other hand, competition reduces profits from innovation (RODRIK, 1995) and prohibits innovation since it destroys monopolistic environments (AGHION/HOWITT, 1998). In the case of developing economies competition can lead to divergence rather than convergence (GROSSMAN/HELPMAN 1991a, RODRIK, 1995). Negative effects also appear in the case of North-South trade (KRUGMAN, 1990).
- Integration helps to avoid the duplication of innovation (KRUGMAN, 1990; GROSSMAN/HELPMAN, 1991a; RODRIK, 1995).
- International trade has an effect on growth through the impact on „static and dynamic comparative advantages" (AGHION/HOWITT, 1998).
- International trade induces learning by doing (DAVIS, 1991; YOUNG, 1991; CHUANG, 1998).
- International trade promotes the diffusion of knowledge (GROSSMAN/HELPMAN, 1991a,b; KRUGMAN, 1990; ROMER, 1992, 1993a; EDWARDS, 1992; BARRO/SALA-I-MARTIN, 1995a,b;

SEGERSTROM/DINOPOULOS, 1990; BREZIS/KRUGMAN/TSIDDON, 1993, LAL, 1992, KUMAR/SIDDHARTHAN, 1997; FEENSTRA, 1996).

4.1.2 Empirical Evidence on Openness and Economic Growth

Many economists find empirical evidence on the positive relationship between openness of the economy and economic growth. To capture this link is important for researchers and policymakers. Only recent theoretical models are able to consider the link between openness and growth. Empirical studies are strongly influenced by serious data problems.

EDWARDS (1992) finds evidence on the impact of trade policies on economic growth. Based on the investigated countries he concludes that open economies with liberal trade policies pursue less distortive policies and tend as a rule to grow faster than those with distortive and more restrictive trade policies. According to EDWARDS (1997), trade has a strong impact on domestic total factor productivity (TFP). He analyzes the relationship between openness and TFP using a data set for 93 countries. TFP growth appears to be faster in more open economies, whereby the results are robust to the openness indicator used, estimation technique, trade period, and functional form. Additionally he finds a positive relationship between the initial level of human capital and TFP growth, which means that countries with more developed educational systems have a greater ability to innovate and absorb new ideas.

FEDER (1982) finds that the export sector is more productive than the non-export sector and hence contributes more to economic growth. His econometric analysis shows that marginal factor productivity is much higher in the export than in the non-export sector. Hence the success of outward oriented economies in comparison to inward oriented is grounded on the more effective or in other words optimal allocation of resources since the export sector is more productive. The differences in productivity appear on the one hand to be according to factors which in common literature make the export sector more productive, such as higher skilled management techniques in production, better trained qualified labor according to international standards, steadier flow of imported inputs, etc.

On the other hand, FEDER finds empirically that export also contributes to growth through the externalities which affect the non-export sector, making it more productive. The effect of this parameter is rather considerable since an increase in exports of 10% causes a growth of approximately 1.3% in the non-export sector. This effect diminishes when the resources from the non-export sector are already reallocated to the export sector.

The studies of some other economists also confirm the existence of the positive link between openness and economic growth. Thus FRANKEL/ROMER (1996), using the gravity model approach, find a large, significant, and robust positive effect of trade on income. In their model trade affects income mostly through induced factor accumulation.

DOLLAR (1992) runs a regression for 95 developing countries for the period 1976-85. The results show that growth rates of countries are highly correlated with the extent of outwards orientation. A sample of the most open economies also experienced the fastest growth. Growth diminished considerably and even turned negative with the reduction of openness. Following the Asian experience, DOLLAR suggests that trade liberalization, devaluation of the real exchange rate, and maintenance of a stable exchange rate would bring other developing countries to a higher growth pace. Thus he estimates for Latin American and African countries the effect of the shift to an Asian level of outward orientation and real exchange rate stability and finds an increase in the per capita growth rate for Latin American countries of 1.5 percent and for African countries for 2.1 percent.

Considering the Asian growth experience FRANKEL/ROMER/CYRUS (1996) investigate how much openness explains the growth of these countries. Using the gravity equation approach they find that openness was a strong explanatory variable for most Asian countries, especially for Hong Kong and Singapore.

BALASSA (1978), investigating a group of eleven developing countries which have already established an industrial base, shows that export-oriented policies provide for higher growth rates than import substitution policies.

There are also estimates which suggest that countries which trade with each other extensively would converge to the same income levels. Thus BEN-DAVID (1996) finds that trade promotes convergence among countries grouped according to their trading partners. Therefore, trade plays a role as an instrument which reduces the income gap between countries. SACHS/WARNER (1995a) also emphasize that developing countries can reach higher than average growth rates by persuading efficient economic policies such as liberalization of foreign trade and protection of private property rights.

LEVINE/RENELT (1992) made a cross-country empirical investigation of growth. They find that trade influences growth through investment. Robust correlation between average growth rates and the average share of investment in GDP on the one hand and a positive and robust correlation between the share of investment in GDP and the average share of trade in GDP on the other hand prove this issue. The accent on capital accumulation is also made in the study of BALDWIN/FORSLID (1996).

One of the most important empirical investigations was made by COE/HELPMAN (1995) and BAYOUMI/COE/HELPMAN (1996). COE/HELPMAN (1995) represent a model of endogenous growth where commercially performed innovation spurs technological progress and economic growth. The authors suggest that TFP growth depends on both domestic and foreign R&D, whereby trade represents a channel by which foreign R&D influences the productivity of a domestic economy. Improvements in domestic R&D lead to the more productive and efficient usage of resources on the one hand, and determine a country's technological capability to learn from foreign experience on the other. The higher domestic R&D the better are the preconditions for adopting more advanced types of technologies.

Empirical evidence on 21 OECD countries plus Israel for the period 1971-90 shows that both domestic and foreign R&D cause an important impact on TFP. This impact appears to be larger the greater the extent of openness. The impact of foreign R&D depends on the size of a country. In the case of large countries the elasticity is larger with respect to the domestic R&D capital stock. In the case of a small country the elasticity seems to be larger with respect to the foreign R&D capital stock. The investigation also shows that the ratio of return on R&D capital is very high, both in terms of domestic output and in terms of international spillovers.

The investigation of COE/HELPMAN shows the impact of spillovers from foreign R&D on domestic productivity for the first time. Thus countries can increase their productivity by not only investing in domestic R&D but also through R&D spillovers coming from trade.

BAYOUMI/COE/HELPMAN (1996) make further investigations on the role of international R&D spillovers for domestic productivity. Their empirical investigation confirms previous findings. Thus countries can boost their productivity by trading with other countries which have accumulated a considerable „stock of knowledge".

In this paper the authors also proclaim other important results. They strengthen the importance of the interplay between R&D and capital accumulation. Foreign R&D provides for an indirect effect on domestic productivity along with the direct effect on productivity, namely through the accumulation of capital. Investment in capital is caused by the increase in productivity, which rises according to foreign R&D spillovers. Increase in output according to investment in capital accounts for one fourth of its total increase (caused by rise in productivity).

They also show an effect of an increase in R&D spending on the domestic economy. They find that *„an increase in US R&D investment equivalent to 0.5 % of GDP raises US real output by about 10% in the long run, while about two-thirds of this gain is coming from increases in productivity and the remainder from investment"* (BAYOUMI/COE/HELPMAN, 1996, p. 2). R&D spending in the US economy would have a spillover effect on other economies as well. The size of these spillovers depends on the extent of trade relations between both countries. They find that R&D spending in the trade partner's country would boost the common effect of R&D spillovers on productivity. They stress that these R&D spillovers are particularly important for developing countries, since there is a large technological gap. The amount of R&D spillovers increases with the intensification of trade relations.

To sum up, empirical evidence shows that openness of the economy has a positive impact on economic growth. In an important study EDWARDS (1997) finds a positive impact of openness on the TFP of the domestic economy. Some studies find a positive influence of openness on growth through the effect on capital accumulation or investment (e.g. LEVINE/RENELT, 1992). However, the most important finding was the study of COE/HELPMAN (1995), where the authors managed for the first time to capture the positive spillover effect of foreign R&D on domestic productivity. Further work of BAYOUMI/COE/HELPMAN (1996) also points to the existence of the link between foreign R&D and increased capital accumulation in the domestic economy, which takes place as a result of increased productivity spurred by foreign R&D.

4.1.3 Economies of Scale and Intra-Industry Trade in Structural Adjustment

The first comprehensive study on intra-industry trade was provided by GRUBEL and LLOYD (1975). According to the OECD (1999, p. 64): *„Simultaneous exports and imports within the same industry are generally labeled intra-industry trade".* Intra-industry trade usually occurs among rich countries with similar levels of development. Intra-industry trade represents the majority of trade among EU member countries. The trade of less developed OECD countries with the EU such as New Zealand, Australia, Greece, Mexico, Korea, and Turkey has more of an inter-industry character which is based on complementarity. Moreover, within the EU trade with products which differ by quality prevails over trade in products which differ by variety. Therefore, intra-industry trade among nations provides consumers not only with a larger variety of products but also with better quality. Additionally, the share of high-technology industries is steadily increasing in the international trade of manufactured goods. The annual growth rate of high-technology industries is much higher than the manufacturing average (OECD, 1999). Therefore, trade among EU countries is mostly intra-industry in nature, whereby product quality plays a decisive role and there is an increasing tendency to trade with high-technology products.

KRUGMAN (1990) tries to find an explanation to the „paradox" of intra-industry trade, which consists of the majority of world trade between countries with similar factor endowments. He finds that intra-industry trade exists according to economies of scale in production. According to the traditional Heckscher-Ohlin trade theory, countries would specialize according to their comparative advantages in products of different industries, which would give rise to inter-industry trade. Scale economies instead only allow countries to specialize on a group of products within the same industry so that there will be intra-industry specialization and trade. Therefore, economies of scale explain trade among countries with similar factor endowments, which is largely intra-industry in character. Intra-industry trade occurs because different countries would trade in different differentiated products. Fixed costs of production prevent countries from producing the whole range of products within a country and economies of scale thus give rise to an intra-industry trade.

KRUGMAN (1990) suggests that the nature of trade between countries depends to a large extent on their similarity in factor endowments. Thus countries similar in factor endowments will engage in intra-industry trade while countries with different factor endowments will engage in Heckscher-Ohlin trade. On the other hand, creating a model with economies of scale, he finds that trade takes place mostly among economies with similar factor endowments and represents a two-way trade in similar products (intra-industry trade).

Specialization, economies of scale, and product differentiation became key words in the modern trade theory. Modern trade theory makes a significant accent on economies of scale and product differentiation in explaining the structure of foreign trade and volumes of trade. HELPMAN (1998) stresses that specialization leads to an increase in international trade. On the other hand, scale economies and product differentiation induce the tendency to specialize. Thus, scale economies and product differentiation provide for larger volumes of trade. Moreover, ROMER (1987) also finds that specialization leads to increasing returns and hence promotes growth. Therefore, scale economies and product differentiation also induce economic growth.

The interplay between product differentiation, economies of scale, and specialization occurs in the following way. Product differentiation involves economies of scale. Economies of scale in turn induce specialization in products which are profitable on the market. Since a brand which should be developed is established and differs from that of rivals, its profitability is first of all determined by the costs of production. Economies of scale determine those brands which are profitable on the market. With international trade, countries specialize in different brands (HELPMAN, 1998).

To sum up, international trade theory emphasizes economies of scale and product differentiation as well as differences in factor composition as the main determinant of world trade. In combination they explain to a large extent the structure of foreign trade, volumes of trade, and patterns of trade among the regions.

Which strategy should transition countries implement in order to increase their volumes of trade and to specialize in manufacturing, and at the same time has a significant impact on? As AGHION/HOWITT (1998) point out, the start position of developing countries provided by the liberalization of trade is to a large extent determined by their initial pattern of specialization. GROSSMAN/HELPMAN (1990) emphasize that cross-country differences in R&D versus manufacturing (comparative advantages) significantly influence the future growth possibilities of the countries and their trade structures. The initial pattern of specialization can lead to divergence or to convergence with more developed countries. Note that trade between highly developed countries is mostly intra-industry in nature. Therefore, transition economies should change their comparative advantages in such a way that they become involved in intra-industry trade. KUMAR/SIDDHARTHAN (1997) point out that countries can change their comparative advantages and therefore their trade positions, affecting their R&D and technological activities as well as the market power of enterprises. Transition economies should move their comparative advantages towards brands of products in industries which would allow them to engage in intra-industry trade with more developed economies. They should encourage specialization in sectors with economies of scale, since economies of scale promote technological progress because a country has to develop differentiated products with techniques of production different from those of rivals and induce intra-industry trade. Specialization in sectors where dynamic gains from international spillovers are significant is also crucial. Thus, according to AGHION/HOWITT (1998), international trade induces the reallocation of resources through technological spillovers and thus changes dynamic comparative advantages towards more technologically intensive industries.

HAKURA/JAUMOTTE (1999)[18] show that engagement in intra-industry trade would also allow transition countries to speed up technology transfer. In their paper they investigate the role of trade as a main channel of technology transfer. They examine in particular the effects of inter- and intra-industry trade on technology transfer. The authors argue that intra-industry trade promotes technology transfer more than inter-industry trade. The main argument is that technology transfer occurs more easily when country's imports are from the same sector as its production and export sector. In this case countries are more able to absorb new technologies.

In their empirical investigation which covers intra- and inter-industry trade in 87 countries over the period 1970-93 they find first of all the confirmation that trade of developing countries with advanced countries enhances technological progress in the first. Secondly, a very important finding is that intra-industry trade seems to have a larger impact on TFP growth in developing countries. Thus, intra-industry trade provides for more technology transfer than inter-industry trade. Therefore, taking part in intra-industry trade would allow transition economies to speed up technological progress and hence convergence in income levels as well as it would allow convergence in trade structures with more advanced countries and would lead to more volumes of trade.

4.2 Progress in the Liberalization of Foreign Trade in Selected CIS and CEECs

This section deals with the dynamics of foreign trade in the investigated CIS and CEECs. The extent of openness of their foreign trade is also discussed. This section follows the changes taken place in the geographical distribution of exports of the investigated economies towards OECD countries during transformation process as well. Finally, the analysis of the adjustment in the specialization pattern in trade with the EU is made.

---

[18] For further reading on intra-industry trade see WOLF (1997) and KRUGMAN (1980).

4.2.1 Foreign Trade Dynamics in Selected CIS and CEECs

Table 10 shows the dynamics in foreign trade for the investigated CIS and CEECs. In Hungary both exports and imports have increased in the period from 1992 to 2000 (projection) by ca. 200%. During this period Hungary was running a trade deficit, which is supposed to diminish in 2000. The share of total trade with non-transition countries remained at approximately the same level: 82.3% in 1991 and 87.9% in 1999 (estimate). The trade to GDP ratio, which deals as a measure of openness to foreign trade, has increased considerably: from 45.9% in 1991 to 93.8% in 1999 (estimate). Since human capital is supposed to induce foreign trade liberalization, the indicators on human capital should also be taken into account. Expenditure on health and education as a percent of GDP decreased in Hungary by a few percentage points but still remained rather high: 11.4% in 1996. The basic school enrollment ratio in Hungary is also high and was equal to 99.2% in 1998.

In Poland exports increased from 1992 to 2000 (projection) by ca. 100%. Imports were growing faster than exports, which resulted in an increased trade deficit which in 2000 was equal to $15,000 mill. The share of total trade with non-transition countries decreased by some percent points: from 83.2% in 1991 to 79.3% in 1999. The trade to GDP ratio increased by ca. 10%, namely from 32.7% in 1991 to 43.6% in 1999. Expenditure on health and education decreased by some percent points and in 1998 was equal to 9.9%. The basic school enrollment ratio is also rather high in Poland and was equal to 98.1% in 1998.

Russia is the only country which was running a trade surplus during the entire period from 1992 to 2000. In 2000 this surplus was equal to $46,000 mill. The share of total trade with non-transition countries increased by some percent points: from 66.6% in 1996 to 70.5% in 1999. The trade to GDP ratio in Russia is rather high. The lowest value of 36.0%. was observed in 1997. In 1999 the share of trade in GDP reached its highest value of 62.7%. In Russia expenditure on health and education is lower than that in Hungary and Poland and was equal in 1999 to only 6.8%. The basic school enrollment ratio is also lower than that of Hungary and Poland by ca. 10%. The basic school enrollment ratio was equal to 89.1% in 1998.

In the Ukraine there was no considerable increase in exports and imports during the whole period. Exports increased from 11,300 mill. in 1992 to 13,300 mill. in 2000. Imports increased from $11,900 mill. in 1992 to 14,000 mill. in 2000. There was a trade deficit of $700 mill. The share of total trade with non-transition countries increased considerably from 38.7% in 1994 to 57.4% in 2000. The trade to GDP ratio in 1999 in the Ukraine was also rather high, equal to 82.5%. Expenditures on health and education and the basic school enrollment ratio were similar to that of Russia and were equal to 6.6% in 1999 and 89.0% in 1998.

In Belarus both exports and imports increased from 1993 to 2000 by about 200%. During the whole period Belarus was running a trade deficit, which in 2000 was equal to $750 mill. The share of total trade with non-transition countries diminished in Belarus from 28.5% in 1993 to 22.6% in 1999. The trade to GDP ratio in Belarus was always high and reached in 2000 its peak point of 158.4%. In Belarus expenditure on health and education is close to that of Hungary and Poland and in 1999 was equal to 11.4%. The basic school enrollment ratio is also high and was equal in 1998 to 96.5%.

Table 10: Foreign Trade Liberalization in Selected CIS and CEECs

	1991	1992	1993	1994	1995	1996	1997	1998	1999 Estimate	2000 Projection
Hungary										
Trade balance (mill. $)		-48	-3,246	-3,635	-2,442	-2,645	-1,963	-2,353	-2,184	-1,748
Merchandise exports (mill. $)		10,028	8,094	7,613	12,810	14,183	19,637	20,749	21,827	29,466
Merchandise imports (mill. $)		10,076	11,340	11,248	15,252	16,828	21,600	23,102	24,011	31,214
Share of total trade with non-transition countries (in percent)	82.3	80.6	78.2	79.1	77.7	77.0	81.2	84.3	87.9	
Trade to GDP ratio (in percent)	54.9	54.0	50.4	45.4	62.8	68.6	90.2	93.3	93.8	
Expenditure on health and education (in percent of GDP)	13.0	14.0	13.5	13.9	12.4	11.4	na	na	na	
Basic school enrollment ratio (in percent)	99.2	99.2	99.1	99.1	99.1	99.2	99.2	99.2	na	
Poland										
Trade balance (mill. $)		500	-2,482	-895	-1,912	-8,179	- 11,320	- 13,720	- 14,462	- 15,000
Merchandise exports (mill. $)		14,000	13,598	17,024	22,878	24,453	27,229	30,122	26,386	28,000
Merchandise imports (mill. $)		13,500	16,080	17,919	24,790	32,632	38,549	43,842	40,848	43,000
Share of total trade with non-transition countries (in percent)	83.2	84.4	87.7	86.3	82.3	79.3	75.5	77.4	79.3	
Trade to GDP ratio (in percent)	32.7	32.6	34.5	37.7	40.0	42.4	48.5	47.0	43.6	
Expenditure on health and education (in percent of GDP)	10.5	10.8	10.4	10.7	9.7	10.8	11.2	9.9	na	
Basic school enrollment ratio (in percent)	97.3	97.1	97.2	97.1	97.2	97.4	98.0	98.1	na	

Table 10: Foreign Trade Liberalization in Selected CIS and CEECs (cont.)

	1991	1992	1993	1994	1995	1996	1997	1998	1999 Estimate	2000 Projection
Russia										
Trade balance (mill. $)		10,634	15,342	17,024	20,151	19,771	14,792	16,896	35,302	46,000
Merchandise exports (mill. $)		53,605	59,646	67,542	81,096	88,599	88,252	74,684	74,663	94,000
Merchandise imports (mill. $)		42,971	44,304	50,518	60,945	68,828	73,460	57,788	39,361	48,000
Share of total trade with non-transition countries (in percent)	na	na	na	66.6	68.2	67.0	65.4	66.9	70.5	
Trade to GDP ratio (in percent)	na	na	61.7	42.6	40.9	37.6	36.0	49.2	62.7	
Expenditure on health and education (in percent of GDP)	na	6.0	7.2	7.7	6.1	6.6	7.0	6.0	6.8	
Basic school enrollment ratio (in percent)	90.0	89.3	88.3	88.6	88.8	88.5	88.2	89.1	na	
Ukraine										
Trade balance (mill. $)		-600	-2,500	-2,575	-2,702	-4,296	-4,205	-2,584	-482	-700
Merchandise exports (mill. $)		11,300	12,800	13,894	14,244	15,547	15,418	13,699	12,463	13,300
Merchandise imports (mill. $)		11,900	15,300	16,469	16,946	19,843	19,623	16,283	12,945	14,000
Share of total trade with non-transition countries (in percent)	na	na	na	38.7	40.3	45.5	57.1	53.6	57.4	
Trade to GDP ratio (in percent)	na	112.3	85.3	80.7	84.3	79.4	69.9	71.7	82.5	
Expenditure on health and education (in percent of GDP)	7.8	10.5	8.5	10.1	10.0	8.7	9.5	7.9	6.6	
Basic school enrollment ratio (in percent)	91.9	91.5	91.0	90.7	90.9	90.8	90.2	89.0	na	

Table 10: Foreign Trade Liberalization in Selected CIS and CEECs (cont.)

	1991	1992	1993	1994	1995	1996	1997	1998	1999 Estimate	2000 Projection
Belarus										
Trade balance (mill. $)		na	-528	-490	-666	-1,149	-1,335	-1,447	-599	-750
Merchandise exports (mill. $)	na	na	1,970	2,510	4,803	5,790	7,383	7,081	5,949	6,000
Merchandise imports (mill. $)	na	na	2,498	3,000	5,469	6,939	8,718	8,528	6,548	6,750
Share of total trade with non-transition countries (in percent)	na	na	na	28.5	20.5	19.0	19.3	17.3	22.6	
Trade to GDP ratio (in percent)	na	na	121.9	113.4	98.8	91.9	118.4	109.3	158.4	
Expenditure on health and education (in percent of GDP)	na	8.7	15.1	12.9	10.4	11.2	13.0	12.1	11.4	
Basic school enrollment ratio (in percent)	93.9	93.8	93.3	93.2	93.7	93.4	93.8	96.5	na	

Source: EBRD (2000), Transition Report 2000

Openness of foreign trade was induced though multilateral commitments. Table 11 shows international commitments of transition economies as of 2000. The commitments on WTO accession, IMF Article VIII on currency convertibility, and EU integration agreements help to adopt trade policies to the international standards and to introduce better transparency and predictability of the trade and payment regimes (EBRD, 2000).

Table 11: International Commitments of Transition Economies as of 2000

	GATT/WTO membership	IMF Article VIII status	EU Association	EU Partnership and Cooperation Agreement	
				Signed	Entered into force
Albania	July-00	--	--	--	--
Bulgaria	Dec-96	Sep-98	Mar-93	--	--
Croatia	July-00	May-95	--	--	--
Czech Republic	Jan-95	Oct-95	Oct-93	--	--
FYR Macedonia	--	Jun-98	--	--	--
Hungary	**Jan-95**	**Jan-96**	**Dec-91**	**--**	**--**
Poland	**Jul-95**	**Jun-95**	**Dec-91**	**--**	**--**
Romania	Jan-95	Mar-98	Feb-93	--	--
Slovak Republic	Jan-95	Oct-95	Oct-93	--	--
Slovenia	Jul-95	Sept-95	Jun-96	--	--
Estonia	Nov-99	Aug-94	Jun-95	--	--
Latvia	Feb-99	Jun-94	Jun-95	--	--
Lithuania	--	May-94	Jun-95	--	--
Armenia	--	May-97	--	Apr-96	Jul-99
Azerbaijan	--	--	--	Apr-96	Jul-99
Belarus	**--**	**--**	**--**	**Mar-95**	**--**
Georgia	Jun-00	Dec-96	--	Apr-96	Jul-99
Kazakhstan	--	Jul-96	--	Jan-95	Jul-99
Kyrgyzstan	Dec-98	Mar-95	--	Feb-95	Jul-99
Moldova	--	Jun-95	--	Nov-94	Jul-98
Russia	**--**	**Jun-96**	**--**	**Jun-94**	**Dec-97**
Tajikistan	--	--	--	--	--
Turkmenistan	--	--	--	May-98	--
Ukraine	**--**	**Sep-96**	**--**	**Jun-94**	**Mar-98**
Uzbekistan	--	--	--	Jun-96	Jul-99

Source: EBRD (2000), Transition Report 2000

Both Hungary and Poland signed the EU Association agreement[19] in Dec-91. In 1995 they became members of GATT/WTO and in 1995/1996 they received IMF Article VIII status. Hungary and Poland are in the first wave of EU eastern enlargement. Both have to transform their economies according to acquis communautaire, which represents the requirements for EU membership. Hungary and Poland have better chances to liberalize their trade towards the EU according to aquis communautaire. Russia signed the EU Partnership and Cooperation Agreement in 1994 which entered into force only in 1997 and received IMF Article VIII status in 1996. The Ukraine signed the EU Partnership and Cooperation Agreement in 1994 which entered into force in 1998 and received IMF Article VIII status in 1996. Belarus only signed the EU Partnership and Cooperation Agreement in 1995 and there has not been any progress since. In the investigated CIS countries there was very slow progress in WTO negotiations. Additionally, the EU association agreement did not have much influence on the

---

[19] EUROPEAN COMMISSION (1998)

(http://europa.eu.int/comm/dg1a/enlarge/index.htm, p. 2) *"On March 25, 1998, the European Commission approved Accession Partnerships for the 10 applicant countries of Central and Eastern Europe (CEEC's). These are a key part of the enhanced pre-accession strategy aimed at guiding the applicants towards European Union (EU) membership. Each Accession Partnership (AP) will support the applicant country in its preparations for membership by setting out both the priority areas for further work identified from the Commission's Opinion and the financial assistance from the EU available to help tackle these problems. The AP's focus on preparing the applicant CEEC's to meet fully the membership criteria set by the Copenhagen European Council. Objectives cover areas such as strengthening democracy and the rule of low, protection of minorities, economic reform, reinforcement of institutional and administrative capacity, preparation for full participation in the internal market, justice and home affairs, agriculture, environment, transport, employment and social affaires, regional policy, and cohesion."*

EUROPEAN COMMISSION (1998)

(http://europa.eu.int/comm/dg1a/en1..access_partnership/intro/index.htm, p.3)

"Principles of the AP's:

The Accession Partnerships are designed to help prepare the Central European applicant countries to meet fully the criteria set by the Copenhagen European Council for membership:

- *stability of institutions guaranteeing democracy, the rule of law, human rights, and respect for and protection of minorities;*
- *the existence of a functioning market economy, as well as the capacity to cope with competitive pressure and market forces within the Union;*
- *the ability to take on the obligations of membership, including adherence to aims of political, economic, and monetary union."*

economies of these CIS countries. A strong impact on liberalization was only possible according to IMF commitment.

To sum up, Hungary shows a very high openness ratio towards foreign trade, which is mostly explainable according to increased trade with the EU. Poland's openness to foreign trade increased but remained on a moderate level. Astonishingly large is the openness ratio for Russia, the Ukraine and Belarus. One explanation of this fact could be that macroeconomic instability in these countries induced foreign trade since it represents the only possibility to earn hard currencies. In the case of Russia the revival of natural resource exports could promote foreign trade. Since these three countries were leading republics in the former Soviet Union, one could suppose that they managed to reestablish old trade links earlier than the others. But CIS countries are also to a much lesser extent involved in international commitments in comparison to Hungary and Poland.

4.2.2 Geographical Distribution of Exports of Selected CIS and CEECs

Figures 13-17 represent exports of the investigated countries to OECD[20] countries and in particular to the following groups of countries: EU-15, EFTA-6, CEE-5[21], Canada and the United States, Asia (Japan and Korea), Australia and New Zealand, and Mexico. The diagrams compare the distribution of export patterns in 1993 and 1997 in absolute terms as well as a share of total exports of the region. The investigation shows that more advanced transition economies such as Hungary and Poland have already reoriented their trade to a considerable extent towards OECD countries.

Hungary is a bright example (Figure 13). Its exports to OECD countries increased both in absolute terms and as a percent of total exports. In absolute terms the rise was on 167%: from $5,963 mill. to $15,907 mill. As a percent of total exports it increased from 69.3% to 83.2%. In 1997 in absolute terms the EU-15 represented the main trading partner of Hungary. Exports to the EU-15 have increased since 1993 by 172%: from $4,984 mill. to $13,604 mill. With a large interval the EU-15 was followed by the EFTA-6. The exports to this group of countries has increased by 119% since 1993, from $1,230 mill. to $2,695 mill.

---

[20] OECD includes Australia, Austria, Belgium, Canada, Czech Republic, Denmark, Finland, France, Germany, Greece, Hungary, Iceland, Ireland, Italy, Japan, Korea, Luxembourg, Mexico, The Netherlands, New Zealand, Norway, Poland, Portugal, Spain, Sweden, Switzerland, Turkey, United Kingdom, United States, Additionally, OECD is extended to Estonia and Slovenia.

[21] CEE-5 consists of Hungary, Poland, Czech Republic, Estonia, and Slovenia.

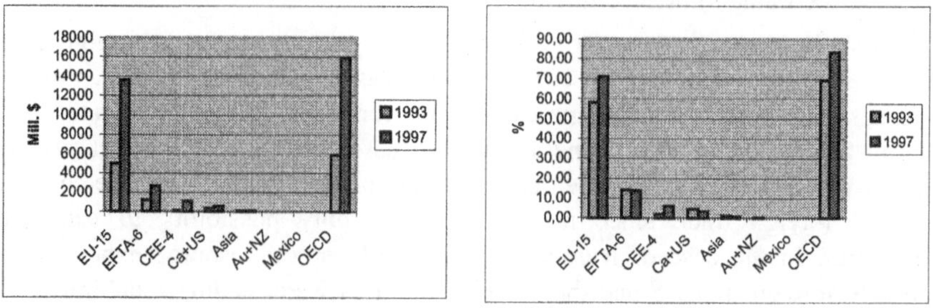

Figure 13: External Trade of Hungary with OECD in $ mill. and as a Percent of Total Trade

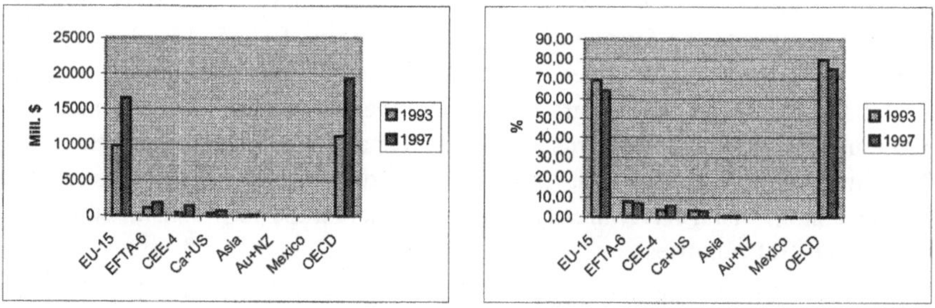

Figure 14: External Trade of Poland with OECD in $ mill. and as a Percent of Total Trade

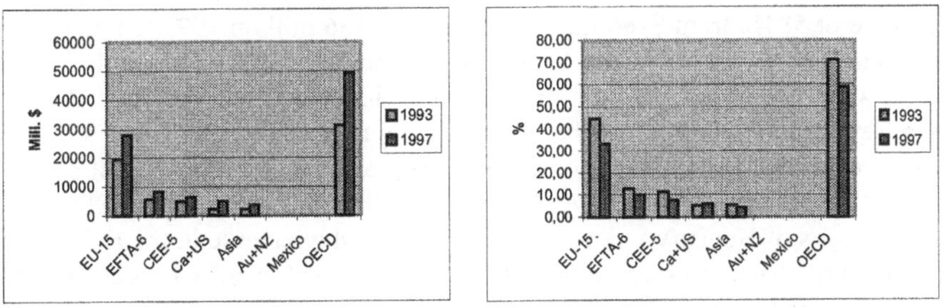

Figure 15: External Trade of Russia with OECD in $ mill. and as a Percent of Total Trade

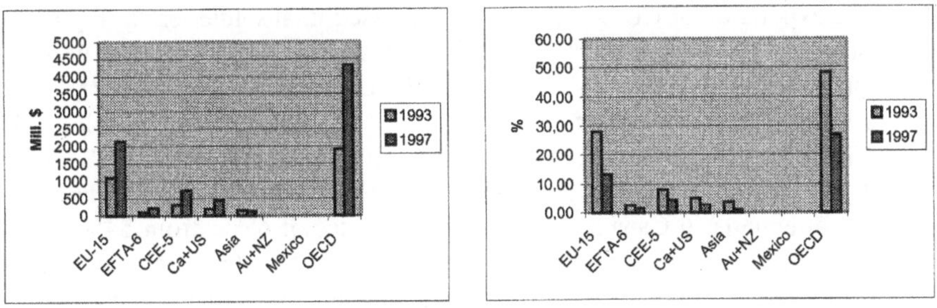

Figure 16: External Trade of Ukraine with OECD in $ mill. and as a Percent of Total Trade

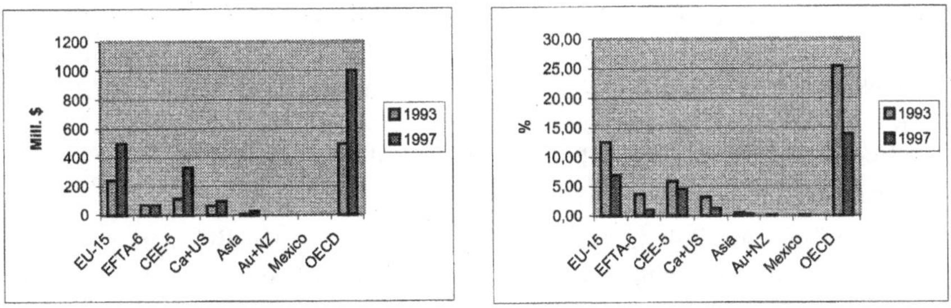

Source: IMF (1998), Directions of Trade Statistics Yearbook 1998, own calculations

Figure 17: External Trade of Belarus with OECD in $ mill. and as a Percent of Total Trade

The exports to CEE-4 also considerably gained in importance. There was an increase of 584% from $166 mill. in 1993 to $1,136 mill. in 1997[22]. The volumes of trade with Canada and the United States increased from $399 mill. to $656 mill., with Asia from $106 mill. to $132 mill. The volumes of trade with Australia and New Zealand remained rather low and accounted for $23 mill. and $5 mill. in 1997, respectively. The diagram, which reflects a share of each group of countries in total exports of Hungary, nevertheless shows that the increase in OECD share in total exports of Hungary was mostly according to the increase in the EU-15 share (13%). The share of other groups of countries in total exports except of CEE-4 decreased in 1997 in comparison to 1993[23].

Thus the increase in the OECD share in total exports of Hungary was mostly according to the increase of Hungary's exports to the EU. The share of the EU-15 in total exports increased from 57.9% in 1993 to 71.2% in 1997. According to EUROPEAN PARLIAMENT (2000), this share accounted for 76.2% in 1999.

Poland's exports to OECD countries also increased in absolute terms (Figure 14). The increase accounted for 72%: from $11,268 mill. to $19,348 mill. The EU-15 accounted for the most exports among the OECD countries. Exports to the EU-15 increased by 69%: from $9,795 mill. to $16,535 mill. The EU-15 was followed by the EFTA-6, with an increase of 64%: from $1,109 mill. to $1,818 mill. Exports to the CEE-4 increase by 161%: from $536 mill. to $1,399 mill. There was also an increase in exports to Canada and the United States of 67%: from $456 mill. to $762 mill. An increase in exports to Asia accounted for 70%: from $90 mill. to $153 mill. The volumes of trade with Australia and New Zealand increased by 50%: from $18 mill. to $27 mill. In exports to Mexico there was a decrease of 56%: from $34 mill. to $15 mill. As in Hungary, there was development of Poland's share of total exports to the OECD. The OECD share of total exports from Poland decreased from 79.6% in 1993 to 75.1% in 1997. The same also concerns all other groups except the CEE-4, whereby the share of the CEE-4 in Poland's total trade increased from 3.7% to 5.4%. The EU-15's share decreased from 69.2% in 1993 to 64.2 % in 1997. Nevertheless, according to EUROPEAN PARLIAMENT (2000), the share of the EU-15 in total trade for Poland increased to 68% in 1999. The intent of Poland to join the EU speaks in favor of further increases in exports to the EU-15.

Thus, Hungary and Poland became very dependent on the EU market with 76% and 68% of their total exports in 1999 going to the EU, respectively. This was not

---

[22] The increase in trade with CEE-4 can be overestimated since the data in 1993 captures only the data on Poland (the data for other CEE was not available). The absent data was assumed to be $1 mill.

[23] The results for CEE-4 are doubtful in this case because of insufficient data for the Czech Republic, Estonia, and Slovenia for 1993. The absent data was assumed to be $1 mill.

the case with the investigated CIS countries. Although Russian exports to the OECD increased considerably in absolute terms, their share in total exports diminished by about 10% (Figure 15). The increase in exports to the OECD accounted for 57%: from $31,435 mill. to $ 49,308 mill. Most of the exports in absolute terms were devoted towards the EU-15. The increase in exports to the EU-15 in absolute terms was 42%: from $19,672 to $28,000 mill. Exports to the EU-15 were followed by the EFTA-6. Exports to this group of countries increased by 51%: from $5,596 to $8,431 mill. The increase in exports to the CEE-5 consisted of 28%: from $5,037 mill. to $6,435 mill. Especially large was the increase in trade with Canada and the United States, which accounted for 126%: from $2,246 to $5,086 mill. The increase in exports to Asia consisted of 57%: from $2,396 mill. to 3,772 mill. The increase of exports to Australia and New Zealand accounted for 25%: from $12 mill. to 15 mill., and the increase of exports to Mexico accounted for 196%: from $27 mill. to $80 mill. On the other hand, the share of the OECD in total exports decreased from 71.3% to 58.5%. Especially large was the decrease in the EU-15's share in total exports, namely from 44.6% in 1993 to 33.2% in 1997. The EFTA-6's share decreased by ca. 3%, the CEE-5's by ca. 4%, and Asia's by ca. 1%. There was only an increase in Canada's and the US's share by ca. 1%, and a very slight increase Mexico's share.

The Ukraine's exports to the OECD increased in absolute terms but decreased by more than 20% as a share of total exports (Figure 16). The EU-15 accounted for most exports from the Ukraine to OECD countries in absolute terms. Exports to the EU-15 increased by 92%: from $1,111 mill. to $ 2,135 mill. The exports to the EFTA-6 increased by 124%: from $102 mill. to $228 mill. The exports to the CEE-5 also increased by 128%: from $314 mill. to $716 mill[24]. There was an increase in exports to Canada and the United Sates in absolute terms, namely by 125%: from $198 mill. to $446 mill., but there was a decrease of exports to Asia, Australia and New Zealand, and Mexico[25]. The share of the OECD in total exports of the Ukraine diminished by approximately 20%. Especially large was the decrease in exports to the EU-15. The share of exports to the EU-15 diminished by ca. 15%. The share of exports to the EFTA-6, the CEE-5, and Canada and the United States also diminished in approximately two times. Much more than that went down the share of Asia, Australia and New Zealand and Mexico.

The situation in Belarus resembles that of the Ukraine. Although there was an increase in exports with OECD countries in absolute terms, the share of the OECD in total exports diminished by approximately 12% (Figure 17). Exports to the OECD increased by 102% in absolute terms: from $494 mill. to $999 mill. The majority of exports in absolute terms were directed towards the EU-15. The

[24] The results for the CEE-5 are doubtful since there was no data for 1993 for Hungary and Slovenia and for the Czech Republic for 1997. The absent data was assumed to be $1 mill.

[25] The results for Asia and Mexico are doubtful since there were no data for Korea and Mexico for 1997. The absent data was assumed to be $1 mill.

exports to the EU-15 increased by 104%: from $244 mill. to $497 mill. The increase in exports to the EFTA-6 in absolute terms was rather small, namely from 72 mill. to 73 mill. The exports to the CEE-5 increased by 191% and equaled $113 mill. in 1993 and $329 mill. in 1997. The increase in exports to Canada and the United States was 56% and increased from $62 mill. to $97 mill. There was a considerable increase in exports directed towards Asia, namely 167%: from $9 mill. to $24 mill. Exports to Australia and New Zealand remained without change, and there was an increase of 100% in exports to Mexico, which accounted in 1997 for $2 mill. On the other hand, the OECD share of total exports for Belarus decreased by ca. 12%. The EU-15's share decreased by ca. 6%. The EFTA-6's share decreased by ca. 3%, and that of the US and Canada by ca. 2%. The shares of all other groups of countries in total Belarus trade have also decreased considerably.

To sum up, Poland and especially Hungary have considerably reoriented their trade towards the EU. This relationship promises to extend further since both countries are candidates of the first EU accession round. But on the other hand, the share of all other OECD groups of countries with the exception of the CEE-4 decreased in total trade of both countries. Thus, both countries have reoriented their trade towards the EU and increased trade with neighboring CEE-4, but this took place to the detriment of the development of trade relations with other groups of OECD countries. Poland and Hungary should put more attention on the development of trade relations with other OECD countries for balanced trade relations with the OECD group as a whole. In the case of Russia, the Ukraine, and Belarus, trade with OECD countries increased in absolute terms but diminished considerably as a share of total trade. For Russia, trade with the United States could play an important role in the future since this share increased in 1997 in comparison to 1993. In the case of the Ukraine and Belarus there was a decrease in the share of trade with all groups of OECD countries. The common economic crisis in the CIS countries and the unwillingness to integrate into the World society in the case of Belarus can explain the emergence of such a situation.

4.2.3 Patterns of Trade Specialization with the EU

Since the EU represents one of the most important trading partners for the investigated CIS and CEECs, the change in the trading structure of these countries with the EU during the transformation process helps to estimate the success of integration with the West, to see the tendencies in structural adjustment which took place in foreign trade in these countries.

The progress in structural adjustment differs from more advanced CEECs to less successful CIS countries. According to UN/ECE (2000b), the trade specialization profile of the investigated CEECs with the EU, which at the beginning of transformation was more of a type of less developed economy, has changed considerably since 1989. This change is associated with an increasing share of capital, and especially R&D and skill-intensive exports to the EU, and at the same time reduction in the share of labor and energy-intensive exports.

Table 12 provides the comparison data on RCA values in trade of CEECs with the EU-12, differentiated according to branches with various factor intensity. The most remarkable example represents Hungary. Hungary managed to transform its sectoral deficits in the capital, R&D, and skill-intensive industries into surpluses and reduce the share of labor and energy-intensive industries in total exports. Although with slightly less success, Poland shows the same tendency. Thus in Poland in the period from 1989 to 1998 the deficits in skill-, R&D-intensive branches have been considerably reduced.

EBRD (1999) represents analysis in RCA for CIS countries (see Table 26 - section 4.5 Appendix). Revealed comparative advantage (RCA) are distinguished for five groups: agriculture, natural resources, capital-intensive goods (such as steel and automobiles), labor-intensive goods (such as clothing), and skill-intensive goods (such as high-tech products). According to EBRD (1999), Russia has strong comparative advantages in resource-intensive branches, strong revealed comparative disadvantage in agriculture, labor, and skill-intensive branches. The Ukraine has a strong revealed comparative advantage in agriculture and diminishing revealed comparative advantage in capital-intensive branches. The Ukraine has also revealed a comparative disadvantage in resource-intensive branches. It has a revealed comparative disadvantage in labor-intensive and a strong revealed comparative disadvantage in skill-intensive branches. Belarus has a revealed comparative advantage in capital-intensive branches, and labor-intensive branches. It has a revealed comparative disadvantage in agriculture and skill-intensive branches (EBRD, 1999). Therefore the investigated CIS countries have mostly revealed comparative advantages in either agriculture or resource and labor-intensive branches. Belarus and the Ukraine have revealed comparative advantages in capital-intensive branches, but no investigated CIS country has a revealed comparative advantage in skill-intensive branches.

Table 12: RCA Values in Trade with the EU-12 of the 30 Most X-factor-intensive Industries

	Bulgaria	Czech Republic	**Hungary**	**Poland**	Romania	Slovakia	Slovenia	Greece	Portugal	Ireland
Capital intensity										
1989	-0.43		**-0.19**	**0.06**						
1993	-0.28	-0.11	**-0.37**	**-0.23**	-0.36	0.22	-0.24	-0.57	-0.41	0.29
1998	0.13	-0.13	**0.16**	**-0.27**	-0.23	0.11	-0.13	-0.63	-0.28	0.19
Skill intensity										
1989	-0.77		**-0.54**	**-0.54**						
1993	-0.54	-0.46	**-0.38**	**-0.53**	-0.60	-0.38	-0.05	-0.82	-0.40	0.22
1998	-0.49	-0.24	**-0.12**	**-0.48**	-0.55	-0.28	-0.11	-0.83	-0.33	0.21
R&D intensity										
1989	-0.84		**-0.59**	**-0.54**						
1993	-0.64	-0.45	**-0.42**	**-0.54**	-0.72	-0.60	-0.16	-0.86	-0.50	0.19
1998	-0.58	-0.14	**0.04**	**-0.47**	-0.62	-0.08	-0.09	-0.87	-0.35	0.13
Labor intensity										
1989	-0.40		**0.13**	**0.17**						
1993	0.12	0.03	**0.16**	**0.26**	0.38	0.18	0.33	-0.16	0.28	-0.05
1998	0.27	0.00	**-0.14**	**0.00**	0.42	0.10	0.09	-0.39	0.13	-0.07
Energy intensity										
1989	-0.49		**-0.15**	**0.09**	0.49					
1993	-0.01	0.07	**-0.18**	**-0.16**	-0.15	0.37	-0.01	-0.52	-0.19	-0.12
1998	0.25	-0.05	**-0.20**	**-0.21**	-0.07	0.10	-0.19	-0.54	-0.19	-0.22

Source: UN/ECE (2000b), Economic Survey of Europe 2000, No. 2/3

According to the UN/ECE (2000b), economies which gained competitive advantages in the medium to high-tech industries and moved away from the low wage, labor-intensive industries also create preconditions for faster catching up, since the productivity increase is larger in the medium- to high-tech industries (e.g. engineering).

The structure of foreign trade with the EU for the investigated CIS and CEEC countries is shown in Tables 13-15. The structure of foreign trade in CEEC countries has exhibited changes during the process of transformation, as CEECs became more involved in the manufacturing and distribution networks of MNCs. At the start of transformation MNCs tried to take use of the comparative advantages of CEECs in cheap and qualified labor. Therefore, at the first stage of transformation these countries were strongly involved in OPT (outward processing trade) like clothing, footwear, furniture, and begging. In the case of OPT, foreign producers do not have large fixed costs, which allows them to move to countries with cheap labor.

In the following years, FDI considerably reshaped the pattern of comparative advantages in some of these countries. Hungary represents a bright example, followed to some extent by Poland. FDI was directed to the car and engineering industries and enforced comparative advantages of these countries in capital, skill and R&D-intensive industries (UN/ECE, 2000a).

Table 13: Structural Analysis of Trade Relations EU - Hungary, 1999

EU-imports (cif)							
	1000 €	%	Main Products (SITC division):	SITC 3 rd rev.	1000 €	%	Intra-Industry Trade Intensity (1)
Total of which:	17 338 084	100.0	Power generating machinery and equipment	71	2 632 100	15.2	157.0
A: Raw materials	1 575 586	9.1	Electr. mach., app. + appliances, N.E.S. + electr. parts thereof	77	2 049 517	11.8	92.6
Food, beverages and tobacco (0+1)	941 535	5.4	Office machines and automatic data-processing machines	75	1 875 578	10.8	122.9
Raw materials (2+4)	384 655	2.2	Road vehicles (including air - cushion vehicles)	78	1 868 321	10.8	75.1
Energy (3)	249 396	1.4	Telecommunic. + sound recording + reprod. apparatus + etc.	76	1 585 319	9.1	125.1
B: Manufactured articles	15 597 549	90.0	Articles of apparel and clothing accessories	84	1 041 157	6.0	147.6
Chemicals (5)	639 670	3.7	General industr. mach. + equipment, N.E.S., machine parts	74	430 106	2.5	55.0
Machinery and transport eq. (7)	10 858 438	62.6	Manufactures of metals, N.E.S.	69	414 765	2.4	75.7
Other manufactured products (6+8)	4 099 441	23.6	Meat and meat preparations	01	383 238	2.2	189.7
			Footwear	85	293 203	1.7	141.0
EU-exports (fob)							
	1000 €	%	Main Products (SITC division):	SITC 3 rd rev.	1000 €	%	Intra-Industry Trade Intensity (1)
Total of which:	18 608 594	100,0	Road vehicles (including air-cushion vehicles)	78	3 106 778	16.7	75.1
A: Raw materials	672 395	3.6	Electr. mach., app. + appliances, N.E.S. + electr. parts .thereof	77	2 374 760	12.8	92.6
Food, beverages and tobacco (0+1)	348 586	1.9	Office machines and automatic data-processing machines	75	1 177 012	6.3	122.9
Raw materials (2+4)	219 793	1.2	General industr. mach. + equipment, N.E.S., machine parts	74	1 133 870	6.1	55.0
Energy (3)	104 016	0.6	Telecommunic., + sound recording + reprod. apparatus +etc.	76	948 295	5.1	125.1
B: Manufactured articles	17 581 563	94.5	Textile yarn, fabrics, made up articles, N.E.S. , + etc.	65	799 865	4.3	44.6
Chemicals (5)	1 708 251	9.2	Textile yarn , fabrics, made up articles, N.E.S., + etc.	89	785 725	4.2	52.4
Machinery and transport eq. (7)	10 667 459	57.3	Power generating machinery and equipment	71	721 794	3.9	157.0
Other manufactured products (6+8)	5 205 853	28.0	Machinery specialized for particular industries	72	693 361	3.7	56.6
			Manufactures of metals, N.E.S.	69	681 640	3.7	75.7

Source: European Parliament (2001), Task Force Enlargement Statistical Annex, http://www.europarl.eu.int/enlargement/briefings/pdf/22a1-en.pdf

(1) The index can vary between 0 and 200: 0 means only exports, 200 only imports and 100 means balance in trade

*Index: (((x+m)-(x-m))/(x+m))*100*

Table 14: Structural Analysis of Trade Relations EU - Poland, 1999

EU-imports (cif)							
	1000 €	%	Main Products (SITC division):	SITC 3 rd rev.	1000 €	%	Intra-Industry Trade Intensity (1)
Total of which:	17 505 391	100.0	Articles of apparel and clothing accessories	84	1 805 013	10.3	159.9
			Road vehicles (including air-cushion vehicles)	78	1 774 115	10.1	70.7
A: Raw materials	2 469 171	14.1	Furnit. + parts thereof; beddg., mattresses, etc.	82	1 521 420	8.7	165.8
Food, beverages and tobacco (0+1)	1 110 383	6.3	Electr. mach., app. + appliances, N.E.S. + electr. parts thereof	77	1 388 221	7.9	79.4
Raw materials (2+4)	570 317	3.3					
Energy (3)	788 471	4.5					
B: Manufactured articles	14 716 485	84.1	Manufacturing of metals, N.E.S.	69	938 736	5.4	91.6
Chemicals (5)	711 807	4.1	Non-ferrous metals	68	707 611	4.0	129.1
Machinery and transport eq. (7)	5 320 208	30.4	Cork and wood manufacturing (excluding furniture)	63	707 349	4.0	159.8
Other manufactured products (6+8)	8 684 470	49.6	Coal, coke and briquettes	32	663 637	3.8	198.6
			Telecommunic. + sound recording + reprod. apparatus + etc.	76	609 737	3.5	66.1
			Iron and steel	67	513 431	2.9	83.6
EU-exports (fob)							
	1000 €	%	Main products (SITC division):	SITC 3 rd rev.	1000 €	%	Intra-Industry Trade Intensity (1)
Total of which:	28 874 051	100.0	Road vehicles (including air-cushion vehicles)	78	3 246 096	11.2	70.7
			Electr. mach., app. + appliances, N.E.S., machine parts thereof	77	2 108 666	7.3	79.4
A: Raw materials	2 411 247	8.4	General indust. mach. + equipment, N.E.S., machine parts	74	2 015 883	7.0	37.0
Food, beverages and tobacco (0+1)	1 264 372	4.4					
Raw materials (2+4)	612 651	2.1					
Energy (3)	534 224	1.9	Textile yarn, fabrics, made-up articles, N.E.S., + etc.	65	1 857 849	6.4	39.2
B: Manufactured articles	25 737 029	89.1	Machinery specialized for particular industries	72	1 559 349	5.4	32.8
Chemicals (5)	4 189 005	14.5	Telecommunic. + sound recording + reprod. apparatus + manufactures of metals, N.E.S.	76	1 235 029	4.3	66.1
Machinery and transport eq. (7)	12 206 733	42.3					
Other manufactured products (6+8)	9 341 292	32.4					
			Manufactures of metals, N.E.S.	69	1 110 663	3.8	91.6
			Miscellaneous manufactures articles, N.E.S.	89	1 090 405	3.8	58.4
			Paper, paperboard + art. of paper pulp, of paper or of pulp	64	979 499	3.4	52.7
			Medical and pharmaceutical products	54	866 842	3.0	4.0

Source: European Parliament (2001), Task Force Enlargement Statistical Annex, http://www.europarl.eu.int/enlargement/briefings/pdf/22a1-en.pdf

(1) The index can vary between 0 and 200: 0 means only exports, 200 only imports and 100 means balance in trade

Index: $(((x+m)-(x-m))/(x+m))*100$

Table 15: Structural Analysis of Trade Relations EU - Russia, 1999

EU-imports (cif)							
	1000 €	%	Main Products (SITC division):	SITC 3 rd rev.	1000 €	%	Intra-Industry Trade Intensity (1)
Total	25 894 775	100.0	Petroleum, petroleum products and related materials	33	10 213 424	39.4	198.8
of which:			Non-ferrous metals	68	2 671 861	10.3	191.5
A: Raw materials	14 534 840	56.1	Gas, natural and manufactured	34	1 117 230	4.3	200.0
Food, beverages and tobacco (0+1)	454 392	1.8	Mettaliferous ores and metal scrap	28	1 013 727	3.9	189.6
Raw materials (2+4)	2 421 198	9.4	Cork and wood	24	936 082	3.6	198.0
Energy (3)	11 659 250	45.0	Non-metallic mineral manufactures, N.E.S.	66	860 996	3.3	158.4
B: Manufactured articles	7 231 638	27.9	Iron and steel	67	845 184	3.3	138.6
Chemicals (5)	1 519 030	5.9	Inorganic chemicals	52	817 908	3.2	192.9
Machinery and transport eq. (7)	438 062	1.7	Fish, crustaceans, and mollusks and preparations thereof	03	402 204	1.6	184.4
Other manufactured products (6+8)	5 274 546	20.4	Organic chemicals	51	286 594	1.1	138.9
EU-exports (fob)							
	1000 €	%	Main products (SITC division):	SITC 3 rd rev.	1000 €	%	Intra-Industry Trade Intensity (1)
Total	14 702 589	100.0	Meat and meat preparations	01	1 004 243	6.8	0.1
of which:			Machinery specialized for particular industries	72	928 638	6.3	12.1
A: Raw materials	3 031 500	20.6	General industr. mach. + equipment, N.E.S., machine parts	74	918 067	6.2	10.2
Food, beverages and tobacco (0+1)	2 433 961	16.6	Electr. mach., app. + appliances, N.E.S. + electric. parts thereof	77	784 964	5.3	13.9
Raw materials (2+4)	535 762	3.6	Office machines and automatic data-processing machine	75	713 149	4.9	3.7
Energy (3)	61 778	0.4	Road vehicles (including air-cushion vehicles)	78	712 444	4.8	14.1
B: Manufactured articles	11 271 092	76.7	Telecommunic. + sound recording + reprod. apparatus + etc.	76	533 268	3.6	7.3
Chemicals (5)	1 726 646	11.7	Articles of apparel and clothing accessories	84	491 370	3.3	46.3
Machinery and transport eq. (7)	5 334 969	36.3	Miscellaneous manufactured articles, N.E.S.	89	486 382	3.3	38.0
Other manufactured products (6+8)	4 209 476	28.6	Paper, paperboard + art. of paper pulp, of paper or of pulp	64	444 763	3.0	65.8

Source: European Parliament (2001), Task Force Enlargement Statistical Annex, http://www.europarl.eu.int/enlargement/briefings/pdf/22a1-en.pdf

(1) The index can vary between 0 and 200: 0 means only exports, 200 only imports and 100 means balance in trade

*Index: (((x+m)-(x-m))/(x+m))*100*

The exports of Hungary to the EU consist of 90% manufactured goods, whereby machinery and transport equipment account for 62.6% (Table 13). Imports from the EU have a similar structure. In imports manufactured goods also represent an absolute majority of 94.5%, and the share of machinery and transport equipment is close to that of exports and equals 57.3%. The share of raw materials in both exports and imports is rather low, 9.1% and 3.6%, respectively. The most exported products from Hungary to the EU are power generating machinery and equipment (15.2% of total), electrical machinery (11.8%), office machines (10.8%), road vehicles (10.8), and telecommunication equipment (9.1%). According to the index of intra-industry trade the intensity of intra-industry trade is especially high if the index approaches 100. Therefore, among the most exported products intra-industry intensity is high in the case of electrical machinery, office machines, road vehicles, and telecommunication equipment. Hungary imports from the EU have a similar structure to exports since 16.7% of imports are road vehicles, 12.8% electrical machinery, 6.3% office machinery, 6.1% general industrial machinery, and 5.1% telecommunication equipment. KAITILA (1999) has investigated in detail the structure of foreign trade between the EU and Hungary and found that intra-industry trade in this case is based more on horizontal intra-industry trade or in other words on two-way trade with the same group of products of similar quality[26].

The structure of Poland's foreign trade with the EU is similar to that of Hungary, but there are some differences. Poland's exports to the EU consist of 84.1% manufactured goods, but the share of machinery and transport equipment is significantly lower than that of Hungary and equals 30.4% (Table 14). The share of other manufactured products accounts for 49.6%. The share of raw materials in exports is also higher than that of Hungary. Thus, it accounts for 14.1%, whereby the share of food, beverages, and tobacco is 6.3%, energy is 4.5%, and raw materials (2+4) 3.3%. Poland's imports from the EU consist mostly of manufactured goods, where the majority is represented by machinery and transport equipment (42.3%), followed by other manufactured products (32.4%) and chemicals (14.5%). The most exported products are represented by apparel and clothing accessories at 10.3%, road vehicles at 10.1%, furniture at 8.7%, electronic machinery at 7.9%, and manufactured metals at 5.4%. Among these product groups the intra-industry intensity is especially large in trade with road vehicles, electronic machinery, and manufactured metals. The main products imported by Poland consist of road vehicles at 11.2%, electrical machinery at 7.3%, general industrial machinery at 7.0%, textiles at 6.4%, and specialized machinery at 5.4%.

---

[26] According to the definition of UN/ECE (2000b), ECONOMIC SURVEY OF EUROPE No. 2/3 (2000, p. 107): *"Vertical product differentiation refers to a situation in which producers are differentiated by the 'quality' of the product variety which they sell as compared with 'horizontal product differentiation' where different consumers prefer one variant over another, but where there is no agreed quality ranking across products".*

The case in Russia is quite different from the previous two. Raw materials predominate in Russia's exports to the EU at 56.1% of total exports (Table 15). Energy represents the largest share of this group with 45.0%. Manufactured goods account for only 30%. The share of machinery and transport equipment is very low at about 2%. The share of other manufactured products accounts for 20.4%. In imports food, beverages, and tobacco are largely present. The share of food, beverages, and tobacco equals to 16.6%, which is twice as much as that of Poland. The majority of imports consist of manufactured goods, namely 76.7%. In imports the share of machinery and transport equipment is rather large and accounts for 36.3%. The share of other manufactured products is 28.6%, followed by chemicals with 11.7%. Among the most exported products are petroleum, petroleum products, and related materials which dominate by a large marginal. This group of products accounts for nearly 40%. Further non-ferrous metals account for 10.3%, gas for 4.3%, etc. The import side is represented by 6.8% meat products, 6.3% specialized machinery, 6.2% general industrial machinery, 5.3% electrical machinery, and 4.9% office machinery. The index of intra-industry intensity points to an absence of intra-industry trade. Since Russia predominately exports raw material (the index on export size is almost always close to 200) and imports manufacturing (the index on import side tends to 0), the trade between Russia and the EU is inter-industry and not intra-industry trade.

There is no available data on exports of the Ukraine and Belarus to the EU, but one problem should be discussed which is associated with these countries in the external sector. Primary commodities dominate the exports of most CIS countries. Therefore, export revenues are highly sensitive to changes in commodity prices (UN/ECE, 2000a). If commodity prices decline as a result of slower global growth, for example, then the impact on the country's external and fiscal balances would be considerable (EBRD, 2000). Table 16 shows the share of commodities in total exports of CIS countries in 1999. All CIS countries except for Belarus and Moldova are highly dependent on commodities.

Table 16: Share of Commodities in Total Exports of CIS Countries in 1999

Country	Main commodities exported	Percentage of total exports
Armenia	Precious stones, minerals, and metals	70.3
Azerbaijan	Oil, metal, and cotton	79.2
Belarus	Metal and wood	12.3
Georgia	Metals, fuels, and tea	58.6
Kazakhstan	Grain, metals, and fuel	77.2
Kyrgyzstan	Gold, metals, and cotton	40.5
Moldova	Metals, minerals, and wood	4.2
Russia	Metal and fuels	64.1
Tajikistan	Cotton and aluminum	59.0
Turkmenistan	Minerals, fuels, and cotton	85.0
Ukraine	Fuel, wood, food, raw materials, and metals	57.5
Uzbekistan	Cotton, gold, and gas	63.0

Source: EBRD (2000), Transition Report 2000

Russia depends strongly on foreign sales of oil and gas products. The Ukraine also depends strongly on primary commodity exports such as fuel, wood, food, raw materials, and metals. Since primary commodities account for 57.5% of total Ukrainian exports, they would also prevail in exports to the EU. The share of primary commodities in total exports of Belarus is not high, only 12.3%. Although manufacturing accounted for 76% of total exports (WORLD BANK, 2000) in Belarus in 1998, its high trade exposure to Russia leads to the conclusion that the structure of Belarussian exports to the EU is rather inter-industry in character.

To sum up, especially significant progress in structural adjustment of foreign trade was observed in Hungary. Hungary reoriented its specialization towards more capital-, skill-, and R&D-intensive industries and took distance from labor and energy-intensive industries. It's foreign trade with the EU is mostly intra-industry in character, where intra-industry trade prevails horizontally. Both exports and imports are app. 60% in machinery and transport equipment. The success of Hungary in structural adjustment of foreign trade is according to a large extent to FDI. Hungary was the largest recipient of FDI, so FDI reshaped the structure of its foreign trade towards intra-industry trade in medium- and high-tech products, which takes place within the channels of MNCs.

Poland follows the pattern of Hungary, although there are still some differences. Poland's exports to the EU, as in the case of Hungary, consist mostly of manufacturing. Standard manufacturing like apparel and furniture stands hand in hand with more sophisticated manufacturing like road vehicles and electronic machinery. The intensity of intra-industry trade, which promotes better technological diffusion, is also larger in the case of such branches as road vehicles and electronic machinery.

The structure of Russian foreign trade with the EU shows a quite different pattern. The trade is strongly inter-industry and not intra-industry. Raw materials, especially energy products, dominate Russian exports to the EU, whereby Russian imports from the EU consist of food and manufactured articles, first of all machinery. Such a structure of foreign trade can considerably impair the future economic growth of Russia since there is a risk of „Dutch disease", which would prevent the development of the manufacturing sector in Russia. The detailed analysis of a possible free trade agreement between Russia and the EU, and among other things the aspects of export structure diversification, trade creation, and trade diversion with the EU in the light of tariff policy are discussed by BRENTON/TOURDYEVA/WHALLEY (1997).

Large dependence on primary commodity exports is also seen in the case of the Ukraine. One could suppose that raw materials and metals and fuel and wood form Ukrainian exports to the EU. Belarus is one of the few countries in the former Soviet Union which exports up to 76% manufacturing, but its strong exposure in trade with Russia prevents the export of manufacturing to the EU. Belarussian exports to the EU are also more inter-industry in character and consist of mostly metal and wood products (EBRD, 2000)[27].

4.3 The Gravity Model of Foreign Trade for Selected CIS and CEECs

The economic relations of the former USSR were concentrated predominately on the CMEA countries. Political reasons distinguished the incentive of the former Soviet Union to limit economic dependence on the West. This resulted in the development of a rather distorted regional structure of foreign trade which was based on political rather then economic principles. After the collapse of the Soviet Union Russia, the Ukraine, and Belarus have inherited the distorted system from their predecessor. Transformation to a market economy in these countries nowadays implies economic opening up and integration with the West which could contribute via trade and foreign direct investment to higher economic growth and welfare in these CIS economies. Using the gravity model it is of great interest to show a "normal" regional pattern for the distribution of foreign trade, a pattern that demonstrates available economic potential for the development of relations between considered economies and the West, and to distinguish the gap

---

[27] It is surprising that there is different information about main export commodity groups for Belarus in EBRD (2000) and EBRD (1999). In EBRD (1999) main commodity exports consist of clothing (21%) and fertilizers (9%) and in EBRD (2000) they consist mostly of metal and wood (12.3%). The specialization pattern in Belarus seems to be rather unstable.

between potential and existing trade patterns to be able to appreciate the success of transformation.

This section discusses the theoretical approach of the gravity model based on previous studies and their results. A new specification of the gravity model is suggested for the investigated CIS and CEECs. Three CIS countries are compared with more advanced CEECs (Hungary and Poland). Finally the results are discussed.

4.3.1 The Gravity Model Approach to Foreign Trade

The gravity model for foreign trade explains the geographical distribution of the bilateral trade of a given country (or region) with it's different trading partners. The gravity model follows Newton's law of gravity, where gravitation forces between different bodies depend on their mass and the distance between them. The gravity model has often been criticized for insufficient theoretical provision as well as for substantial abstraction from reality (VAN SELM (1995), DEARDORFF (1995), BREUSS/EGGER (1999)). The gravity model tries to explain trade flows using some geographical, macroeconomic, and cultural factors, but ignores for example some aspects of trade theory. Therefore, comparative advantages, factor endowments, and patterns of intra- or inter-industrial trade are not the focus of the gravity model. Advantages of the model, on the other hand, are its empirical robustness and clear interpretation of attained results. Gravity models have been used over decades and have not lost their attractiveness.

Theoretical foundations for gravity models are provided by GROS/DAUTREBANDE (1992), WANG/WINTERS (1992), BALDWIN (1993), and HOLZMANN/ZUKOWSKA-GAGELMANN (1998). The gravity equation assumes that the amount of bilateral trade between two countries is determined by their „size" and the „distance" between them (GROS/DAUTREBANDE, 1992). Economic growth or „size" emphasizes the role of *GNP* and *GNP per capita* of both exporting and importing countries in explaining the value of trade. In some cases income and population are used not in combination, (i.e. income/income per capita), but separately. The larger both countries are in terms of income and income per capita, the more trade there should be between them. The increase in income would lead to more opportunities for intra-industrial trade, conditioned by more differentiated consumer preferences emerging with higher per capita income.

„Distance" includes both restricting and stimulating factors. „Distance" explains trade flows using such factors as geographical distance (affecting costs of transportation), common frontier, trade policy (whether or not the countries participate in a preferential trade agreement), and cultural affinity (whether or not the countries share a common language or have similarities in legal systems, etc.). There are several restricting factors, such as costs of transportation and protectionist measures. Stimulating factors for trade are membership in common regional integration agreements, a common language, historical ties, and similar legal systems. BALDWIN (1994) offers an intuitive summary. The „size" of the importing country determines its demand for goods, while the „size" of the exporting country determines its supply of goods. Distance is a proxy for transportation costs.

A number of estimations for Central and Eastern European countries were carried out based on the gravity model approach. All of them show that Eastern Europe and the EU are „natural" trading partners. WANG/WINTERS (1992), using a gravity model, found the potential trade between Central and Eastern Europe and the EU to substantially higher than the actual. The gap ranges from about 30 percent for Hungary to almost 650 percent for Bulgaria. COLLINS/RODRIK (1991) arrived at a relatively similar conclusion. AHMAD/YANG (1998), whose investigation was also based on the gravity approach, came to the result that Central and Eastern Europe's trade with the EU has the highest proportion in the long run.

Some economists who oppose the above mentioned studies argue that trade adjustment for some transition economies has already been accomplished. Thus GROS/GONCIARZ (1996) found no unused potential in trade for Central and Eastern European Countries. HOLZMANN/ZUKOWSKA-GAGELMANN (1998) showed in their investigation of this question that the trade adjustment for Central and Eastern European countries is far from being exhausted and varies considerably from the advanced reform countries in Central Europe (Poland, Czech Republic, Hungary, and Slovenia) to the less developed transition economies.

4.3.1.1 Overview of Selected Previous Studies

In order to look at the most often used determinants of geographical distribution of trade it is useful to discuss some model specifications. One should note that in order to estimate the shift in trade of CIS and CEECs it is necessary to use a gravity model with parameter estimates for Western market economies and data about the income, population of the CIS and CEECs, and the distance to their main markets, assuming that trade of CIS and CEECs follows the same pattern as trade among market economies. In other words, it means that parameter estimates from recent empirical studies on the geographical distribution of international trade based on data from market economies should be multiplied with actual values on income, population, and distance (and that of all/between its potential trading partners) of a given CIS/CEE-country in order to carry out a prediction about its future distribution of trade pattern. The next step would be a comparison of the predictions based on the gravity approach with the actual pattern.

GROS/DAUTREBANDE (1992) carried out estimations of the determinants of the distribution of inter-republican trade in the former Soviet Union (see equation 4.1). The gravity model describes the trade flows, say exports, from a particular country i to another country j. Exports from country i are assumed to depend on national income in i (to proxy for the supply of exportables) and national income in j (to proxy for the demand for i's exportables in country j). Per capita output is also used to reflect the idea of increase in the share of tradables in overall income with the increase in income. In other words, a country with a higher per capita income should trade more intensively (have more exports and imports) than a poorer country. The same arguments are relevant for the distribution of imports. The other variables used in the gravity model are the distance and area of the importing or exporting country. The latter should have a negative effect on trade, as does distance, because it proxies the transportation costs from the hinterland to the economic center. A variable which reflects the presence/absence of a common border (adjacency variable) is expected to have a positive sign.

The estimated equation is:

$$\begin{aligned} Ln\left(EX_{ij}\right) &= CONST + \beta_1 \ln\left(NMP_i\right) + \beta_2 \ln\left(NMP_j\right) + \\ &\beta_3 \ln\left(NMP_i / POP_i\right) + \beta_4 \ln\left(NMP_j / POP_j\right) + \\ &\beta_5 \ln\left(DIST_{ij}\right) + \beta_6 \ln\left(AREA_i\right) + \beta_7 \ln\left(AREA_j\right) + \beta_8 \left(A_{ij}\right) \end{aligned} \tag{4.1}$$

where: EX_{ij} are exports from country i to country j, *CONST* is a constant, NMP_i is National Material Product of country i, NMP_j is National Material Product of country j, NMP_i/POP_i is per capita output in county i, NMP_j/POP_j is per capita output in country j, $DIST_{ij}$ is distance between countries i and j, $AREA_i$ is the area of country i from a hinterland to the economic center, $AREA_j$ is the area of country j, and A_{ij} is an adjacency dummy variable.

WANG/WINTERS (1992) estimate the gravity model equation for a sample of 76 countries, 19 industrial and 57 developing (see equation 4.2). Since the purpose was to investigate trade patterns for market economies, the East European countries, China, and oil exporting countries have been excluded. In the model WANG/WINTERS estimate imports from country i to country j. The imports are expected to positively depend on the Gross Domestic Product of both countries. Additionally, the population variable is taken into account. The population variable represents a proxy for the physical size of the economy and is expected to have a negative sign. The population variable reflects the self-sufficiency of the economy in terms of economies of scale and natural resource endowments in the situation of autarky, and is supposed to have a negative effect on the openness ratio. Imports are presumed to negatively depend on distance, while the adjacency variable is presumed to have a positive sign and becomes 1 if i and j share a common border. WANG/WINTERS also introduce a series of dummy variables which reflect preferential trading arrangements. The purpose of the dummy variables for preferential trading arrangements is to take into account a favorable trade climate among some countries and trade restrictions between others. Since it is not possible to introduce tariff and/or non-tariff barriers, preferential trading arrangements carry out this role. The trade between two countries is supposed to be stronger if they are members of the same trading area.

The equation of WANG/WINTERS is as follows:

$$Ln(IM_{ij}) = CONST + \beta_1 \ln(GDP_i) + \beta_2 \ln(GDP_j) + \beta_3 \ln(POP_i) + \\ \beta_4 \ln(POP_j) + \beta_5 \ln(DIST_{ij}) + \beta_6 (A_{ij}) + \beta_7 (PREF_{kij}) \quad (4.2)$$

where: IM_{ij} are imports from country i to country j, *CONST* is a constant, GDP_i is Gross Domestic Product of country i, GDP_j is Gross Domestic Product of country j, POP_i is population of county i, POP_j is population of country j, $DIST_{ij}$ is distance between countries i and j, A_{ij} is an adjacency dummy variable, and $PREF_{kij}$ is a dummy variable representing the kth preference relationship between countries i and j.

BALDWIN's (1993) model specification is based on the WANG/WINTERS (1992) model (see equation 4.3). The goal of his paper was to investigate potential trade between CEECs and the EFTA. BALDWIN (1993) updated the WANG/WINTERS model to 1989. He excluded all non-European nations from the sample of 76 countries and considered 12 CEECs as well as 11 EC countries and 6 members of EFTA. BALDWIN proposed to rearrange the WANG/WINTERS equation into an equation with total and per capita income in both countries. Without dummy variables it yields:

$$Ln(IM_{ij}) = CONST + \beta_1 \ln(GDP_i) + \beta_2 \ln(GDP_j) + \beta_3 \ln(GDP_i / POP_i) + \\ \beta_4 \ln(GDP_j / POP_j) + \beta_5 \ln(DIST_{ij}) \quad (4.3)$$

HOLZMANN/ZUKOWSKA-GAGELMANN (1998) investigate the potential in trade between OECD countries and reform economies in Eastern Europe. The HOLZMANN/ZUKOWSKA-GAGELMANN model differs from the ordinary specification in one important point, namely it takes into account over and under-valuation of exchange rates and represents the log of the nominal dollar value of GDP as a sum of two terms: the log of PPP (purchasing power parity)-converted GDP (GDP^P) and the log of the exchange rate mark-up (*MU*) (see equation 4.4). The specification of their model appears as follows:

$$Ln(EX_{ij}) = CONST + \beta_1 \ln(GDP^P{}_i) + \beta_2 \ln(GDP^P{}_j) + \beta_3 \ln(POP_i) + \\ \beta_4 \ln(POP_j) + \beta_5 \ln(MU_i) + \beta_6 \ln(MU_j) + \beta_7 \ln(DIST_{ij}) + \\ \beta_8 \ln(AREA_i) + \beta_9 \ln(AREA_j) + \beta_{10} (A_{ij}) + \beta_{11} (EU_{ij}) + \\ \beta_{12} (EFTA_{ij}) \quad (4.4)$$

They suppose that national income ($GDP^P{}_{i,j}$), population ($POP_{i,j}$), an adjacency variable (A_{ij}), and a common membership in preferential trade areas (EU_{ij} and $EFTA_{ij}$) would have a positive impact on trade. On the other hand, distance

($DIST_{ij}$), the exchange rate ($MU_{i,j}$) , and area ($AREA_{i,j}$), where the latter reflects dependence on trade of large countries, would negatively effect trade.

4.3.1.2 Comparison of Estimation Results

For an overview of the most important determinants of trade flows we will look at Table 17 which allows us to compare the results of estimations. Table 17 represents the results of the gravity models of GROS/DAUTREBANDE (1992), WANG/WINTERS (1992), BALDWIN (1993), and HOLZMANN/ZUKOWSKA-GAGELMANN (1998). In these studies, approximately the same variables were used. In some cases income and population are used separately, and not income and output per capita. The most used export estimates for the gravity model (the exception is WANG/WINTERS, which used import estimates). Export and import estimates should be identical, apart from some difficulties, which can cause small differences in coefficients. Thus, there are differences in valuation and minor differences according to the time-lag between the recording of exports and imports. These differences exhibit only little influence on the coefficients, therefore one can choose to use export or import estimates.

The most significant explanatory variable in all studies is income. The elasticity of income varies from 0.66 according to the estimation of HOLZMANN/ZUKOWSKA-GAGELMANN to 1.17 according to WANG/WINTERS. The other explanatory variable, which is not less important than income, is distance. For instance, the impact of distance on trade in the HOLZMANN/ZUKOVSKA-GAGELMANN model is even larger than that of income. Its elasticity varies form -0.39 according to GROS/DAUTREBANDE to -1.05 according to HOLZMANN/ZUKOWSKA-GAGELMANN.

The GROS/DAUTREBANDE model was estimated with ordinary least squares (OLS). In their model the import and export coefficients are mostly identical, therefore they use only the export equation. Most of the variables are highly significant and have an expected sign. Thus, trade increases if countries have a common border and decreases with distance. The impact of the variable distance is much less than in other studies. Since GROS/ DAUTREBANDE investigate inter-republican trade of the former Soviet Union, this could be explained by a lack of attention paid by Soviet planners to the transportation costs. The variable with the largest impact on trade is *GDP* (this variable is also highly significant). The hypothesis about the impact of output per capita was not confirmed by the Soviet data, since per capita output of the partner country j does not have a significant coefficient. The estimation results of the variable *AREA* are also not plausible. Thus, trade is supposed to decrease with the area of the home country, i, but increase with the area of the partner country, j.

Table 17: Gravity Model For Foreign Trade (Comparison of Studies)*

Explanatory Variables	GROS/ DAUTRE-BANDE (1992) (Inter-republican trade of the former Soviet Union)	WANG/ WINTERS (1992) (76 market economies)	BALDWIN (1993)[28] (12 CEECs, 11 EU, 6 EFTA)	HOLZMANN/ZUKOWSKA-GAGELMANN (1998)[29] (OECD economies 1988-1995)		
	OLS	OLS	OLS	OLS	SUR	SUR/ IVS
CONST	-10.48	-12.49	-12.5	7.17	7.56	7.31
	(-7.9)	(32.42)		(15.91)^{3*}	(13.34)^{3*}	(12.92)^{3*}
ln (GDP_i)	1.01	1.17	0.79	0.65	0.63	0.66
	(19.1)	(58,19)		(6.61)^{3*}	(24.48)^{3*}	(26.87)^{3*}
ln (GDP_j)	0.69	1.02	0.80	0.91	0.69	0.71
	(13.2)	(42.75)		(9.07)^{3*}	(26.62)^{3*}	(29.24)^{3*}
ln (GDP_i/POP_i)	0.32		0.38			
	(2.7)					
ln (GDP_j/POP_j)	-0.06		0.22			
	(-0.5)					
ln (POP_i)		-0.38		0.09		
		(15.67)		(0.90)		
ln (POP_j)		-0.22		-0.20		
		(8.19)		(-1.90)^{1*}		
ln $(DIST_{ij})$	-0.39	-0.75	-0.75	-1.09	-1-07	-1.03
	(-6.3)	(22.28)		(-30.70)^{3*}	(-15.70)^{3*}	(-16.06)^{3*}
ln $(AREA_i)$	-0.11			-0.04	-0.00	
	(-3.0)			(-1.91)^{1*}	(-0.07)	
ln $(AREA_j)$	0.16			0.03	0.05	
	(4.4)			(1.54)	(1.31)	

---

[28] Since the equation is rearranged in total and per capita income, the t-statistics are no longer applicable.

[29] ^{3*} denotes significance at the 1 per cent level, ^{2*} denotes significance at the 5 per cent level, and ^{1*}denotes denotes significance at the 10 per cent level.

Table 17: Gravity Model For Foreign Trade (Comparison of Studies)* (cont.)

Explanatory Variables	GROS/ DAUTRE-BANDE (1992) (Inter-republican trade of the former Soviet Union)	WANG/ WINTERS (1992) (76 market economies)	BALDWIN (1993)[30] (12 CEECs, 11 EU, 6 EFTA)	HOLZMANN/ZUKOWSKA-GAGELMANN (1998)[31] (OECD economies 1988-1995)		
	OLS	OLS	OLS	OLS	SUR	SUR/ IVS
Dummy (A_{ij})	0.59	0.78	0.78	0.31	0.35	0.36
	(3.1)	(3.27)		(5.37)^{3*}	(2.75)^{3*}	(2.86)^{3*}
ln (MU_i)				-0.86	-0.50	-0.51
				(-7.94)^{3*}	(-8.17)^{3*}	(-5.09)^{3*}
ln (MU_j)				0.09	-0.37	-0.32
				(0.83)	(-6.08)^{3*}	(-3.22)^{3*}
Dummy ($PREF_{ij}$)		0.99[32]				
Dummy (EU_{ij})		0.70**		0.11	0.13	0.17
		(2.17)		(2.58)^{3*}	(4.70)^{3*}	(4.40)^{3*}
Dummy ($EFTA_{ij}$)		-0.02**		-0.09	-0.03	
		(0.05)		(-1.52)	(-0.82)	
R^2	0.92	0.70		0.90	0.89	0.89
S.E.	0.47					
F-values				1235		
DW				1.56	1.56	1.57
Observations	210	4320				

* *In brackets: t-statistics*

** *Dummy variables are included into* $PREF_{ij}$

[30] Since the equation is rearranged in total and per capita income, the t-statistics are no longer applicable.

[31] ^{3*} denotes significance at the 1 per cent level, ^{2*} denotes significance at the 5 per cent level, and ^{1*}denotes denotes significance at the 10 per cent level.

[32] The coefficient for $PREF_{ij}$ is taken as an average of all the coefficients for the k PREF-dummy variables. Therefore, the t-statistic is not mentioned, since it is no longer plausible.

WANG/WINTERS (1992), using OLS, found a strong income effect on trade as well as a moderate but rather significant population effect. Distance and adjacency dummy variables are also significant and have the expected signs. WANG/WINTERS tested a number of economic integration dummy variables. Among them are: EC, European Free Trade Association (EFTA), the Economic Community of the West African States (ECOWAS), the South African Developing Co-Ordination (SADCC), the Central American Common Market (CACM), the Andean Group (AG), Latin American Integration Association (LAIA), and Association of South East Asian Nations (ASEAN). Additionally, they considered British and French colonies, EC preferences for the African, Caribbean, and Pacific developing countries under the Lome Conversion and all industrial countries' Generalized Systems of Preferences. Some of the $PREF_{ij}$ dummy variables were not statistically significant. Concentrating on the sample of variables in the table one should note that they also found a significant impact of *EU* dummy variables on foreign trade, with the coefficient of 0.70. The dummy *EFTA* variable was insignificant.

The BALDWIN (1993) gravity model, which rearranges the WANG/WINTERS equation, makes it comparable to the GROS/DAUTREBANDE equation. In the WANG/WINTERS equation, per capita output has the expected sign for both countries, whereas in the case of GROS/DAUTREBANDE, the output per capita variable for country j has a negative sign and insignificant t-statistic.

HOLZMANN/ZUKOWSKA-GAGELMANN (1998) used the seemingly unrelated regression method (SUR) along with the OLS procedure. Since OLS estimation provided different income elasticities and the wrong sign for one *MU*-variable, they regard the OLS procedure as inappropriate for the estimation of their gravity model. They re-estimated the parameters with the SUR method. Additionally, they eliminated the population variable from the equation in order to prevent correlation with the *GDP*-variable. As a result, HOLZMANN/ ZUKOWSKA-GAGELMANN attain highly significant coefficients for the important variables with the correct sign. They re-estimated the parameters once again to improve fit, omitting all insignificant variables (*POP*, *AREA*, *EFTA*). The variable *POP* is eliminated to escape the correlation between *POP* and *GDP*. The impact of variables *AREA* and *EFTA* on trade can be set apart. As a result they receive parameter estimates, which all have significant impact on foreign trade. The effect of income and distance variables on foreign trade is quite large, which corresponds to the results of the other studies. The variable *MU* also has a considerable effect. The *MU*-coefficients are statistically different. Thus, under valuation reduces exports, since it has a negative impact on both export supply and import demand. A lower coefficient for *MU* in comparison to GDP^p elasticities shows that the growth of nominal GDP with currency depreciation at the same time increases exports.

To summarize: What combines all the previous studies mentioned above is the sufficient and highly significant impact of the variables income and distance (which varies from 0.66 to 1.17 for income and from -0.39 to -1.05 for distance). The impact of population or income per capita according to WANG/WINTERS and BALDWIN can be close to 0.3. Additionally, HOLZMANN/ZUKOWSKA-GAGELMANN found evidence that the effect of the exchange rate on international trade is negative and close to -0.5 for MU_i and -0.3 for MU_j (see SUR/IVS). Among dummy variables the impact of the adjacency dummy and *EU* dummy should be taken into account. The impact of the adjacency dummy varies between 0.36 (HILZMANN/ZUKOWSKA-GAGELMANN) and 0.78 (WANG/ WINTERS). The *EU* variable varies between 0.17 (HOLZMANN/ZUKOWSKA-GAGELMANN) and 0.70 (WANG/WINTERS).

4.3.2 *Specification of the Gravity Model for Selected CIS and CEECs*

It is of great interest to consider trade potential for the investigated CIS and CEECs with seven blocks of countries, namely EU-15, EFTA-6, and the CEE-5[33] (the candidate countries of the first accession round), Asia (Japan, Korea), Canada and the United States, Australia and New Zealand, and Mexico.

Since the gravity model should predict trade potential between countries and represents a kind of deviation from a market economy's pattern, one should apply the coefficients from the equation for market economies to the data for the developing countries.

We suggest to assume that the most advanced transition economies have already considerably re-oriented their trade relations towards the West and hence can be taken into the gravity model together with the developed market economies (OECD countries)[34]. Some recent investigations based on the gravity model show that more advanced transition economies have already exhausted or nearly exhausted their potential in trade and FDI inflows from developed economies (see for trade GROS/GONCIARZ (1996), HOLZMANN/ZUKOWSKA/GAGEL-MANN (1998), and DOEHRN/VON WESTERNHAGEN (2001) for FDI). Therefore, the sample of OECD countries, which is usually used in the gravity model to attain coefficients for market economies, can be extended to the more advanced transition economies (CEE-5).

It is of great interest, given the growing role of the internet, to introduce the *INTERNET* variable into the gravity equation among standard variables, as it will test the influence of the internet on trade. „Distance" is an abstract subject which proxies the economic horizon of a country (WANG/WINTERS, 1992). Economic horizon includes how much the people are informed about the business conditions in other countries. Nowadays one can find a lot of business information

---

[33] CEE-5 include Czech Republic, Poland, Hungary, Slovenia and Estonia.

[34] Mexico and South Korea are excluded from the estimation because of insufficient data base.

concerning institutions, lows, business habits, and language in the internet. In an economic sense the internet considerably reduces the distance between countries. Thus, the more internet users both countries have, the more trade between two countries will take place, while countries with fewer internet users will be placed at a disadvantage.

It is also of great interest to introduce an *AGENDA* variable into the gravity equation, which will reflect the impact of the accession process on trade between candidate countries and EU member-countries. EU membership implies that accession countries will enforce market reforms, adopt their legal, political, and economic systems to EU standards, and implement *acquis communautaire*, which is supposed to sufficiently improve institutional rules and norms crucial for the functioning of a market economy (PIAZOLO, 1997). Including advanced transition countries (CEE-5) in the model would allow us to test the impact of the *AGENDA* variable on trade, since anticipated accession to the EU greatly stimulates the re-orientation of trade towards the EU.

It is of additional interest to test the impact of a *CMEA* variable, which is supposed to reflect historical ties between former *CMEA* countries, which nowadays influences business relationships between these countries. Close neighborhood, common history, and better understanding in conducting business speak in favor of further economic relations between former *CMEA* countries.

The gravity model is estimated for 1997 at the 5 per cent significance level. We consider two model specifications: one with the sample of standard variables and one with the *INTERNET* variable. Since the test of the *INTERNET* variable is a new approach and represents a topic for further research, it is worthwhile to compare the results attained with this model with the results attained with the model which includes standard variables. Additionally, the use of the *INTERNET* variable for CIS and CEECs can lead to underestimated results since the internet is not sufficiently spread in these economies. All variables except *DIST* are expected to have a positive sign.

The estimation 1 with a sample of standard variables appears as follows (see equation 4.5):

$$Ln(EX_{ij}) = CONST + \beta_1 \ln(GDP_i) + \beta_2 \ln(GDP_j) + \beta_3 \ln(GDP_i / POP_i) + \beta_4 \ln(GDP_j / POP_j) + \beta_5 \ln(DIST_{ij}) + \beta_6 EU_{ij} + \beta_7 AGENDA_{ij} + \beta_8 CMEA_{ij} + \beta_9 A_{ij} + \beta_{10} LANG_{ij} \quad (4.5)$$

where: EX_{ij} are exports from country i to coutry j, *CONST* is a constant, GDP_i is the Gross Domestic Product of country i, GDP_j is the Gross Domestic Product of country j, GDP_i/POP_i is the Gross Domestic Product per capita of county i, GDP_j/POP_j is the Gross Domestic Product per capita of country j, $DIST_{ij}$ is the distance between countries i and j, EU_{ij} is a dummy variable for EU membership (it is 1 if both countries are EU members and 0 otherwise), $AGENDA_{ij}$ is a dummy variable indicating whether or not the countries belong to the first accession round (it is 1 in the case of combination of one accession country and EU country and 0 otherwise), $CMEA_{ij}$ is a dummy variable indicating whether or not the countries belong to the former CMEA countries (it is 1 if both countries are former CMEA members and 0 otherwise), A_{ij} is an adjacency dummy variable (it is 1 if countries have a common border and 0 otherwise), and $LANG_{ij}$ is a dummy variable which indicates whether or not the countries speak the same language (it is 1 if both countries speak the same language and 0 otherwise).

Estimation 2 with the *INTERNET* variable appears as follows (see equation 4.6):

$$\begin{aligned} Ln(EX_{ij}) = CONST + \beta_1 \ln(GDP_i) + \beta_2 \ln(GDP_j) + \beta_3 \ln(INTERNET_i) + \\ \beta_4 \ln(INTERNET_j) + \beta_5 \ln(DIST_{ij}) + \beta_6 EU_{ij} + \beta_7 AGENDA_{ij} + \beta_8 CMEA_{ij} + \\ \beta_9 A_{ij} + \beta_{10} LANG_{ij} \end{aligned} \quad (4.6)$$

where: EX_{ij} are exports from country i to coutry j, *CONST* is a constant, GDP_i is the Gross Domestic Product of country i, GDP_j is the Gross Domestic Product of country j, $INTERNET_i$ is the number of internet hosts per 10,000 people in county i, $INTERNET_j$ is the number of internet hosts per 10,000 people in country j, $DIST_{ij}$ is the distance between countries i and j, EU_{ij} is a dummy variable for EU membership (it is 1 if both countries are EU members and 0 otherwise), $AGENDA_{ij}$ is a dummy variable indicating whether or not the countries belong to the first accession round (it is 1 in the case of combination of one accession country and EU country and 0 otherwise), $CMEA_{ij}$ is a dummy variable indicating whether or not the countries belong to the former CMEA countries (it is 1 if both countries are former CMEA members and 0 otherwise), A_{ij} is an adjacency dummy variable (it is 1 if countries have a common border and 0 otherwise), and $LANG_{ij}$ is a dummy variable which indicates whether or not the countries speak the same language (it is 1 if both countries speak the same language and 0 otherwise).

The variables $GDP_{i,j}$ and $GDP_{i,j}/POP_{i,j}$ are measured in billions of dollar, the variable $INTERNET_{i,j}$ is measured in internet hosts per 10,000 people, the variable $DIST_{ij}$ is measured in kilometers, the other variables are dummy variables.

It is not a good idea to introduce both *GDP per capita* and *INTERNET* variables into the same model specification since they are correlated and lead to biased coefficients. The measurement of the *INTERNET* variable could also be a subject for further research. The number of internet users could provide a more real picture about the impact of internet on trade since the intensity of internet usage depends more on the number of people which have internet access rather then on the number of internet providers. We used the data for internet hosts as a proxy since we did not have the data on internet users at our disposal.

The coefficients of both estimations are shown in Table 18. Most of them are significant and have the expected sign. The model is estimated with ordinary least squares. The R^2 in estimation 1 is 88% and R^2 in estimation 2 is 89%. Both estimations provide robust and stable results for the most important variables such as income and distance. Income and distance have the largest impact on foreign trade in both estimations and are highly significant. The elasticity of income in estimation 1 is 0.84 for country i and 0.85 for country j. The elasticity of income in estimation 2 is 0.90 for country i and 0.87 for country j. The elasticity of distance is -0.90 in estimation 1 and -0.93 in estimation 2.

Estimation 1 shows a moderate positive impact of income per capita for country i on foreign trade, while the elasticity of income per capita for country j is rather low and insignificant. This corresponds to the results obtained in other studies. The elasticity of income per capita for country i is 0.37 and 0.07 for country j. Estimation 2 provides stable results for the *INTERNET* variable, which are not sensible to the omission or conclusion of additional variables. According to estimation 2, the *INTERNET* variable has a moderate impact on trade. Both *INTERNET* variables are significant. The elasticity of the *INTERNET* variable for country i equals 0.21 and is higher than that for country j, which is 0.09. The other method of measurement of the *INTERNET* variable could lead to different results. That's why it is of interest to measure the *INTERNET* variable for a number of internet users rather than internet hosts.

Table 18: Estimates of a Gravity Model for Foreign Trade (1997)[35]*

Estimation 1		Estimation 2	
Constant	2.65	Constant	2.22
	(7.45)		(6.81)
GDP_i	0.84	GDP_i	0.90
	(37.64)		(44.27)
GDP_j	0.85	GDP_j	0.87
	(37.68)		(40.88)
GDP_i/POP_i	0.37	$INTERNET_i$	0.21
	(7.67)		(9.08)
GDP_j/POP_j	0.07	$INTERNET_j$	0.09
	(1.25)		(3.71)
$DIST_{ij}$	-0.90	$DIST_{ij}$	-0.93
	(-23.75)		(-25.21)
EU_{ij} (Dummy variable)	0.31	EU_{ij} (Dummy variable)	0.40
	(4.29)		(5.92)
$AGENDA_{ij}$ (Dummy variable)	0.26	$AGENDA_{ij}$ (Dummy variable)	0.37
	(2.19)		(3.72)
$CMEA_{ij}$ (Dummy variable)	0.84	$CMEA_{ij}$ (Dummy variable)	0.77
	(4.46)		(4.49)
A_{ij} (Dummy variable)	0.27	A_{ij} (Dummy variable)	0.29
	(2.53)		(2.91)
$LANG_{ij}$ (Dummy variable)	0.48	$LANG_{ij}$ (Dummy variable)	0.39
	(3.78)		(3.30)
R^2	0.887		0.891
R^2 adj.	0.886		0.890
number of observations	756		756

**In brackets: t-statistics*

The impact of other variables is relatively close in both estimations, but there are still some differences. The impact of the *EU* variable is larger in estimation 2 and equals 0.40 rather than the 0.31 in estimation 1. The impact of the *AGENDA* variable is also higher in estimation 2. The elasticity of the *AGENDA* variable is

[35] In Table 18 t-statistics are corrected for white heteroskedasticity.

0.37 in estimation 2 and 0.26 in estimation 1. Both estimations provide very close results for the adjacency variable. The elasticities are 0.28 according to estimation 1 and 0.29 according to estimation 2. The impact of the *CMEA* and *LANG* variables tends to be higher in estimation 1 and is equal to 0.84 (0.77 - estimation 2) for the *CMEA* variable and 0.48 (0.39 - estimation 2) for the *LANG* variable.

4.3.3 Gravity Model Results for Selected CIS and CEECs

The gravity model results for 1997 for more advanced transition economies (Hungary and Poland) are represented in Table 19 and Table 20, respectively. The gravity model results for three CIS countries, Russia, the Ukraine, and Belarus are represented in Table 21, Table 22, Table 23, respectively. The Tables are structured in such a way as to show the trade pattern of a particular country with seven blocks of countries such as: EU-15, EFTA-6, CEE-5, Canada and the United States, Asia (Japan and Korea), Australia and New Zealand, and the Western Hemisphere (Mexico). The Tables compare actual trade flows with estimated according to both estimation 1 and estimation 2. A country has a potential in trade with another country or a group of countries if the estimated trade flows exceeds the actual. The gravity model provides not only evidence on potential trade volume in absolute terms, but also under market conditions („optimal" distribution of trade flows), which is reflected in the tables, where percent from OECD whole trade is calculated for each group of countries under actual and potential conditions.

For further research on the gravity model one should apply confidence intervals in order to judge about the precision of estimation. The problem of confidence intervals is known in the theoretical and empirical literature (BREUSS/EGGER, 1999; GROS/DAUTREBANDE, 1992; HAMILTON/WINTERS, 1992; DOEHRN, 2000; GREENE, 2000). There are different opinions on this problem. Thus e.g. BREUSS/EGGER (1999) obtained rather large confidence intervals for their gravity model which did not allow for plausible conclusions about the absolute trade potentials. Additionally, the estimation results of BREUSS/EGGER were highly sensitive with respect to dummy variables. Thus the change in dummy variable could shift potential exports over actual. The problem is that in the gravity model we deal with cross-sectional and not with time series data. The data in the gravity model varies very much from the center of the data. It is so far important, since the width of the confidence interval depends on the distance of the observations from the center of the data (GREENE, 2000). The large variance in the data used in the gravity model leads to the large confidence intervals and it becomes difficult to judge about the estimated results with the help of the confidence intervals. Moreover, this study represents also relative distribution of predicted exports over the main groups of OECD countries (as a percentage of total OECD trade). The relative distribution additional to absolute values allows it to better judge about the existing potential in trade. The main goal of this study was to receive plausible estimates on the potential trade flows for the investigated

CIS and CEECs which provide for approximation of the real situation and allow for consequent policy options.

Starting with more advanced transition economies, one could say Hungary has already exhausted it's potential in trade with the EU-15 group of countries. It's potential trade flows account for $6,097 mill. or $7,746 mill. according to estimation 1 and 2, respectively. Actual trade flows ($13,604) exceed potential on 123% (estimation 1) or 76% (estimation 2), respectively. This result is, however, not surprising since Hungary has already to a large extent liberalized and reoriented it's foreign trade towards the EU. Additionally, one should not forget that Hungary is a country which attained the most FDI among all transition economies, which could also lead to the increased export flows. Therefore, the goal to enter the EU on the one hand, and ample FDI inflows on the other, spurred considerable trade flows towards the EU, but there is still some potential in trade with particular EU countries. There is, for example, potential in trade with Denmark, Finland (only according to estimation 2), France, Greece, Portugal, Sweden, and the United Kingdom (only according to estimation 2).

There is also no potential in trade with the EFTA-6 group of countries since actual trade flows ($2,695 mill.) exceed the estimated ($1,394 mill. for estimation 1 and $1,814 mill. for estimation 2) on 93% or 49%, respectively. This potential is mostly exhausted according to trade with Austria. Therefore, there is still considerable potential in trade with other EFTA-6 countries. There is potential in trade with Finland (only according to estimation 2), Iceland, Norway, Sweden, and Switzerland (only according to estimation 2).

Hungary's trade with the CEE-4 also lies above the potential values, as a group and concerning particular countries. Actual trade flows ($1,136 mill.) exceed predicted values on 83% or 77%, respectively.

Table 19: Gravity Model Results for Hungary*

Country i	Country j	Exij actual ($ mill.)	Exij est. 1 ($ mill.)	Exij est. 2 ($ mill.)	% of OECD		% actual from potential	
					act.	est.[1]	est. 1	est. 2
Hungary	**EU-15**	13,604	6,097	7,746	86	76	223	176
	Austria	2,188	875	1,152				
	Belgium-Luxembourg	473	196	255				
	Denmark	71	**143**	**189**				
	Finland	92	77	**112**				
	France	719	**737**	**879**				
	Germany	7,107	1,777	2,311				
	Greece	81	**96**	**107**				
	Ireland	68	40	48				
	Italy	1,176	920	1,089				
	The Netherlands	537	249	336				
	Portugal	19	**39**	**42**				
	Spain	287	206	239				
	Sweden	147	**150**	**206**				
	United Kingdom	639	591	**781**				
Hungary	**EFTA-6**	2,695	1,394	1,814	17	18	193	149
	Austria	2,188	875	1,152				
	Finland	92	77	**112**				
	Iceland	2	**3**	**3**				
	Norway	37	**76**	**94**				
	Sweden	147	**150**	**206**				
	Switzerland	229	213	**246**				
Hungary	**CEE-4**	1,136	620	641	7	8	183	177
	Czech Republic	322	186	201				
	Estonia	13	8	8				
	Poland	510	313	307				
	Slovenia	291	112	124				
Hungary	**Canada+ United States**	656	565	**713**	4	7	116	92
	Canada	37	**60**	**71**				
	United States	619	505	**642**				

Table 19: Gravity Model Results for Hungary* (cont.)

Country i	Country j	Exij actual ($ mill.)	Exij est. 1 ($ mill.)	Exij est. 2 ($ mill.)	% of OECD		% actual from potential	
					act.	est.[1]	est. 1	est. 2
Hungary	**Asia**	132	**288**	**302**	0.8	4	46	44
	Japan	101	**251**	**265**				
	Korea	31	**37**	**38**				
Hungary	**Australia+ New Zealand**	23	23	**28**	0.1	0.3	99	83
	Australia New Zealand	21 2	19 **4**	**23** **4**				
Hungary	**Western Hemisphere (Mexico)**	5	**22**	**20**	0.03	0.3	23	26
Hungary	**OECD[2]**	15,907	7,986	9,869	100	100	199	161

Source: IMF (1998), Directions of Trade Statistics Yearbook 1998; own calculations

* *Potential is marked fat*

[1] *Est. is based on est. 1 since both est. 1 and est. 2 provide for similar results*

[2] *OECD includes additionally to 29 countries also Slovenia and Estonia. OECD includes also Turkey*

Table 20: Gravity Model Results for Poland*

Country i	Country j	Exij actual ($ mill.)	Exij est. 1 ($ mill.)	Exij est. 2 ($ mill.)	% of OECD		% actual from potential	
					act.	est.[1]	est. 1	est. 2
Poland	**EU-15**	16,535	15,094	**18,362**	85	80	110	90
	Austria	479	**667**	**789**				
	Belgium-Luxembourg	563	445	542				
	Denmark	757	494	620				
	Finland	332	284	**392**				
	France	1,139	**1,570**	**1,754**				
	Germany	8484	7,003	**8,783**				
	Greece	99	**157**	**162**				
	Ireland	71	**95**	**109**				
	Italy	1,515	1,339	1,468				
	The Netherlands	1,203	606	767				
	Portugal	28	**81**	**83**				
	Spain	287	**416**	**450**				
	Sweden	610	563	**733**				
	United Kingdom	968	**1,376**	**1,709**				
Poland	**EFTA-6**	1,818	**2,154**	**2,628**	9	11	84	69
	Austria	479	**667**	**789**				
	Finland	332	284	**392**				
	Iceland	5	**7**	**8**				
	Norway	217	**246**	**286**				
	Sweden	610	**563**	**733**				
	Switzerland	175	**388**	**419**				
Poland	**CEE-4**	1,399	901	909	7	5	155	154
	Czech Republic	912	487	501				
	Estonia	55	31	30				
	Hungary	383	286	282				
	Slovenia	49	**96**	**96**				
Poland	**Canada+ United States**	762	**1,336**	**1,584**	4	7	57	48
	Canada	85	**143**	**158**				
	United States	677	**1,193**	**1,426**				

Table 20: Gravity Model Results for Poland* (cont.)

Country i	Country j	Exij actual ($ mill.)	Exij est. 1 ($ mill.)	Exij est. 2 ($ mill.)	% of OECD		% actual from potential	
					act.	est.[1]	est. 1	est. 2
Poland	**Asia**	153	**699**	**690**	0.8	4	22	22
	Japan	58	**609**	**604**				
	Korea	95	90	86				
Poland	**Australia+ New Zealand**	27	**54**	**61**	0.1	0.3	50	44
	Australia	20	**45**	**51**				
	New Zealand	7	**9**	**10**				
Poland	**Western Hemisphere (Mexico)**	15	**51**	**43**	0.1	0.3	29	35
Poland	**OECD[2]**	19,348	18,931	**22,498**	100	100	102	86

Source: IMF (1998), Directions of Trade Statistics Yearbook 1998; own calculations

* *Potential is marked fat*

[1] *Est. is based on est. 1 since both est. 1 and est. 2 provide for similar results*

[2] *OECD includes additionally to 29 countries also Slovenia and Estonia. OECD includes also Turkey*

On the other hand, according to estimation 2, Hungary has potential in trade with Canada and the United States, where actual trade accounts for 92% of potential. Estimation 1, on the other hand, only shows potential in trade with Canada. Hungary has a considerable potential in trade with both Japan and Korea. It's actual trade with Asian countries only accounts for 46% or 44% from potential, according to estimation 1 and estimation 2, respectively. There is some potential in trade with Australia and New Zealand. Actual trade values account for 99% or 83% of the potential value, according to estimation 1 and 2, respectively. There is much potential in trade with Mexico (the actual value is only 23% or 26% of the potential one).

If we judge about the trade of Hungary with OECD countries then these estimations show that potential in trade with OECD group of countries is already exhausted and is 99% (estimation 1) or 61% (estimation 2) higher than the actual trade flows. But on the other hand, the trade distribution pattern among OECD countries shows that Hungary's actual trade is already redistributed too much towards the EU-15 (10% more than predicted by the gravity model) in detriment to other groups of countries. Hungary's trade with the EFTA-6 as a percentage of OECD trade corresponds to the share predicted by the gravity model. (18%). One could call the trade share between the CEE-5 and Hungary close to „normal" (7%-

actual; 8%-potential), but there is a considerable catching up needed in trade with Canada and the United States (4%-actual; 7%-potential), Asian countries (0,8%-actual; 4% potential), Australia and New Zealand (0,1%-actual; 0,3%-potential), and Mexico (0,03%-actual; 0,3%-potential).

Poland's trade potential with the EU-15 is close to the actual value according to estimation 1 and is higher than that according to estimation 2. The predicted value according to estimation 1 is $15,094 mill., 10% lower than the actual value of $16,535 mill., but the actual trade value is 90% of the potential $18,362 mill. according to estimation 2. Thus, the results for Poland point to more potential in trade with the EU than for Hungary. One should mention that Poland represents a much larger market and hence is more attractive for trade than Hungary. Poland shows trade potential with a number of EU countries. There is potential in trade with Austria, Finland (only according to estimation 2), France, Germany and Greece (only according to estimation 2), Ireland, Portugal, Spain, Sweden (only according to estimation 2), and the United Kingdom.

Poland also has trade potential with the EFTA-6 group of countries. This potential is $2,154 mill. according to estimation 1 and $2,628 mill. according to estimation 2. The actual trade value amounts to $1,818 mill. and is 84% or 69% of estimated values, respectively. According to estimation 2 there is potential for Poland in trade with all EFTA-6 countries. Finland and Sweden represent exceptions according to estimation 1.

On the other hand, Poland still trades more with CEE-4 countries than the gravity model predicts. The actual trade value is 55% or 54% higher than the potential value for this group of countries. There is only trade potential in the case of Slovenia.

Poland has much potential in trade with Canada and the United States. Actual trade with this group of countries accounts for only 57% or 48% of the potential values according to estimation 1 and 2, respectively. Poland also shows considerable potential in trade with Asian countries, mostly with Japan. Unrealized potential in trade with Japan is about 90%. A large lag can also be observed in trade with Australia and New Zealand. Actual trade with this group of countries accounts for 50% or 44% from potential, respectively. Trade with Mexico follows the same path. Potential in trade with Mexico accounts for about 70% or 65%.

Polish trade with OECD countries is close to the actual value according to estimation 1 and shows some potential according to estimation 2. According to the trade distribution pattern among OECD countries, Poland has redistributed its trade, as Hungary, to a large extent towards the EU. The actual trade with the EU is larger than predicted by the gravity model's distribution pattern (85%-actual; 80%-potential). Poland's trade with EFTA-6 countries has instead some space to grow (9%-actual; 11%-potential). The estimations show that Poland still relies much on its former relations with CEE-4 countries. Its trade share with the CEE-4 as a % of the OECD total is still larger than predicted by the gravity model (7%-

actual; 5%-potential). Poland requires considerable catching up in trade with other groups of countries. Thus, actual trade for Poland with Canada and the United States accounts for 4% against a potential 7%; actual trade with Asia accounts for 0.8% of the OECD total and potential trade is 4%; for Australia and New Zealand and Mexico, 0.1% and 0.3%, respectively.

Russia's trade with the EU exceeds its potential. The actual value, which is \$28,000 mill., exceeds the potential, which is \$13,393 mill. (estimation 1) or \$13,946 (estimation 2) on 109% and 101%, respectively. The actual values for Russia generally look very high. Since Russia is the largest oil exporter it might be that oil prices very much influence the values of Russian exports in dollars. So as world oil prices went up during the last years (the gravity model does not account for this aspect), potential values tend to be much lower than actual ones. Still, Russia shows some potential in trade with Denmark, France, Greece, and Portugal (according to both estimations).

Russia's trade with EFTA-6 group also exceeds its potential. The actual trade value of \$8,431 mill. for this group of countries exceeds the predicted value of \$3,036 mill. or \$3,423 mill. on 178% or 146%, respectively. There is some potential in trade with Iceland and Norway.

Russia's actual trade with the CEE-5 is also much higher than the predicted values. This shows that historical ties are still very strong for Russia. The actual trade of \$6,435 mill. is 194% or 218% higher than the predicted values, \$2,187 mill. or \$2,025 mill, respectively.

There is much potential in trade with Canada, which remains unrealized for unclear reasons. Russia exceeds potential trade with Asia as well. Russia has a considerable potential in trade with Australia and New Zealand, which is close to 90%. There is some potential in trade with Mexico. Actual trade values for Mexico account for 64% or 78% of potential ones according to estimation 1 and 2, respectively.

Russia does not show any undeveloped potential in trade with the OECD group of countries. The actual trade value with OECD countries is twice as large as the predicted one. It is general very difficult to judge the estimation results since oil prices can considerably influence the dollar value of Russian exports. A trade distribution pattern could really help to analyze the situation with Russia. According to the predicted distribution pattern Russia still has some room for trade with the EU (57%-actual; 60%-potential). On the other hand, it trades with the EFTA-6 rather too much, (17%-actual; 14%-potential). It's trade with CEE-5 is still larger as it should be according to „normal" distribution (13%-actual; 10%-potential). The trade sample with Asian countries is close to the „normal" (8%-actual; 9%-potential). Catching up in trade is needed with Canada and the United States (10%-actual; 14%-potential), Australia and New Zealand (0.03-actual; 0.7-potential), and Mexico (0.2-actual; 0.6-potential).

The Ukraine's actual trade with the EU-15 group of countries equals \$2,135 mill. and is 43% or 24% higher than the predicted value which is \$1,495 mill. or \$1,722 mill. according to estimation 1 and estimation 2, respectively. There is trade potential among the EU-15 with Finland, France, Ireland, Sweden, and the United Kingdom (according to both estimations).

The Ukraine shows potential in trade with most EFTA-6 countries. Actual trade with the EFTA-6 is $228 mill. and accounts for 81% or 67% of the potential value, which is $280 mill. or $341 mill. according to estimation 1 and estimation 2, respectively. There is trade potential with 5 EFTA countries: Finland, Iceland, Norway, Sweden, and Switzerland (according to both estimations).

Ukraine's trade with the CEE-5 group of countries considerably exceeds the predicted value. Actual trade is 125% or 116% more than predicted trade, which is $318 mill. or $331 mill. according to estimation 1 and estimation 2, respectively. There is some potential in trade among the CEE-5 countries with the Czech Republic and Slovenia.

There is some potential in trade with Canada, although the potential in trade with the United States is exhausted. The Ukraine's potential in trade with Asia (both Japan and Korea) is far from being exhausted. The actual trade value equals $129 mill. and accounts for 76% or 71% of the predicted value, which is $170 mill. according to estimation 1 and $183 mill. according to estimation 2. There is large potential in trade with Australia and New Zealand, as well as with Mexico. The potential in trade with Australia and New Zealand is right about 85% and 90% in the case of Mexico.

In trade with the OECD group of countries the Ukraine shows no undeveloped potential. Its actual trade, which is $4,321 mill., exceeds the potential by 76% or 54%, which is $2,448 mill. or $2,804 mill. according to estimation 1 and estimation 2, respectively. Nevertheless, the actual distribution of trade flows does not correspond to the potential or „normal" distribution. Thus, in trade with the EU-15, the Ukraine could move from 49% to 61% of total OECD trade. It also has a large gap in trade with the EFTA-6 and could move from 5% to 11%. On the other hand, the share of trade with the CEE-5 is still larger than „normally" necessary and represents 17% instead of 13%. There is a large lag in trade with other groups of countries. The share of trade with Canada and the United States should be 12% instead of 10%. The share of trade with Asia in total OECD trade should be 7% instead of 3%. In trade with Australia and New Zealand the level is defined as 0.5% instead of the actual 0.05%. And in trade with Mexico the potential level is defined by 0.5% opposed to 0.02%.

Table 21: Gravity Model Results for Russia*

Country i	Country j	Exij actual ($ mill.)	Exij est. 1 ($ mill.)	Exij est. 2 ($ mill.)	% of OECD		% actual from potential	
					act.	est.[1]	est. 1	est. 2
Russia	**EU-15**	28,000	13,393	13,946	57	60	209	201
	Austria	735	509	518				
	Belgium-Luxembourg	859	481	509				
	Denmark	167	443	480				
	Finland	2,774	711	884				
	France	1,626	**1,805**	**1,753**				
	Germany	6,531	3,802	4,006				
	Greece	202	**232**	**210**				
	Ireland	2,500	127	127				
	Italy	3,564	1,575	1,502				
	The Netherlands	4,554	646	710				
	Portugal	27	**116**	**104**				
	Spain	630	569	537				
	Sweden	985	728	828				
	United Kingdom	2,846	1,648	1,780				
Russia	**EFTA-6**	8,431	3,036	3,423	17	14	278	246
	Austria	735	509	518				
	Finland	2,774	711	884				
	Iceland	13	**16**	**18**				
	Norway	192	**538**	**620**				
	Sweden	985	728	828				
	Switzerland	3,732	534	557				
Russia	**CEE-5**	6,435	2,187	2,025	13	10	294	318
	Czech Republic	1,823	341	328				
	Estonia	553	96	93				
	Hungary	1,417	301	283				
	Poland	2,514	1,330	1,206				
	Slovenia	128	119	114				
Russia	**Canada+ United States**	5,086	3,141	3,646	10	14	162	140
	Canada	135	**335**	**365**				
	United States	4,951	2,805	3,281				

Table 21: Gravity Model Results for Russia* (cont.)

Country i	Country j	Exij actual ($ mill.)	Exij est. 1 ($ mill.)	Exij est. 2 ($ mill.)	% of OECD		% actual from potential	
					act.	est.[1]	est. 1	est. 2
Russia	**Asia**	3,772	2,013	1,955	8	9	187	193
	Japan	2,935	1,750	1,707				
	Korea	837	263	248				
Russia	**Australia+ New Zealand**	15	**146**	**163**	0.03	0.7	10	9
	Australia	6	**123**	**137**				
	New Zealand	9	**23**	**26**				
Russia	**Western Hemisphere (Mexico)**	80	**125**	**103**	0.2	0.6	64	78
Russia	**OECD[2]**	49,308	22,463	23,350	100	100	220	211

Source: IMF (1998), Directions of Trade Statistics Yearbook 1998; own calculations

** Potential is marked fat*

[1] Est. is based on est. 1 since both est. 1 and est. 2 provide for similar results

[2] OECD includes additionally to 29 countries also Slovenia and Estonia. OECD includes also Turkey

Table 22: Gravity Model Results for Ukraine*

Country i	Country j	Exij actual ($ mill.)	Exij est. 1 ($ mill.)	Exij est. 2 ($ mill.)	% of OECD		% actual from potential	
					act.	est.[1]	est. 1	est. 2
Ukraine	**EU-15**	2,135	1,495	1,722	49	61	143	124
	Austria	154	71	81				
	Belgium-Luxembourg	72	53	63				
	Denmark	67	47	57				
	Finland	10	**41**	**54**				
	France	124	**200**	**217**				
	Germany	589	455	536				
	Greece	240	31	31				
	Ireland	1	**13**	**14**				
	Italy	547	199	212				
	The Netherlands	121	71	86				
	Portugal	26	12	12				
	Spain	121	62	65				
	Sweden	5	**65**	**82**				
	United Kingdom	58	**175**	**211**				
Ukraine	**EFTA-6**	228	**280**	**341**	5	11	81	67
	Austria	154	71	81				
	Finland	10	**41**	**54**				
	Iceland	1**	**1**	**2**				
	Norway	37	**38**	**48**				
	Sweden	5	**65**	**82**				
	Switzerland	21	**63**	**74**				
Ukraine	**CEE-5**	716	318	331	17	13	225	216
	Czech Republic	1**	**44**	**48**				
	Estonia	69	6	6				
	Hungary	259	60	65				
	Poland	378	191	195				
	Slovenia	9	**16**	**17**				
Ukraine	**Canada+ United States**	446	288	371	10	12	155	120
	Canada	19	**31**	**37**				
	United States	427	258	334				

Table 22: Gravity Model Results for Ukraine* (cont.)

Country i	Country j	Exij actual ($ mill.)	Exij est. 1 ($ mill.)	Exij est. 2 ($ mill.)	% of OECD		% actual from potential	
					act.	est.[1]	est. 1	est. 2
Ukraine	**Asia**	129	**170**	**183**	3	7	76	71
	Japan	128	**148**	**160**				
	Korea	1**	**22**	**23**				
Ukraine	**Australia+ New Zealand**	2	**13**	**16**	0.05	0.5	15	12
	Australia	1	**11**	**14**				
	New Zealand	1	**2**	**3**				
Ukraine	**Western Hemisphere (Mexico)**	1**	**11**	**10**	0.02	0.5	9	10
Ukraine	**OECD[2]**	4,321	2,448	2,804	100	100	176	154

Source: IMF (1998), Directions of Trade Statistics Yearbook 1998; own calculations

** Potential is marked fat*

*** There was no available data. The absent data was assumed to be $1 mill.*

[1] Est. is based on est. 1 since both est. 1 and est. 2 provide for similar results

[2] OECD includes additionally to 29 countries also Slovenia and Estonia. OECD includes also Turkey

Table 23: Gravity Model Results for Belarus*

Country i	Country j	Exij actual ($ mill.)	Exij est. 1 ($ mill.)	Exij est. 2 ($ mill.)	% of OECD		% actual from potential	
					act.	est.[1]	est. 1	est. 2
Belarus	**EU-15**	497	**1,379**	**786**	50	62	36	63
	Austria	16	**60**	**33**				
	Belgium-Luxembourg	24	**48**	**28**				
	Denmark	16	**50**	**30**				
	Finland	4	**49**	**33**				
	France	20	**176**	**94**				
	Germany	217	**449**	**260**				
	Greece	2	**21**	**10**				
	Ireland	1	**12**	**6**				
	Italy	64	**154**	**81**				
	The Netherlands	83	65	39				
	Portugal	1**	**10**	**5**				
	Spain	7	**51**	**26**				
	Sweden	6	**76**	**47**				
	United Kingdom	36	**158**	**93**				
Belarus	**EFTA-6**	73	**280**	**170**	7	13	26	43
	Austria	16	**60**	**33**				
	Finland	4	**49**	**33**				
	Iceland	1**	1	1				
	Norway	24	**40**	**25**				
	Sweden	6	**76**	**48**				
	Switzerland	22	**54**	**31**				
Belarus	**CEE-5**	329	319	163	33	14	103	202
	Czech Republic	27	**40**	21				
	Estonia	16	7	4				
	Hungary	39	36	18				
	Poland	245	223	112				
	Slovenia	2	**13**	**7**				
Belarus	**Canada+ United States**	97	**242**	**153**	10	11	40	63
	Canada	4	**26**	**15**				
	United States	93	**217**	**138**				

Table 23: Gravity Model Results for Belarus* (cont.)

Country i	Country j	Exij actual ($ mill.)	Exij est. 1 ($ mill.)	Exij est. 2 ($ mill.)	% of OECD		% actual from potential	
					act.	est.[1]	est. 1	est. 2
Belarus	**Asia**	24	**138**	**72**	2	6	17	33
	Japan	8	**120**	**63**				
	Korea	16	**18**	**9**				
Belarus	**Australia+ New Zealand**	2	**10**	**6**	0.2	0.5	19	32
	Australia	1	**9**	**5**				
	New Zealand	1**	**2**	**1**				
Belarus	**Western Hemisphere (Mexico)**	2	**9**	**4**	0.2	0.4	21	47
Belarus	**OECD**[2]	999	**2,223**	**1,255**	100	100	45	80

Source: IMF (1998), Directions of Trade Statistics Yearbook 1998; own calculations

** Potential is marked fat*

*** There was no available data. The absent data was assumed to be $1 mill.*

[1] *Est. is based on est. 1 since both est. 1 and est. 2 provide for similar results*

[2] *OECD includes additionally to 29 countries also Slovenia and Estonia. OECD includes also Turkey*

Belarus is the only country which exhibits considerable trade potential with almost all groups of OECD countries except the CEE-5. This shows that Belarus continues to trade with it's former trade partners and did not open up and liberalize it's trade to other OECD countries.

Belarus has a large potential in trade with the EU-15 group of countries. It's actual value, which is $497 mill., accounts for only 36% or 63%, which corresponds to a potential trade value of $1,379 mill. or $786 mill., according to estimation 1 and estimation 2, respectively. Belarus exhibits trade potential with all EU-15 countries except the Netherlands.

The same is true for the case of EFTA-6 countries. In trade with the EFTA, the actual trade value accounts for only 26% or 43% of the potential one according to estimation 1 and 2, respectively. The actual value is $73 mill. and the predicted is 280 $mill. or 170 mill., respectively. There is a large trade lag with all EFTA-6 countries.

Belarus concentrates predominately on the trade with the CEE-5 countries among OECD countries. The trade with the CEE-5 equals $329 mill. and is 3% or 102% larger than potential. Among this group of countries there is potential in trade with the Czech Republic and Slovenia.

Belarus has considerable trade lag with Canada and the United States. Actual trade with this group of countries equals $97 mill., which is 40% or 63% of the potential value, equal to $242 mill. or $153 mill. according to estimation 1 and estimation 2. There is a large trade potential in trade with Asian countries (especially Japan). The actual trade value with Asian countries accounts for 17% or 33% of the predicted one. Also considerable is potential with Australia and New Zealand and equals about 80% or 70%. There is a large lag in trade with Mexico, where an actual trade value of $2 mill. accounts for 21% or 47% of the potential value of $9 mill. or $4 mill. respectively.

In OECD trade Belarus still has an ample potential. The actual trade value of $999 mill. accounts for 45% or 80% of the potential value of $2,223 mill. or $1,255 mill. according to estimation 1 and estimation 2, respectively. The actual foreign trade of Belarus is still to a large extent redistributed towards trade with CEE-5 countries (33%-actual, 14%-potential). On the other hand, there is a lag in trade with the EU-15, where actual trade could be 12% more redistributed towards the EU-15. There is also space to catch up in the EFTA, from 7% to 13%. It could be, according to the trade distribution pattern, 4% more redistributed towards Asian countries, 1% towards Canada and the United States, 0.3% towards Australia and New Zealand, and 0.2% towards Mexico.

Table 24 and Table 25 represent trade potential according to three scenarios. They are the *no change scenario*, *scenario 2007 I,* and *scenario 2007 II.* These scenarios show how trade potential changes under the assumption that the investigated countries would catch up with OECD countries in terms of GDP. The *no change scenario* is the scenario without catching up, which shows potential for the year 1997 and deals as a clue for further scenarios. *Scenario 2007 I* assumes that countries would exhibit a catching up process during the next 10 years with GDP growth of 2 percentage points above the OECD average, which for 1997 equals 3.7%. *Scenario 2007 II* assumes that countries would grow 4% above the OECD average for the next 10 years.

Table 24: Deviation of Actual Trade Flows from Potential for Hungary and Poland*

	EU-15	EFTA-6	CEE-4	Ca+ US	Asia	Au +NZ	Western Hemisph. (Mexico)	OECD
Hungary observed in 1997 ($ mill.)	13,604	2,695	1,136	656	132	23	5	15,907
no change								
Estimation 1 ($ mill.)	6,097	1,394	620	565	288	23	22	7,986
Estimation 2 ($ mill.)	7,746	1,814	641	713	302	28	20	9,869
Act. from pot. %, (est. 1)	*223%*	*193%*	*183%*	*116%*	*46%*	*99%*	*23%*	*199%*
Act. from pot. %, (est. 2)	*176%*	*149%*	*177%*	*92%*	*44%*	*83%*	*26%*	*161%*
2007 I								
Estimation 1 ($ mill.)	11,916	2,725	1,211	1,104	563	45	43	15,608
Estimation 2 ($ mill.)	12,782	2,994	1,057	1,177	499	46	32	16,284
Act. from pot. %, (est. 1)	*114%*	*99%*	*94%*	*59%*	*23%*	*51%*	*12%*	*102%*
Act. from pot. %, (est. 2)	*106%*	*90%*	*107%*	*56%*	*26%*	*50%*	*15%*	*98%*
2007 II								
Estimation 1 ($ mill.)	14,946	3,418	1,519	1,385	706	57	54	19,578
Estimation 2 ($ mill.)	15,140	3,546	1,252	1,394	591	54	38	19,289
Act. from pot. %, (est. 1)	*79%*	*92%*	*75%*	*47%*	*19%*	*41%*	*9%*	*81%*
Act. from pot. %, (est. 2)	*76%*	*90%*	*91%*	*47%*	*22%*	*42%*	*13%*	*82%*

Table 24: Deviation of Actual Trade Flows from Potential for Hungary and Poland (cont.)*

	EU-15	EFTA-6	CEE-4	Ca+ US	Asia	Au +NZ	Western Hemisph. (Mexico)	OECD
Poland								
observed 1997 ($ mill.)	16,535	1,818	1,399	762	153	27	15	19,348
no change								
Estimation 1 ($ mill.)	15,094	2,154	901	1,336	699	54	51	18,931
Estimation 2 ($ mill.)	18,362	2,628	909	1,584	690	61	43	22,498
Act. from pot. %, (est. 1)	*110%*	*84%*	*155%*	*57%*	*22%*	*50%*	*29%*	*102%*
Act. from pot. %, (est. 2)	*90%*	*69%*	*154%*	*48%*	*22%*	*44%*	*35%*	*86%*
2007 I								
Estimation 1 ($ mill.)	29,501	4,210	1,761	2,611	1,366	105	101	37,000
Estimation 2 ($ mill.)	30,298	4,337	1,500	2,614	1,138	101	71	37,123
Act. from pot. %, (est. 1)	*56%*	*43%*	*79%*	*29%*	*11%*	*26%*	*15%*	*52%*
Act. from pot. %, (est. 2)	*55%*	*42%*	*93%*	*29%*	*13%*	*27%*	*21%*	*52%*
2007 II								
Estimation 1 ($ mill.)	37,004	5,281	2,208	3,275	1,714	132	126	46,409
Estimation 2 ($ mill.)	35,888	5,137	1,777	3,096	1,348	119	84	43,973
Act. from pot. %, (est. 1)	*45%*	*34%*	*63%*	*23%*	*9%*	*20%*	*12%*	*42%*
Act. from pot. %, (est. 2)	*46%*	*35%*	*79%*	*25%*	*11%*	*23%*	*18%*	*44%*

**Ca+US means Canada + United States and Au + NZ means Australia and New Zealand*

Hungary will only reach trade potential with the EU-15 if it grows according to *scenario 2007 II*. The potential trade value in this case will equal $14,946 mill. or $15,140 mill. according to estimation 1 and estimation 2, respectively. It has some potential in trade with EFTA-6 countries in the case of *scenario 2007 I* and *2007 II*. The potential value will reach $2,725 mill. or $2,994 mill. according to estimation 1 and estimation 2 in *scenario 2007 I* and, in *scenario 2007 II* $3,418 mill. and $3,546 mill., respectively. Potential trade with CEE-4 countries can be reached according to *scenario 2007 I* according to estimation 1 and according to *scenario 2007 II* according to both estimations. This potential varies from $1,211 mill. to $1,519 mill. There is potential in trade with Canada and the United States according to estimation 2 in *no change scenario,* which becomes larger in both scenarios and reaches the value of $1,394 mill. The potential will also increase with other groups of countries. It reaches the value of $706 mill. for Asia, $57 mill. for Australia and New Zealand, and $54 mill. for Mexico. Hungary has potential in trade with the OECD group of countries according to estimation 2 in *scenario 2007 I,* and according to both estimations in *scenario 2007 II.* The potential can increase to $19,578 mill.

Poland already exhibits trade potential with the EU-15 in the *no change scenario* according to estimation 2. This potential increases in the following scenarios and can reach the value of $37,004 mill. Poland also has some potential in trade with the EFTA-6 in the *no change scenario.* This potential can reach the value of $5,281 mill. with the catching up process. Poland shows some potential in *scenario 2007 I* and *scenario 2007 II* in trade with the CEE-4 group of countries. The potential can reach the maximum value of $2,208 mill. All scenarios point to a considerable potential in trade with other groups of countries which increases with the catching up process. The potential increases to $3,275 mill. in trade with Canada and the United States, to $1,714 mill. in trade with Asia, to $132 mill. in trade with Australia and New Zealand, and to $126 mill. in trade with Mexico. Poland already shows some potential in trade with OECD countries in the *no change scenario* according to estimation 2. This potential increases further to $46,409 mill.

Russia only shows some potential in trade with the EU-15 in scenario 2007 II according to estimation one. The potential equals $32,834 mill. Russia shows no potential in trade with EFTA-6 and CEE-5 countries in all scenarios. This speaks in favor of the assumption that Russia has a strong surplus in trade with EFTA-6 countries on the one hand, and relies too much on trade with the CEE-5 on the other. There is some potential in trade with Canada and the United States in *scenario 2007 I* and *scenario 2007 II.* This potential can increase to $7,699 mill. Estimation results point to some potential in trade with Asia in *scenario 2007 I* according to estimation 1 and in *scenario 2007 II* according to both estimations. This potential can reach $4,935 mill. Russia has a considerable potential in trade with Australia and New Zealand, as well as Mexico according to the *no change scenario.* Trade potential with Australia and New Zealand can reach $359 mill., and $306 mill. with Mexico. Russia's trade with the OECD total only shows some potential in scenario 2007 II according to estimation 1, which equals $55,069 mill.

Table 25: Deviation of Actual Trade Flows from Potential for CIS Countries*

	EU-15	EFTA-6	CEE-4	Ca+ US	Asia	Au +NZ	Western Hemisph. (Mexico)	OECD
Russia								
observed 1997 ($ mill.)	28,000	8,431	6,435	5,086	3,772	15	80	49,308
no change								
Estimation 1 ($ mill.)	13,393	3,036	2,187	3,141	2,013	146	125	22,463
Estimation 2 ($ mill.)	13,946	3,423	2,025	3,646	1,955	163	103	23,350
Act. from pot. %, (est. 1)	*209%*	*278%*	*294%*	*162%*	*187%*	*10%*	*64%*	*220%*
Act. from pot. %, (est. 2)	*201%*	*246%*	*318%*	*140%*	*193%*	*9%*	*78%*	*211%*
2007 I								
Estimation 1 ($ mill.)	26,176	5,934	4,275	6,138	3,935	286	244	43,904
Estimation 2 ($ mill.)	23,011	5,648	3,342	6,016	3,226	268	170	38,528
Act. from pot. %, (est. 1)	*107%*	*142%*	*151%*	*83%*	*96%*	*5%*	*33%*	*112%*
Act. from pot. %, (est.2)	*122%*	*149%*	*193%*	*85%*	*117%*	*6%*	*47%*	*128%*
2007 II								
Estimation 1 ($ mill.)	32,834	7,443	5,362	7,699	4,935	359	306	55,069
Estimation 2 ($ mill.)	27,257	6,690	3,959	7,126	3,821	318	201	45,638
Act. from pot. %, (est. 1)	*85%*	*113%*	*120%*	*66%*	*76%*	*4%*	*26%*	*90%*
Act. from pot. %, (est.2)	*103%*	*126%*	*163%*	*71%*	*99%*	*5%*	*40%*	*108%*
Ukraine								
observed 1997 ($ mill.)	2,135	228	716	446	129	2	1	4,321
no change								
Estimation 1 ($ mill.)	1,495	280	318	288	170	13	11	2,448
Estimation 2 ($ mill.)	1,722	341	331	371	183	16	10	2,804
Act. from pot. %, (est. 1)	*143%*	*81%*	*225%*	*155%*	*76%*	*15%*	*9%*	*176%*
Act. from pot. %, (est.2)	*124%*	*67%*	*216%*	*120%*	*71%*	*12%*	*10%*	*154%*
2007 I								
Estimation 1 ($ mill.)	2,923	548	621	564	332	26	22	4,785
Estimation 2 ($ mill.)	2,841	563	546	612	302	27	17	4,627
Act. from pot. %, (est. 1)	*73%*	*42%*	*115%*	*79%*	*39%*	*8%*	*4%*	*90%*
Act. from pot. %, (est.2)	*75%*	*40%*	*131%*	*73%*	*43%*	*8%*	*6%*	*93%*
2007 II								
Estimation 1 ($ mill.)	3,666	687	778	707	417	32	28	6,002
Estimation 2 ($ mill.)	3,366	667	647	725	357	32	20	5,481
Act. from pot. %, (est. 1)	*58%*	*72%*	*92%*	*63%*	*31%*	*6%*	*4%*	*72%*
Act. from pot. %, (est.2)	*63%*	*79%*	*111%*	*61%*	*36%*	*6%*	*5%*	*79%*

Table 25: Deviation of Actual Trade Flows from Potential for CIS Countries (cont.)

	EU-15	EFTA-6	CEE-4	Ca+ US	Asia	Au +NZ	Western Hemisph. (Mexico)	OECD
Belarus								
observed 1997 ($ mill.)	497	73	329	97	24	2	2	999
no change								
Estimation 1 ($ mill.)	1,379	280	319	242	138	10	9	2,223
Estimation 2 ($ mill.)	786	170	163	153	72	6	4	1,255
Act. from pot. %, (est.1)	*36%*	*26%*	*103%*	*40%*	*17%*	*19%*	*21%*	*45%*
Act. from pot. %, (est.2)	*63%*	*43%*	*202%*	*63%*	*33%*	*32%*	*47%*	*80%*
2007 I								
Estimation 1 ($ mill.)	2,695	548	623	474	269	20	18	4,345
Estimation 2 ($ mill.)	1,297	280	268	253	120	10	7	2,071
Act. from pot. %, (est.1)	*18%*	*13%*	*53%*	*20%*	*9%*	*10%*	*11%*	*23%*
Act. from pot. %, (est.2)	*38%*	*26%*	*123%*	*38%*	*20%*	*19%*	*29%*	*48%*
2007 II								
Estimation 1 ($ mill.)	3,381	687	782	594	337	25	23	5,450
Estimation 2 ($ mill.)	1,536	332	318	299	142	12	8	2,453
Act. from pot. %, (est.1)	*15%*	*11%*	*42%*	*16%*	*7%*	*8%*	*9%*	*18%*
Act. from pot. %, (est.2)	*32%*	*22%*	*104%*	*32%*	*17%*	*16%*	*24%*	*41%*

**Ca+US means Canada + United States and Au + NZ means Australia and New Zealand*

The Ukraine shows some trade potential with the EU-15 in *scenario 2007 I* and *scenario 2007 II.* This potential can reach the maximum value of $3,666 mill. The Ukraine already exhibits considerable potential in trade with EFTA-6 countries in the *no change scenario.* This potential can increase to $687 mill. The Ukraine only exhibits potential in trade with the CEE-5 in *scenario 2007 II,* according to estimation 1. This potential is equal to $778 mill. This supports the assumption about the strong historical ties which bind these countries. The potential in trade with Canada and the United States can be reached in *scenario 2007 I* and *scenario 2007 II* and equals a maximum of $725 mill. The Ukraine has considerable potential with Asian countries, which can reach $417 mill. The Ukraine exhibits a considerable potential in trade with Australia and New Zealand, as well as Mexico according to the *no change scenario.* The potential in trade with Australia and New Zealand can increase to $32 mill., and to $28 mill. with Mexico. The Ukraine has potential in trade with OECD in *scenario 2007 I* and *scenario 2007 II.* This potential can reach $6,002 mill.

Belarus exhibits potential with almost all groups of countries according to the *no change scenario.* The only exception is trade with the CEE-5, which only exhibits potential *in scenario 2007 I* and *scenario 2007 II,* which shows that Belarus still relies to a large extent on it's old trading partners in the framework of the CMEA agreement. It's trade with the EU-15 can potentially reach $3,381 mill., trade with the EFTA-6 $687 mill., trade with the CEE-5 $782 mill., with Canada and the United States $594 mill., with Asian countries $337 mill., with Australia and New Zealand $25 mill., and with Mexico $23 mill. Belarus's trade with the OECD also shows potential according to the *no change scenario,* which can reach $5,450 mill.

To sum up, the investigation shows that Poland to some extent and Hungary to a large extent have already adjusted their trade towards the EU. Trade with the EU, which is accelerated by the accession process (and FDI), considerably exceeds „normal" trade flows, especially in the case of Hungary. The trade distribution pattern confirms this view since the share of EU-15 trade in Hungary's total trade with the OECD exceeds the share predicted by the gravity model by 10%. There is still some potential in trade with the EU-15 in the case of Poland according to estimation 2, since Poland represents a larger market than Hungary. Hungary and Poland have much in common. Both show an especially large trade potential with Southern European countries such as Greece, Portugal (for both Hungary and Poland), and Spain (for Poland). Both countries point to trade potential with France and the United Kingdom. Hungary exhibits additional potential with Denmark, Poland, Germany, and Ireland.

Both countries show a considerable potential in trade with EFTA-6 countries. Poland has potential in trade with all EFTA-6 countries. This point is also underlined by the trade distribution pattern, which shows that the share of Poland's trade with the EFTA-6 in total OECD trade could increase by 2 percent. Hungary shows trade potential with all EFTA-6 countries except Austria.

Poland does not exhibit undeveloped potential in trade with CEE-4 countries. Poland already has a lot of trade with the CEE-4. The trade distribution pattern shows that the share of CEE-4 trade in total OECD trade could sink by 2%. There is no undeveloped potential in trade between Hungary and the CEE-4. The trade distribution pattern shows that trade between Hungary and the CEE-4 is close to the „normal" share in total OECD trade, or could even increase by 1%. Both countries exhibit a large potential in trade with Asian countries and Mexico and some potential in trade with Canada and the United States, Australia and New Zealand.

Thus, Hungary has already exhausted its trade potential with the EU-15. Poland still has some potential in trade with the EU since it represents a larger market, but other country groups such as the EFTA-6; Canada and the United States, Asian countries, Australia and New Zealand, and Mexico point in some cases to a considerable potential. The CEE-4 country group still plays a considerable role in Polish trade.

Russia does not exhibit any undeveloped potential in absolute terms with most of the country groups. There is only evidence of more trade potential with Australia and New Zealand and Mexico. The trade distribution pattern shows that there is some space for increase of the EU-15 trade share in total OECD trade, namely by

3%. Russia, like Poland and Hungary, exhibits an especially large amount of trade potential with Southern European countries such as Greece and Portugal. Additionally, it has trade potential with France and Denmark.

Russia does not show any potential in trade with EFTA-6 countries. There is an assumption that Russia has excessively redistributed its trade towards EFTA-6 countries, as is the assumption that Poland and especially Hungary already excessively redistributed their trade towards the EU-15. The trade distribution pattern shows that the actual share of EFTA-6 trade in total OECD trade is 3% higher than predicted by the gravity model. Nevertheless, Russia points to some potential in trade with Iceland and Norway.

Russia still relies too much on it's trade with CEE-5, just like Poland. The CEE-5 share in total OECD trade is 3% more than predicted by the gravity model. There is some potential in trade with Canada. The share of Canadian and US trade in total OECD trade could rise by 4%. Russia's trade with Asia, according to the trade distribution pattern, is close to „normal".

The Ukraine shows no potential in trade with the EU-15. The trade distribution pattern suggests in turn that the share of EU-15 trade in the OECD total could rise by 12%. There is trade potential with France, Ireland, and the United Kingdom among the EU-15 countries. The Ukraine has potential with almost all EFTA-6 countries except Austria. The share of EFTA-6 trade in total OECD trade could rise by 6%.

The Ukraine's trade with the CEE-5 is much more than predicted by the gravity model. This shows that the Ukraine relies too much on trade with the CEE-5, since the share of CEE-5 trade in total OECD trade should diminish by 4%. There is still some potential with the Czech Republic and Slovenia. There is a large trade potential with Asian countries, Australia and New Zealand, and Mexico. There is some potential in trade with Canada.

Belarus shows large potential in trade with all groups of countries except the CEE-5, as it relies especially strong on trade with this country group.

4.4 Tentative Conclusions

There are many positive links between openness and growth discussed in the theoretical literature. Especially new growth theory provides new insights into the effects of openness on growth, namely through innovation, knowledge spillovers and externalities, learning by doing, diffusion of knowledge, etc. On the other hand, integration may imply a reallocation effect for developing countries towards industries with low R&D intensity, which could impair long run growth. It might be a task of the government in these countries to direct certain resources towards industries which spur economic growth.

The transformation process induces the opening up of transition economies and the reorientation of their trade towards the West. Transition economies should take into account that trade inside the OECD is mostly intra-industry in character. Therefore, an intensification of trade relations with OECD countries implies a challenge for transition economies to move their specialization pattern towards more intra-industry trade. Transition economies should encourage industries with economies of scale and industries which provide for dynamic gains from trade like medium and high-tech manufacturing in order to become involved in intra-industry trade. Intra-industry trade in turn can raise the possibilities of technology transfer.

The data on foreign trade openness shows that Hungary has an especially high openness ratio among the investigated CEECs. This is mostly to be explained by the induced trade of Hungary with the EU. The openness ratio of Poland increased, but remained on a moderate level. The openness ratio is relatively large for three CIS countries (Russia, the Ukraine, and Belarus). There are different explanations for this. These three countries might have managed to reestablish old trade links earlier than the other post-socialist countries. In the case of Russia increased exports of oil products also played a considerable role. One important aspect was not considered in this chapter. This aspect reflects the influence of the real exchange rate movements on trade flows. Thus the depreciation of the real exchange rate would promote exports since exported products would become cheaper for foreign importers (WELFENS, 1999b; HISHOW, 1998). Exchange rate volatility has in turn a negative impact on trade (CHOU, 2000; GOTUR, 1985; BAILEY/TAVLAS/VLAN, 1987).

The geographical pattern of foreign trade shows Poland and Hungary have considerably reoriented their trade towards EU. Trade has also increased with neighboring CEE-4 countries. This took place to some extent in detriment to trade with other OECD countries. The trade of three CIS countries with OECD countries increased in absolute terms but decreased considerably as a percent of total trade. The decrease took place with all groups of OECD countries and especially with the EU-15[36].

In this chapter patterns of trade specialization of the investigated countries with the EU were also discussed. Hungary has managed to change its specialization pattern and to become involved in intra-industry trade with the EU. Poland is to a large extent similar to Hungary. Poland's exports to the EU can be placed into two groups: to the first accounts traditional manufacturing which took place as a result of OPT, and the second group represents more sophisticated manufacturing. Intra-industry intensity is especially high in the second group of products. The exports of the three CIS countries to the EU are inter-industry in character. They consist mostly of primary commodities. These are, in the case of Russia, primarily energy products. In the case of the Ukraine, supposedly, raw materials and metals, fuels

---

[36] The following groups of OECD countries were considered: EU-15, EFTA-6, CEE-5, Canada and the United States, Asia (Japan and Korea), Australia and New Zealand, and Mexico.

and wood. Belarus's high trade exposure to Russia suggests that this is mostly inter-industry trade between Belarus and the EU, although Belarus specializes up to 78% in manufacturing.

At the end of the chapter the investigation on trade potential between selected CEECs, CIS, and Western countries was made. The investigation is carried out with the gravity model. Two model specifications were considered: one with standard variables and the other with the *INTERNET* variable. Both estimations provide for plausible coefficients. The gravity model results were discussed for CEECs and CIS. The gravity model results show that especially Hungary has already exhausted its potential in trade with the EU-15. Poland still exhibits some potential since Poland represents a larger market than Hungary. Increased trade with the EU reduced trade flows to other OECD countries. Thus, both Hungary and Poland show considerable potential in trade with other OECD country groups, i.e. the EFTA-6, Canada and the United Sates, Asian Countries, Australia and New Zealand, and Mexico. The CEE-5 proceed to play a considerable role in Polish trade.

The actual trade flows for Russia are supposed to be influenced by oil prices since they are mostly very high. There is unrealized potential in absolute terms only with Australia and New Zealand and Mexico. Since Russia does not exhibit any potential in absolute terms, its trade distribution pattern helps to understand the situation. Thus Russia still trades less than predicted with the EU. Its trade with the EFTA-6, on the other hand, exceeds the potential ratio as a percent of total OECD trade. Russia also trades more than predicted with CEE-5 countries. There is potential in trade with Canada, according to the distribution pattern. Russia's trade with Asia is close to „normal".

The Ukraine does not show any untapped potential in trade with the EU-15 in absolute terms. It could increase by 12% as a percent of total OECD trade. The Ukraine exhibits a large potential in trade with the EFTA-6. It relies much on its trade relations with the CEE-5. There is potential in trade with Asian countries, Australia and New Zealand, Mexico, and some potential in trade with Canada.

Belarus in the only country which shows a lot of potential in trade with all OECD countries, except with the CEE-5. It relies especially strong on trade with this group of OECD countries.

One should note that realization of trade potential for CIS and CEECs means a deeper integration with the world economy and thus induces dependence on the conditions of world markets. Countries with a diversified export structure are better able to cope with external shocks.

4.5 Appendix

Table 26: Revealed Comparative Advantage (RCA) and Exports

Sectors	Agricul-ture RCA	Resources RCA	Capital RCA	Labor RCA	Skills RCA	Main export commodity groups
Central Europe				**(+)**	**(-)**	
Croatia	(-)	(+)	(-)	(+)	(-)	Clothing (24%), footwear (9%)
Czech Republic	(-)				(-)	Vehicles (12%), electrical machinery (9%)
Hungary	(+)	(-)	(-)		(+)	Electrical (12%), power machinery (12%)
Poland	(+)	(+)	(-)	(+)	(-)	Clothing (11%), vehicles (8%)
Slovak Republic	(-)	(-)	(+)	(+)	(-)	Iron & steel (13%), vehicles (12%)
Slovenia	(--)	(-)		(+)		Vehicles (13%), electrical machinery (10%)
Baltic States	**(-)**	**(+)**	**(-)**		**(-)**	
Estonia	(-)	(+)	(-)		(-)	Oil (23%), wood (14%)
Latvia	(-)	(+)	(-)		(--)	Oil (41%), wood (23%)
Lithuania	(-)	(+)	(-)	(+)	(--)	Clothing (23%), oil (10%)
South-eastern Europe	**(-)**		**(-)**	**(+)**	**(--)**	
Albania	(-)	(+)	(-)	(+)	(--)	Clothing (28%), footwear (22%)
Bosnia and Herzegovina	(--)	(+)	(-)	(+)	(--)	Clothing (28%), footwear (22)
Bulgaria	(+)	(-)	(+)		(--)	Clothing (18%), non-ferrous metals (11%)
FYR Macedonia				(+)	(--)	Clothing (34%), iron & steel (20)
Romania				(+)	(--)	Clothing (30%), iron & steel (10%)

Table 26: Revealed Comparative Advantage (RCA) and Exports (cont.)

Sectors	Agricul-ture RCA	Resources RCA	Capital RCA	Labor RCA	Skills RCA	Main export commodity groups
Western CIS					**(--)**	
Armenia		(+)	(-)	(-)	(--)	Diamonds (74%), metaliferous ores (9%)
Azerbaijan		(++)	(-)	(-)	(--)	Cotton (29%), oil (21%)
Belarus	**(-)**		**(+)**	**(+)**	**(-)**	**Clothing (21%), fertilizers (9%)**
Georgia	(-)	(+)		(+)	(-)	Oil (23%), iron & steel (18%)
Moldova	(++)	(--)	(-)		(--)	Clothing (25%), iron & steel (19%)
Ukraine	**(++)**	**(-)**	**(+)**	**(-)**	**(--)**	**Iron & steel (27%), metaliferous ores (15%)**
Russia	**(--)**	**(++)**		**(--)**	**(--)**	**Oil (32%), non-ferrous metals (20%)**
Central Asia		**(++)**	**(--)**	**(-)**	**(--)**	
Kazakhstan		(++)	(--)	(-)	(--)	Non-ferrous metals (39%), oil (29%)
Kyrgyzstan	(+)	(++)	(-)	(--)	(--)	Gold (27%), cotton fibres (25%)
Tajikistan	(-)	(++)	(--)	(+)	(--)	Cotton (62%), textiles (17%)
Turkmenistan	(-)	(++)	(--)	(-)	(--)	Cotton (56%), textiles (18%)
Uzbekistan	(-)	(++)	(--)	(-)	(--)	Cotton (82%), non-ferrous metals 87%)

Source: EBRD (1999), Transition Report 1999

Note:

RCA:

(++) strong revealed comparative advantage

(+) revealed comparative advantage

(-) revealed comparative disadvantage

(--) strong revealed comparative disadvantage

Revealed comparative advantage is a normalized measure of net exports. Formula: RCAi = (ESi - ISi)/(ESi - ISi) for sector i, where ES is the export share and IS is the import share in each commodity group. Data is obtained from partner countries in SITC - 2 digit (rev.3) and commodity groups are: agriculture - 0, 1, 4, 22, 29; Skill-intensive - 54, 72, 75, 76, 87, 88; Labor-intensive - 26, 60, 61, 65, 77, 80-85, 89 (textiles, clothes, footwear, other); Natural resources - 21, 24, 26, 27, 28, 32-35, 63, 66, 68 (wood, oil, gas, electricity, coal, stone, non-ferrous metals, skins and furs, textiles fibers); Capital-intensive - 23, 25, 51-53, 55-59, 64, 67, 69-71, 73, 74, 78, 79 (paper, chemicals, rubber, plastic, ferrous metals, transport and industrial machinery).

5 The Role of FDI in the Transition Process of Selected CIS and CEECs

Transformation from a centrally planned to a market-based economy brings about considerable changes in external relations with the rest of the world; transformation also brings about obsolescence of part of the existing capital stock. In this context structural adjustment and opening up to foreign direct investment (FDI) is necessary in order to achieve rapid capital accumulation and growth.

The Central and Eastern European countries (CEECs) and Commonwealth of Independent States (CIS) have inherited a rather distorted economic system after the collapse of the command economy and the CMEA. The main distortions which influenced these countries' external relations were concerned with special distribution networks of foreign trade; foreign trade only took place in the framework of CMEA block-countries. There was a high level of specialization and integration among the countries of the former USSR. There was a distorted pattern of sectoral structure with an oversized industry sector and underdeveloped services as well as a large CMEA military-industrial sector. CMEA trade in combination with poor integration with market economies led to the development of the distortional regional distribution of foreign trade without taking into account economic, geographical, and cultural aspects (POZNANSKI, 1987; MURELL, 1990; WELFENS, 1992b;). Specialization and integration occurred for political reasons, not according to comparative advantages. The former USSR created a biased domestic and foreign trade pattern. The USSR, richly endowed with natural resources, took advantage of this situation by exporting raw materials, which is a contrast to trade among Western economies, where the most trade between OECD countries is intra-and not inter-industry trade. The other CIS countries were strongly dependent on natural resources from Russia. Moreover, the production in CIS countries was predominately oriented towards the CIS (to a large extent Russian market) and did not correspond to international standards, which made these countries uncompetitive in the world markets after the collapse of the Soviet Union. Thus, the collapse of the Soviet Union and the break-up of the former economic relations partly led to the necessity of foreign trade reorientation towards the West, changes in specialization patterns, and the search for new financing opportunities for the emerging production.

Foreign direct investment should play a decisive role in regards to the modernization of production and the tradable sector. FDI is important as it brings not only additional capital but also technology transfer and knowledge spillovers. Mostly negligible for political reasons in the past, FDI patterns, similar to foreign trade, follow economic, geographic, and cultural principles. This chapter consists of three sections. The first section deals with the impact of FDI on economic growth. In the first section the positive impact of FDI on economic growth in transition economies is analyzed. Additionally, possible negative affects of FDI are also taken into account. The possible negative effect of FDI on the balance of payments in transition economies is discussed in this section as well. The growth spiral, which represents the interplay of foreign trade and FDI in their impact on growth is also regarded in this section. The second section analyses trends and fluctuations of FDI in five selected transition countries, where three CIS countries including Russia, the Ukraine, and Belarus are compared with more advanced transition economies, namely Poland and Hungary. The conditions for FDI created through privatization are also covered by this section as well as the impact of FDI on structural adjustment. The third section is an empirical investigation of potential FDI inflows for the selected countries, where analysis carried out is based on the gravity model. At the end some conclusions are made with respect to the role of FDI in the restructuring of the economy during the transformation process and in the long run.

5.1 FDI and Growth Perspectives of Transition Economies

This section provides an overview of the role of FDI for catching up in transition economies from the perspective of neoclassical and new growth theory. It points to the special role of FDI as a channel for technology transfer carried out mostly by MNCs. The OLI-bahavior of MNCs is therefore regarded in this section, since it is of crucial importance for transition economies to know the motives and incentives of MNCs which promote their investment activities. The impact of FDI on growth in transition economies is regarded both positively and negatively. Besides, the impact of FDI on the balance of payments is taken into account. Finally, since FDI and foreign trade are closely connected with each other in their impact on economic growth, the interplay between FDI and trade and their impact on growth is covered by this section as well.

5.1.1 The Role of FDI in the Catching up Process of Transition Economies

The new theory of economic growth emphasizes the crucial role of technological progress in the catching up process of developing countries. In contrast to the neoclassical framework of the Solow growth model, where technology is supposed to be „equally given" for all countries, recently developed new growth theory emphasizes the dependence of the growth rates on the state of the technological change in the countries in comparison to the technological progress worldwide. New growth theory explains the growth rates in developing countries, in part, through catching up in the level of technologies.

In general there are two possibilities for countries to move up the technological ladder. The first possibility is to develop the advanced technologies that provide an internationally competitive position in world markets, and the other possibility is to import the technologies from abroad. Developing new technologies by own forces demands high innovation capabilities based on a high level of indigenous resources and highlights the special role of high-skilled human capital. Therefore, the process of innovation can be carried out only by those countries which already have the position of a technological leader. More advanced knowledge allows these countries to develop new technologies at a lower cost.

The transformation countries, on the other hand, have a considerable productivity and technology gap. The technology gap is reflected in the trade structure of these economies. Therefore, the catching up opportunities for transition economies are closely connected with the ability of these countries to switch to the pool of the advanced knowledge and technologies developed by leading nations. Since it is cheaper to imitate existing products than to produce the products at the frontier of innovation, the process of imitation and adaptation of advanced technologies rather than innovation is more relevant for these countries. The level of human capital in this context determines the start-off position for these countries and is one of the major factors in attracting and adopting advanced technologies.

FDI carried out by Multinational Corporations (MNCs) is considered to be a major channel for the access to advanced technologies by transformation countries. FDI takes place when investors, usually MNCs, situated in one country (the country of head-quarter) establish foreign investment enterprises (FIEs) in the other country (the host country) and exhibit managerial control over FIEs. Technological assets are provided by the MNCs since they have technological comparative advantages over local firms. MNCs are among the most technologically advanced firms which carry out a substantial part of the world's research and development (R&D) investment (BORENSZTEIN etc., 1995). Besides technology transfer, which has to be considered as a „direct" effect of FDI, FDI also leads to „indirect" productivity gains associated with the realization of the external economies. The „indirect" effect is referred to as „spillovers", which are available to the economy in general and rise it's productivity as a whole. Therefore, the ability of countries to attract FDI distinguishes the future economic growth and prosperity of the country. This ability is limited by the absorptive capability of the transition economies, which requires first of all the presence of a sufficient level of human capital in the host country. Only the minimum available stock of human capital will make it possible to absorb and adopt new technologies and make FDI more productive than domestic investment. The higher the level of human capital in the country, the higher the effect of FDI on the growth rate of the economy. The countries with different levels of human capital have different effects of FDI on growth rates. In fact, the countries with a low level of human capital exhibit a negative effect of FDI.

The role of FDI is also enforced by the process of globalization. For transition economies, FDI becomes an opportunity to be deeply involved in the international network, opposed to the case of economic isolation, which predicts their being cut off from international resources and the advantages of the liberalized world.

5.1.2 FDI and the OLI-Behaviour of MNCs

Since MNCs are the firms which provide most of the world's FDI, it is of great importance for transition countries (most of which have only little experience with FDI) to understand the motives and incentives that induce MNCs to invest in particular countries, as well as to gain insight into the organizational structure of MNCs, which determines their behavior worldwide and explains intra-firm trade and FDI flows prevailing in the developed world.

The following Ownership - Location - Internalization (OLI) model of FDI highlights these questions (DUNNING, 1988; EDEN, 1991).

This model assumes that MNCs organize their activities according to the following three factors:

1) Ownership advantages: MNCs possess ownership or firm-specific advantages (FSAs) which allow them to produce abroad in that they receive rents in foreign locations which are high enough to overcome certain disadvantages of producing in foreign markets. FSAs represent privileges acquired by MNCs in comparison to domestic firms. These owner-specific advantages can usually be divided into knowledge or oligopoly-based advantages and can be quickly transferred within MNCs at low costs. Knowledge-based advantages are associated with product and process innovations and allow MNCs to become technological leaders in local markets and introduce new products at relatively low costs. Oligopoly-based advantages include economies of scale and scope, as well as privileged access to raw materials and financing.

2) Internalization advantages: Internalization advantage consists of opportunities received by MNCs from arranging their activities in host markets through subsidiaries rather than from being involved in other contractual arrangements. The explanation of such preference includes exogenous market imperfections on the one hand and the desire to gain from oligopolistic imperfections on the other. Such natural exogenous market imperfections like transaction costs and government-imposed imperfections like tariff barriers, exchange controls, and subsidies discourage MNCs to serve foreign markets through exports from the parent company. From the other side the intent to gain use of the endogenous oligopolistic imperfections which include exertion of monopoly power, cross-subsidization of markets, and opportunistic exploitation of suppliers and buyers enforce MNCs to spread their networks over new markets. Internalization thus helps MNCs spread their activities all over the world, receiving rents from owner-specific advantages and taking gains from imperfect competition.

3) Locational advantages: Locational advantages or country-specific advantages (CSAs) determine which countries are attractive for the investment and production activities of MNCs. Broadly the CSAs can be divided into tree categories: Economic advantages, social advantages, and political advantages.

Economic advantages: Economic CSAs include first of all such factors as the market size of the country. Market size plays a role for *Market-seeking* MNCs which are motivated to enter new markets and expand their market share.

The attractiveness of the country for MNCs depends not in the least on it's country's factor endowment of labor, capital, technology, managerial skills, natural resources, and infrastructure (transportation, communications). Country's factor endowments are important for *Resource/asset seeking MNCs,* which are primarily interested in the availability in the host country of raw materials, low-cost and/or skilled labor, infrastructure, and specific technological assets. The classical example is the reallocation of production into countries with low labor costs.

For the *Efficiency-seeking* MNCs which take their advantage from the availability of resources, their relative productivity of high-skilled labor and management, the appropriate level of existing technologies, a sufficient stock of physical capital, and a developed infrastructure, the introduction of new technologies is easier and raises the productivity of production. Developed infrastructure is important as it lowers the costs of market transactions.

Social advantages: Noneconomic or social CSAs refer both to the „physical" and „cultural" distance between countries in form of differences in languages, culture, ethnicity, and business customs.

Political advantages: Political factors include first of all the attitude of the government towards MNCs. The FDI climate, i.e. regulations on foreign trade and capital flows, reflects the readiness of government to invite MNCs and attract FDI.

Therefore FDI is likely to be attracted to the geographically close countries with similar cultural and business habits with good factor endowments and low factor costs. Integration and globalization that reduce transaction costs and make capital flows easier between countries open new possibilities for large MNCs and create favourable conditions for FDI.

5.1.3 Theoretical Considerations of the Impact of FDI on Economic Growth in Transition Economies

FDI is associated with many positive effects on economic growth in transition economies but there are also negative effects, especially in the case of insufficient competition in domestic markets. This, of course, assumes that no monopoly positions of MNC subsidiaries are allowed in the host country. Multinational Corporations (MNCs) sometimes take advantage of their economic power and create distorted conditions in which domestic firms are not able to compete. Thus, there could be some negative or „courteous" FDI effects.

5.1.3.1 The Positive Relationship Between FDI and Economic Growth

The effect of FDI on economic growth was described in the theoretical literature and analyzed empirically with the evidence of positive results. One should differentiate between greenfield investment, which directly adds to the capital stock, and M&E, where positive productive effects are mainly related to knowledge transfer.

FDI can contribute to growth in CIS and in investigated CEECs through the following channels relevant in particular for low income host countries:

- *FDI contributes to the capital stock in the host countries and increases employment.* The upgrading possibilities of countries depend on their local factors such as stock of human and physical capital. FDI helps in increasing and modernizing physical capital and creating new working places to parallel the increase of production (BELLAK, 1998). Investments in physical capital and increase in employment in turn create positive real income effects, which raises demand for the products of domestic firms.

- *FDI is a channel of technology transfer.* An important contribution of FDI to economic growth consists in the characteristic of FDI as a vehicle for knowledge and technology transfer. On the one side, FDI through knowledge and technology transfer as well as through better managerial skills makes foreign investment enterprises (FIEs) more productive than domestic firms. In other words, FDI is more productive than domestic investment. From the other side, it contributes to the expansion of domestic firms through positive spillover-effects and externalities which arise from the nonrival nature of technology and the presence of FIEs in the local market thus increasing the total level of investment in the host country. The increase of total capital accumulation assumes that FDI does not „crowd out" an equal amount of investment made by domestic firms by competing on product and financial markets (BORENSZTEIN etc., 1995).

- *FDI raises the productivity of the FIEs.* Productivity, which means more efficient use of inputs, will accelerate the catching up process. More efficient use of inputs by FIEs in comparison to domestic firms will be reached through the combination of advanced managerial skills and technology with domestic labor and inputs. As a result, higher productive efficiency allows FIEs to produce products at lower costs than domestic firms. Thus FIEs are more productive than domestic firms. But FIEs can only be more productive in comparison to domestic firms if the host country possess a minimum threshold stock of human capital. FDI interacts with the stock of human capital to influence economic growth (BELLAK, 1998, and BORENSZTEIN etc., 1995).

- *Intra-firm spillover efficiency.* MNCs, in order to avoid leaks, are eager to transfer modern and complex technologies only through wholly or majority-owned subsidiaries and less willing to accept any other arrangements. Transfer of technologies on an intra-firm basis is the fastest way of know-how transfer across borders. In other words, it allows host countries to get new technologies within a considerably shorter period of time than the other ways of technology transfer (BLOMSTROEM, 1991).

- *Restructuring effect.* Integration into the MNCs' networks is an important impulse for the restructuring of the enterprises which enforces the competitiveness of the enterprises on the world markets and makes them stronger against domestic firms (BELLAK, 1998). The restructuring effect also plays a role when FDI means just a change of ownership and not connected with a transfer of capital. The importance of *the restructuring effect* for transformation economies is especially meaningful in the context of privatization since state enterprises during the Soviet era were oversized and characterized by insufficient structures with weak control possibilities (WELFENS, 2000).

- *Economies of scale.* FIEs are normally larger than domestic firms and have a higher R&D intensity which allows them to exploit economies of scale in host markets (BELLAK, 1998).

- *FDI intensifies competition against local firms.* Introduction of new management, increased specialization, and restructuring, as well as new knowledge and technologies give FIEs competitive advantages against local firms. The question is whether MNCs displace domestic firms from the local market. There is evidence that FDI does not „crowd out" domestic investment, but instead makes domestic firms more competitive and productive (BORENSZTEIN etc., 1995; BLOMSTROEM, 1991).

- *FDI increases the productivity of local firms.* Borensztein found empirical evidence that FDI increases total investment in the economy more than one for one, which speaks in favor of the complementary effect of FDI with domestic investment[37]. FDI increases the total investment in the economy through complementary effects in production and through spillover-effects and externalities from knowledge and technology transfer, which raises the productivity of domestic firms thus providing their expansion.

- The most important spillover-effects which bring productivity gains to local firms are (BLOMSTROEM, 1991).

- *-The increased competition between FIEs and local firms.* Competition between FIEs and domestic firms forces inefficient local firms to become more productive by investing in physical and human capital. The increased competition also allows for the reallocation of resources from insufficient to competitively stronger domestic firms.

- *-Spillovers from labor and management training.* MNCs often provide labor and management training that represents spillovers which spread throughout the economy. Many managerial people who started their careers at the FIEs may later change to locally-owned firms or establish their own firms. Host

---

[37] Borensztein, E. etc. (1995, p. 3):"*...a one dollar increase in the net inflow of FDI is associated with an increase in total investment in the host economy of more than one dollar".*

countries receive important spillovers in this way. Such spillovers are especially crucial in the case of developing countries.

- -„*Supplier" spillover-effect.* MNCs tend to upgrade the local facilities and enforce local suppliers of intermediate products to improve quality standards, reduce delivery time, and exhibit stricter quality control in order to meet the requirements of the technology or operating methods of the FIEs. Therefore, MNCs increase competition among suppliers which forces them to introduce lower costs in order to compete for MNC's. Thus the „*supplier" spillover-effect* improves the functioning of the whole economy.

- *MNCs tend to speed up the technological upgrading of domestic firms.* Considering transfer of technology as a main activity of MNCs, domestic firms would in turn speed up the access to particular technologies, the existence and profitability of which are demonstrated by the MNCs. Productivity has exhibited approximately the same effect on new products introduced by MNCs and purchased by local firms. Technological gains appear here through technological spillovers inferred in new products (BLOMSTROEM, 1991).

- *FDI changes the specialization pattern.* With further development the share of intra-industry FDI as well as intra-industry trade would increase as it is in highly developed countries which represent competitors of similar differentiated products. The network channels of MNCs and intra-firm trade are likely to provide these changes. By contrast, domestic firms are too technologically and financially weak to initiate structural changes (BELLAK, 1998).

- *FDI increases trade.* FDI carried out first of all by MNCs serves as a conduit for exports from the host country. FDI creates secondary flows in the form of exports of machinery and other capital goods, and also creates demand for manufactured production imports as well as for imports of services (expertise, finance, accounting and so on). FDI provides a positive effect on the balance of payments in the long run: each dollar of outward FDI is associated with $2 of additional exports and with a bilateral trade surplus of $1.7 dollars. Since FDI is associated with industrialization and change of the specialization pattern it hastens the expansion of the „increasingly technologically-sophisticated manufactured exports" (OECD, 1998). However, FDI inflows can go along with net imports (mainly capital goods) in the medium term.

Figure 18 once again summarizes the impact of FDI on growth. FDI contributes to economic growth through two main channels. First, by adding to the stock of physical capital and increasing employment in the host country with a positive real income effect that raises demand for the products of domestic firms, thus promoting their expansion. Second, by the productivity gains attained from the technology transfer and „spillovers" that bring technological gains to the whole economy. Knowledge and technology transfer, higher managerial skills, and restructuring effects, as well as intra-firm spillover efficiency, make FIEs more productive in comparison to domestic firms. Higher productivity and economies of scale give FIEs additional competitive advantages in the host market. But there is evidence that FIEs do not „crowd out" domestic firms from the local market. Spillover effects such as increased competition, knowledge spillovers, and technology transfer, as well as „supplier" spillover effects raise, in turn, the productivity of domestic firms. Increased competition provides for the reallocation of resources from insufficient to more sufficient firms, and stimulates firms to be more productive and furthermore invest in physical and human capital. Through labor training and transfer of managerial skills domestic firms "import" significant organizational knowledge and labor skills which have a positive effect on the productivity of domestic firms. Technological upgrading is also reinforced by domestic firms's desire to switch from available to the MNC technologies. Buying new products developed by FIEs also allows for technology transfer incorporated in these products. „Supplier" spillover effects improve the „business environment" not only for MNCs but also for domestic firms. The „business environment" includes lower costs, higher quality standards, and shorter delivery time by suppliers as a result of stronger competition. All these factors together raise the productivity of FIEs and domestic firms, provide technological catching up, increase both foreign and domestic investment, and hence promote economic growth.

FDI initiates changes of the specialization pattern. In the long term, assuming per capita income growth, the transition countries will switch from inter to intra-industry trade, which is typical for the developed world. Rising exports, as a reaction to the increased FDI, will represent increasingly technologically sophisticated manufactured products accompanied by the adjustment of import structure.

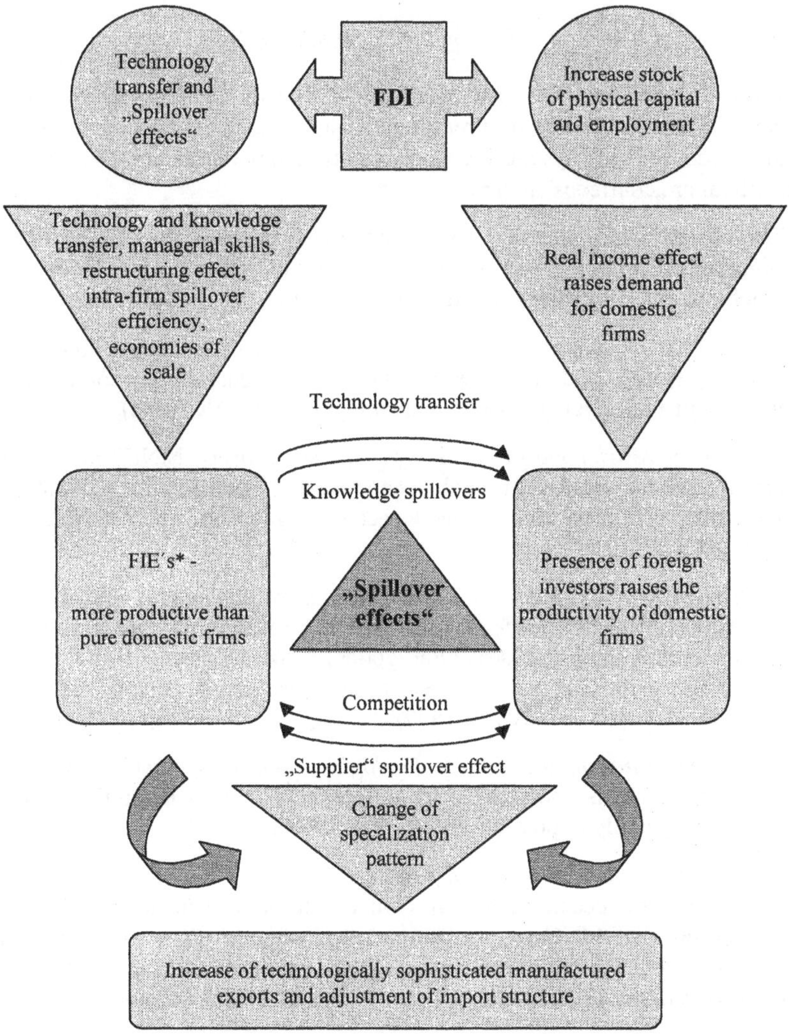

*FIE´s - Foreign Investment Enterprises

Figure 18: The Effect of FDI on Economic Growth

5.1.3.2 Negative Impact of FDI on the Economies of Host Countries

Alongside with the possible positive effects of FDI on economic growth in the host countries, FDI may also be a reason for distortions in the host countries. This side of FDI does not always receive much attention in the literature. Here there are some critical or „courteous" points:

- *FDI may reduce competition.* Due to the intense desire of the FIEs profit from oligopolistic imperfections, FIEs tend to use their market power in a way which distorts competition and thus leads to welfare loss (BELLAK, 1998).
- *FIEs get tax privileges and subsidies.* FIEs get favorable opportunities from FDI tax regimes and subsidies schemes in the transition economies which gives them additional competitive advantages (BELLAK, 1998).
- *MNCs may restrict market access for domestic firms.* MNCs may restrict access to the market through economies of scale and technological requirements because they prefer to act in oligopolistic markets (HUNYA, 1999; BURGER, 1999).
- *Insufficient factor markets may limit competitive advantages of local firms.* Distortions of factor markets (insufficient allocation of financial capital, human capital, and infrustructural goods) make domestic firms weak in competition with FIEs as the latter can use resources available through the networks of MNCs (BURGER, 1999).
- *Weak competition may reduce technological spillovers.* A small number of market participants and weak price competition may make spillover-effects from FDI factually impossible (BURGER, 1999).
- *Restructuring effect at the initial period of FDI is not a guarantee for further success.* Future success of foreign owned enterprises depends first of all on the decisions of MNCs as a reaction on changes in domestic and foreign demand and can limit „the choice of future company strategies" (HUNYA, 1999; BELLAK, 1998).
- *FDI affects only a small sector of the economy.* In transition economies FDI is concentrated only on a part of the economy which represents mostly the „best-of" privatized firms and foreign investors seem not to be motivated to make further investments in the host economy (BELLAK, 1998).
- *FIEs may ignore domestic suppliers.* FIEs may only use already existing supplier „schemes" in their activities, for example exporting intermediate products from neighboring and more advanced transition economies, and not involve domestic suppliers in their activities. Although it could have technological advantages for MNCs, it restricts „supplier" effects on the economy with it's price and quality effects on the intermediate products in the host country and may kill domestic suppliers (BELLAK, 1998).

- *FDI reinforces polarization between high and low-income regions.* As FDI is directed to the regions with abundant factor endowments, human capital, and technologies, spillover effects in these regions strengthen their economic growth. On the other hand the limited diffusion of knowledge and unwillingness of MNCs to invest into regions with poor factor endowments will lead to the further lagging behind of poor regions (HUNYA, 1999).
- *FIEs may limit local R&D activity.* FIEs limit local R&D activity as the highly skilled human resources reallocated towards MNCs and competition for high-standard products within MNCs is much stronger relative to domestic firms (HUNYA, 1999).
- *Local companies may not be able to adsorb and imitate technologies.* Local companies that don't invest in learning are not able to gain from opportunities from externalities and spillover effects. In this case MNCs should not be afraid of technological leakages and „borrow" more than „give" to the host markets (BURGER, 1999).
- *The conflict of interests between MNCs and domestic firms.* MNCs try to prevent positive technology spillovers and externalities to domestic firms (BELLAK, 1998).

5.1.4 The Impact of FDI on the Balance of Payments

A positive impact of FDI flows on the host country if we just regard FDI like a „supply" of foreign currency at the domestic market is first of all associated with the increase in the currency reserves which help the country to finance foreign deficits. An increase in currency reserves also lowers the vulnerability of the country to currency crises. On the other hand, strong inflows of FDI over a long period of time create inflation pressures by raising the amount of money circulating in the economy. Moreover, by flexible exchange rates there is the possibility of an appreciation of the currency with negative effects on domestic producers and the export capacity of the country (HUNYA, 1999; WELFENS/GANUSCHTSCHENKO, 1999).

The Effect of FDI on Current Account Balance:

Besides the above illustrated impact, FDI flows also have an effect on current account balance. The effect on current account balance might be positive or negative. In a short period of time strong FDI inflows may cause current account deficit which is a serious problem for transformation economies which in fact used to have current account deficit independently from FDI inflows. Thus FDI could deepen current account deficit, which has a negative impact on the catching up possibilities of transition countries.

- *Trade balance deficit in the short run.* In the short run it seems plausible to assume that FDI could be responsible for foreign trade deficit as FIEs would import more machinery and other capital goods in order to set-up new production which does not yet bring returns in the form of exports.

- *Services account deficit.* On the side of services it is also plausible to expect deficits as FIEs generally tend to import more services than domestic firms.
- *Trade balance surplus in the long run.* Only in the long run could FDI contribute to trade balance surplus in exporting manufacturing products from the expanding production.
- *Repatriation of profits.* FIEs transfer profits more often abroad than domestic firms. The repatriation of profits for example from Hungary doubled in 1998 to $1 bill. against 0.5 bill. in 1997. The repatriation of profits accounted for almost half of Hungary's $4.2 bill. current account deficit in 1998.

5.1.5 The Relationship between FDI and Trade: Growth Spiral

The relationship between trade and FDI represents a very interesting aspect in the context of „new" growth theory and „new" international trade theory. This question is of special interest in the case of transition countries. Transition economies on the way of catching up intend to receive productivity gains both from openness of trade and connected with the liberalization of trade FDI inflows. The economic practice shows that openness of trade and FDI can not be regarded separately but represents a combination of impulses and incentives called to initiate changes in the specialization pattern and give rise to economic growth. Therefore understanding the relationship between FDI and trade, and associated with this relationship economic growth, is of primary importance for economic policies in these countries.

Neoclassical trade theory was not able to explain the factually existing trade flows between countries as it did not correspond to the tendencies of global economic growth. Thus the standard Heckscher-Ohlin-Samuelson model, based on the principle of comparative advantage, with the assumption of perfect competition and identical technology in all countries was simply broken by the reality. „New" international trade theory based on economies of scale and imperfect competition better suits the tendencies of the world's trade distribution and economic growth. There is no explicit „new" theory on FDI that would clearly describe the place of FDI in „new" growth and „new" trade theories, but FDI in the framework of the neoclassical model obviously does not provide sufficient explanation for the real distribution of FDI between countries, especially if we want to understand FDI flows to developing countries. According to the strict neoclassical model where only capital and labor factors are included and the assumption about identical technologies across countries is true, the poorest countries should attract most of the foreign capital. ZEBREGS (1998) extended this neoclassical model in his empirical work to country-specific technologies and showed that under this alternative specification poor countries do not necessarily attract most of the world's FDI. Instead, FDI would rather be directed to richer countries which possess more capital-intensive technologies and have higher total factor productivity.

But if we regard FDI in the context of „new" trade theory, it can give us powerful insights into the relationship between FDI and trade as well as show its impact on economic growth. As a considerable amount of FDI is carried out by MNCs, it seems plausible to combine the OLI-behavior of MNCs with the principles of „new" trade theory. If we add to the new trade theory MNCs with typical features of economies of scale, imperfect competition, strategic considerations, technological change, and diffusion we would make interesting conclusions about the impact of FDI and internalization of the pattern of specialization and trade in the host countries (ETHIER/MARKUSEN, 1996). Opposite to the „new" trade theory, the Dunning eclectic OLI - FDI theory with an accent on owner-specific advantages contradicts the comparative-advantage trade theory, which does not take into account external economies, imperfect competition, and economies of scale. Therefore neoclassical trade theory rules out technological change and external economies and ignores those technology and knowledge effects responsible for positive welfare changes in host countries. The other aspect that gives reasons for the introduction of MNCs behavior into the „new" trade theory is the fact that FDI tendencies between countries look considerably like trade patterns.

The largest part of world FDI and the fastest growing part is carried out between developed market economies; it is not directed form developed countries to the least developed countries. Figure 19 shows the distribution of FDI between developed and developing countries in 1997. Worldwide stock of FDI in 1997 amounted for $3,456 million, 70% of which were directed towards developed market economies and only 30% to developing countries. Therefore, developed economies are the largest donor-countries of FDI and at the same time the largest recipients of FDI.

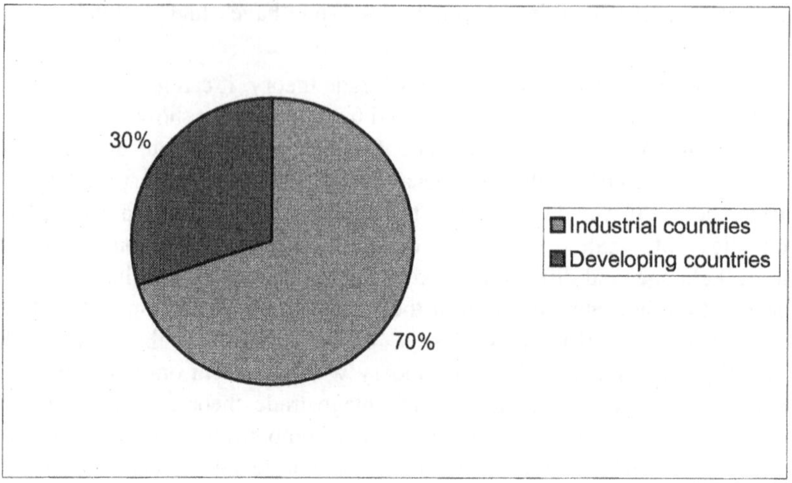

Source: World Bank (1999/2000), World Development Report 1999/2000

Figure 19: Distribution of FDI between Developed and Developing Countries in 1997 (Worldwide stock of FDI in 1997 ($3,456 billion)

Such FDI behavior corresponds considerably to trade patterns as a large share of trade is now intra-firm (particularly intra-industry) trade. Since World War II there has been a change from vertically-integrated firms in raw material based sectors to horizontally-integrated manufacturing firms, as manufacturing won on importance in international trade. Nowadays 2/3 of trade in the leading OECD countries is intra-industry trade where 1/3 is intra-firm trade. Therefore the distribution of FDI and foreign trade demonstrates the connection between FDI and trade, as well as the behavior of MNCs is successfully enrolled in the „new" trade theory.

The question is whether this relationship is growth enhancing and whether liberalization of trade leads to more FDI while FDI in turn aggregates export growth, and whether FDI and trade are *substitutes* or *complements.* The question of whether FDI and trade are *substitutes* or *complements*, or whether the inflows of FDI lead to decreases or increases in exports has a considerable importance for policy makers as possible negative effects of FDI upon a country's balance of payments should be taken into account. Moreover, increasing FDI and trade could have a positive impact in the long run on economic growth in transition economies.

Due to OLI advantages MNCs are eager to produce locally those products they would usually export from the „home" country to the „host" country. In this sense the outward FDI and exports of the „home" country could be regarded as *substitutes*. From the other side MNCs arrange strongly export oriented activities in the host country where FDI leads to the export of goods and services to the other nations. From this point of view FDI and trade become *complements*.

Both theoretical considerations and most of the empirical investigations speak in favor of the complementary relationship between FDI and trade.

Here there are some arguments in favor of complementary effects between FDI and trade (GRAHAM, 1999):

- As „home" MNC and „host" firms are involved in vertical links through FDI, the increase in the efficiency of local FIEs in the production of final goods would create demand for the intermediate goods produced by the „home" MNC. Increased demand would stimulate the efficiency of the „home" MNC in the production of intermediate goods and increase exports of intermediate goods from the „home" to the „host" country. The relationship between FDI and exports for both „home" and „host" firms would become complementary despite substitute effects for the „home" firm in the past.
- Owner-specific advantages and economies of scale allow MNCs to get large market shares which has an increase effect on both trade and FDI. In combination with the increased efficiency of „host" firms the relationship between additional FDI and trade would be increasingly complementary.
- Outward FDI tends to mostly stimulate the export of capital goods and intermediate goods from the „home" country.
- Especially there is an increase in the intra-firm exports strengthening the special importance of vertical relationship among the various international affiliates of MNC's.

Most empirical studies support theoretical considerations that FDI and foreign trade are more complements then substitutes and hence associated with an increase of exports. GRAHAM (1999) showed the relationship between FDI and trade using the gravity model approach where he assumed that a positive correlation between coefficients for FDI and trade suggests complementarity and a negative coefficient substitutability. Gravity model results for the United States and Japan as well as for Taiwan and Korea suggest that FDI and trade are complements and not substitutes (GRAHAM, 1999; GRAHAM/LUI, 1998). These results proclaim that outward FDI from developed or newly industrialized countries does not lead to the „deindustrialization" and „hollowing up" of the „home" industry, but is instead associated with the further growth of manufactured exports.

While Graham showed the complementary relationship for the source country, BRENTON/DI MAURO/LUECKE (1998) investigated additionally complementary relationship between FDI and trade for recipient countries taking into consideration FDI flows from EU countries to the Central and Eastern European countries (CEECs). They found empirical confirmation of a complementary relationship between FDI inflows from the EU and the CEEC's exports. Let us consider the last case more precisely, the case where the relationship between FDI and trade bear economic growth in the recipient country. Figure 20 represents *trade-investment spiral* which shows the stages of structural adjustment initiated by liberalization of foreign trade and FDI inflows, the change of the specialization pattern, the movement from inter-to intra-trade and from inward to outward FDI, and effects on economic growth.

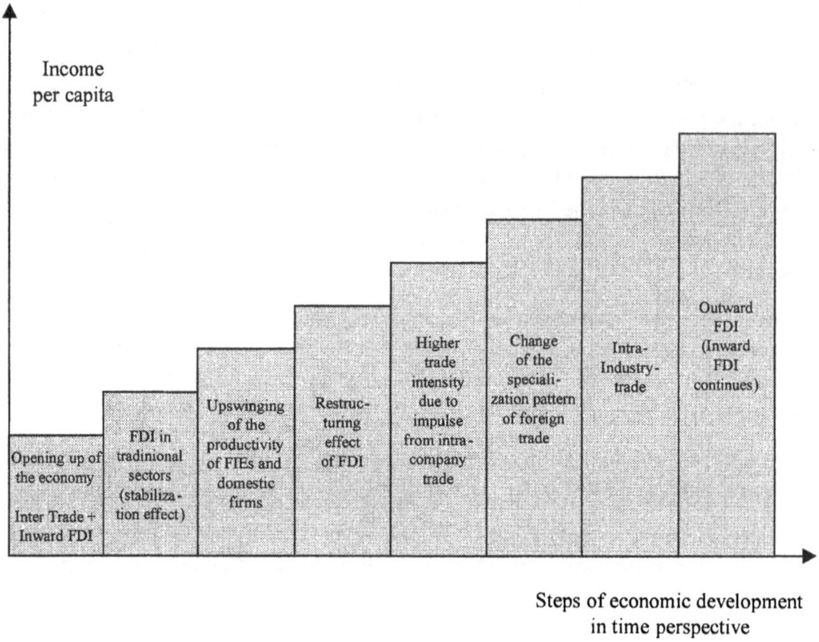

Figure 20: Trade - Investment Spiral of Economic Growth

Trade - Investment Spiral of Economic Growth:

- *Opening up of the economy.* Opening up of the economy is associated with efficiency gains, better exploitation of economies of scale, adoption of more efficient technologies, higher trade intensity necessary to import capital, intermediate goods, and raw materials. All these factors create conditions for MNCs activities and FDI inflows. On the first stage the trade between Western and transition economies is still characterized by inter rather than intra-industry trade as well as inward FDI predominates outward FDI, which is supposed to change with further development.

- *Inflow of FDI to the traditional sectors.* FDI plays a different role in different stages of transformation (BELLAK, 1998). The contribution of FDI to economic growth in the first stage consists of the stabilization effect by maintaining already existing firms and modernizing capital stock. Therefore in the fist stage FDI would primarily be concentrated on traditional sectors.

Privatization can considerably exaggerate this process. FDI in the first stage is thus responsible for the recovery of the traditional sector. Stabilizing of the traditional sector is an important prerequisite for further economic growth.

- *Upswing in productivity.* The rise in the productivity of FIEs creates through technology and knowledge spillovers as well as through competitive impulses from producer and supplier sides the conditions for an upswing in the productivity of domestic firms. Higher total productivity, efficiency, and increased competition promotes the reallocation of resources to more productive sectors, encouraging the creation of new innovative firms.

- *Restructuring effect of FDI.* Rises in the productivity of FIEs and domestic firms together with the stabilization effect of FDI creates conditions for the next contribution of FDI to economic growth. This contribution consists in the restructuring effect which means flows of FDI into new growing industries. FDI would be directed to capital intensive industries with higher R&D and economies of scale (such as automotive industry, mechanical engineering, electronic industry, and manufacturing) and move out of labor intensive and raw material based industries.

- *Higher trade intensity due to impulse from intra-company trade.* As FIEs and subsidiaries become more efficient there is an increase in „demand" for imports of intermediate goods which in turn raises the „supply" of final goods produced and exported by local subsidiaries.

- *The change of the specialization pattern of foreign trade.* FDI would initiate the change of the specialization pattern of foreign trade and move it from exports of the primary commodity sector goods towards exports of manufactured goods. The contribution of manufactured exports to economic growth is much higher than that of the primary sector as the manufactured export sector is associated with increasing returns and higher productivity efficiency. *„The manufactured export sector is more than twice as productive as the rest of the economy"* (LEVIN/RAUT, 1997, p. 162). FIEs are also financially stronger in initiating structural changes than domestic firms.

- *Intra-industry trade.* The change in the specialization pattern as well as higher trade intensity with the special accent on intra-firm trade would lead to the movement from inter to intra-industry trade, trade with similar differentiated products.

- *Outward FDI.* Higher innovation intensity and the development of ownerspecific advantages would lead to outward FDI. At the same time the inward FDI from Western to transition countries would continue to take place as empirical investigations approve that similarities in factor endowments generated by MNCs following their locational behavior may promote direct investment (ETHIER/MARKUSEN 1996).

5.2 FDI in Selected CIS and CEECs

In the 1990s CEECs accounted for the majority of FDI in comparison to CIS with the situation slightly changing recently. FDI was directed towards economies with a successful record in market reforms. Privatization and improvements in property rights as well as adequate economic policy encouraged this process. Channeling FDI to the „right" sectors of the economy reinforced the positive effect of FDI, those with considerable backward and forward linkages. From the other side, financial crisis, e.g. Asian and Russian Crises in 1998 enhanced the risk of new investment into the region.

5.2.1 The Impact of the Russian Financial Crisis on FDI in Investigated Economies

In Russia there was a decline in FDI during 1998 when Russia faced a major crisis. The countries with large GDP exposure in trade with Russia were especially affected by the Russian crisis (WELFENS/GANUSCHTSCHENKO (1999)). This refers to Belarus and the Ukraine with GDP exposure equal to 41% and 8% respectively (see Table 36 - section 5.5. Appendix). Although the Ukraine's GDP exposure in trade with Russia does not seem to be that large, the trade linkages between Ukraine and Russia still remain large enough (share of exports of goods from Ukraine to Russia consists 22% and 27% to both Russia and Belarus). The share of exports from Belarus to Russia is 59%, representing the second highest share in trade with Russia among CIS countries after Moldova. Although Hungary and Poland have reoriented their economies for trade primarily with the West during the period of transformation, the impact of the Russian crisis through trade linkages on these countries was still remarkable (GDP exposure for Hungary 3% and for Poland 2%, with the total share of exports of goods to Russia, Belarus, and Ukraine, 7% and 10% respectively). One should notice that the data represented in the table only refers to merchandise trade exposure, not capturing service trade which includes, above all, transport of energy so essential for Belarus and Ukraine. In Poland there is substantial trade exposure through cross-border trade which is not reflected in the trade statistics. For Hungary indirect trade exposure through intermediary markets was estimated at 30 percent of total exports (EBRD, 1998). The other channels of impact from the Russian crisis such as the banking sector exposure, capital markets, and a potential world economic slowdown are discussed in the literature.

The Russian financial crisis also had a negative effect on the exchange rate movements in many transition economies. The sharp devaluation of the Russian ruble caused a parallel depreciation in exchange rates against the dollar in most investigated countries (see Table 27). Thus in 1998, as compared to 1997, with exchange rates taken for the end of the period, the depreciation of the Belorussian ruble was higher than that of the Russian with 86% and 71% respectively, followed by the Ukrainian hryvnia with 44%. The impact was more modest in more advanced market economies. Thus, Hungary proclaimed depreciation of only 7% while in Poland there was no large negative impact on the exchange rate other than a 0.46% revaluation.

Table 27: Depreciation of Exchange Rate Against Dollar

	Exchange rate - end of period		% (98/97)
	1997	1998	%
Russia	5,96	20,65	-71
Belarus	30740	220000	-86
Ukraine	1,899	3,427	-45
Poland	3,52	3,504	0.46
Hungary	203,5	219,03	-7

Source: IMF (1999), International Financial Statistics Yearbook 1999; own calculations

Exchange rate movements are important as FDI stocks reported in dollar terms at the end of the year include depreciation of the exchange rate and lead to capital losses according to the official stock statistics (see exchange rate change above). Additionally one should note that high volatility of exchange rate like it is the case in Russia reduces stability in this country and can damage both trade and FDI inflows (IMF, 2000). CORKER/BEAUMONT/VAN ELKAN/IAKOVA (2000) discuss in detail the questions of exchange rate regimes in transition economies. EDWARDS (1998) provides also an important paper on this topic.

In Table 28 one can clearly see the impact of the Russian crisis on FDI inflows. In 1998 FDI inflows to Russia accounted for $2,183 mill. in comparison with 1997, where FDI accounted for $6,243 mill., meaning a fall of 65%. One should, however, mention that in 1997 FDI in Russia had reached a peak level and in previous years the amount of FDI was close to $2 bn. Therefore one could say it returned to the previous value in 1998. The fall in FDI inflows in 1998 was also observed in Belarus and reached 28%. In Ukraine FDI continued to grow. The same was relevant for Poland. One should mention that Poland is the only country with very stable FDI growth. Hungary experienced a small drop of 7% in 1998. The peak of FDI inflows in Hungary was observed in 1995.

5.2.2 Comparison of Country's FDI

To compare FDI inflows in transition economies one should take into account that statistical systems of these countries also undergo transformation and that the countries use various approaches to measure FDI. In some cases there is tendency to overestimate FDI inflows as an indicator of successful reforms.

5.2.2.1 Measurement Problems

Measuring FDI is a difficult task. In transition economies these difficulties are also reinforced by the transformation of their statistical systems. The term FDI is defined for balance of payment purposes. According to the IMF definition, FDI represents capital flows that create „a lasting interest of an entity resident in one economy (direct investor) in an entity resident in another economy (direct investment enterprise)". To secure the control of the investor over the company the share of the investor should be more than 10 percent-guarantee for a voice in company decisions.

As DOEHRN (2000) points out, measuring FDI is also difficult in a technical sense. Thus even in developed countries the actual FDI can be substantially misrepresented in the official statistics. In Germany's case, incoming FDI is underreported by a factor of 4 to 6 and outflows seem to be overestimated to some extent. For transformation countries the incentive to overstate the incoming FDI is stronger as FDI serves as an indicator of successful transformation process.

The Russian example shows the disparity of the data on FDI according to official Russian sources and the data of OECD countries (see Figure 21). The common approach to find out the error is to compare inward investment in the recipient country with the data on outward investment in the investor's countries. The information on Russia's inward FDI is taken from IMF source and corresponds to the data of Russian central bank. The figures on outflow to Russia are taken from 18 OECD countries. The deviation between the two sources is astonishingly large. According to the Russian sources the inflows in Russia in 1997 achieved more than $6 bn., the outflow from the OECD countries-based on OECD figures - at the same time fell to only approximately $1 bn. The large discrepancy is a testament to the fact that Russia considerably overstates the inflow of FDI into the country (DOEHRN/GANUSCHTSCHENKO, 2000; DOEHRN/VON WESTERN-HAGEN, 2001).

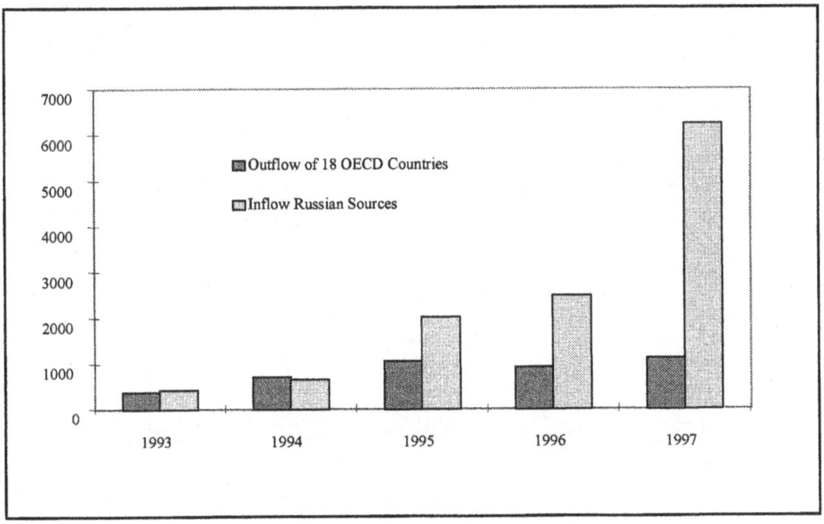

Source: Doehrn/Von Westernhagen (2001)

Figure 21: Measuring FDI in Russia: National and International Sources, 1993 - 1997; US - $ mill.

Some factors could help to explain these differences. The figure on inflows might contain Russian money reinvested in the economy in the form of FDI. Furthermore, tax preferences might make it favorable for Russian investors to involve a foreign partner, even if the latter does not make an investment in the end, and finally, the inflows reflected in Russian statistics could consist of planned FDI not yet reflected in the statistics of most OECD countries.

The other method to judge the quality of the data to compare FDI stocks with FDI inflows, where the inflows are adjusted for exchange rate movements (see Figure 22). In Russia, where insignificant FDI was made before 1990, cumulated inflows adjusted with exchange rate movements should come close to stocks. But, in 1997, cumulated inflows were more that 10 times larger than stocks, although Russian authorities publish both figures.

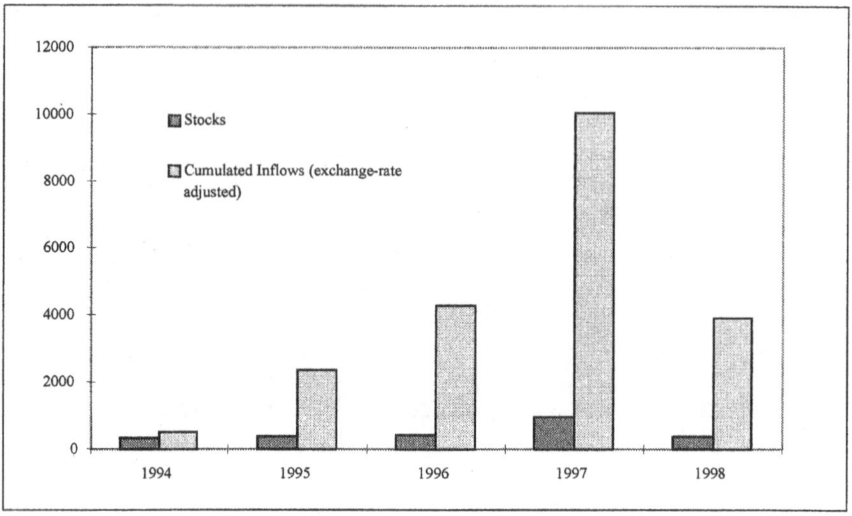

Source: Doehrn/Von Westernhagen (2001)

Figure 22: Comparison of Stock of FDI in Russia and Cumulative Inflows, 1994 - 1998, US - $ mill.

This calculation shows another problem, especially relevant for a country that exhibited considerable exchange rate movements in the past. As a result of market devaluation of the ruble in 1998, FDI stock measured in dollars dropped down to almost one third of the 1997 value. As no substantial outflows of FDI took place, the changes in stock reflected exchange rate movement rather than changes in foreign held equities (DOEHRN/VON WESTERNHAGEN, 2001).

5.2.2.2 Country's FDI

Before 1989 FDI into CEECs and CIS countries was almost negligible. During the period of transformation to a market economy the amount of FDI to CEECs and CIS has considerably increased, from ca. 10% of the world's total FDI since 1989 to 28% in 1996. Thus, in the period from 1989 to 1998, FDI into this region accounted for $74.5 bn. (WESTIN, 1999). The distribution of FDI directed to CEECs and CIS did not equally occur among the economies so that a considerable part of this FDI flowed to Hungary ($16.9 bn.) and Poland ($12.4 bn.), followed by the Czech Republic ($8.5 bn.) (see Table 37 - section 5.5. Appendix).

Table 28: Foreign Direct Investment, (US - $ mill.)

	1989	1990	1991	1992	1993	1994	1995	1996	1997	1998
Hungary										
FDI Inflows	184	311	1,462	1,480	2,350	1,144	4,519	1,982	2,079	1,936
FDI Inflows per capita	18	30	141	144	228	112	443	196	206	192
FDI Cum. Inflows	184	495	1,957	3,437	5,787	6,931	11,450	13,432	15,511	17,447
FDI per capita	18	48	188	334	562	680	1,123	1,330	1,536	1,727
FDI Cum. Inflows, adjusted	174	497	1,849	3,057	4,695	5,357	8,324	8,873	9,099	10,350
FDI per capita, adjusted	17	48	178	297	456	525	816	879	901	1,025
Population (mill.)	10,4	10,4	10,4	10,3	10,3	10,2	10,2	10,1	10,1	10,1
Poland										
FDI Inflows	11	89	291	678	1,715	1,875	3,659	4,498	4,908	5,217
FDI Inflows per capita	0,3	2	8	18	45	49	95	117	127	135
FDI Cum. Inflows	11	100	391	1,069	2,784	4,659	8,318	12,816	17,724	22,941
FDI per capita	0,3	2,6	10	28	72	121	215	332	458	593
FDI Cum. Inflows, adjusted	2	90	359	833	2,077	3,560	7,108	10,307	13,005	18,239
FDI per capita, adjusted	0,1	2,4	9,4	22	54	92	184	267	336	471
Population (mill.)	38	38,2	38,3	38,4	38,5	38,6	38,6	38,6	38,7	38,7

Table 28: Foreign Direct Investment, (US - $ mill.) (cont.)

	1989	1990	1991	1992	1993	1994	1995	1996	1997	1998
Russia										
FDI Inflows					400	637	2,017	2,479	6,243	2,183
FDI Inflows per capita					3	4	14	17	42	15
FDI Cum. Inflows					400	1,037	3,054	5,533	11,776	13,959
FDI per capita					3	7	21	38	80	95
FDI Cum. Inflows, adjusted					311	505	2,368	4,259	10,033	3,922
FDI per capita, adjusted					2	3	16	29	68	27
Population (mill.)					148	148	148	147,5	147,2	146,7
Ukraine										
FDI Inflows						159	267	521	623	743
FDI Inflows per capita						3	5	10	12	15
FDI Cum. Inflows						159	426	947	1,570	2,313
FDI per capita						3	8	18	31	46
FDI Cum. Inflows, adjusted						159	312	800	1,407	1,311
FDI per capita, adjusted						3	6	16	28	26
Population (mill.)						51,9	51,7	51,3	50,9	50,1
Belarus										
FDI Inflows					18	11	15	73	200	144
FDI Inflows per capita					2	1	1	7	20	14
FDI Cum. Inflows					18	28	43	115	315	459
FDI per capita					2	3	4	11	31	45
FDI Cum. Inflows, adjusted					9	6	23	81	41	92
FDI per capita, adjusted					1	1	2	8	4	9
Population (mill.)					10,4	10,3	10,2	10,2	10,2	10,2

Source: UN/ECE (1998), Economic Survey of Europe, No. 3, p. 124; UN/ECE (1999), Economic Survey of Europe, No. 1, p. 170; IMF (1999), International Financial Statistics Yearbook 1999; own calculations

Table 28 represents FDI figures for the five investigated countries. It shows FDI inflows from 1989 to 1998, cumulative FDI, cumulative FDI with exchange rate movements adjusted, which functions as a proxy for the data on FDI stocks, and FDI in per capita terms. The FDI stocks in dollar terms are reflected as it is used later in the gravity model. The only difference from the cumulative FDI are the incorporated exchange rate movements[38]. In the 1990s Hungary and Poland were the prior destinations of FDI inflows among the most advanced transition economies. At the first stage of transformation until the year 1995 Hungary held the leading position in attracting FDI, reaching it's peak of $4.5 bn. in 1995. After 1995, Poland accumulated the most FDI including 1998, where $5.2 bn. was accounted for. In 1997 Russia surpassed Poland with FDI reaching $6.2 bn., which declined considerably after the Russian crisis in 1998 to a mere $2.1 bn. FDI inflows to the Ukraine remained small but increased continuously while the FDI inflows to Belarus also went back in the crisis year 1998. Cumulative FDI inflows in Hungary accounted for $17.4 bn. in 1998, and for $22.9 bn. in Poland. Cumulative FDI inflows reached $13.9 bn. in Russia, $2.3 bn. in the Ukraine, and only $459 mill. in Belarus. The FDI stocks in $ (cum. FDI inflows adjusted with exchange rate) reflect exchange rate movements and therefore lead to considerable capital losses in the countries that experienced depreciation in their exchange rates. Thus, 1998 FDI stocks in Hungary accounted for $10.3 bn. instead of $17.4 bn., in Russia FDI stocks equaled only $3.9 bn. instead of $13.9 bn., and FDI stocks in Belarus equaled only $45 mill. instead of $459 mill. Although these figures do not really reflect the loss of FDI in real terms it still allows one to compare the data among transition economies; one should use the data on FDI stocks in $ terms with incorporated exchange rate movements.

Hungary still held the leading position in per capita terms in 1998 with $1.7 bn. FDI per capita. Poland reported $593 mill. in per capita terms while Russian FDI per capita did not correspond to the size and demand of the Russian market. The Ukraine and especially Belarus are far behind in per capita terms. Thus Russia accounted for only $95 mill. FDI per capita, the Ukraine $46 mill., and Belarus $45 mill. If one compares the Ukraine with Poland and Belarus with Hungary in terms of population then the Ukraine accounted for only ca. 7.7% of Polish FDI per capita and Belarus only 2.6% of Hungarian figures.

[38] To make FDI stocks data comparable among transition economies one should take FDI stocks in one common currency, say in $. From the one side, FDI stocks reflect the data on FDI inflows which while collected by national authorities is expressed in national currency and should be transferred to $ at the average exchange rate for the used period. From the other side, FDI stocks reflect the share of foreign investors in FIEs and should be reported at the end of a calendar year. As the balances of enterprises are given in national currency, the data should be converted into $ with the exchange rate at the end of the calendar year. Thus, data on FDI stocks in $ has also incorporated influence of exchange rate movements and does not always correspond to the data on FDI inflows (DOEHRN/VON WESTERNHAGEN, 2001).

As has already partly been discussed above, there are several problems in measuring FDI. One more problem is that not all transition economies capture reinvested earnings and capital loans in the balance of payments statistics on FDI. Most transition economies record only the equity capital component of FDI (see Table 37 - section 5.5. Appendix). Some countries in the region have begun to alter the FDI statistics. For example, Poland (since 1990) recorded reinvested earnings and inter-company debt. Calculating the data, we used the IMF definition so that the data for Poland might appear to be overestimated in comparison to other countries, which in turn represent lower figures[39].

5.2.3 Privatization and FDI

Based on the definition of FDI it is definitely in the interest of foreign investors to have long-term cooperation with substantial influence on the management of enterprises. Long-term cooperation is an attractive factor for an investor for other reasons as well, where the incentive to earn management fees and other sorts of income is especially strong as enterprises often represent units of multinational corporations where profitability depends strongly on performance of a particular enterprise. Therefore privatization and property rights play a distinguishing role for FDI.

In many transformation countries investment related to privatization accounted for a bulk in the overall amount of investment. The reason for the privatization related FDI lies in the fact that FDI was first of all attracted by the possibility of

---

[39] *"Direct investment is the category of international investment that reflects the objective of obtaining a lasting interest by a resident entity in one economy in an enterprise resident in another economy. (The resident entity is the direct investor and the enterprise is the direct investment enterprise.) The lasting interest implies the existence of a long-term relationship between the direct investor and the enterprise and a significant degree of influence by the investor on the management of the enterprise. Direct investment comprises not only the initial transaction establishing the relationship between the investor and the enterprise but also all subsequent transactions between them and among affiliated enterprises, both incorporated and unincorporated"* (IMF, 1993, p. 86). Furthermore, according to the IMF definition *"... a direct investment enterprise is defined ...as an incorporated or unincorporated enterprise in which a direct investor, who is resident in another economy, owns 10 percent or more of the ordinary shares or voting power (for an incorporated enterprise) or the equivalent (for an unincorporated enterprise"*. There are three main components to FDI: *"(i) equity capital - the purchase of shares of the investor in a foreign country; (ii) reinvested earnings; and (iii) capital loans - the borrowing and lending of funds between direct investors and affiliates"* (EBRD Transition Report 1998, p. 82).

participating in the privatization of state-owned enterprises rather than by the existing GDP growth. Thus, e.g., in Russia, FDI inflows increased steadily from 1994 to the crisis 1998 year, while GDP did not recover until 1997. By contrast, the restructuring and upgrading of inefficient state-owned enterprises associated with the privatization process contributes to the GDP growth in transition economies. Thus there was a boom of FDI in Hungary in 1995, while GDP growth was considerable only in 1997.

The extreme example of privatization related FDI is Hungary, which in 1999 had already almost exhausted its potential for privatization related investment. The privatization of both small and large enterprises as well as infrastructure privatization was nearly completed in Hungary in 1999. The share of privatization related FDI in Hungary decreased from 68 percent in 1995 to 13 percent in 1997, giving space for the other FDI inflows (UNCTAD, 1998). The majority of FDI inflows (more than 60%) realized in Hungary were greenfield investments and reinvested profits, not payments for privatized assets (CSAKI, 1998). The amount of foreign capital represented 70% of privatization revenues in 1990 - 1997. In Poland in the period from 1990 to 1996 foreign investors bought 45,1% of the total number of state-owned enterprises. The privatization process in Poland is not yet fully completed. It was planned to reinforce the privatization in 1999, where many sales should represent strategic stakes for foreign investors. At the same time, Poland made progress in the sense of creating favorable conditions for foreign investors to participate in the privatization of state-owned enterprises. Thus in Poland there are no limitations on the foreign capital stake. Non-residents may acquire or purchase up to 100% of the company's assets. Along with that, the principle of national treatment is valid which provides equal conditions for companies with foreign investment and local firms (WARESA, 1998).

The investigated CIS countries experienced considerable difficulties in attracting foreign strategic investors. In Russia the privatization of large oil companies according to the privatization program of the 1998 has been postponed. The major privatization event at the end of 1998 was the sale of 2.5% of Gasprom. Given low dollar asset prices, the sale of state companies is not a top priority in Russia. In the Ukraine, large scale privatization was realized only to some extent, where 53 of the 200 largest enterprises were privatized. Attracting strategic foreign investors was difficult because of relatively high share prices and the lack of transparency in the procedure. In Belarus the progress in small as well as large privatization is still incomplete and hence there was only little possibility for strategic foreign investors. The lack of market oriented land code and constraints on the sale of land prevented the privatization in the agricultural sector and represented an obstacle on the urban and the rural land markets (EBRD, 1999).

5.2.4 Sectoral Aspects

The success in transformation depends heavily upon in which sectors FDI is directed. FDI should be allocated to the right" sectors. It is a difficult task to find comparable data on sectoral reallocation of FDI in investigated countries. As a reference one could take UNCTAD as a source although it differs in the definition of FDI from the IMF approach as portfolio investment and bank credits are also covered to some extent. Table 29 represents sectoral and industrial distribution of inward FDI stock in five transformation countries. The data for Belarus is a special case as it refers to the percentage of total foreign investing firms (BELARUS ECONOMIC TRENDS, 1999).

In regard to the „right" sectors, the term „right" changes along with the transformation process (BELLAK, 1998). Thus FDI tends to play a different role at different stages of transformation. During the early stage, it contributes to the stabilization of the economy by supporting existing firms and modernizing their capital stock. The early stage is characterized by investments in typical sectors but provides little input to the restructuring of the economy in the form of moving from resource and labor intensive industries to R&D and capital intensive industries. In the second stage, investment will focus on restructuring and will later be directed predominately towards growing industries.

The more advanced transformation economies such as Hungary and Poland have already overcome the first stage and moved up to the next „restructuring" ladder. The data on reallocation of FDI in Hungary and Poland confirms this suggestion. Such former targets as food industry and textiles were consequently replaced by investment in machinery and equipment industry as well as the chemical industry which are the most skill- and technology-intensive, and are the major contributors to economic growth in some transition economies. The investment in machinery, equipment industry, and chemical industry was simultaneously followed by investment in services: wholesale and distributive trade, finance (banking and insurance) sector, transport, and telecommunications sector which are initially supposed to support the restructuring process.

The tendencies for the three CIS countries are less dynamic and show that FDI is primarily directed into traditional sectors. 16% of FDI in Russia in 1997 was made in the fuel industry, a considerably high figure in comparison to the other transition economies (this figure will be even higher if we consider FDI without banking credits). FDI in machinery and equipment still remains very low, which is a serious obstacle on the way towards restructuring and sustainable growth. An astonishing amount of FDI was made in the finance sector, which shows an existing misbalance between real and monetary sectors in Russia. FDI as a whole and distributive trade are also considerable. Some large projects were started in infrastructure coinciding with the interest of investors in infrastructure potential in basic telecommunications.

Table 29: Central and Eastern Europe: Sectoral and Industrial Distribution of Inward FDI Stock in Selected Countries, 1997 (Percentage)

Sector/Industry	Hungary	Poland[a]	Russia	Ukraine	Belarus*
Primary sector	**2**	**2**	**16**	**2**	**2**
Agriculture, hunting, forestry & fishing	1	0	..	2	2
Mining, quarrying & petroleum	1	2	16[b]	..	0
Secondary sector	**39**	**61**	**23**	**50**	**34**
Food, beverages & tobacco	9	21	9	20	7
Textiles, leather & clothing	2	3[d]	..	2[d]	4
Wood, paper, publishing & printing	3	5	4	3	11
Chemicals, chemical products 6 coke &, petroleum products	8	5	3	7	3
Non-metallic mineral products (cement & building materials)	3	6	..	7	1
Basic metals & metal products	2	1	3	3	2
Machinery and equipment	12[e]	17[e]	4[f]	9	4
Electrical machinery & apparatus	..	..	..	..	2
Automotive	..	..	..	..	0
Unspecified secondary	0	3	..	..	0

Table 29: Central and Eastern Europe: Sectoral and Industrial Distribution of Inward FDI Stock in Selected Countries, 1997 (Percentage) (cont.)

Sector/Industry	Hungary	Poland[a]	Russia	Ukraine	Belarus*
Tertiary sector	**59**	**38**	**51**	**40**	**65**
Electricity & water distribution	14	..	..	..	0
Construction	4	5	..	..	3
Wholesale trade & distributive trade	12	6	11	19	45
Hotels &restructuring (tourism)	2	..	5	..	1
Transport, storage & telecommunications	8	5	2	5	6
Finance (& banking & insurance)	9	21	32	9	0
Real estate, rental activities & business services	8	..	..	2	6
Public administration, health & social services	2	0	1	5	3
Unspecified	**-**	**-**	**10**	**8**	**0**

Source: UNCTAD (1999), World Investment Report 1999; Belarus Economic Trends (1999), April - June 1999

These estimates are based on national statistical surveys and are not necessarily comparable with FDI data based on balance - of - payments figures;

a End 1996.

b Fuel industry.

c Includes „consumer goods"

d Includes other light industries

e Includes electrical machinery & automotive industries.

f Includes basic metals & metal products.

g Includes trade in vehicles and gases.

** The data for Belarus is taken as % of total foreign investing firms.*

Ukraine shows some slight signs of change with 9% of FDI made in the machinery and equipment industry and 7% in the chemical industry (Table 29). But on the other hand, the food industry is still the major recipient of FDI in the Ukraine. From the service side considerable FDI was directed towards the whole and distributive trade followed by banking, transport, and the telecommunications sectors. In Belarus FDI was based on the amount of firms in the food industry, textiles, and wood industry, where the latter accounts for 11% of FDI. The contribution of FDI remains small in Belarus when it comes to the machinery, equipment, and chemical industries. A large share consists of whole trade and the distributive trade sector. Some FDI was made in transport and telecommunications as well as in business services (including engineering and information services), which are supposed to support successful transition.

Except for Russia, where FDI in the primary sector accounts for a large share, FDI in other investigated countries in equal importance were made predominately in the secondary and tertiary sectors. The tertiary sector accounts for a leading position in Hungary, Russia, and Belarus. Manufacturing dominates FDI in Poland and the Ukraine.

The FDI made up to now in the investigated CIS was predominately directed towards traditional sectors which were very well developed before and are also further called upon to play an important role in the economy (VON WESTERNHAGEN, 2000). A shift towards new industries and above all towards manufacturing is not observed at the present (except for the Ukraine to some extent). There is a slight improvement tendency in the service sector in the Ukraine and Belarus (in the banking sector in Ukraine; in the transport and telecommunications sector in both the Ukraine and Belarus). High FDI in Russia into the banking sector was not supported by FDI in manufacturing, chemicals, and other services necessary for a balanced development. By contrast, Hungary and Poland showed first steps in restructuring by increasing investment in machinery and equipment, chemicals, and at the same time in service sectors.

5.3 Empirical Investigation of the FDI Potential

This paper estimates potential FDI stocks for the investigated transition economies in order to determine the backlog the countries have in attracting FDI. The next step is to examine the role FDI could play in gross fixed capital formation in the long run and its contribution to the restructuring of the economy in the process of transition.

5.3.1 Specification of the Gravity Model for FDI

The estimates for potential FDI stocks in more advanced CEECs, (Hungary and Poland, as well as in CIS countries with little market experience) Russia, the Ukraine, and Belarus are based on the work of DOEHRN (2000). Doehrn derives coefficients from investment of 15 OECD countries in 25 industrialized and emerging economies. He uses data on FDI-stocks abroad in 1995 that are taken from OECD sources. The coefficients from his estimation of the „normal" pattern are used to make statements on FDI stocks in investigated economies.

The regression of Doehrn includes the following parameters (see equation 5.1):

$$FDI_{ij} = F\left(GDP_i, GDP_j, DIST_{ij}, R\&D_i, WAGE_i, WAGE_j, LANG_{ij}, ENGLANG_j\right) \quad (5.1)$$

where:

FDI_{ij} = FDI from country i into country j
GDP_i and GDP_j = GDP in the source and the host country, respectively
$DIST_{ij}$ = The distance between country i and country j
$R\&D_i$ = Expenditure on R&D in investing country
$WAGE_i$ and $WAGE_j$ = Wage level in investor and host country, respectively
$LANG_{ij}$ = Dummy variable for common language
$ENGLANG_j$ = Dummy variable for English language spoken in recipient country

GDP as a proxy for the „size" of the market and *R&D* intensity in the investor country are considered as the main „push" factors responsible for investment activities abroad. Thus *R&D* would allow multinational corporations to use their owner-specific advantages which encourages them to produce abroad. *GDP* in a recipient country is a main „pull" factor for FDI, therefore emphasizing market penetrating as a major incentive for making FDI. The impact of wage levels in investor and host countries on FDI was argued in the literature. It is commonly expected that low wages in the host county is a stimulating factor for the reallocation of production and hence for FDI flows. A dummy variable for a common language is a cultural stimulating factor responsible for better understanding in conducting business. Doehrn also includes a dummy variable for the English language in his estimation. English spoken in the recipient country should also promote FDI.

The variables *GDP* of investor's country and *GDP* of host country are measured in billions of dollar, the variable $DIST_{ij}$ is measured in kilometers, the variable *R&D* represents expenses on research and development as a percent from *GDP* in an investors country, the variable $WAGE_{i,j}$ is measured in 1000 dollars per worker and the variables *LANG* and *ENLANG* are dummy variables.

Doehrn introduced new estimation techniques in his gravity model approach. He uses a nonlinear estimator as an alternative to the OLS procedure. OLS estimates, through the attempt to linearize the specification of the model by means of logarithms, aggregates multiplicative error-term. The minimization of multiplicative error-term in the OLS procedure is the same as the minimization of a percentage error. From this it follows that small figures in a sample could have an enormous impact on the coefficients associated with large percentage errors. An alternative to the OLS procedure could be to introduce an additive error term in the gravity equation and to carry out estimation applying non-linear estimation techniques.

The other problem to be discussed is connected with the estimation procedure used in the case of an insufficient database. In having to estimate FDI Doehrn was confronted with the problem of lack of information in some cases in the data matrix. Under the assumption that the data is missing in the cases of very small FDI records in the recipient county he estimates the equation with minimal possible values for FDI in every particular case possible with a Tobit-estimator in the linear model framework. Available software only allows for the application of the Tobit-estimator in linear, not in non-linear models.

The coefficients of both linear and non-linear estimations are shown in Table 30. The R^2 in the non-linear estimation is 83% and the R^2 in the linear estimation is 69%. Although both estimators have common features there are some differences in the impact of such variables as *WAGE* and *DIST*. Non-linear estimation shows no evidence that wages in investor and host countries play any significant role for FDI. The impact of wage level in the host country on FDI according to the linear estimation also exhibits very low results. It shows however that low wages are not really a primary incentive for FDI but the market penetration (market size, market share) plays the major role. The variable *DIST* also becomes a different importance according to both estimators.

Table 30: Estimates of a Gravity Model of FDI Stock*

	estimation 1: Non-linear	estimation 2: Tobit
Constant	0.025	-4.850
	(2.1)	(3.6)
GDP of Investor's country	0.833	1.064
	(18.4)	(12.4)
GDP of Host country	0.868	1.302
	(25.4)	(14.6)
Distance	-0.178	-1.353
	(6.3)	(14.6)
Expenses on Research and Development, investors country	1.492	1.336
	(5.8)	(4.1)
Wages investors' country	-	1.504
		(4.9)
Wages host country	-	0.078
		(0.6)
Common language (Dummy-variable)	0.979	1.164
	(12.2)	(3.6)
Official language English in host country (Dummy-variable)	1.007	2.161
	(12.0)	(8.7)
R^2 adj.	0.830	0.696
number of observations	395	464

Source: Doehrn (2000)

* *In brackets: t-statistics*

Thus the non-linear estimator depicts smaller influence of distance on FDI as the linear estimator. The differences in influence are also observable for other elasticities where elasticity with respect to market size in the host country is less then unity in equation 1 but above in equation 2. However, these differences refer to different methods. There is not enough empirical evidence to say which estimator provides better estimation results so both estimators are used to predict „normal" FDI pattern between Hungary, Poland, CIS countries - Russia, the Ukraine, Belarus, and OECD countries. Since Hungary and Poland represent more sophisticated transition economies it is worth comparing them to the situation in CIS countries in terms of FDI.

5.3.2 Gravity Model Results

The gravity model results for five countries are represented in Table 31. The table is structured in a way that shows the potential FDI pattern under the assumption that transformation countries would follow the „normal" sample characteristic for developed market economies, the *no change scenario*. It also represents two more scenarios where it is assumed that these countries would exhibit a light catching up process during the following ten years with GDP growth in the *scenario 2005 I* of 2 percentage points above OECD growth equal to 2.5% - points, and in the *scenario 2005 II* of 4 percentage points above the OECD. The catching up scenarios, however, look too optimistic for some countries and too pessimistic for others. Thus, the growth rate of Hungary in 1997 was 4.4%, for Poland 6.9%, for Russia it was only 0.8%, the Ukraine 3.2%, and Belarus 10%, where the situation for the CIS countries has changed drastically lately. The same catching up scenario is chosen for all five countries in order to provide a better comparison basis. The next part of the table shows FDI inflows per year necessary to compensate for the lag in FDI stocks (cumulated inflows) [40] and reach the potential level according to the three scenarios.

The obtained results for Hungary proclaim an interesting picture which, however, is not surprising if we take into account the unequal distribution of FDI among the CEECs and CIS as mentioned above, where Hungary was a „champion" in the amount of attracted FDI. The gravity model results for Hungary show that the accumulated FDI pattern is far above its potential level. It is so large that it overcomes the predicted level for the *scenario 2005 II* on 42% according to the estimator 1, and on 108% according to the estimator 2 (see Table 32). One could guess that ample FDI inflows into Hungarian economy are primarily related to the transformation process in this country and in the long run would come down to its „normal" level which is also relevant as the catching up gap between Hungary and OECD countries diminishes. In other words, the FDI inflows during the initial stage of catching up always tend to be much larger so that the gravity model which shows „normal" patterns among developed market economies predicts long run FDI composition which looks underestimated for successful transformation economies at their initial stage. One could expect that FDI into the Hungarian economy had already exhibited its peak point and will shrink down approaching its normal pattern in the long run[41].

---

[40] We use cum. inflows as a proxy for FDI stocks since there are no available data on stocks for all investigated countries.

[41] Average yearly inflows of FDI to Hungary is not possible to distinguish with this gravity model.

Table 31: Projections of FDI, 1995 - 2005, US - $ mill.

		observed 1995	scenarios		
Country	Estimate	cum. inflows	no change	2005 I	2005 II
Hungary	Estimate 1	8,324	2,756	4,962	5,850
	Estimate 2	8,324	933	3,120	3,994
	Average yearly inflows required to reach				
	cumulated inflows[1], estimate 1		...	...	...
	cumulated inflows[1], estimate 2		...	...	...
Poland	Estimate 1	7,108	7,973	14,354	16,922
	Estimate 2	7,108	5,360	17,926	22,946
	Average yearly inflows required to reach				
	cumulated inflows[1], estimate 1		87	725	981
	cumulated inflows[1], estimate 2		...	1082	1,584
Russia	Estimate 1	2,368	19,475	35,059	41,332
	Estimate 2	2,368	7,330	24,514	31,378
	Average yearly inflows required to reach				
	cumulated inflows[1], estimate 1		1,711	3,269	3,896
	cumulated inflows[1], estimate 2		496	2,215	2,901
Ukraine	Estimate 1	312	2,799	5,039	5,941
	Estimate 2	312	457	1,530	1,958
	Average yearly inflows required to reach				
	cumulated inflows[1], estimate 1		249	473	563
	cumulated inflows[1], estimate 2		15	122	165
Belarus	Estimate 1	23	992	1,785	2,105
	Estimate 2	23	165	552	706
	Average yearly inflows required to reach				
	cumulated inflows[1], estimate 1		97	176	208
	cumulated inflows[1], estimate 2		14	53	68

Source: Doehrn/Von Westernhagen (2001)

[1] *Exchange rate adjusted*

Table 32: Deviation of County's Cumulated Inflows from Its Potential

	Russia	%	Ukraine	%	Belarus	%	Poland	%	Hungary	%
observed 1995	2,368		312		23		7,108		8,324	
no change										
Estimate 1	19,475	12	2,799	11	922	2.5	7,973	89	2,756	302
Estimate 2	7,330	32	457	68	165	13.9	5,360	133	933	892
2005 I										
Estimate 1	35,059	7	5,039	6	1,785	1	14,354	50	4,962	168
Estimate2	24,514	10	1,530	20	552	4	17,926	40	3,120	267
2005 II										
Estimate 1	41,332	6	5,941	5	2,105	1	16,922	42	5,850	142
Estimate 2	31,378	8	1,958	16	706	3	22,946	31	3,994	208

Source: Von Westernhagen (2000)

The results for Poland tend to be close to that of Hungary but still predict considerable unused potential. Note that Poland represents substantially larger market than Hungary and consequently might be a more attractive goal for FDI. Part of differences between these two countries can be explained above all by the relative progress in privatization in these countries. The level of FDI observed in 1995 looks higher than the potential in the *no change scenario* according to estimator 2, but accounts for only 50% and 40% from the estimated potential level in the *scenario 2005 I* due to estimators 1 and 2 respectively. The *scenario 2005 II* is closer to the real situation for Poland now. To preserve the situation, higher GDP would lead to more potential FDI whereas actual FDI accounts for only 42% and 31% of the predicted by the *scenario 2005 II* level. Thus, the gravity model results for Poland still show considerable potential. In order to reach this potential, Poland should accumulate between $87 mill. to $981 mill. per year according to the estimator 1 and between $1,082 mill. to $1,584 mill. according to the estimator 2.

Russia's 1995 actual FDI accounts for 12% or 32% from potential FDI in the *no change scenario*, 7% or 10% in the *2005 I scenario,* and 6% or 8% in the *2005 II scenario* according to the estimators 1 and 2 respectively, therefore indicating a rather substantial lag from the potential level.

According to estimator 1 the necessary volume of FDI per year consists of $1,711 mill. in the *no change scenario* and goes up to $3,896 mill. in the *2005 II scenario*. However, estimate 2 represents lower figures from \$496 mill. to \$2,901 mill. necessary to invest per year to reach „normal" stocks (cum. inflows).

Ukraine's cumulated inflows in 1995 account for 11% or 68% of the potential pattern in the *no change scenario*, 6% or 20% in the *2005 I scenario,* and 5% or 16% in the *2005 II scenario* according to estimators 1 and 2 respectively. To compensate for the lag, the Ukraine should accumulate between \$249 mill. to \$563 mill. per year according to estimator 1 and from \$15 mill. to \$165 mill. according to estimator 2.

Belarus shows the largest lag. It's cumulative FDI in 1995 is only 2.5% or 14% of that in the *no change scenario*, 1% or 4% in the *2005 I scenario*, and 1% or 3% in the *2005 II scenario*. The FDI necessary to reach „natural" FDI stock varies from \$97 mill. to \$208 mill. according to estimator 1 and from \$14 mill. to \$68 mill. according to estimator 2.

5.3.3 FDI and Capital Formation

Several aspects have to be taken into account when analyzing the impact of FDI on capital formation and thus on the restructuring of the economies in investigated countries. First of all, the size of gross fixed capital formation necessary to bring the investigated countries forward in transformation should be discussed. Secondly, the contribution of FDI to gross fixed capital formation has to be examined. A comparative perspective is useful.

5.3.3.1 Investment and Growth

The growth rate is mainly influenced by the investment/GDP ratio and the marginal product of capital. The ratio of GFCF to GDP and marginal capital for selected countries is indicated in Table 33. The marginal capital for Hungary and Poland is close to that of South Korea and Malaysia. High marginal capital for Belarus is doubtful as the official figures on economic growth in Belarus are not reliable. The figures for Russia and the Ukraine are difficult to interpret since they are negative.

There is no reliable information concerning the size and structure of capital stocks in investigated countries. Therefore the suggestions about the size of capital formation can not be derived from considerations about the difference between existing and necessary capital stock. One could guess only about the necessary investment ratio in the countries taking as a reference the investment ratios from other emerging economies.

Table 33 shows the share of gross fixed capital formation (GFCF) in several Asian emerging economies and in some European transition countries. The data for these two regions is considerably different. The Asian countries exhibit GFCF between 35% and 42% of GDP, whereas the ratio in CEECs is between 15% and slightly more that 30%, with Russia approaching a ratio similar to that in Hungary and Poland. However, the development in Russia was rather different from other

European countries. While the above considered CEECs experienced upwards tendencies, only Russia had a relative fall in investment from nearly 24% in 1992 to less than 19% in 1997, and 1998 data indicates a further decline (DOEHRN/ VON WESTERNHAGEN, 2001).

Table 33: Share of Gross Fixed Capital Formation in GDP in Selected Emerging Economies, 1992 - 1997,%

	1992	1993	1994	1995	1996	1997	g_y 96 - 97	GFCF/Y 96 - 97	dY/dK 96 - 97
South Korea	36.6	36.0	35.7	36.6	36.9	35.0	4.8	35.95	0.13
Malaysia	36.0	38.3	40.1	43.0	42.3	42.8	7.5	42.55	0.18
Thailand	39.3	39.4	39.9	41.8	40.8	35.6	-0.4	38.2	-0.01*
Czech Republic	-	28.0	29.6	32.8	33.0	30.7	0.7	31.85	0.02
Estonia	20.9	13.3	20.5	26.0	33.1	-	6.4	33.1	0.2
Hungary	19.9	18.9	20.1	19.1	21.5	22.3	3.9	21.9	0.18
Poland	16.8	15.9	16.2	16.9	19.0	21.2	6.8	20.1	0.34
Belarus	25.4	33.9	33.2	25.0	21.8	26.0	11.1	23.9	0.46
Russia	23.9	20.4	21.8	20.3	20.4	18. 8	-1.3	19.6	-0.07*
Ukraine	27.4	24.5	23.7	23.4	20.9	18.4	-3.0	19.65	-0.15*

Source: Doehrn/Von Westernhagen (2001); World Bank (1998/1999), World Development Report 1998/1999; EBRD (1999), Transition Report 1999; own calculations

* *Negative figures*

It is clear that more investment is needed than the recently observed amount to modernize the investigated CIS countries within a reasonable period of time. It is assumed, for simplicity, that the ratio of investment to GDP in the investigated countries should be 30%, which is admittedly arbitrary, but it may be a good guess.

5.3.3.2 *The Contribution of FDI to Gross Fixed Capital Formation*

To analyze which role FDI plays in the restructuring of transition economies, the contribution of FDI to the gross fixed capital formation in the long run should be estimated. For the estimation the results for potential FDI inflows attained from the gravity model are being used (see Table 35). Under the assumption that a ratio of investment to GDP showed to be close to 30% for successful transformation, the results for investigated countries were attained, which show that long run FDI plays a moderate role in gross fixed capital formation, where the ratio tends to be higher for smaller economies.

If one refers to the data represented in Table 34, one would find substantially higher results for Hungary and Poland for the data period from 1994 to 1996 where for Russia, the Ukraine, and Belarus the data according to the gravity model results could be under the „normal" long run level.

Table 34: Central and Eastern Europe: Selected Indicators of the Importance of Inward FDI by Country

Country	FDI inward stock over GDP, 1996 (Per cent)	FDI inward stock per capita, 1996 (Dollars)	FDI inflows over gross fixed capital formation, 1994 - 1996 (Per cent)
Central and Eastern Europe average[a]	6[b]	151[b]	8[b]
Hungary	34	1,490	30
Estonia	19	551	23
Latvia	17	335	
Albania	11	84	
Czech Republic	11	537	11
Poland	11	339	18
Moldova, Republic of	9	34	36
Slovakia	5	161	4
Bulgaria	4	51	5
Lithuania	4	80	
Romania	4	55	6
Croatia	4	185	
Slovenia	4	366	5
Ukraine	3	26	4
Russian Federation	1	45	2
FYR Macedonia	1	20	
Belarus	-	6	1
Reference group[c]			
Trinidad and Tobago	77	2,996	46
Grenada	71	2,016	22
Malaysia	49	2,014	12
Fiji	39	925	21

Table 34: Central and Eastern Europe: Selected Indicators of the Importance of Inward FDI by Country (cont.)

Country	FDI inward stock over GDP, 1996 (Per cent)	FDI inward stock per capita, 1996 (Dollars)	FDI inflows over gross fixed capital formation, 1994 - 1996 (Per cent)
Costa Rica	36	915	22
Botswana	33	942	31
Chili	27	1,356	17
Mexico	22	783	15
Panama	22	646	13
Tunisia	22	470	7
Belize	15	762	15
Peru	15	374	23
Thailand	12	328	3
Colombia	11	261	16
Mauritius	7	252	2
Turkey	3	92	2
Syrian Arab Republic	2	74	1
Lebanon	2	61	2
Average, reference group	26	848	15

Source: UNCTAD (1998), World Investment Report 1998

a Including Croatia, Slovenia and TFYR Macedonia.

b Unweighted averages (ratios for the region or group taken as a whole).

c This group, selected for comparison, includes countries with GDP per capita ranging from $2,000 to $5, 000 per anuum.

Thus Hungary's FDI inflows indicator on gross fixed capital formation in the period of 1994 - 1996 is the highest among all Central and Eastern European countries, far above average (8%) and equal to 30%. The same indicator for Poland is 18%, which is also a considerable value. The figures for Russia, the Ukraine, and Belarus are 2%, 4%, and 1% respectively (see Table 35).

Gravity model results for Poland show that FDI in gross fixed capital formation could vary from 0.2% (c1) to 3.1% (c2) in the long run. For Russia from 0.5% (c2) to 2.6% (c1), for the Ukraine - from 0.1% (c2) to 3.5% (c1), and for Belarus from 0.5% (c2) to 4.8% (c1) (see Table 35). The results for Hungary do not have any economic information but it is plausible to assume that further FDI inflows into the Hungarian economy will be much less than before and the contribution of FDI to gross fixed capital formation will become moderate.

The interpretation of these figures depends on a number of factors. First of all, the gravity model represents the „normal" pattern characteristic for the long run so that this data could be, however, bad compared with the data representing a specific period of time. The high ratios for Hungary and Poland are to be explained through the catching up process of these countries where there was a bump up of FDI in the given period and GDP did not yet grow enough to compensate growth of FDI. The actual share of gross fixed capital formation in GDP for these countries is also considerably lower than admitted in the gravity model. High ratios of FDI in gross fixed capital formation for Hungary and Poland could also be an effect of overall increasing importance of FDI in the global economy. The share of FDI in gross fixed capital formation is not high for CIS countries because of legal and regulatory problems and long situations of recession connected with political instability, as well as a prolonged privatization process.

Table 35: Contribution of FDI to Gross Fixed Capital Formation, 1995 to 2005 averages, %

		scenario		
Country	assumptions	no change	2005 I	2005 II
Hungary	c1	...	...	...
	c2	...	...	...
Poland	c1	0.2	1.6	1.9
	c2	...	2.4	3.1
Russia	c1	1.6	2.4	2.6
	c2	0.5	1.7	1.9
Ukraine	c1	2.2	3.3	3.5
	c2	0.1	0.9	1.0
Belarus	c1	3.2	4.6	4.8
	c2	0.5	1.4	1.6

Source: Von Westernhagen (2000)

In general in the economic history there are very different country experiences in importance of FDI for the transformation and restructuring of the economy. The Asian countries such as China, Malaysia, and Singapore reported high figures reaching 60% for Singapore in the period from the mid eighties to the begin of the nineties. On the other hand, Austria's catching up after World War II was successfully carried out without attracting much FDI. The ratio of FDI in gross fixed capital formation in Austria still remains rather low, only 1.8% in the mid nineties. The experience with FDI seems to vary strongly from country to country where the incentives to invest on one hand and the ability of the country to attract investments on the other play a decisive role. High ratios of FDI over gross fixed capital formation are more typical for the countries in the early stage of their transformation where the countries possess attractive incentives at the same time which are able to cause high FDI inflows. In this period of transformation the countries have low saving rates and do not have enough capital needed for the restructuring of the economy. This tendency seems to change in the long run where FDI plays only a moderate role in gross fixed capital formation and country's savings come to play the primary role. The experience also shows that the importance of FDI seems to be larger for small countries than for large countries in the transformation stage as well as in the long run.

5.4 Tentative Conclusions

FDI is associated with the positive impact on economic growth in terms of additional capital but foremost in consideration of technology transfer and knowledge spillovers, which bring productivity gains to the economy as a whole. On the other hand economic growth would in turn lead to more FDI as it is one of the major factors distinguishing FDI inflows between countries. FDI may, under circumstances of insufficient competition policy, lead to negative effects on domestic firms where it limits, first of all, access to the domestic market, reduces competition, and hence possibilities for technology transfer. Thus domestic countries should look for a balanced competition policy between MNCs and domestic firms.

FDI patterns vary considerably between more advanced transition economies like Hungary and Poland and the investigated CIS countries. Cumulative FDI inflows in CIS countries do not correspond to the size and demand of these markets, although official statistics tend to overestimate actual FDI inflows. To create favorable conditions for attracting FDI, privatization is expected to play a decisive role. In this respect, it is especially important to make privatization objects available to strategic foreign investors since the evidence shows that FIEs are more productive and efficient than domestic firms. In order to make FDI successful it should be directed to the „right" sectors of the economy. Sectoral analysis for more advanced transition economies witnesses that they have already surpassed the first stage associated with the investments in the traditional sectors of the economy and moved up to the sectors that contribute considerably to the restructuring of the economy. Thus in Hungary FDI grows in machinery, equipment industry, and chemical industry, which are the most skill and technology intensive ones. FDI made in CIS until now has been predominately directed towards traditional sectors. Little remains of the FDI share in machinery and equipment while FDI in food, textile industries, and, particularly in Russia's case, fuel industry still prevail.

This chapter also examines the potential of FDI inflows into investigated transition economies with the gravity model. The gravity model results for Hungary and Poland reflect unequal distribution of FDI between CEECs. Thus, Hungary according to the gravity model, has already exhausted it's potential. Gravity model results point to a considerable potential in FDI inflows for the CIS countries, but the contribution of FDI to gross fixed capital formation in the long run according to the gravity model tends to be moderate.

One should take into account the static character of the model, which does not cover policy decisions of the country to attract FDI. Thus, the intense need of the country to attract more FDI e.g. though privatization policy can considerably stimulate FDI inflows; the opposite is valid for restrictive policy. An important aspect not treated here is the link between FDI and the real exchange rate; according to FROOT/STEIN (1991) a real depreciation of the currency leads to higher FDI inflows since capital equipment (and firms) become relatively cheaper for foreign investors. Thus the contribution of FDI to gross fixed capital formation and hence to the restructuring of the economy during the period of transition can be high once the countries create attractive conditions for foreign investors, but in the long run the contribution of FDI to gross fixed capital formation will be moderate and the saving rate of a country is supposed to play a more decisive role. Even with very optimistic projections for GDP growth, the role of FDI, although important, can not initiate a process of sustained growth in the long run and the considerable share of capital formation should still be financed through domestic savings.

5.5 Appendix

Table 36: Trade Exposure to Russia (in percent)

Central and eastern Europe and the Baltic states[1]	Share of exports of goods to Russia[2]	Share of exports of goods to Ukraine[2]	Share of exports of goods to Belarus[2]	Total	Share of exports in GDP[2]	GDP exposure[3]
Bulgaria	7	3	0	10	47	5
Croatia	4	0	0	4	22	1
Czech Republic	2	1	-	4	43	2
Estonia	6	5	2	13	49	6
FYR Macedonia	2	8	1	11	36	4
Hungary	5	1	0	7	43	3
Latvia	21	4	3	28	32	9
Lithuania	7	9	12	28	44	12
Poland	4	5	1	10	20	2
Romania	3	1	0	4	28	1
Slovak Republic	3	3	-	6	45	3
Slovenia	4	1	-	5	47	2
Average	6	4	2	11	38	4

Table 36: Trade Exposure to Russia (in percent) (cont.)

Central and eastern Europe and the Baltic states[1]	Share of exports of goods to Russia[2]	Share of exports of goods to Ukraine[2]	Share of exports of goods to Belarus[2]	Total	Share of exports in GDP[2]	GDP exposure[3]
Commonwealth of independent States						
Armenia	23	2	1	26	14	4
Azerbaijan	23	4	0	28	21	6
Belarus	59	15	-	74	55	41
Georgia	30	4	0	34	9	3
Kazakhstan	39	3	-	42	30	13
Kyrgyzstan	21	1	1	23	37	9
Moldova	63	5	2	70	38	26
Russia	-	9	6	15	20	3
Tajikistan	8	1	1	10	60	6
Turkmenistan	5	-	-	5	41	2
Ukraine	22	-	5	27	31	8
Uzbekistan	31	6	2	39	26	10
Average	29	5	2	33	32	11

Source: EBRD (1998), Transition Report 1998

1 Data for Albania and Bosnia and Herzegovina were not available from the IMF. National sources for Albania indicate only minor trade exposure to Russia.

2 Exports of merchandise only. Figures from national authorities for total exports give considerably higher figures for all three Baltic countries.

3 Calculated as the total share of exports of goods to Russia, Belarus, and the Ukraine multiplied with the share of exports of goods in GDP.

Table 37: Foreign Direct Investment (net inflows of equity capital recorded in the balance of payments)

	(in millions of US dollars)							(in US dollars)		
	1993	1994	1995	1996	1997 (revised)	1998 (projected)	Cumulative FDI-inflows 1989 - 1998	Cumulative FDI-inflows 1989 - 1997 per capita	FDI-inflows per capita in 1997	FDI-inflows as % of GDP in 1997
Albania	45	65	89	97	42	95	473	148	13	1.9
Bulgaria	40	105	82	100	497	300	1,222	147	60	4.8
Croatia	77	95	83	509	196	450	1,422	297	41	1.0
Czech Republic	552	749	2,526	1,388	1,275	1,000	8,473	823	124	2.4
Estonia	157	215	199	111	128	200	1,010	695	88	2.7
Hungary	2339	1,097	4,453	1,986	2,100	1,500	16,903	1,667	207	4.6
Latvia	40	238	180	210	347	300	1,358	543	139	6.3
Lithuania	30	31	65	127	218	800	1,271	344	59	2.3
FYR Macedonia	na	24	13	12	30	45	124	59	14	0.9
Poland	580	542	1,134	2,741	3,044	4,000	12,442	321	79	2.2
Romania	97	341	417	263	1,224	900	3,370	149	54	3.5
Slovak Republic	107	236	194	199	51	220	1,223	227	9	0.3
Slovenia	111	128	176	186	321	200	1,274	639	161	1.8
CEEC and Baltic states	4,175	3,866	9,610	7,928	9,473	10,010	50,566	439	82	2.4
Armenia	na	3	19	22	51	170	265	72	14	3.1
Azerbaijan	20	22	282	661	1,093	1,155	3,233	425	144	28.4
Belarus	18	11	7	70	190	50	346	34	19	1.4
Georgia	na	8	6	54	189	255	512	95	35	3.6
Kazakh-stan	473	635	964	1,137	1,320	1,200	5,729	365	84	5.9
Kyrgyz-stan	10	45	96	46	83	29	309	67	18	4.9
Moldova	14	18	73	56	64	100	342	80	15	2.9

Table 37: Foreign Direct Investment (net inflows of equity capital recorded in the balance of payments) (cont.)

	(in millions of US dollars)							(in US dollars)		
	1993	1994	1995	1996	1997 (revised)	1998 (projected)	Cumulative FDI-inflows 1989 - 1998	Cumulative FDI-inflows 1989 - 1997 per capita	FDI-inflows per capita in 1997	FDI-inflows as % of GDP in 1997
Russia	na	539	1,710	1,700	3,752	1,500	9,201	63	25	0.8
Tajikistan	9	12	17	20	11	18	87	15	2	1.0
Turkme-nistan	79	103	233	129	108	110	762	162	23	5.9
Ukraine	200	100	400	526	600	700	2,696	53	12	1.2
Uzbeki-stan	48	73	-24	90	167	60	423	18	7	1.2
CIS	871	1,569	3,783	4,511	7,628	5,347	23,905	84	27	1.3
Total	5,046	5,435	13,393	12,439	17,101	15,357	74,471	187	43	1.8

Source: EBRD (1998), Transition Report 1998

Note:

For most countries, figures cover only investment in equity capital and in some cases contributions - in - kind. For those countries where net investment into equity capital was not easily available (e.g. Estonia and the Slovak Republic), more recent data include reinvested earnings as well as inter-company debt transactions.

6 Lessons and Policy Options for CIS and CEECs

The experience of CEECs and CIS countries in transition, the analysis of economic growth theories, openness of the economy, and FDI and its impact on economic growth, as well as the situation in the investigated countries helps to draw lessons and policy options which these countries should follow to reach higher economic growth in the future. This chapter is divided into four sections: the first section derives conclusions and policy options which are a result of the transition experience; the second section provides lessons and policy options which are a result of different theories on economic growth; the third section covers lessons and policy options which are specifically connected with openness of the economy, and the fourth section derives lessons and policy options which are directed towards the creation of an appropriate investment climate and the attraction of more FDI.

6.1 Transition - Lessons and Policy Options

Since the late 1980s and CEECs and CIS have been involved in the transition process. Transition was caused by the collapse of the old socialist system and was directed towards the establishment of a new, well functioning market economy. In the first stages of transition, all transition countries experienced rapid output declines (EBRD, 1999). Output declines took place on the one hand due to inefficiencies inherited from the old socialist system and on the other hand due to shocks connected with the transition process itself. Transition shocks also occurred due to the breakup of the former economic relations among CMEA countries and the disintegration of the USSR. Therefore, integration of CEECs and CIS countries into the global market economy has gained in importance as it plays an important role in compensating for the significant decline in the old economic relations with CMEA countries and in stimulating economic reforms in transition economies.

Not all CEECs and CIS countries have been equally successful in transition. The success in transition varies from more advanced transition economies such as Hungary and Poland to less advanced CIS economies such as Russia, the Ukraine, and Belarus. CIS countries have experienced particularly severe and prolonged output declines and have proclaimed only slow progress in reforms. Hungary and Poland instead managed relatively quickly to overcome recession and to reach sustained progress in reforms. The success of Poland and Hungary in transition could be partly a model for less successful transition economies. This analysis compares the transition effort in three CIS countries and in more advanced transition economies like Hungary and Poland and analyzes the preconditions for future economic growth.

Differing levels of progress in reforms, lies to some extent in differing initial conditions. CEEC countries benefited from favorable starting conditions before transition, however success depends to a large degree on the countries' desire to implement reforms and on the different speeds of reforms. Quick reorientation of countries towards Western markets is also supposed to induce reforms. The speed of reforms depends on whether countries implemented „shock therapy", a method of quick reform, or the „gradualist approach", a step by step introduction of reforms. Poland is an example of a country which used „shock therapy" and Hungary is an example of a country which followed the „gradualist approach".

Despite different strategies Poland and Hungary became front runners in reforms. The recession in both countries was not prolonged and the recovery of GDP had already started in 1992 in Poland and in 1994 in Hungary. Favorable initial conditions and prudent policies allowed Hungary to reach economic growth relatively quickly implementing the gradualist approach. CIS countries chose the gradualist approach, but the reforms were rather slow and inconsistent, the recession and transition crisis rather prolonged (EBRD, 1999).

Following either „shock therapy" or the „gradualist approach", the transition countries should implement such market reforms as liberalization, stabilization, privatization, and the establishment of market institutions. The sequence of implementation of reforms is prone to controversy, for instance whether liberalization, stabilization, and privatization should be carried out first followed by the establishment of institutions, or whether the institutional frame should be created first before the introduction of other reforms (SIEBERT, 1997). Sequencing issues are indeed of importance.

The experience of transition has shown that those countries which had success in transition had reached sustained liberalization and stabilization, comprehensive privatization, and opened their markets towards international trade and investment. The development of institutions, presents a more complicated process and even more advanced transition economies still face challenges in developing stable, efficient and credible institutions. The development of institutions is an evolutionary process as institutions should become accepted in society in order to have an influence on the economic practices in these countries. Changing attitudes and behavioral problems obviously takes time.

While Hungary and Poland, according to the EBRD transition indicators, have had high levels of progress in terms of liberalization, stabilization and privatization, and have already made considerable progress in institutional reforms, CIS countries still have to make strong efforts in the following directions:

- liberalization, in particular in the field of trade and capital flows
- sustainable stabilization - a moderate level of inflation, a sustainable fiscal deficit
- privatization of large enterprises - increasing the share of strategic investors

- institutional reforms - legal infrastructure, protection of property rights and effective contract laws, reduction of bureaucratic red tape and corruption, implementation of hard budget constraints, promotion of effective and efficient corporate governance, competition policy, banking reform, and the creation of stable security markets and non-banking financial institutions

Although Russia has already made considerable progress in the liberalization of both domestic and external markets, it was backtracked temporarily after the crisis of 1998. The Ukraine also had reversals in liberalization following the Russian crisis. Belarus still shows strong signs of catching up in terms of liberalization. The crisis of 1998 in Russia considerably destabilized economies of the other two CIS countries, the Ukraine and Belarus. In Belarus inflation was still very high in 2000/01. The only form of privatization which really improved the performance of privatized enterprises was the sale of assets to strategic investors, however it was not implemented sufficiently in the CIS countries being examined (EBRD, 2000).

The need to improve the performance of key institutions is of particular urgency (DERYABINA, 2001). Therefore, such basic reforms as liberalization, stabilization, and privatization create preconditions for the establishment and expansion of market enterprises which in their turn raise demand for market institutions. Increased foreign trade and foreign direct investment (FDI) can also promote the creation of institutions (WELFENS, 2000). Foreign trade and FDI intensify competitive pressures on local producers, thus strengthening demand for more efficient institutions, foreign MNCs also encourage the development of modern standards in both the business community and government (GORODETSKII, 2000). Additionally, foreign trade and FDI provide for knowledge spillovers and externalities which improve the ability of a domestic economy to introduce efficient institutional arrangements and practices. It is also difficult to reduce macroeconomic imbalances without institutions, since the financial sector is vulnerable to internal instability and external shocks.

Governmental support plays a crucial role in the implementation of reforms. Governments should show a strong commitment to market oriented reforms to support economic, social, and political development. Participation in international organizations also induces reforms since it stimulates the import of adequate rules and laws (WELFENS, 2000). The EU accession process strongly supports candidate countries in their reform efforts (EBRD, 2000).

Adequate market reforms lay foundations for sustainable growth in transition economies. Therefore, it is important not only to reach progress in reforms but also to be able to sustain those reforms. Participation in international organizations like the WTO and multilateral commitments like IMF Article on currency convertibility as well as the EU agreements on regional integration and free trade can help to prohibit the reversals in reforms.

In 2000, three CIS countries experienced significant positive growth rates for the first time since the beginning of transition. Russia grew in 2000 with a rate of 6.5%, even higher than that of Poland, 6.0%, the second largest country of the region. Hungary grew at 6.0%. Growth in Poland and Hungary was strongly supported by the increase in EU demand. The Ukraine also woke up from a recession and grew in 2000 at 3.0%. Belarus grew at 2.0%. Belarus is the only country which has experienced positive growth rates since 1996, in 1997 even reaching 11.4%. It is, however, doubtful that the official statistics in Belarus provide for reliable figures. The lack of reforms also explains the declining growth tendency in Belarus (EBRD, 2000).

It is of crucial importance for these countries to sustain economic growth. There were favorable conditions for economic growth in CIS countries in 2000/2001. High prices of commodities generated high export revenues on the one hand, large deprecations of real exchange rates in some transforming countries stimulated growth of exports on the other. However, there is evidence that this situation also stimulated the emergence of import substitution since sharp real exchange rate depreciations gave domestic producers large cost advantages over imports (IMF, 2000; SAMOKHVALOV, 2001). Therefore, in 2000/2001 the opportunity to grow appeared for the first time for light consumer goods industries (industries which normally grow at the start of transition) such as the food industry, textiles, etc.

Real exchange rate depreciations and high oil prices obviously backed up the growth success of the CIS in 2000. High oil prices helped to considerably improve external and fiscal accounts and to support macroeconomic stability in Russia and other oil and gas exporting CIS countries. On the other hand, a high dependence on exports of commodities makes CIS countries vulnerable to changes in world market prices and represents a major threat to sustainable economic growth in the future (ILLARIONOV, 2001). Additionally, with the stabilization of real exchange rates, the viability of domestic enterprises in the tradables sector will be proven. Therefore, it is of crucial importance for CIS countries to further proceed with market reforms, as these countries will only reach sustainable economic growth if reforms in the field of liberalization, stabilization, privatization, and the establishment of market institutions are sustained (MAU, 2000). It seems that under president Putin both the business community and bureaucracy have started to consider a more long-term perspective which should contribute to gains in efficiency.

6.2 Economic Growth - Lessons and Policy Options

Market reforms represent a base for economic growth in CIS and other CEECs, however to sustain economic growth transition countries should also take into account factors which generate long run economic growth in market economies. These factors are the topic of different economic growth theories. Starting with the neoclassical growth theory and going towards issues of the recently developed new growth theory, and additionally to the technological gap theory, one understands the strategic factors which lay behind long run economic growth and the possibilities for catching up of transition countries.

The discussion on the role of technological progress for economic growth represents a core issue of economic growth theories. Neoclassical growth theory exogenizes technological progress and assumes that different countries have equal technological possibilities at their disposal (SOLOW, 1956). New growth theory looks instead for the reasons which lie behind technological change and explains different growth capabilities of countries through the differences in their technological capabilities (ROMER, 1986, 1990, 1994; GROSSMAN, 1996; LUCAS, 1988; GROSSMAN/HELPMAN, 1991b, 1994; BARRO/SALA-I-MARTIN, 1995a; AGHION/HOWITT, 1998; TROFIMOV, 2000 etc.). The technological gap theory considers the possibilities for catching up of developing countries which emerge through technology transfer (ABRAMOWITZ, 1986; BELL/PAVITT, 1992; FAGEBERG, 1994; etc.).

Neoclassical growth theory does not explain long run growth but provides for transitional dynamics, the movement from one steady state to another. In a steady state, countries grow at the exogenous rate of technological progress, at the same time not excluding diminishing returns to capital and hence transitional dynamics. New growth theory explains the long run growth of countries. In the models of new growth theory, governmental policies, investment in physical and human capital, and investment in R&D influence the long run growth capabilities of a country.

Since catching up to the income levels of the industrialized countries for CIS and CEECs represents a major challenge, it is important to analyze this issue from the point of view of different growth theories. According to the neoclassical growth theory, countries converge to their own steady state level. Therefore, neoclassical growth theory predicts convergence between countries and regions. New growth theory does not predict unconditional convergence. In many new growth theory models, different technological capabilities lead to permanently different productivity levels and hence different growth rates in the long run. According to the technological gap theory, countries can converge through knowledge diffusion (which takes place due to technology transfer between countries). Imitation rather than innovation activities explain caching up opportunities of countries. In the technological gap theory, external factors such as foreign trade and foreign direct investment play a considerable role in technology transfer between countries.

It is important to analyze the historical aspects of economic growth of CIS and CEECs in order to develop policy options for the future growth strategy of these countries (OL'SEVICH, 2000). Economic growth in the former Soviet Union was extensive with minimal technological change. Insufficient technological progress, low incentives for adoption of new technologies and innovation, and extensive reliance on such factors of production as physical capital and labor, where the input of labor was declining, led to diminishing returns to physical capital and the decline of economic growth. The presence of diminishing returns to capital in combination with insufficient technological change supports the explanation of output decline in the former Soviet Union predicted by the neoclassical growth theory (EASTERLY/FISCHER, 1992; WEITZMAN, 1990). However, on the other hand, distortionary policies, the absence of innovation, and poor conditions for adoption of new technologies provide an explanation for declining economic growth from the point of view of new growth theory (EASTERLY, 1993; BARRO, 1991; ROMER, 1993b). Taking historical analysis into account, technological progress will be of prime importance for future economic growth in CIS and CEECs.

The analysis of theories on economic growth helps to develop policy options on growth strategy for CIS and CEECs. The neoclassical model provides inadequate policy applications for these countries. According to the neoclassical approach, government should stimulate investment in physical (through savings) or human capital in order to reach a higher steady state level, whereby investment in capital does not have an impact on the long run growth rate of an economy. New growth theory provides for many more policy applications. Thus, governmental policies such as liberalization, lower capital taxation, and stronger property rights can have a positive impact on the long run growth rate of an economy. Moreover, investment in physical and human capital generates knowledge spillovers and externalities and thus raises the productivity level of the whole economy and therefore its rate of economic growth. Most important is to create incentives for innovation and the adoption of new technologies which induce technological change in an economy and thus spur economic growth. Investment in R&D should encourage innovation activities. The accumulation of physical and human capital would promote innovation as well, since physical and human capital incorporate knowledge needed for further innovations. New growth theory emphasizes the special role of human capital for the first time (NUREEV, 2000). In the new growth theory human capital is not simply accumulated, but provides for knowledge spillovers and externalities, generates innovations, and attracts physical capital.

Technological gap theory emphasizes the importance of technological catching up. Using the „advantage of backwardness", less developed countries can improve their productivity levels through imitation activities and thus catch up with more advanced countries. In order to be able to adopt and implement foreign technologies, the countries should possess „social capability", „technological capability" or „opportunity", and support „indigenous innovation". „Social capability" refers to education, infrastructure, and a country's institutions. „Technological capability" or „opportunity" represents the effort a country should be able to make for the adoption and improvement of gained technologies. „Indigenous innovation" is also supposed to induce technology transfer since successful imitation often contains innovative activities. The technological gap theory also pays much attention to the role of human capital in technological catching up. Human capital forms a precondition for „social capability",

„technological capability"/„opportunity", and „indigenous innovation" and thus induces technology transfer.

Table 38 presents an overview of the most important economic indicators for selected CIS and CEECs and shows that Russia, Ukraine and Belarus were on average behind the examined CEECs in terms of human capital (poverty, gross primary enrollment, expenditure on health and education), investment-GDP ratio, whereby the indicator for the patent applications filed remains low for both CIS and CEECs.

Table 38: Selected CIS and CEECs at a Glance in 1999

	Hungary	Poland	Russia	Ukraine	Belarus
Poverty and social					
Population, mid-year (millions)	10.1	38.7	146.2	50.0	10.2
GNP per capita (Atlas method, US$)	4,640	3,990	2,250	750	2,450
GNP (Atlas method, US$ billions)	46.7	154.2	329.0	37.5	25.02
Average annual growth, 1993-99					
Population (%)	-0.4	0.1	-0.3	-0.7	-0.2
Labor force (%)	0.3	0.4	0.0	-0.4	-0.2
Most recent estimate					
Poverty (% of population below national poverty line)	**9**	**24**	**30**	**27**	**23**
Urban population (% of total population)	64	65	73	68	71
Life expectancy at birth (years)	71	73	66	67	68
Infant mortality (per 1,000 live birth)	9	10	16	14	11
Child malnutrition (% of children under 5)	..	..	3	..	..
Access to improved water source (% of population)	..	..	..	..	..
Illiteracy (% of population age 15+)	1	0	1	0	1
Gross primary enrollment (% of school-age population)	**103**	**96**	**109**	**87**	**98**
Male	104	97	109	87	100
Female	102	96	108	87	96
Expenditure on health and education (in per cent of GDP)	**11.4****	**9.9***	**6.8**	**6.6**	**11.4**
Patent applications filed					
Residents	**751***	**2,410***	**16,630***	**5,327***	**919***
Non-residents	**37,956***	**38,942***	**41,902***	**36,623***	**34,350***

Table 38: Selected CIS and CEECs at a Glance in 1999 (cont.)

	Hungary	Poland	Russia	Ukraine	Belarus
Key economic ratios and long-term trends					
GDP (US$ billions)	48.4	152.6*	184.6	30.8	26.8
Gross domestic investment/GDP	**28.8**	**26.4***	**15.5**	**19.8**	**24.0**
Exports of goods and services/GDP	52.6	28.4*	45.7	52.8	61.8
Gross domestic savings/GDP	26.3	21.1*	32.9	20.9	21.1
Gross national savings/GDP	23.7	21.6*	26.7	22.5	21.1
Current account balance/GDP	-4.3	-4.5*	11.2	2.7	-1.0
Interest payments/GDP	..	0.9*	1.6	2.5	0.2
Total debt/GDP	60.0	31.3*	95.8	40.8	..
Total debt service/exports	26.1	12.4*	11.6	14.4	..
Present value of debt/GDP	..	28.9*	..	37.3	..
Present value of debt/exports	..	120.8*	..	68.7	..
(average annual growth)					
GDP	4.5	4.1	3.2	-0.4	3.4
GNP per capita	5.6	3.3	0.7	-0.7	-0.7
Exports of goods and services	11.3	..	-3.0	-7.9	3.3

Source: EBRD (2000), Transition Report 2000; World Bank (2000), World Bank Development Indicators 2000, http://www.worldbank.org

**The data is for 1998*

*** The data is for 1996*

When discussing the possibilities of economic growth for CIS countries, one should pay attention to the special case of a large country such as Russia, which is well endowed with natural resources. Government advisors in Russia should be aware of the danger of „Dutch Disease", which leads to the reallocation of resources from the manufacturing sector to the resource sector and thus prohibits economic growth in the long run. There is also the potential danger of immiserizing growth where deterioration of term of trades can lead to welfare losses (SACH/WARNER, 1995, 1999; VAN WIJNBERGEN, 1984, 1987; KRUGMAN, 1987; SMITS/DE JONG/VAN ARK, 1999; LINDERT/PUGEL, 1992).

To sum up, new growth theory provides broader policy options for CIS and CEECs than the neoclassical growth theory since technological progress is of primary importance for the further development of these countries in order to achieve economic growth. Moreover, because these countries are in the initial stages of the catching up process, imitation and non-innovation activities are important for these countries in order to gain compatibility with world markets and catch up technologically to the levels of advanced market economies.

To achieve economic growth in the long run CIS and CEECs should:

- increase and invest savings in an efficient manner; still insufficient reform in the financial sector in the period 1999 – 2001.
- implement market-enhancing governmental policies such as liberalization, lower capital taxation, and induce stronger property rights.
- induce investment in physical capital since this will not only raise capital intensity, but also generate knowledge spillovers and externalities and promote innovation because accumulation of physical capital contains embodied knowledge needed for further innovations.
- induce investment in human capital. Human capital is not only the basis for knowledge spillovers and externalities, it represents the main input in R&D and hence innovation. Human capital also attracts investment in physical capital. Therefore, countries which promote the creation of human capital will also be able to attract more FDI.
- create preconditions for the innovation and adoption of new technologies and promote investment in R&D since it will induce innovation activity within a country.

To encourage technology diffusion CIS and CEECs should:

- invest in education and infrastructure and promote the establishment of institutions in order to create conditions for „social capability".
- improve the quality of the workforce through training (vocational training and on-the-job training).
- invest in education, science and engineering in order to promote „technological capability"/„opportunity" and encourage „indigenous innovation".
- promote openness of the economy and FDI since they are the main channels of technology transfer. New investment also creates conditions for new jobs and the introduction of new equipment and new technologies attained through openness and FDI create demand for highly skilled labor. This, naturally, raises challenges for Russia's education system.

Additionally, Russia should:

- be aware of the risks connected to the „Dutch Disease" and immiserizing growth. Therefore, a resource rich country should not only rely on its resource sector but rather promote the development of different industry sectors and diversify its export structure over time. A strong expansion of the resource sector also diverts efforts from development of job skills and prohibits the development of human capital.

Special attention should be devoted to the development of human capital. Human capital plays a crucial role for technology transfer, the adoption of new technologies, and the introduction of innovations. Although in the former Soviet states the workforce was well qualified and investment in training and education was high, transition has shown that many specialists were not adequately prepared for the special requirements of the market economy. Therefore, it is important to rapidly introduce market reforms because they create demand for market oriented specialists. Moreover, openness and FDI will provide rapid transfer of new technologies into transition economies. Adoption of new technologies will increase pressure on the development of advanced skills.

Table 39 and Table 40 present a comparison of the situation in regards to human capital in Hungary and Russia. Table 39 shows that although in Russia the provision of education was relatively wide, the quality of the workforce did not correspond to the requirements of a market economy. The main challenge lies in the lack of worker adaptability, since the skills are tied to a particular firm or process. Additionally, inadequate IT knowledge of workers also represents a serious obstacle for conducting business in Russia. Therefore, it is essential for Russia to induce provision of basic business training and finance skills, to encourage the incentives for firms to provide training.

Table 39: Obstacles to Future Development of Business (percentage of firms citing each factor as significant obstacle)

	Hungary		Russia	
	Manufacturing	Services	Manufacturing	Services
Adaptability of workers	40	29	16	13
Inadequate IT knowledge of workers	34	28	20	20
Insufficient public resources for training	27	18	47	27
Lack of incentives for firm to provide training	26	25	47	24

Source: EBRD (2000), Transition Report 2000

Table 40 shows the percentage of the workforce that requires training in Hungary and Russia. The share of the workforce requiring training is much higher in Russia than in Hungary. This difference is especially large in the case of managers and white-collar workers.

Table 40: Percentage of Workforce that Requires Training

	Language	PC/IT skills	Management	Client training
Hungary				
Managers	7	11	12	2
White-collar workers	3	15	0	2
Blue-collar skilled workers	1	1	na	0
Unskilled blue-collar workers	0	0	na	0
Russia				
Managers	22	30	38	30
White-collar workers	17	34	26	23
Blue-collar skilled workers	na	11	na	na
Unskilled blue-collar workers	na	1	na	na

Source: EBRD (2000), Transition Report 2000

The time lag between the beginning of the recession and the introduction of market reforms and measures which promote economic growth and technology transfer could be large. The more the losses in physical capital, the more difficult it will be to introduce new capital and adopt new technologies. The technological lag could grow over time as human capital has the potential to deteriorate as a result of, for instance, lost skills. If the time lag between the beginning of the recession and the introduction of these measures is large, then the advantages that CIS and CEECs had before the transition will erode and narrowing the technological gap would become more difficult.

6.3 Openness - Lessons and Policy Options

In our analysis special attention is devoted to external economic factors such as foreign trade and foreign direct investment and their impact on economic growth. The debate on whether economic openness has a positive impact on economic growth or not received a positive confirmation in the economic and empirical literature of the last few years. Therefore, CIS and CEECs should promote openness of their economies since it provides a positive impact on economic growth and brings about other positive gains from trade. The positive static gains from openness are primarily associated with increased capital accumulation, factor price equalization, more efficient price system, efficiency gains from increased competition, and consumer welfare gains (AGHION/HOWITT, 1998; HECKSCHER, 1919; OHLIN, 1993; SAMUELSON, 1948, 1949; RUFFIN, 1987, WARZIARG, 1998; VENTURA, 1997; OECD, 1998, etc.).

The new growth theory allows a deeper analysis of the impact of openness on economic growth. New growth theory allows one to analyze the impact of openness on long run economic growth and to develop appropriate policy options. According to new growth theory, economic openness allows countries to better exploit economies of scale, get access to new technologies, increase the scope of knowledge spillovers and positive externalities which induce technology diffusion and innovation, increase the scope of possible innovations and returns from innovation, induce accumulation of capital, help to avoid duplication of innovation, induce adjustment of specialization pattern, induce learning by doing and promote diffusion of technologies (AGHION/HOWITT, 1998; GROSSMAN/HELPMAN, 1991a,b, 1994; RIVERA-BATIZ/ROMER, 1991, KRUGMAN, 1990; RODRIK, 1995, DAVIS, 1991, YOUNG, 1991, SEGERSTROM/DINOPOULOS, 1990, etc.).

However, openness of the economy could in certain cases have a negative impact on long run growth (GROSSMAN/HELPMAN, 1991a). Since CIS and CEECs do not have a comparative advantage in R&D intensive sectors before the liberalization of foreign trade, openness of the economy can induce further specialization of these countries in labor intensive and energy intensive industries (SHMELEV, 2000). CIS and CEEC governments should support gradual efforts to reallocate resources to „growth" sectors in order to stimulate long run economic growth (SMIRNOV, 2000). Otherwise, economic openness can impair economic growth and lead to divergence rather than to convergence with OECD countries.

Since CIS and CEEC countries wish to catch up to the income levels of the advanced OECD countries they should also take into account that trade between OECD countries is mostly intra- and not inter-industry trade. Therefore, in order to promote trade with OECD countries, CIS and CEECs should adjust their specialization pattern in such a way that they become more involved in intra-industry trade. Intra-industry trade occurs due to product differentiation, economies of scale, and specialization (GRUBEL/LLOYD, 1975; KRUGMAN, 1990; HELPMAN, 1998, etc.). Specialization leads to an increase in international trade. Since product differentiation and economies of scale induce specialization they also lead to increased volumes of trade. Thus, product differentiation and scale economies also promote growth. Moreover, intra-industry provides for more technology transfer than inter-industry trade. Therefore, it is important for poor catching up countries to become involved in intra-industry trade because it induces economic growth and speeds up convergence with the income levels of OECD countries.

Governments of the examined CIS countries should support the Heckscher-Ohlin-Schumpeter process through such economic policies as promoting competition, encouraging free trade and inducing growth-enhancing policies. At the fist stage of transformation and liberalization the expansion of labor- and resource-intensive exports could make sense as it would allow for capital-intensive imports. During the second stage of transformation it is of crucial importance to use capital-intensive imports in combination with human capital in order to promote trade in skill- and R&D-intensive products. Trade with low-income countries at the first stage of transition also makes sense if it promotes growth dynamics in a domestic economy.

Since the most important contribution of economic openness is its the role in innovation activities and technology transfers, and since it is important for CIS and CEECs to reallocate resources towards technology intensive sectors and to become involved in intra-industry trade, they should:

- promote the tradable sector and the export sector, since productivity is higher in the export sector than in the non-export sector.
- trade strongly with more technologically advanced countries. Since there is an impact of foreign R&D on domestic productivity CIS and CEECs can boost their productivity by trading with more technologically advanced countries; here both the export and import side are important.
- specialize in sectors with greater potential for innovation. International trade raises returns to innovation and encourages R&D activities and hence economic growth. It is therefore important to specialize in sectors with a greater potential for innovation.
- specialize in sectors with positive spillovers and externalities. Technological spillovers and externalities have a positive impact on technological progress and hence economic growth. Human capital plays a special role for international spillovers and externalities. To induce spillovers and externalities CIS and CEECs should choose trading partners with higher levels of human capital. Dynamic gains from international spillovers and externalities are also important since international trade induces the reallocation of resources through technological spillovers and thus changes dynamic comparative advantages towards more technologically intensive industries.
- specialize in sectors with a greater potential for learning by doing. International trade reinforces the effects of learning by doing in sectors with a greater potential for this process. Trade with more technologically advanced countries would also induce learning by doing.

- specialize in sectors with economies of scale. Economies of scale promote technological progress because countries should specialize in differentiated products different from those of rivals. Economies of scale lead to increased volumes of trade and promote the development of intra-industry trade. Intra-industry trade in its turn induces technology transfer and spurs economic growth.
- specialize in sectors with a greater diffusion of knowledge. Specialization in sectors with a greater diffusion of knowledge would allow CIS and CEECs to better absorb, adopt, and imitate foreign technologies; it is however, necessary to reorganize R&D policies.

Geographical and specialization patterns of trade were analyzed in this study since regional reorientation and composition of trade are of importance. The specialization pattern was analyzed in trade with the EU as the EU represents a major trading partner of the countries being examined. The largest adjustment in the pattern of specialization was observed in Hungary. The specialization pattern in Hungary was reshaped to a large extent by FDI. In Eastern Europe Hungary was the largest recipient of FDI and trade within MNCs moved foreign trade of Hungary towards intra-industry trade in high quality products. Thus, Hungary became increasingly an exporter of capital-, skill-, and R&D-intensive products and moved away from labor- and energy-intensive products. Poland follows Hungary's example. Although Poland still exports standard manufacturing products such as apparel, clothing, and furniture, the exports of more sophisticated products such as road vehicles and electronic machinery are expanding. Poland is also becoming more involved in intra-industry trade.

The situation is different with CIS countries. CIS countries show extensive dependence on the export of primary commodities. These are mostly exports of oil and gas in the case of Russia. In the case of the Ukraine these are mostly raw materials, metals, fuel, and wood. Although Belarussian exports are 76% manufacturing, its exports to the EU consist mostly of metal and wood products. The exports of primary commodities restricts technological progress and reduces economic growth in these countries in the long run. The predominance of natural resource exports may lead to the „Dutch Disease" and in the case of Russia to immiserizing growth. Moreover, export of primary commodities makes CIS countries highly dependent on world commodity prices.

Further involvement in global trade would also make these countries more vulnerable to external shocks. Trade to GDP ratios are already rather high in these CIS countries, which shows their dependence on external markets. The change of their specialization patterns to more capital-, skill-, and R&D-intensive goods on the one hand, and the diversification of their export structures on the other, would induce economic growth and make the CIS countries less vulnerable to external shocks. Therefore, CIS countries should make an effort to attract more FDI, which would help to reshape their specialization patterns and help them to understand the importance of a diversified export structure.

The analysis of the geographical trade pattern with OECD countries has shown that Poland and especially Hungary have considerably reoriented their trade towards the EU. Trade has also increased with the neighboring CEE-4, but the share of other OECD groups of countries in total trade of Hungary and Poland has diminished. In the case of the CIS countries, trade with OECD countries, although it increased in absolute terms, decreased considerably as a share of total trade. Participation in world organizations and multilateral commitments such as WTO membership, IMF Article VIII, EU Association, as well as EU Partnership and Cooperation Agreement exercises much influence on trade relations between countries (EBRD, 2000). The intensified relations between Hungary, Poland, and the EU took place to a large extent because the CEEC countries became candidate countries of the first accession round. Up till now the CIS countries have made little progress in WTO negotiations and they were barely influenced by the EU Partnership and Cooperation Agreement. IMF commitments were seen to have the strongest impact on liberalization of the CIS. Therefore, CIS countries should place more attention on participation in international organizations and should reinforce WTO negotiation and make more efforts in cooperation with the EU.

In this work potential in foreign trade between the investigated CEECs and CIS was estimated in their trade with different groups of OECD countries such as the EU-15, EFTA-6, CEE-5, Canada and the United States, Asia (Japan and Korea), Australia and New Zealand, and the Western Hemisphere (e.g. Mexico). The estimation was made with the gravity model for 1997. Two model specifications were used, one with standard variables and the other with the *INTERNET* variable. Both estimations yield similar results.

According to the gravity model results, Hungary has already exhausted its potential in trade with the EU-15. Poland still exhibits some potential since Poland represents a much larger market than Hungary. The CEE-4 also play a considerable role in trade with Poland, however, on the other hand, both Hungary and Poland show considerable potential in trade with other OECD groups of countries. Since the gravity model allows the identification of deviation from a „normal" trade pattern, Hungary's and Poland's trade with some OECD groups of countries is far from being „normal". Both Hungary and Poland should increase their trade with the EFTA-6, Canada and the United States, Asian countries, Australia and New Zealand, and Mexico.

The actual trade flows for Russia seem to be strongly influenced by oil prices. Therefore, in our interpretation of the results we rely not on the data in absolute terms but on the trade share of total OECD trade. Thus, Russia should increase its trade with the EU, with Canada, and to some extent with Asia. Russia also shows potential in absolute terms, in trade with Australia and New Zealand and Mexico. On the other hand, Russia trades more than predicted by the gravity model with the EFTA-6 and CEE-5 groups of countries.

The Ukraine also relies heavily on its previous relations with the CEE-5. Although the Ukraine does not exhibit potential in trade with the EU in absolute terms, it shows potential as a percent of total OECD trade. Moreover, the Ukraine should intensify trade relations with the EFTA-6 countries, where it experiences a very large lag. The Ukraine also has a large potential in trade with Asian countries, Australia and New Zealand, Mexico, and some potential in trade with Canada.

Belarus is a country which until now made very little effort to intensify its trade relations with OECD countries. Belarus exhibits a lot of potential in trade with all OECD groups of countries except the CEE-5. In Belarus trade relations remain strongly influenced by political rather than by economic principles. Belarus still relies heavily on its previous economic relations. This inhibits considerably Belarus's future economic growth and its integration into international global markets.

6.4 FDI - Lessons and Policy Options

FDI is associated with many positive effects on economic growth. Thus FDI increases capital stock in a host country and creates new employment. However, the most important role played by FDI is as a channel of technology transfer. Additionally, FDI brings about spillovers which raise productivity in the sectors concerned and - in the presence of spillovers - in the whole economy. For the realization of spillover effects, the available stock of human capital is of special importance. The ability to absorb new technologies and to realize spillover effects is not only closely connected with the level of human capital, but also with labor mobility across sectors. Therefore, the effect of FDI on economic growth of the country is larger the larger the level of human capital and the more flexible labor markets are.

The effect of FDI on the domestic economy shows up in host countries in the form of increases in productivity, increases in the FIEs expenditure, intra-firm spillover efficiency gains; it also induces the restructuring of domestic enterprises, helps to exploit economies of scale, intensifies competition, increases the productivity of local firms, and speeds up their technological upgrading (BELLAK, 1998; BORENSZTEIN etc. 1995; BLOMSTROEM, 1991; WELFENS, 2000). Moreover, FDI changes the specialization pattern of a domestic country towards more intra-industry trade (BELLAK, 1998). FDI also provides for secondary flows in terms of exports and creates demand for imports and hence increases trade. In the long run FDI could have a positive impact on the balance of payments; FDI provides in the long run an increasing share of technologically sophisticated exports since it changes the specialization pattern towards intra-industry (OECD, 1998).

However, on the other hand, FDI can also be associated with different distortions in the host countries (BELLAK, 1998; HUNYA, 1999; BURGER, 1999). Thus, because of the larger market power, FIEs may reduce competition in domestic markets, which in turn can reduce the amount of technological spillovers to domestic firms through economies of scale and technological requirements. FIEs may restrict market access for domestic firms. Moreover, FIEs often receive tax privileges and subsidies which provide for additional competitive advantages. Additionally, FDI is often only directed to limited sectors of the economy. FDI is also often only directed to particular regions which are better endowed with human capital and technologies. The restructuring effect induced by FIEs in the initial period does not provide for the success of an enterprise with FDI in the long run. FIEs are often eager to ignore domestic suppliers and tend to use their own supplier schemes. FIEs may limit local R&D activity though the reallocation of human resources towards FIEs, and may also try to prevent positive technology spillovers and externalities to domestic firms.

Therefore, the numerous advantages of FDI show that the governments of transition economies should try to attract more FDI; at the same time, they should also provide an appropriate competition environment and create favorable conditions for technology transfer from FIEs to domestic firms.

Neoclassical and new growth theory also provide controversial explanations as to which countries should be more successful in attracting FDI. According to neoclassical growth theory, FDI should go to the countries where capital is scarce. According to new growth theory, FDI would go to the countries with low political risk and a high level of human capital (ZEBREGS, 1998; LUCAS, 1990; GARIBALDI/MORA/SAHAY/ZETTELMEYER, 1999). Therefore, human capital plays a complementary role for FDI. This view is supported by the figures on FDI inflows for transition economies. Among transition economies, the most advanced countries such as Hungary, Poland, and the Czech Republic attracted the majority of FDI. The CIS countries being examined only reported small figures of FDI inflows with FDI inflows per capita being particularly insufficient.

An important effect of FDI on economic growth is seen through the inducement of foreign trade and the effect of FDI on the specialization pattern. There is evidence that there is a complementary relationship between FDI and trade (BRENTON/DI MAURO/LUECKE, 1998; GRAHAM, 1999; GRAHAM/LIU, 1998). This means that FDI leads to more trade in the long run and trade to more FDI. The effect of FDI on the specialization pattern is important in that it stimulates a change from inter- to intra-industry trade with an increasing role of technologically sophisticated products in exports. At the initial stage of transformation CIS and CEECs were used to being involved in inter-industry trade with OECD countries. The liberalization of foreign trade leads in the early stages of transformation to more FDI inflows into traditional sectors of the economy. Furthermore, FDI speeds up the productivity of FIEs and domestic firms and induces the restructuring of domestic enterprises. Since FDI is mostly carried out by MNCs, intra-company trade within MNCs provides for technology transfer to domestic firms and spillover effects and contributes to the change of the specialization pattern in a domestic economy. The specialization pattern moves towards more intra-industry trade. With time, outward FDI also takes place, while inward FDI continues. With liberalization of their economies, transition countries would also become more vulnerable to macroeconomic and financial instabilities which hurt economic development. There is evidence that FDI is less volatile (as measured by the coefficient of variation) than commercial bank loans and foreign portfolio flows (EBRD, 2000).

Among CEECs, FDI was predominately directed towards Hungary, Poland and Czech Republic. FDI in the investigated CIS countries does not correspond to the demand and the size of their markets. The main obstacle for FDI inflows into the CIS countries was unfavorable investment climate (NOSOVA, 2000; STRUCHINEVSKII, 2000).

At the fist stage of transformation, privatization of domestic enterprises plays a considerable role in attracting FDI. The experience of Hungary shows that much FDI in Hungary was connected with the privatization of state-owned enterprises rather than being attracted by GDP growth. Since foreign investors have a long term interest in the privatized enterprises with substantial influence on the management of enterprises, it is of crucial importance for governments of transition economies to provide for property rights in order to attract more FDI. Additionally, foreign majority ownership is also important. The main difference in privatization policy between Hungary and later Poland and the CIS countries consisted in the sale of strategic stakes to foreign strategic investors. Foreign strategic investors may provide a larger impact on productivity, induce the restructuring of state-owned enterprises, and induce technological changes within enterprises (LIPSITS/VIGDORCHIK/NESHCHADIN/EIKEL'PASH/RYBAKOVA, 1998). In the CIS countries privatization took place through domestic sources. The participation of foreign strategic investors was made more difficult because there was no transparency in the procedure, the lack of market oriented land code and constraints on the sale of land prevented privatization in the agriculture sector, and in urban and rural land markets (EBRD, 1999).

It is also of crucial importance for future economic growth into which sectors of the economy FDI is directed. Whether it is directed into „growth" sectors of the economy or not. FDI also plays a different role at different stages of transformation (BELLAK, 1999, DOEHRN/GANUSCHTSCHENKO, 2000). At the first stage it contributes to the stabilization of the economy and helps to finance imports and build up foreign exchange reserves at the central bank. At this stage FDI is directed into traditional sectors of the economy which used to play an important role and will play this role in the future. With further transformation, FDI contributes more to the restructuring of the economy and stimulates movement from resource- and labor- intensive sectors to more capital-, skill- and R&D-intensive sectors of the economy.

The evidence shows that FDI in Hungary and Poland already contributes to the restructuring of the economy since it is directed into the machinery, equipment, and chemical industries. Another situation is evident in the CIS countries. In the CIS, FDI is still to a large extent directed towards traditional sectors and a shift towards more investment into manufacturing is not to be seen (except to some extent in the Ukraine). In Russia FDI mostly goes to the oil and gas industry. In the Ukraine the food industry is the main recipient of FDI, although some FDI was also received by machinery and equipment and chemical industries. In Belarus, FDI went to the food, textiles, and wood industries (UNCTAD, 1999; BELARUS ECONOMIC TRENDS, 1999).

In this study, potential FDI inflows were estimated with the gravity model for CEECs and CIS countries. Hungary has already exhausted its FDI potential. This is not surprising if one considers that Hungary received the most FDI among the transition countries. The results for Poland are similar to those of Hungary, however Poland still shows some excess potential. Poland also represents a substantially larger market than Hungary and hence is a more attractive goal for FDI. The estimations point to considerable potential for the CIS countries in obtaining FDI. Among the investigated CIS Belarus shows the largest lag. Cumulative FDI inflows in CIS countries do not correspond to the size and demand of these markets.

The impact of FDI on gross fixed capital formation was also analyzed using the gravity model. The results show that FDI tends to play a moderate role in gross fixed capital formation in the long run. In judging the gravity model results one should take into account the static character of the model. The model does not explicitly cover the policies directed to attract more FDI. Thus, privatization with participation of foreign strategic investors is supposed to strongly induce FDI. The opposite is valid for restrictive policies. Real depreciation of the exchange rate can attract more FDI too. The data for Hungary and Poland for the period 1994 - 1996 supports this view. Thus, FDI inflows over gross fixed capital formation in this period was equal to 30 percent for Hungary and 18 percent for Poland. The high ratios can be explained through the high level of FDI which Hungary and Poland achieved in the early stages of transformation. Therefore, in the transformation phase, when transition countries have low saving rates and need the inflow of capital from abroad for the restructuring and modernizing of the economy, FDI can play a very important role. The impact of FDI on the economy depends on the investment climate in these countries and their ability to attract high FDI inflows. But according to the gravity model results, the role of FDI in the long run tends to become moderate and a considerable share of gross fixed capital formation will be financed though domestic savings.

To attract more FDI CEECs and CIS should adopt the following policy options:

- carry out macroeconomic reforms - liberalization, macroeconomic stabilization, and privatization. Macroeconomic reform is the first step in creating a favorable climate for FDI. Improving the financial system is particularly important, through structural reforms in banking, improving corporate governance, and improving the regulation of securities markets. Much attention should also be devoted to tax policy.

- ensure property rights and abolish constraints on the sale of land. Since foreign direct investors are interested in the long term participation in an enterprise it is important to ensures them first of all such basic rights as property rights and abolish constraints on the sale of land.

- establish a legal framework for FDI inflows. National policies and institutions are responsible for the creation of an investment climate. To attract FDI it is important to develop legislation concerning FDI and to clearly define rights and obligations of MNCs (FIEs) in a domestic economy.

- restrict corruption, red tape, and bureaucratic delays. Corruption, red tape, and bureaucratic delays make it more difficult for foreign investors get a foot in a domestic market. In some cases corruption and red tape aggravate the situation to such an extent that foreign direct investors decide to leave the market.

- diminish political risk and increase the credibility of the government. Political risk is an important factor which prohibits the inflow of FDI into a country. Therefore, it is very important to reduce political risk and to ensure foreign direct investors of the stability of political decisions made by governments of transition economies.

- liberalize foreign trade first. Since MNCs operate in global markets and are strongly export oriented they are more interested in investing in countries which promote exports instead of in countries which follow import-substitution policies. Therefore, openness of the economy is a very important precondition for FDI.

- encourage cooperation with the EU. Accession to the EU has a strong positive effect on FDI inflows. Accession to the EU is associated with stability, removal of barriers to market entry, and increases in trade flows, and therefore increases in FDI inflows.

- adopt complementary human capital policies (to improve local systems of education and training). Since human capital attracts FDI and the adoption of new technologies and realization of spillovers strongly depends on the level of human capital, an appropriate level of human capital is an important precondition for attracting FDI.

- carry out small scale and large scale privatization with attraction of foreign strategic investors. Privatization of state-owned enterprises often represents the first possibility for FIEs to get a foothold in domestic markets. Moreover, FIEs are more productive and efficient than domestic firms and can afford the restructuring and modernizing of an enterprise more effectively and quickly than domestic firms.

- attract more greenfield FDI. Greenfield FDI, which represents the establishment of a new plant, is supposed to have a larger impact on the restructuring of the domestic economy than M&E and privatization-related FDI.

- promote FDI in capital-, skill-, and R&D-intensive sectors of the economy, since it is important in which sectors of the economy FDI is directed. It should be directed to sectors which contribute to the economic growth of the economy, i.e. manufacturing, equipment industry, electronic industry, chemical industry, etc.
- avoid inducements for FIEs which bring welfare losses for society. To attract FDI, some governments create favorable conditions for FIEs. However on the other hand, policies such as protection against imports of goods which compete with the goods produced by FIEs and financial inducements such as subsidies and tax holidays, although they may encourage FDI, may bring about considerable losses to the society as a whole.
- create a balanced competition policy between FIEs and domestic firms since FIEs should not enjoy a monopolistic position in domestic markets and prevent competition and effective technology transfer as well as the technological upgrading of domestic firms.

This analysis has revealed a complex set of problems. Initial distortions and policy pitfalls have caused slow or even sustained negative growth over some period in Russia, the Ukraine and Belarus. Considering the conclusions drawn here should allow crucial improvement of economic performance in the first decade of the 21st century.

List of Abbreviations

% from pot.	% from potential
act.	actual
AG	Andean Group
$AGENDA_{ij}$	dummy variable indicating whether or not the countries belong to the first accession round
A_{ij}	adjacency dummy variable
AP	accession partnership agreement
$AREA_i$	area of country i from a hinterland to the economic center
$AREA_j$	area of country j from a hinterland to the economic center
ASEAN	Association for South East Asian Nations
Au+NZ	Australia and New Zealand
bn.	billions
ca.	circa
Ca+US	Canada and United States of America
CACM	Central American Common Market
CBRF	Central Bank of Russian Federation
CEE-5	Central and Eastern European countries which tend to join the EU in the first accession round (Poland, Czech Republic, Estonia, Hungary, Slovenia)
CEECs[42]	Central and Eastern European countries
CES	constant elasticity of substitution production function
CIA	Central Intelligence Agency
CIS[43]	Commonwealth of Independent States (which includes as full or associate members all countries of the former Soviet Union, except the Baltic states)

---

[42] Central and Eastern European countries (CEECs): Albania, Bosnia and Herze-govina, Bulgaria, Croatia, Czech Republic, FYR Macedonia, Hungary, Poland, Romania, Slovak Republic and Slovenia

CMEA	Council for Mutual Economic Assistance
$CMEA_{ij}$	dummy variable indicating whether or not the countries belong to the former CMEA countries
CONST	constant
CSAs	country-specific advantages
CSFR	Czech and Slovak Republic
Cum. Inflows	cumulated inflows
$DIST_{ij}$	distance between two countries
DW	Durbin Watson statistics
e.g.	exemplum gratia
EBRD	European Bank for Reconstruction and Development
EC	European Community
ECE	Economic Commission for Europe
ECOWAS	Economic Community of the West African States
EFTA	European Free Trade Area
EFTA-6	EFTA's member countries (Austria, Finland, Iceland, Norway, Sweden, Switzerland)
$EFTA_{ij}$	dummy variable for membership in EFTA
EME	entrepreneurial market economy
$ENGLANG_j$	dummy variable for English language spoken in recipient country
E-OECD	European OECD countries
est.	estimated
est. 2	estimation 2
est.1	estimation 1
et al.	et altera
etc.	et cetera
EU	European Union

[43] Commonwealth of Independent States (CIS): Armenia, Azerbaijan, Belarus, Georgia, Kazakhstan, Kyrgyzstan, Moldova, Russia, Tajikistan, Turkmenistan, Ukraine and Uzbekistan

EU-15	EU's member countries (Austria, Belgium-Luxembourg, Denmark, Finland, France, Germany, Greece, Ireland, Italy, The Netherlands, Portugal, Spain, Sweden, United Kingdom)
EU_{ij}	dummy variable for membership in the EU
Ex.	exports
Ex_{ij}	exports from country i to country j
FDI	foreign direct investment
FDI_{ij}	foreign direct investment from country i to country j
FIEs	foreign investment enterprises
FRG	Federal Republic of Germany
FSAs	firm-specific advantages
FYR	former Yugoslav Republic
GATT	General Agreement on Tariffs and Trade
GDP	gross domestic product
GDP_i	gross domestic product of country i
GDP_j	gross domestic product of country j
GDP^p_i	gross domestic product of country i in purchasing power parity
GDP^p_j	gross domestic product of country j in purchasing power parity
GFCF	gross fixed capital formation
GNP	gross national product
i.e.	id est
ICT	information and computer technology
IMF	International Monetary Fund
$INTERNET_i$	number of internet hosts in country i per 10,000 people
$INTERNET_j$	number of internet hosts in country j per 10,000 people
IT	information technology
LAIA	Latin American Integration Association
$LANG_{ij}$	dummy variable for common language
LDCs	least developed countries
mill.	millions

MNCs	Multinational Corporations
MU_i	exchange rate in country i
MU_j	exchange rate in country j
na	not available
NATO	North Atlantic Treaty Organization
NEP	new economic policy
NICs	Newly Industrializing Countries
NMP	national material product
NMP_i	national material product of country i
NMP_i/POP_i	per capita output of country i
NMP_j	national material product of country j
NMP_j/POP_j	per capita output of country j
OECD	Organization for Economic Cooperation and Development
OLI model	Ownership-Localization-Internalization model
OLS method	ordinary least squares method
OPT	outward processing trade
P&A	permanent residence
p.a.	per annum
PCs	personal computers
POP_i	population of country i
POP_j	population of country j
PPP	purchasing power parity
$PREF_{ij}$	dummy variable representing the kth preference relationship between two countries
R&D	research and development
R&D&E	research and development and engineering
$R\&D_i$	expenditure on R&D in investing country
R^2	fit of the regression
R^2 adj.	R^2 adjusted
RCA	revealed comparative advantages
S&T	science and technology

S.E.	standard error
SADCC	South African Developing Co-Ordination
SITC	Standard International Trade Classification
SUR	seemingly unrelated regression method
SUR/IVS	seemingly unrelated regression method with important variables
TFP	total factor productivity
t-statistics	level of significance
UK	United Kingdom
UN	United Nations
UN/ECE	United Nations Economic Commission for Europe
UNCTAD	United Nations Conference on Trade and Development
US	United States of America
USSR	Union of Soviet Socialist Republics
$WAGE_i$	wage level in investor country i
$WAGE_j$	wage level in host country j
WIPO	World Intellectual Property Organization
WTO	World Trade Organization

List of Tables

List of Figures

References

ABALKIN, L. (2000): Cmena Tysyacheletii i Sotsial'nye Al'ternativy. Voprosy Ekonomiki, Vol. 9, pp. 27 - 40

ABRAMOVITZ, M. (1986): Catching Up, Forging Ahead, and Falling Behind. The Journal of Economic History, Vol. XLVI, No. 1, March 1986, pp. 385 - 406

ADES, A.F., GLAESER, E.L. (1994): Evidence on Growth, Increasing Returns and the Extent of the Market. NBER Working Paper No. 4714, April 1994, Cambridge

AGENOR, P.R., MCDERMOTT, J.C., PRASAD, E.S. (1999): Macroeconomic Fluctuations in Developing Countries: Some Stylized Facts. IMF Working Paper No. 35, March 1999, Washington, D.C.

AGHION, P., BLANCHARD, O.J. (1994): On the Speed of Transition in Eastern Europe. In: FISCHER, S., ROTEMBERG, J.J. (Eds.): NBER Macroeconomics Annual 1994. MIT Press, Cambridge, Mass., pp. 283 - 320

AGHION, P., BLANCHARD, O.J. (1996): On Insider Privatization. European Economic Review, Vol. 40, No. 3 - 5, April 1996, pp. 759 - 766

AGHION, P., HOWITT, P. (1998): Endogenous Growth Theory. MIT Press, Cambridge Mass.

AHMAD, J., YANG, J. (1998): Trade Liberalization in Eastern European Countries and the Prospects of their Integration into the World Trading System. In: PARASKEPOULUS, C. (Ed.): Global Trading Arrangements in Transition. Studies in Economic Transformation and Public Policy under the Auspices of the Athenian Policy Forum. Cheltenham, Edward Elgar Published ltd, U.K., pp. 1 - 16

ANDERSON, J., CITRIN, D.A., LAHIRI, A.K. (1995): The Output Decline. In: CITRIN, D.A., LAHIRI, A.K. (Eds.): Policy Experiences and Issues in the Baltics, Russia, and Other Countries of the Former Soviet Union. International Monetary Fund, Washington, D.C., pp. 28 - 43

ANDERSON, R.W., BERGLOF, E., MITZSEI, K. (Eds.) (1996): Banking Sector Development in Central and Eastern Europe. Forum Report of the Economic Policy Initiate No. 1. CEPR, London

ANDERSON, R.W., KEGELS, C. (1998): Transition Banking: Financial Development of Central and Eastern Europe. Clarendon Press, Oxford

ARROW, K.J. (1962): The Economic Implications of Learning by Doing. Review of Economic Studies, Vol. 29, June 1962, pp. 155 - 173

ASLUND, A., BOONE, P., JOHNSON, S. (1996): How to Stabilize: Lessons from Post - communist Countries. Brookings Papers of Economic Activity No. 1, pp. 217 - 291

BAI, C., WANG, Y. (1998): Bureaucratic Control and the Soft Budget Constraint. Journal of Comparative Economics, Vol. 26, No. 1, March 1998, pp. 41 - 61

BAILEY, M.J., TAVLAS, G.S., VLAN, M. (1987): The Impact of Exchange-Rate Volatility on Export Growth: Some Theoretical Considerations and Empirical Results. Journal of Policy Modeling, Vol. 9, No. 1, pp. 225 - 243

BALASSA, B. (1978): Exports and Economic Growth. Journal of Development Economics, Vol. 5, pp. 181 - 189

BALDWIN, R.E. (1992): Measurable Dynamic Gains from Trade. Journal of Political Economy, Vol. 100, No. 1, pp. 162 - 174

BALDWIN, R.E. (1993): The Potential for Trade Between the Countries of EFTA and Central and Eastern Europe. CEPR Discussion Paper No. 853, London

BALDWIN, R.E. (1994): Towards an Integrated Europe. Center for Economic Policy Research, London

BALDWIN, R.E., FORSLID, R. (1998): Trade and Growth: Any Unfinished Business? European Economic Review, Vol. 42, pp. 695 - 703

BALZER, H. (1993): Science, Technology, and Education in the Former U.S.S.R. In: KAUFMAN, R.F., HARDT, J.P. (Eds.): The Former Soviet Union in Transition. M.E. Sharpe, New York, pp. 889 - 908

BARRO, R.J. (1991): Economic Growth in a Cross Section of Countries. The Quarterly Journal of Economics, Vol. 106, No. 2, May 1991, pp. 407 - 443

BARRO, R.J. (1992): Human Capital and Economic Growth. In: Policies for Long - Run Economic Growth. Symposium Series. Federal Reserve Bank of Kansas City, pp. 199 - 216

BARRO, R.J., MANKIW, N.G., SALA-I-MARTIN, X. (1995): Capital Mobility in the Neoclassical Models of Growth. American Economic Review, Vol. 85, No. 1, pp. 103 - 115

BARRO, R.J., SALA-I-MARTIN, X. (1992): Convergence. Journal of Political Economy, Vol. 100, No. 2, April 1992, pp. 223 - 251

BARRO, R.J., SALA-I-MARTIN, X. (1995a): Economic Growth. McGraw - Hill, New York

BARRO, R.J., SALA-I-MARTIN, X. (1995b): Technological Diffusion, Convergence, and Growth. NBER Working Paper No. 5151, Cambridge

BAYOUMI, T., COE, D.T., HELPMAN, E. (1996): R&D Spillovers and Global Growth. CEPR Discussion Paper No. 1467, London

BELARUS ECONOMIC TRENDS (1999): April - June 1999, Minsk

BELL, M., PAVITT, K. (1992): Two Strategies for Economic Development: Using Ideas and Producing Ideas. In: The World Bank Annual Conference on Development Economics. The World Bank, Washington, D.C., pp. 257 - 281

BELLAK, C. (1998): Lessons from Austria's Postwar Pattern of Inward FDI for CEECs. WIIW Research Reports No. 251, Vienna

BEN-DAVID, D. (1996): Trade and Convergence Among Countries. Journal of International Economics, Vol. 40, pp. 279 - 298

BEN-DAVID, D., LOEWY, M.B. (1996): Free Trade and Long-Run Growth. Working Paper No. 32 - 96. The Foerder Institute for Economic Research, Tel-Aviv University, Israel

BEN-DAVID, D., LOEWY, M.B. (1998): Free Trade, Growth and Convergence. Journal of Economic Growth, Vol. 3, June 1998, pp. 142 - 170

BENHABIB, J., SPIEGEL, M.M. (1994): The Role of Human Capital in Economic Development: Evidence from Aggregate Cross-Country Data. Journal of Monetary Economics, Vol. 34, pp.143 - 173

BERG, A. (1995): Supply and Demand Factors in Output Decline in Central and Eastern Europe. In: HOLZMANN, R., GACS, J., WINCKLER, G. (Eds.): Output Decline in Eastern Europe: Unavoidable, External Influence or Homemade? London, pp. 3 - 36

BERGLOF, E., ROLAND, G. (1998): Soft Budget Constraints and Banking in Transition Economics. Journal of Comparative Economics, Vol. 26, No. 1, March 1998, pp. 18 - 40

BERGSON, A. (1978): Productivity and the Social System - the USSR and the West. Harvard University Press, Cambridge, Mass.

BERGSON, A. (1987): Comparative Productivity: The USSR, Eastern Europe, and the West. The American Economic Review, Vol. 77, No. 3, pp. 342 - 357

BERGSON, A. (1991a): The USSR Before the Fall: How Poor and Why. Discussion Paper No. 1540. Harvard Institute of Economic Research, March 1991. Harvard University Press, Cambridge, Mass.

BERGSON, A. (1991b): Communist Economic Efficiency Revised. Discussion Paper No. 1581. Harvard Institute of Economic Research, December 1991. Harvard University Press, Cambridge, Mass.

BERKOWITZ, D., DE JONG, D.N., HUSTED, S. (1998): Quantifying Price Liberalization in Russia. Journal of Comparative Economics, Vol. 26, pp. 735 - 760

BLANCHARD, O.J. (1996): Assessment of the Economic Transition in Central and Eastern Europe: Theoretical Aspects of Transition. AER Papers and Proceedings, Vol. 86, No. 2, May 1996, pp. 117 - 122

BLANCHARD, O.J. (1997): The Economics of Post-Communist Transition. Oxford University Press, Oxford, U.K.

BLEJER, M.I., SKREB, M. (1999): Financial Sector Transformation-Lessons from Economies in Transition. Cambridge University Press, Cambridge, Mass.

BLOMSTROEM, M. (1991): Host Country Benefits of Foreign Investment. In: MCFETRIDGE, D. (Ed.): Foreign Investment, Technology and Economic Growth. University of Calgary Press, Calgary, Mass., pp. 93 - 110

BOESMAN, W. (1993): Science and Technology in the Former Soviet Union: Capabilities and Needs. In: KAUFMAN, R.F., HARDT, J.P. (Eds.): The Former Soviet Union in Transition. M.E. Sharpe, New York, pp. 610 - 628

BONIN, J. et al. (1998): Banking in Transition Economies: Developing Market Oriented Banking Sectors in Eastern Europe. Elgar, Cheltenham

BOONE, P., GOMULKA, S., LAYARD, R. (Eds.) (1998): Emerging from Communism: Lessons from Russia, China, and Eastern Europe. MIT Press, Cambridge, Mass.

BORENSZTEIN, E. etc. (1995): How Does Foreign Direct Investment Affect Economic Growth? NBER Working Paper No. 5057, Cambridge

BRADA, J.C., KING, A.E., KUTAN, A.M. (2000): Inflation Bias and Productivity Shocks in Transition Economies, The Case of the Czech Republic. Economic Systems, Vol. 24, No. 2, pp. 119 - 138

BRADA, J.C., SCHOENFELD, R., SLAY, B. (1995): The Role of International Financial Institutions in Central and Eastern Europe. Journal of Comparative Economics, Vol. 20, pp. 49 - 56

BRENTON, P., DI MAURO, F., LUECKE, M. (1998): Economic Integration and FDI: An Empirical Analysis of Foreign Investment in the EU and in Central and Eastern Europe. Kiel Working Paper No. 890, Kiel

BRENTON, P., TOURDYEVA, N., WHALLEY, J. (1997): The Potential Trade Effects of an FTA Between the EU and Russia. Weltwirtschaftliches Archiv, Vol. 133, No.2, Kiel

BRETSCHGER, L. (1998): Wachstumstheorie, 2 Auflage. Oldenburg

BREUSS, F., EGGER, P. (1999): How Reliable are Estimations of East - West Trade Potential Based on Cross-Section Gravity Analysis? Empirica, Vol. 26, No. 2, pp. 81 - 94

BREZIS, E.S., KRUGMAN, P.R., TSIDDON, D. (1993): Leapfrogging in International Competition: A Theory of Cycles in National Technological

Leadership. The American Economic Review, Vol. 83, No. 5, pp. 280 - 289

BROADBERRY, S.N. (1994): Technological Leadership and Productivity Leadership in Manufacturing Since the Industrial Revolution: Implication for the Convergence Debate. The Economic Journal, Vol. 104, March 1994, pp. 291 - 302

BRODSKII, B.E. (1998): Transformatsionnye Krizisy. Ekonomicheskii Zhyrnal Vysshei Shkoly Ekonomiki, Vol. 2, No. 3, pp. 322 - 341

BRUNO, D., LUIGI, M. (Eds.) (1996): Economic Institutions, Markets and Competition: Centralization and Decentralization in the Transformation of Economic Systems. Cheltenham, Edward Elgar, U.K.

BUCH, C.M. (1996): Creating Efficient Banking System: Theory and Evidence from Eastern Europe. Kieler Studien Nr. 277. Mohr, Tübingen

BULATOV, A. (2001): Kapitaloobrazovaniya v Rossii. Voprosy Ekonomiki, Vol. 3, pp. 54 - 68

BURGER, B. (1999): Importance of FDI for Late Industrializing Countries. HWWA Intereconomics, Vol. 34, May/June 1999, pp. 115 - 123

BZHILIANSKAYA, L. (1996): The Transformation of Technological Capabilities in Russian Defense Enterprises, with Special Reference to Dual - Use Technology. STEEP Discussion Paper No. 31, Brington

CAMPBELL, R.W. (1991): The Socialist Economies in Transition. Indiana University Press, Bloomington and Indianapolis

CENTRAL BANK OF RUSSIAN FEDERATION (CBRF) (1997): Annual Report, http://www.cbr.ru

CENTRAL BANK OF RUSSIAN FEDERATION (CBRF) (1998): Annual Report, http://www.cbr.ru

CENTRAL BANK OF RUSSIAN FEDERATION (CBRF) (2001): Social and Economic Situation in Russia in March, http://www.cbr.ru

CENTRAL INTELLIGENCE AGENCY (CIA) (1984): Handbook of Economic Statistics (HB), Washington, D.C.

CENTRAL INTELLIGENCE AGENCY (CIA) (1986): Handbook of Economic Statistics (HB), Washington, D.C.

CHOU, W.L. (2000): Exchange Rate Variability and China's Exports. Journal of Comparative Economics, Vol. 28, pp. 61 - 79

CHRISTENSEN, B.V. (1994): The Russian Federation in Transition. External Developments. International Monetary Fund, Washington, D.C.

CHUANG, Y. (1998): Learning by Doing, the Technology Gap, and Growth. International Economic Review, Vol. 39, No. 3, August 1998, pp. 697 - 497

CKLYAR, M. (1999): Sovremennyi Etap Ekonomicheskikh Reform v Rossii. V: MEN'KOV i dr. (Red.): Sotsial'no - Ekonomicheskie Reformy v Rossii i Germanii: Itogi i Perspektivy. Isd - vo RGPU im. A.I. Gerzsena, SPb., pp. 6 - 15

COE, D.T., HELPMAN, E. (1995): International R&D Spillovers. European Economic Review, Vol. 39, pp. 859 - 887

COLLINS, S., RODRICK, D. (1991): Eastern Europe and the Soviet Union in the World Economy. Policy Analysis in International Economics No. 32. Institute of International Economics, Washington, D.C.

CORKER, R., BEAUMONT, C., VAN ELKAN, R., IAKOVA, D. (2000): Exchange Rate Regimes in Selected Advanced Transition Economies - Coping with Transition, Capital Inflows, and EU Accession. IMF Policy Discussion Paper No. 00/3, Washington, D.C.

CORNWALL, J. (1977): Modern Capitalism: Its Growth and Transformation. Martin Robertson, London

CSAKI, G. (1998): Foreign Direct Investment in Hungary. In: Foreign Direct Investment in the CEFTA Countries. Economic Trends and Research Summaries No. 1, Budapest, pp. 1 - 11

DAVIS, D.R. (1991): Mutual Dynamic Gains from Trade Due to Specialization in Learning. Journal of Development Economics, Vol. 37, pp. 351 - 367

DE LONG, B.J., SUMMERS, L.H. (1991): Equipment Investment and Economic Growth. The Quarterly Journal of Economics, Vol. 106, No. 2, May 1991, pp. 445 - 502

DEARDORFF, A.V. (1995): Determinants of Bilateral Trade: Does Gravity Work in a Neoclassical World? NBER Working Paper No. 5377, Cambridge

DERYABINA, M. (2001): Institutsional'nye Aspekty Postsotsialisticheskogo Perekhodnogo Perioda. Voprosy Ekonomiki, Vol. 2, pp. 108 - 124

DESAI, P. (1976): The Production Function and Technological Change in Postwar Soviet Industry: A Reexamination. The American Economic Review, Vol. 66, No. 3, pp. 372 - 381.

DINOPOULOS, E., THOMPSON, P. (1999): Reassessing the Empirical Validity of the Human-Capital Augmented Neoclassical Growth Model. Journal of Evolutionary Economics, Vol. 9, pp. 135 - 154

DMITRIEV, M.E., KARCEV, N. (1996): Fiscal Policy of CIS Countries in 1993 - 1995. Studia i Analizy: Centrum Analiz Spoleczno-Ekonomicznych. Fundacja Naukowa, Vol. 84, Warsaw

DOEHRN, R. (2000): Foreign Direct Investment in Russia - An Engine of Structural Adjustment? In: WELFENS, P.J.J., GAVRILENKOV, E. (Eds.): Restructuring, Stabilizing and Modernizing the New Russia. Springer, Heidelberg and New York, pp. 127 - 147

DOEHRN, R., GANUSCHTSCHENKO, N. (2000): Pryamye Inostrannye Investitsii v Vyborochnykh Stranakh SNG - Dvigatel' Strukturnykh Peremen?. V: GAVRILENKOV, E., WELFENS, P.J.J. (Red.), Rossiiskaya Ekonomika: Opyt Transformatsii 1990-kh Godov i Perspektivy Rasvitiya. GU – VSHE, M., pp. 7 - 18

DOEHRN, R., VON WESTERNHAGEN, N. (2001-forthcoming): Foreign Direct Investment in Selected CIS Countries and Eastern European Countries: Perspectives from the Gravity Model. In: WELFENS, P.J.J., GAVRILENKOV, E. (Eds.): Proceedings of the Conference at the Leontief Center: Economic Development and Modernization in Russia and Eastern Europe, St. Petersburg

DOLLAR, D. (1992): Outward-oriented Developing Economies Really Do Grow More Rapidly: Evidence from 95 LDCs, 1976-1985. Economic Development and Cultural Change, Vol. 40, pp. 523 - 544

DUNNING, J. (1988): Explaining International Production. London: Unwin Hyman

EASTERLY, W. (1993): How Much Do Distortions Affect Growth? Journal of Monetary Economics, Vol. 32, pp. 187 - 212

EASTERLY, W., FISCHER, S. (1992): Growth Prospects for the Ex-Soviet Republics: Lessons from Soviet Historical Experience. In: ATKINSON, A.B. (Eds.): Economics in a Changing World, Proceedings of the Tenth World Congress of the International Economic Association, Vol. 1, Moscow, pp. 59 - 86

EASTERLY, W., FISCHER, S. (1994): The Soviet Economic Decline: Historical and Republican Data. NBER Working Paper No. 4735, Cambridge

EASTERLY, W., KING, R., LEVINE, R., REBELO, S. (1994): Policy, Technology Adoption and Growth. Centre for Economic Policy Research (CEPR) Discussion Paper No. 957, London

EATON, J., KORTUM, S. (1995): Engines of Growth: Domestic and Foreign Sources of Innovation. NBER Working Paper No. 5207, Cambridge

EBRD (1998): Transition Report 1998, London

EBRD (1999): Transition Report1999, London

EBRD (2000): Transition Report 2000, London

EDEN, L. (1991): Multinational Responses to Trade and Technology Changes: Implications for Canada. In: MCFETRIDGE, D. (Ed.): Foreign Investment,

Technology and Economic Growth. University of Calgary Press, Calgary, Mass., pp. 133 - 172

EDWARDS, S. (1992): Trade Orientation, Distortions and Growth in Developing Countries. Journal of Developing Economics, Vol. 39, No. 1, July 1992, pp. 31 - 57

EDWARDS, S. (1997): Openness, Productivity and Growth: What Do We Really Know? NBER Working Paper No. 5978, Cambridge

EDWARDS, S. (1998): Interest Rate Volatility, Capital Controls and Contagion. NBER Working Paper No. 6756, October 1998, Cambridge

ESTRIN, S., WRIGHT, M. (1999): Corporate Governance in the Former Soviet Union: An Overview. Journal of Comparative Economics, Vol. 27, pp. 398 - 421

ETHIER, W.J., MARKUSEN, J.R. (1996): Multinational Firms, Technology Diffusion and Trade. Journal of International Economics, Vol. 41, pp. 1 - 28

EUROPEAN COMMISSION (1998): Accession Partnerships with the Central European Applicant Countries, Principles of the AP's, http://europa.eu.int/comm/dg1a/en1...access_partnership/intro/index.htm, p.3

EUROPEAN COMMISSION (1998): Enlarging the European Union, Accession Partnerships, http://europa.eu.int/comm/dg1a/enlarge/index.htm, p.2

EUROPEAN PARLIAMENT (2001): Task Force Enlargement Statistical Annex, http://www.europarl.eu.int/enlargement/briefings/pdf/22a1-en.pdf

FAGEBERG, J. (1987): A Technology Gap Approach to Why Growth Rates Differ. Research Policy, Vol. 16, pp. 87 - 99

FAGEBERG, J. (1988): Why Growth Rates Differ. In: DOSI, G., FREEMAN, C. et al. (Eds.): Technical Change and Economic Growth. Printer Publishes, London and New York, pp. 432 - 457

FAGEBERG, J. (1994): Technology and International Differences in Growth Rates. Journal of Economic Literature, Vol. XXXII, September 1994, pp. 1147 - 1175

FAN, C.S., OVERLAND, J., SPAGAT, M. (1999): Human Capital, Growth, and Inequality in Russia. Journal of Comparative Economics, Vol. 27, pp. 618 - 643

FEDER, G. (1982): On Exports and Economic Growth. Journal of Development Economics, Vol. 12, pp. 59 - 73

FEENSTRA, R. (1996): Trade and Uneven Growth. Journal of Development Economics, Vol. 49, pp. 229 - 256

FISCHER, S., SAHAY, R., VEGH, C.A. (1996): Stabilization and Growth in Transition Economies: The Early Experience. Journal of Economic Perspectives, Vol. 10, No. 2, pp. 45 - 66

FISCHER, S., SAHAY, R., VEGH, C.A. (1998): From Transition to Market: Evidence and Growth Prospects. IMF Working Paper No. 52, Washington, D.C.

FRANKEL, J.A., ROMER, D, CYRUS, T. (1996): Trade and Growth in East Asia Countries: Cause and Effect? NBER Working Paper No. 5732, August 1996, Cambridge

FRANKEL, J.A., ROMER, D. (1996): Trade and Growth: An Empirical Investigation. NBER Working Paper No. 5476, March 1996, Cambridge

FROOT, K.A., STEIN, J.C. (1991): Exchange Rates and Foreign Direct Investment: an Imperfect Capital Markets Approach. The Quarterly Journal of Economics, Vol. 106, No. 4, pp. 1191 - 1217

FRYDMAN, R., PISTOR, K., RAPACZYNSKI, A. (1996): Investing in Insider-Dominated Firms: A Study of Russian Voucher Privatization Funds. In: FRYDMAN, R., GRAY, C., RAPACZYNSKI, A. (Eds.): Corporate Governance in Central Europe and Russia, Vol. 1, Banks, Funds, and Foreign Investors, Chap. 5. Central European University Press, Budapest, pp. 187 - 241

GACS, J. (1995): The Effects of the Demise of the CMEA and the USSR on Output in Hungary. In: HOLZMANN, R., GACS, J., WINCKLER, G. (Eds.): Output Decline in Eastern Europe: Unavoidable, External Influence or Homemade? London, pp. 161 - 184

GACS, J., PECK, M.J. (Eds.) (1996): International Trade Issues of the Russian Federation. Luxemburg, IIASA Press, Austria

GADDY, C.G. (1996): The Price of the Past: Russia's Struggle with the Legacy of a Militarized Economy. Brookings Institution, Washington, D.C.

GARIBALDI, P., MORA, N., SAHAY, R., ZETTELMEYER, J. (1999 - Draft): What Moves Capital to Transition Economies? International Monetary Fund, July 1999, Washington, D.C.

GAVRILENKOV, E. (1999): Permanent Crisis in Russia: Selected Problems of the Macroeconomic Performance. Hitotsubashi Journal of Economics, Vol. 40, pp. 41 - 57

GERSCHENKRON, A. (1962): Economic Backwardness in Historical Perspective. Harvard University Press, Cambridge Mass.

GLAZ'EV, S. (2000): Pyti Preodoleniya Investitsionnogo Krizisa. Voprosy Ekonomiki, Vol. 11, pp. 13 - 26

GOKHBERG, L. (1997): Russian R&D: A Sectoral Analysis. STEEP Discussion Paper No. 40, Bringron

GOMULKA, S. (1971): Inventive Activity, Diffusion, and the Stages of Economic Growth. Institute of Economics. University of Aarhus, Aarhus

GORODETSKII, A. (2000): Ob Osnovakh Institutsional'noi Transformatsii (Teoreticheskii Aspekt). Voprosy Ekonomiki, Vol. 10, pp. 118 - 133

GOTUR, P. (1985): Effects of Exchange Rate Volatility on Trade: Some Further Evidence. IMF Staff Papers No. 32, September 1985, pp. 475 - 512

GRAHAM, E.M. (1999): The Relationships Between Trade and Foreign Direct Investment in the Manufacturing Sector: Empirical Results for the United States and Japan. Institute for International Economics, Washington, D.C.

GRAHAM, E.M., LUI, L. (1998): The Relationship Between Trade and Foreign Direct Investment: Empirical Results for Taiwan and South Korea. Institute for International Economics, Washington, D.C.

GREENE, W.H. (2000): Econometric Analysis. 4th Edition. Prentice Hall Internat, London

GRIES, T., JUNGBLUT, S. (1997): Catching Up of Economies in Transition. In: WELFENS, P.J.J., WOLF, H.C. (Eds.): Banking, International Capital Flows and Growth in Europe. Springer, Heidelberg, pp. 297 - 313

GRILICHES, Z. (1995): Technology, Education, and Productivity. International Center for Economic Growth Occasional Paper No. 18. ICS Press, San Francisco, California

GRINBERG, R. (2000): Desyt' Let Rynochnykh Preobrazovanii v Stranach Zentral'noi i Vostochnoi Evropy i v Rossii: Itogi i Uroki. V: GAVRILENKOV, E., WELFENS, P.J.J. (Red.): Rossiiskaya Ekonomika: Opyt Transformatsii 1990-kh Godov i Perspektivy Rasvitiya. GU - VSHE, M., pp. 7 - 18

GRISHIN, L. (2000): My kak Uchastniki Rynochnykh Otnoshenii. Voprosy Ekonomiki, Vol. 8, pp. 31 - 37

GROS, D, GONCIARZ, A. (1996): A Note on the Trade Potential of Central and Eastern Europe. European Journal of Political Economy, Vol. 12, pp. 709 - 721

GROS, D., DAUTREBANDE, B. (1992): International Trade of Former Republics in the Long Run: an Analysis Based on the „Gravity" Approach. CEPS Working Document No. 71, Brussels

GROSSMAN, G.M. (1996): Economic Growth: Theory and Evidence, Vol. I and Vol. II. Edward Elgar Publishing Company, Cheltenham, U.K.

GROSSMAN, G.M., HELPMAN, E. (1990): Comparative Advantage and Long-Run Growth. The American Economic Review, Vol. 80, No. 4, pp. 224 - 243

GROSSMAN, G.M., HELPMAN, E. (1991a): Innovation and Growth in the Global Economy. MIT Press, Cambridge Mass.

GROSSMAN, G.M., HELPMAN, E. (1991b): Quality Ladder in the Theory of Growth. Review of Economic Studies, Vol. 58, pp. 43 - 61

GROSSMAN, G.M., HELPMAN, E. (1991c): Trade, Knowledge Spillovers, and Growth. European Economic Review, Vol. 35, pp.517 - 526

GROSSMAN, G.M., HELPMAN, E. (1994): Endogenous Innovation in the Theory of Growth. Journal of Economic Perspectives, Vol. 8, No. 1, pp. 23 - 44

GRUBEL, H., LLOYD, P. (1975): Intra-Industry Trade: The Theory and Measurement of International Trade in Differentiated Products. MacMillian, London

GRUNDLACH, E. (1997): Openness and Economic Growth in Developing Countries. Weltwitschaftliches Archiv, Vol. 133, No. 3, Kiel

GRUNDLACH, E., NUNNENKAMP, P. (1996): Falling Behind or Catching Up? Developing Countries in the Era of Globalization. Kiel Discussion Paper No. 263, Kiel

HAKURA, D., JAUMOTTE, F. (1999): The Role of Inter- and Intra-industry Trade in Technology Diffusion. IMF Working Paper No. 58, Washington, D.C.

HALL, R., JONES, C. (1997): What Have We Learned from Recent Empirical Growth Research. Levels of Economic Activity Across Countries. AER Papers and Proceedings, Vol. 87, No. 2, May 1997, pp. 173 - 177

HAMILTON, C.B., WINTERS, L.A. (1992): Opening up International Trade with Eastern Europe. Economic Policy, Vol. 14, pp. 78 - 104

HANSON, P. (1997): What Sort of Capitalism is Developing Russia? Communist Economies, Vol. 9, No. 1, March 1997, pp. 27 - 42

HARE, P., REVESZ, T. (1992): Hungary's Transition to the Market: the Case Against a „Big-Bang". Economic Policy, Vol. 14, April 1992, pp. 228 - 264

HAVRYLYSHYN, O., IZVORSKI, I., VAN ROODEN R. (1998): Recovery and Growth in Transition Economies 1990 - 1997: A Stylized Regression Analysis. IMF Working Paper No. 141, Washington, D.C.

HECKSCHER, E.F, OHLIN, B. (1991): Heckscher-Ohlin Trade Theory. In: FLAM, H., FLANDERS, J.M. (Eds.). MIT Press, Cambridge Mass.

HECKSCHER, E.F. (1919): The Effect of Foreign Trade on the Distribution of Income. Ekonomisk Tidskrift 21, Printed (1950). In: AER Readings in the Theory of International Trade. Blakiston, Philadelphia, pp. 1 - 32

HELPMAN, E. (1992): Innovation, Imitation, and Intellectual Property Rights. NBER Working Paper No. 4081, Cambridge

HELPMAN, E. (1998): Explaining the Structure of Foreign Trade: Where Do We Stand? Lecture Delivered at the Kiel Institute of World Economics on the Occasion of Being Awarded the Bernhard Harms Prize on June 27, Kiel

HELPMAN, E., KRUGMAN, P.R. (1993): Market Structure and Foreign Trade: Increasing Returns, Imperfect Competition, and the International Economy. MIT Press, Cambridge Mass.

HELPMAN, E., RANGEL, A. (1999): Adjusting to a New Technology: Experience and Training. Journal of Economic Growth, Vol. 4, December 1999, pp. 359 - 383

HIRSCHMAN, A. O. (1958): The Strategy of Economic Development. Yale Studies in Economics, No. 10. Yale University Press, New Haven

HISHOW, O. (1998): Wechselkursentwicklung im östlichen Europa. Bestimmungsfaktoren und transformationspolitischer Stellenwert. BIOst Bericht Nr. 23, Köln

HOLZMANN, R., ZUKOWSKA-GAGELMANN, K. (1998): Trade Adjustment in Eastern Europe During Transition: The Determined, Sophisticated and Proximate. Journal of Public Policy, Vol. 18, No. 1, January-April 1998, pp. 29 - 52

HUANG, H., XU, C. (1999): Institutions, Innovations and Growth. IMF Working Paper No. 34, Washington, D.C.

HUNYA, G. (1999): Central Europe Catching Up Through FDI? The Vienna Institute for International Economic Studies, Vienna

ILLARIONOV, A. (2001): Ekonomicheskaya Politika v Usloviyakh Otkrytoi Ekonomiki so Znachitel'nym Syr'evym Sektorom. Voprosy Ekonomiki, Vol. 4, pp. 4 - 31

IMF (1993): Balance of Payments Manual, Fifth Edition, Washington, D.C.

IMF (1998): Directions of Trade Statistics Yearbook 1998, Washington, D.C.

IMF (1999): International Financial Statistics Yearbook 1999, Washington, D.C.

IMF (2000): Russian Federation: Staff Report for the 2000 Article IV Consultation and Public Information Notice Following Consultation. IMF Staff Country Report No. 00/145, Washington, D.C.

IMF et al. (1991): A Study of the Soviet Economy, Vol. 1, Washington, D.C.

IYIGUN, M.F., OWEN, A.L. (1999): Entrepreneurs, Professional, and Growth. Journal of Economic Growth, Vol. 4, June 1999, pp. 213 - 232

JONES, A. (1994): The Educational Legacy of the Soviet Period. In: JONES, A. (Ed.): Education and Society in the New Russia. M.E. Sharpe, New York, pp. 3 - 23

JONES, C. (1995a): Time Series Tests of Endogenous Growth Models. The Quarterly Journal of Economics, Vol. 110, No. 2, May 1995, pp. 495 - 525

JONES, C. (1995b): R&D-Based Models of Economic Growth. Journal of Political Economy, Vol. 103, No. 4, pp. 759 - 784

JONES, C. (1998): Introduction to Economic Growth. Norton, New York

JONES, C.I., BERNARD, A.B. (1996): Technology and Convergence. The Economic Journal, Vol. 106, July 1996, pp. 1037 - 1044

JONES, L.E., MANUELLI, R. (1990): A Convex Model of Equilibrium Growth: Theory and Policy Implications. Journal of Political Economy, Vol. 98, No. 5, pp. 1008 - 1038

KAITILA, V. (1999): Trade and Revealed Comparative Advantage: Hungary, the Czech Republic, and the European Union. BOFIT Discussion Papers No. 8, Helsinki

KATZ, B.G., OWEN, J. (2000): Choosing Between Big-Bang and Gradualist Reforms: An Option Price Approach. Journal of Comparative Economics, Vol. 28, pp. 95 - 107

KELLER, W. (1996): Absorptive Capacity: On the Creation and Acquisition of Technology in Development. Journal of Development Economics, Vol. 49, pp. 199 - 277

KITAEV, I.V. (1994): The Labor Market and Education in the Post-Soviet Era. In: JONES, A. (Ed.): Education and Society in the New Russia. M.E. Sharpe, New York, pp. 311 - 333

KNEZO, G.J. (1993): Science and Technological Collaboration with Former Soviet Countries. In: KAUFMAN, R.F., HARDT, J.P. (Eds.): The Former Soviet Union in Transition. M.E. Sharpe, New York, pp. 648 - 664

KOLODKO, G. (2001): Globalizatsiya i Sblizhenie Urovnei Ekonomicheskogo Razvitiya: ot Spada k Rosty v Stranakh s Perekhodnoi Ekonomikoi. Voprosy Ekonomiki, Vol. 10, pp. 4 - 26

KORNAI, J. (1994): Transformational Recession: The Main Causes. Journal of Comparative Economics, Vol. 19, pp. 39 - 63

KORNAI, J. (1998): The Place of the Soft Budget Constraint Syndrome in Economic Theory. Journal of Comparative Economics, Vol. 26, No. 1, March 1998, pp. 11 - 17

KORNAI, J. (1999): Hardening the Budget Constraint: The Experience of Postsocialist Countries. Collegium Budapest. Discussion Paper Series No. 59, July 1999, Budapest

KOSSOV, R.V. (1998): Investitsii kak Rychag dly Pod'ema Ekonomiki Rossii iz Krizisa. Ekonomicheskii Zhyrnal Vysshei Shkoly Ekonomiki, Vol. 2, No. 3, pp. 308 - 321

KOTZ, D. (1997): Revolution from Above: The Demise of the Soviet System. Routledge, London and New York

KRASNIKOVA, E. (2001): Rynochnaya Tranformatsiya Rossiiskoi Ekonomiki kak Protsess Pervoklasnogo Hakopleniya Kapitala. Voprosy Ekonomiki, Vol. 2, pp. 142 - 154

KRUEGER, G., CIOLKO, M. (1998): A Note on Initial Conditions and Liberalization During Transition. Journal of Comparative Economics, Vol. 26, pp. 718 - 734

KRUGMAN, P. (1980): Scale Economies, Product Differentiation, and the Pattern of Trade. Journal of Development Economics, Vol. 70, No. 5, pp. 950 - 959

KRUGMAN, P. (1990): Rethinking International Trade. MIT Press, Cambridge Mass.

KRUGMAN, P.R. (1987): The Narrow Moving Band, The Dutch Disease, and The Competitive Consequences of Mrs. Thatcher. Journal of Development Economics, Vol. 27, pp. 41 - 55

KUMAR, N., SIDDHARTHAN, N.S. (1997): Technology, Market Structure and Internationalization: Issues and Policies for Developing Countries. UNU Press, London and New York

LAL, D. (1992): Does Openness Matter? How to Appraise the Evidence. In: SIEBERT, H. (Ed.): Economic Growth in the World Economy. Symposium 1992. Institute für Weltwirtschaft an der Universität Kiel, Kiel, pp. 115 - 131

LEIJONHUFVUD, A., RUEHL, C. (1997): Russian Dilemma. AER Papers and Proceedings, Vol. 87, No. 2, May 1997, pp. 344 - 348

LESHCHENKO, L., REVENKO, V. (1999): Privatization in Ukraine: Stages, Actors and Outcomes. In: HARE, P., BATT, J., CAVE, M., ESTRIN, S. (Eds.): Reconstituting the Market: The Political Economy of Microeconomic Transformation. Harwood Academic, London, pp. 315 - 335

LEVIN, A., RAUT, L. (1997): Complementarities Between Exports and Human Capital in Economic Growth: Evidence from the Semi-industrialized Countries, Economic Development and Cultural Change. The University of Chicago, Chicago

LEVINE, R., RENELT, D. (1992): A Sensitivity Analysis of Cross-Country Growth Regressions. The American Economic Review, Vol. 82, No. 4, pp. 943 - 963

LINDERT, P.H., PUGEL, T.A. (1996): International Economics. IRWIN, London

LIPSITS, I.V., VIGDORTSIK, E.A., NESHCHADIN, A.A., EIKEL'PASH, A. RYBAKOVA, T.A. (1998): Vybor Konkyrentnykh Strategii dly Privatizirovannykh Predpriytii: Sravnitil'noe Isselodavie na Materialakh Vostochnoi Germanii i Rossii. Ekonomicheskii Zhyrnal Vysshei Shkoly Ekonomiki, Vol. 2, No. 4, pp. 476 - 499

LLEWELLYN, G.E.J., PESARAN, M.H. (1976): Diffusion, Convergence and Kaldor's Laws. The Economic Journal, Vol. 86, June 1976, pp. 307 - 314

LUCAS, R. (1988): On the Mechanics of Economic Development. Journal of Monetary Economics, Vol. 22, pp. 3 - 42

LUCAS, R. (1990): Why Doesn't Capital Flow from Rich to Poor Countries? The American Economic Review, Vol. 80, No.2, pp. 92 - 96

LUCAS, R. (1993): Making a Miracle. Econometrica, Vol. 61, No. 2, March 1993, pp. 251 - 272

MANKIW, G.N., ROMER, D., WEIL, D.N. (1992): A Contribution to the Empirics of Economic Growth. Quarterly Journal of Economics, Vol. CVII, No. 2, May 1992, pp. 407 - 437

MASKIN, E. (1999): Recent Theoretical Work on the Soft-Budget Constraint. American Economic Review, Vol. 89, No. 2, May 1999, pp. 421 - 425

MAU, V. (2000): Ekonomicheskaya Politika v Rossii: v Nachale Novoi Fazy. Voprosy Ekonomiki, Vol. 3, pp. 4 - 22

MURELL, P. (1990): The Nature of Socialist Economies. Princeton University Press, Princeton

NELSON, R.R., PHELS, E.S. (1966): Investment in Humans, Technological Diffusion, and Economic Growth. The American Economic Review, Vol. LVI, No. 2, May 1996, pp. 69 - 82

NIKOLIC, M. (2000): Money Growth-Inflation Relationship in Postcommunist Russia. Journal of Comparative Economics, Vol. 28, pp. 108 - 133

NOSOVA, O. (2000): Pryamye Inostrannye Investitsii i Ekonomicheskii Rost v Rosii, Pol'she i Ukraine. V: GAVRILENKOV, E., WELFENS, P.J.J. (Red.): Rossiiskaya Ekonomika: Opyt Transformatsii 1990-kh Godov i Perspektivy Rasvitiya. GU - VSHE, M., pp. 79 - 85

NUREEV, R. (2000): Teorii Razvitiya: Novye Modeli Ekonomicheskogo Rosta (Vklad Chelovecheskogo Kapitala). Voprosy Ekonomiki, Vol. 9, pp. 136 - 157

OECD (1994): Science, Technology and Innovation Policies: Federation of Russia, Vol. II, Paris

OECD (1998): The Benefits of Trade and Investment Liberalization, Paris

OECD (1999): OECD Science, Technology and Industry Scoreboard, Paris

OFER, G. (1987): Soviet Economic Growth: 1928 - 1985. Journal of Economic Literature, Vol. 15, December 1987, pp. 1767 - 1833

OHLIN, B. (1933): Interregional and International Trade. Cambridge, UNU Press, Mass.

OL'SEVICH, YU. (2000): Nuzhno li Zanovo Issledovat' Ekonomicheskuyu Istoriyu SSSR? Voprosy Ekonomiki, Vol. 11, pp. 79 - 90

PACK, H. (1992): Technology Gaps Between Industrial and Developing Countries: Are There Dividends for Latecomers. In: The World Bank Annual Conference on Development Economics. The World Bank, Washington, D.C., pp. 283 - 302

PAN, H. (1999): Openness, Capital Mobility and Global Convergence. In: ADAMS, J., PIGLIARU, F. (Eds.): Economic Growth and Change: National and Regional Patterns of Convergence and Divergence. Edward Elgar, Cheltenham, pp. 102 - 126

PAVITT, K., SOETE, L.L.G. (1981): International Differences in Economic Growth and the International Location of Innovation. In: GIERSCH, H. (Ed.): Emerging Technologies: Consequences for Economic Growth, Structural Change, and Employment. Symposium, Institute für Weltwirtschaft an der Universität Kiel, Kiel, pp. 105 - 133

PIAZOLO, D. (1997): Gaining Credibility and Enhancing Economic Growth through Regional Integration. The Case for EU Membership of Eastern Europe. Kiel Working Paper No. 837, October 1997, Kiel

POOPER, S.W. (1993): A Note on the Emigration of Russia's Technical Intelligentsia. In: KAUFMAN, R.F., HARDT, J.P. (Eds.): The Former Soviet Union in Transition. M.E. Sharpe, New York, pp. 820 - 839

POZNANSKI, K. (1987): Technology, Competition & the Soviet Bloc in the World Market. Institute for International Studies, Berkeley

PREZ, C., SOETE, L. (1988): Catching up in Technology: Entry Barriers and Windows of Opportunity. In: DOSI, G., FREEMAN, C. et al. (Eds.): Technical Change and Economic Growth. Printer Publishes, London and New York, pp. 458 - 479

RADOSEVIC, S. (1992): Transformation of Science and Technology Systems into Systems of Innovation in Central and Eastern Europe: The Emerging Patterns of Recombination, Path-Dependency and Change. Electronic Working Paper No. 9, Brington

RAJAN, R.G., ZINGALES, L. (1998): Financial Dependence and Growth. The American Economic Review, Vol. 88, No. 3, June 1998, pp. 559 - 586

RANDALL, F.K., HANOUSEK, J. (2000): Output Changes and Inflationary Bias in Transition. Economic Systems, Vol. 24, No. 3, pp. 285 - 294

REBELO, S. (1991): Long-Run Policy Analysis and Long-Run Growth. Journal of Political Economy, Vol. 99, No. 31, pp. 500 - 621

RIVERA-BATIZ, L., ROMER, P.M. (1991): Economic Integration and Endogenous Growth. The Quarterly Journal of Economics, Vol. CVI, Issue 1, May 1991, pp. 531 - 555

RODRIK, D. (1992): Making Sense of the Soviet Trade Shock in Eastern Europe: A Framework and Some Estimations. NBER Working Paper No. 4112, Cambridge

RODRIK, D. (1995): Trade and Industrial Policy Reform. In: BEHRMAN, J., SRINIVASAN, T.N. (Eds.): Handbook of Development Economics, Vol. III A. Amsterdam: North-Holland, pp. 2925 - 2997

ROMER, P. (1992): Two Strategies for Economic Development: Using Ideas and Producing Ideas: In: The World Bank Annual Conference on Development Economics. The World Bank, Washington, D.C., pp. 63 - 91

ROMER, P.M. (1986): Increasing Returns and Long-Run Growth. Journal of Political Economy, Vol. 94, No. 5, pp. 1002 - 1037

ROMER, P.M. (1987): Growth Based on Increasing Returns Due to Specialization. The American Economic Review, Vol. 77, No. 2, May 1987, pp. 56 - 67

ROMER, P.M. (1990): Endogenous Technological Change. Journal of Political Economy, Vol. 98, No. 5, Part 2, October 1990, pp. 71 - 102

ROMER, P.M. (1993a): Idea Gaps and Objects Gaps in Economic Development. Journal of Monetary Economics, Vol. 32, pp. 543 - 547

ROMER, P.M. (1993b): New Goods, Old Theory, and The Welfare Costs of Trade Restrictions. NBER Working Papers Series No. 4452, Cambridge

ROMER, P.M. (1994): The Origins of Endogenous Growth. Journal of Economic Perspectives, Vol. 8, No. 1, Winter 1994, pp. 3 - 22

RUFFIN, R.J. (1988): The Missing Link: The Ricardian Approach to the Factor Endowments Theory of Trade. The American Economic Review, Vol. 78, No. 4, pp. 759 - 772

RUTZHENKOV, A. (1995): Technology Policy for a Future-oriented Social Market Economy in Russia. Materialien des Universitätsschwerpunktes Internationale Wirtschaftsbeziehingen und Internationales Management, Band 6. Universität Bremen, Bremen

SACHS, J.D. (1995): Russia's Struggle with Stabilization: Conceptual Issues and Evidence. In: BRUNO, M., PLESKOVIC, B. (Eds.): Proceedings of the World Bank Annual Conference on Development Economies 1994. World Bank, Washington, D.C., pp. 57 - 80

SACHS, J.D. (1996): The Transition at Mid Decade. AER Papers and Proceedings, Vol. 86, No. 2, May 1996, pp. 128 - 133

SACHS, J.D., WARNER, A.M. (1995a): Economic Convergence and Economic Policies. Discussion Paper No. 1715. Harvard Institute of Economic Research. Harvard University Press, Cambridge, Mass.

SACHS, J.D., WARNER, A.M. (1995b): Natural Resource Abundance and Economic Growth. NBER Working Paper No. 5398, Cambridge

SACHS, J.D., WARNER, A.M. (1996): Achieving Rapid Growth in the Transition Economies of Central Europe. Mimeo, January 1996. Harvard University, Harvard

SACHS, J.D., WARNER, A.M. (1999): The Big Push, Natural Resource Boom and Growth. Journal of Development Economics, Vol. 59, pp. 43 - 76

SAMOKHVALOV, A. (2001): O Vozmozhnosti i Neizbezhnosti Ekonomicheskogo Pod''ema v Rossii. Voprosy Ekonomiki, Vol. 4, pp 139 - 144

SAMUELSON, P.A. (1948): International Trade and the Equalization of Factor Prices. Economic Journal, Vol. 58, pp. 163 - 184

SAMUELSON, P.A. (1949): International Factor-Price Equalization Once Again. Economic Journal, Vol. 59, pp. 181 - 197

SCHNEIDER, C. M. (1994): Research and Development Management: From the Soviet Union to Russia. Springer, Heidelberg

SCHULZE, T.W. (1961): Investment in Human Capital. The American Economic Review, Vol. LI, No. 1, March 1961, pp. 1 - 17

SEGERSTROM, P.S., DINOPOULOS, E. (1990): A Schumpetetian Model of the Product Life Cycle. The American Economic Review, Vol. 80, No. 5, pp. 290 - 304

SELOWSKY, M., MARTIN, R. (1997): Policy Performance and Output Growth in the Transition Economies. AER Papers and Proceedings, Vol. 87, No. 2, May 1997, pp. 349 - 353

SHMELEV, N. (2000): Rossiya i Evropa na Poroge XXI Veka. Voprosy Ekonomiki, Vol. 9, pp. 120 - 134

SIEBERT, H. (1997): Weltwirtschaft. Lucius und Lucius, Stuttgart

SIMANOVSKY, S. (1998): Science and Technology in Russia: Problems and Prospects. Berichte des Bundesinstituts für ostwissenschaftliche und internationale Studien Nr. 18. BIOst, Koeln

SINGER, H.W., REYNILDS, L. (1975): Technological Backwardness and Productivity Growth. The Economic Journal, Vol. 85, December 1975, pp. 873 - 876

SMIRNOV, S. (2000): Promyshlennaya Politika: Problemy i Perspektivy. Voprosy Ekonomiki, Vol. 9, pp. 4 - 17

SMITS, J.P., DE JONG, H., VAN ARK, B. (1999): Three Phases of Dutch Economic Growth and Technological Change, 1815 - 1997. Research Memorandum. Groningen Growth and Development Centre, Vol. 42, Groningen

SOLOW, R. (1956): A Contribution to The Theory of Economic Growth. Quarterly Journal of Economics, Vol. LXX, No. 278, February 1956, pp. 65 - 94

STREPETOVA, M. (1995): The Brain Drain in Russia. Working Paper No. 55. Institute for World Economics. Hungarian Academy of Sciences, Budapest

STRUCHENEVSKII, A. (2000): Real'nye i Finansovye Investitsii v Rossiiskoi Ekonomike. V: GAVRILENKOV, E., WELFENS, P.J.J. (Red.): Rossiiskaya Ekonomika: Opyt Transformatsii 1990-kh Godov i Perspektivy Rasvitiya. GU - VSHE, M., pp. 115 - 149

TEMPLE, J. (1999): The New Growth Evidence. Journal of Economic Literature, Vol. XXXVII, March 1999, pp. 112 - 156

THIRLWALL, A.P. (1999): Growth and Development with Special Reference to Developing Economies, 6th Edition. MacMillian Press ltd, Houndmills

TROFIMOV, F. (2000): O Rezhimakh Dolgovremennogo Ekonomicheskogo Rosta. Voprosy Ekonomiki, Vol. 11, pp. 27 - 45

UN/ECE (1998): Economic Survey of Europe 1998, No. 3, New York and Geneva

UN/ECE (1999): Economic Survey of Europe 1999, No. 1, New York and Geneva

UN/ECE (2000a): Economic Survey of Europe 2000, No.1, New York and Geneva

UN/ECE (2000b): Economic Survey of Europe 2000, No. 2/3, New York and Geneva

UNCTAD (1998): World Investment Report 1998, New York and Geneva

UNCTAD (1999): World Investment Report 1999, New York and Geneva

VAN SELM, B. (1995): The Economics of Soviet Break-up. Labyrint Publ., Capellee aan de Ijssel, The Netherlands

VAN WIJNBERGEN, S. (1984): The „Dutch Disease": A Disease After All? The Economic Journal, Vol. 94, March 1984, pp. 41 - 55

VENTURA, J. (1997): Growth and Interdependence. Quarterly Journal of Economics, Vol. 112, No. 1, pp. 57 - 84

VON WESTERNHAGEN, N. (2000): The Role of FDI in the Transition Process of Selected CIS and Eastern European Countries. EIIW Discussion Paper No. 73. University of Potsdam, Potsdam

WACZIARG, R. (1998): Measuring the Dynamic Gains from Trade. Mimeo. May 1998, Stanford University, Stanford

WANG, Z.K., WINTERS, A.L. (1992): The Trading Potential of Eastern Europe. Journal of Economic Integration, Vol. 7, No. 2, Autumn 1992, pp. 113 - 136

WARESA, M. (1998): Foreign Direct Investment in Poland in the 1990's. In: Foreign Direct Investment in the CEFTA Countries. Economic Trends and Research Summaries No. 1, Budapest, pp. 37 - 68

WEITZMAN, M.L. (1970): Soviet Postwar Economic Growth and Capital - Labor Substitution. American Economic Review, Vol. 60, No. 5, December 1970, pp. 676 - 92

WELFENS, P.J.J. (1992a): Market-oriented Systemic Transformation in Eastern Europe: Problems, Theoretical Issues, and Policy Options. Springer, Heidelberg and New York

WELFENS, P.J.J. (1992b): Internationalization of Production, Investment and European Integration: Free Trade in Goods, Technology and Assets. In: KLEIN, M.W., WELFENS, P.J.J. (Eds.): Multinationals in the New Europe and Global Trade. Springer, Heidelberg and New York, pp. 9 - 63

WELFENS, P.J.J. (1999a): The Russian Transformation Crisis: Origins, Analysis and New Policy Requirements. EIIW Discussion Paper No. 57, University of Potsdam, Potsdam

WELFENS, P.J.J. (1999b): Die Russische Transformationskrise: Monetäre und reale Aspekte sowie Politikoptionen. Kredit und Kapital, 32. Jahrgang 1999, Heft 3. Duncker und Humboldt, Berlin, pp. 331 - 368

WELFENS, P.J.J. (2000): Instituty i Transformatsiya: na Puti k Rynochnoi Ekonomike - Teoriya i Prilozhenie k Usloviyam Rossii. V: GAVRILENKOV, E., WELFENS, P.J.J. (Red.): Rossiiskaya Ekonomika: Opyt Transformatsii 1990-kh Godov i Perspektivy Rasvitiya. GU – VSHE, M., pp. 19 - 54

WELFENS, P.J.J., GANUSCHTSCHENKO, N. (1999): Eastern EU Enlargement and the Russian Transformation Crisis, prepared for 2nd EACES Paris Workshop: The European Union Enlargement to the East, but at What Speed? March, 22 - 23, Paris

WESTIN, P. (1999): Foreign Direct Investments in Russia. Russian Economic Trends, March 1999

WOLF, H.C. (1997): Patterns of Intra- and Inter-State Trade. NBER Working Paper No. 5939, Cambridge

WORLD BANK (1996): Statistical Handbook, Washington, D.C.

WORLD BANK (1998/1999): World Development Report 1998/1999, Washington, D.C.

WORLD BANK (1999/2000): World Development Report 1999/2000, Washington, D.C.

WORLD BANK (2000): World Bank Development Indicators 2000, http://www.worldbank.org

YOUNG, A. (1991): Learning by Doing and the Dynamic Effects of International Trade. The Quarterly Journal of Economics, Vol. 106, No. 2, pp. 369 - 405

ZEBREGS, H. (1998): Can the Neoclassical Model Explain the Distribution of Foreign Direct Investment Across Developing Countries. IMF Working Paper No. 139, Washington, D.C.

ZECCHINI, S. (1995): The Role of International Financial Institutions in the Transition Process. Journal of Comparative Economics, Vol. 20, pp. 116 – 138

Contributions to Economics

Stefan Baumgärtner
Ambivalent Joint Production and the Natural Environment
2000. ISBN 3-7908-1290-0

Henri Capron, Wim Meeusen (Eds.)
The National Innovation System of Belgium
2000. ISBN 3-7908-1308-7

Tobias Miarka
Financial Intermediation and Deregulation
2000. ISBN 3-7908-1307-9

Chisato Yoshida
Illegal Immigration and Economic Welfare
2000. ISBN 3-7908-1315-X

Nikolaus Thumm
Intellectual Property Rights
2000. ISBN 3-7908-1329-X

Max Keilbach
Spatial Knowledge Spillovers and the Dynamics of Agglomeration and Regional Growth
2000. ISBN 3-7908-1321-4

Alexander Karmann (Ed.)
Financial Structure and Stability
2000. ISBN 3-7908-1332-X

Joos P.A. van Vugt/Jan M. Peet (Eds.)
Social Security and Solidarity in the European Union
2000. ISBN 3-7908-1334-6

Johannes Bröcker/Hayo Herrmann (Eds.)
Spatial Change and Interregional Flows in the Integrating Europe
2001. ISBN 3-7908-1344-3

Kirstin Hubrich
Cointegration Analysis in a German Monetary System
2001. ISBN 3-7908-1352-4

Nico Heerink et al. (Eds.)
Economic Policy and Sustainable Land Use
2001. ISBN 3-7908-1351-6

Friedel Bolle/Michael Carlberg (Eds.)
Advances in Behavioral Economics
2001. ISBN 3-7908-1358-3

Volker Grossmann
Inequality, Economic Growth, and Technological Change
2001. ISBN 3-7908-1364-8

Thomas Riechmann
Learning in Economics
2001. ISBN 3-7908-1384-2

Miriam Beblo
Bargaining over Time Allocation
2001. ISBN 3-7908-1391-5

Peter Meusburger/Heike Jöns (Eds.)
Transformations in Hungary
2001. ISBN 3-7908-1412-1

Claus Brand
Money Stock Control and Inflation Targeting in Germany
2001. ISBN 3-7908-1393-1

Erik Lüth
Private Intergenerational Transfers and Population Aging
2001. ISBN 3-7908-1402-4

Nicole Pohl
Mobility in Space and Time
2001. ISBN 3-7908-1380-X

Pablo Coto-Millán (Ed.)
Essays on Microeconomics and Industrial Organisation
2002. ISBN 3-7908-1390-7

Mario A. Maggioni
Clustering Dynamics and the Locations of High-Tech-Firms
2002. ISBN 3-7908-1431-8

Ludwig Schätzl/Javier Revilla Diez (Eds.)
Technological Change and Regional Development in Europe
2002. ISBN 3-7908-1460-1

Alberto Quadrio Curzio/Marco Fortis (Eds.)
Complexity and Industrial Clusters
2002. ISBN 3-7908-1471-7

Friedel Bolle/
Marco Lehmann-Waffenschmidt (Eds.)
Surveys in Experimental Economics
2002. ISBN 3-7908-1472-5

Pablo Coto-Millán
General Equilibrium and Welfare
2002. ISBN 7908-1491-1

Wojciech W. Charemza/
Krystyna Strzała (Eds.)
East European Transition and EU Enlargement
2002. ISBN 3-7908-1501-2

GPSR Compliance

The European Union's (EU) General Product Safety Regulation (GPSR) is a set of rules that requires consumer products to be safe and our obligations to ensure this.

If you have any concerns about our products, you can contact us on ProductSafety@springernature.com

In case Publisher is established outside the EU, the EU authorized representative is:

Springer Nature Customer Service Center GmbH
Europaplatz 3
69115 Heidelberg, Germany

Batch number: 10725973

Printed by Printforce, the Netherlands